MEDIA
CANADA
An Introductory Analysis

MEDIA CANADA
An Introductory Analysis

Walter I. Romanow

Walter C. Soderlund

University of Windsor

Copp Clark Pitman Ltd.

ISBN: 0-7730-5187-2

EDITOR: Deborah Viets
TEXT AND COVER DESIGN: Liz Nyman
COVER PHOTOGRAPH: "Telecommunications, Abstract"
           by Steven Hunt, from The Image Bank
TYPESETTING: Marnie Morrissey
PRINTING AND BINDING: Best Gagne Book Manufacturers

Canadian Cataloguing in Publication Data

Romanow, W.I., 1924–
  Media Canada

Includes bibliographical references and index.
ISBN 0-7730-5187-2

1. Mass media - Canada. I. Soderlund, W.C.
(Walter C.). II. Title.

P92.C3R65 1992   302.23'0971   C91-095078-4

Copp Clark Pitman Ltd.
2775 Matheson Blvd. East
Mississauga, Ontario
L4W 4P7

Associated companies:
Longman Group Ltd., London
Longman Inc., New York
Longman Cheshire Pty., Melbourne
Longman Paul Pty., Auckland

Printed and bound in Canada

1 2 3 4 5   5187-2   96 95 94 93 92

T A B L E   O F   C O N T E N T S

Preface

The purpose of this book is to examine, historically and developmentally, mass media systems in Canada. This examination flows out of university curricular studies that began in Canada following World War II and accelerated dramatically during the past quarter century. It is important to point out that such studies are not necessarily recognized as a developed and clearly focussed discipline: rather communication studies is a developing area of study. The essential problem with this definitional difficulty revolves around the many research facets of the broad area of communication. For example, these facets include engineering, law, journalism, psychology, sociology, history, economics, and political science, among others. The focus of this book, in the light of the developmental concept, is in the traditional social sciences rather than in engineering or the law.

At the same time, because of this multidimensional character, the approach frequently taken to the area is a multidisciplinary one. The multidisciplinary characterization of the field is indeed a valid one. When programs of communication across Canada are studied, they tend to be of three different types: programs in which several departments offer courses, but in which these courses remain under the control of their respective departments (for example, sociology, political science, philosophy, and English); departments that have been established as autonomous academic units, but where the departmental faculty membership is as multidisciplinary as in the case above; and departments/schools of journalism and communication that have been established primarily to train professional journalists, both print and broadcast. Until such time as Canadian colleges and universities are staffed by graduates in communications per se, it is difficult to use a term other than a developing discipline to describe this area of study. It must be added that what is an encouraging sign concerning the future is that professional colleagues in the country are actively involved in research activities that focus on communication processes and institutions. Thus, while such research tends to be based in a number of disciplines, the focal points at least are uniform.

Evidence of such research activities is to be found first in two Canadian journals: *Canadian Journal of Communication* and *Communication Information*, the former published in English and the latter published in French. These journals emphasize Canadian studies in communication research. Both journals have been publishing for over a decade, and increasingly are gaining recognition as they are abstracted in international indexes. Secondly, the Canadian Communication Association, which became affiliated with the Canadian Learned Societies in 1980, has provided a forum for colleagues to meet with regularity to present papers, discuss instructional strategies, and assess developments in the media telecommunications industries. Membership in the association, in addition to academics, includes representatives from various media industries and federal and provincial agencies associated with communications. Thus, while there are signs that the discipline is maturing, at this point in time, its multidisciplinary character is still its predominant feature.

It is the goal of this book to bring to beginning students an overview that is both comprehensive and understandable with respect to mass communication systems as they have functioned and continue to function in Canada. While the authors advance no personal ideological position, it is obvious that many important questions in Canadian mass communications are caught up in ideological controversy. These controversies and conflicts will not be avoided, but rather will be explained, we hope, from a detached stance.

If on occasion our views of media events differ from those of our colleagues, it should be understood that we comment on those events from a perspective that has been shaped by particular research, study, and work experiences. In this sense, one of our purposes in the text is to add our perspective to a slowly accumulating body of knowledge about Canadian mass media with a view to helping students as they seek to formulate their own understandings of Canadian society and its media institutions.

We've identified our text as an historical and developmental exam-

ination of media systems in Canada. While we do so, we are fully aware of the implicit dangers in such reviews when all of the historical parts have not yet fallen into place. These dangers might be particularly emphasized, given the dynamic nature of the media industries where change is more characteristic of the infrastructure than is stability. At this time of writing, for example, shifts in the economic bases of media are occurring; extensions of media ownership beyond national boundaries are commonplace; and the regulatory patterns for Canadian media, which we've taken for granted, might well be becoming obsolete due to the rapid and constant developments in delivery systems for media content. And all of this is set in a highly volatile political context where the future of what we know as Canada is uncertain. Yet if one were to wait for a settling of conditions in the mass media environment, precious little would be done in documenting characteristics of that environment. This text, then, is our statement of the conditions and the environment in which mass media in Canada have developed and function as we've recognized these at the time of writing.

We wish to stress that the selection of material, the emphasis placed on it, as well as interpretations of it, are our responsibilities. We thank the editorial staff of Copp Clark Pitman, especially Deborah Viets and Barbara Tessman, for their advice, as we do our colleagues Stan Cunningham and Stu Surlin, who generously gave of their time and expertise to comment on portions of the manuscript. We are also indebted to Lucia Brown, Diane Dupuis and Pat Jolie of the University of Windsor Word Processing Centre for their tireless and cheerful efforts in getting the manuscript ready for publication, as well as to cartographer Ronald Welch. Finally we owe a debt of gratitude to our families, who perhaps didn't see as much of us as they may have wished over the past two and a half years.

The authors have found the subject of mass communication tremendously interesting and important and hope that some of this interest and enthusiasm, as well as insights gained over years of teaching and research, is passed on to students reading this book.

About the Authors

Professor Walter I. Romanow entered university teaching following a career in television broadcasting, which included bringing the first T.V. signal to Saskatoon. Receiving his Ph.D. in communication from Wayne State University, he founded the department of communication studies at the University of Windsor in 1968. Professor Walter C. Soderlund received his Ph.D. in political science from the University of Michigan, and his interests have focussed on international communication and the role of media in Canadian political processes. Professor Romanow has taught introductory communication studies, communication policy, consumer behaviour, and advertising, while Professor Soderlund has taught courses in public opinion, the media and Canadian politics, and research methods. They have collaborated in research and writing since the mid-1970s.

The Historical and Theoretical Context

C H A P T E R I

The Canadian Media–Telecommunications Context

Introduction

Because the central focus of this book is the functioning of Canada's mass media systems, it is important at the outset to describe the conditions, historical and current, within which these systems have developed and currently function. An appropriate beginning for this description, then, is the historical context, for it is in our history that the basic operational principles of media–telecommunications systems originated and were nurtured.

It should be understood that when we speak of an historical overview, the period of time involved has been relatively brief.

While newspapers and magazines formed a part of Canada's legacy during the colonial period (the first newspaper was published in 1752), the cinematic arts were popularized only in the early 1900s, while the broadcasting media date from the early 1920s (radio from 1922, television from 1952).

At this point some basic definitions of key terms are in order.

When we speak of media–telecommunications systems, we refer to the instruments of mass media—print, broadcast, cinematic—as well as to distribution systems such as cable television wired systems,[1] and satellites. It is important to be aware of the dynamic nature of mass media due to constant technological development and growth. Even as you read this, breakthroughs are occurring concerning broadcasting–telecommunications, and any applications of technology that can be imagined today are likely to be realized tomorrow.

Historical Overview

As historian and journalism professor Wilfred Kesterton has so aptly pointed out, the establishment of the press in Canada was a rebirth rather than a new enterprise. Traditions of a free press had their origin in Western Europe and were transplanted to the colonies, first to what is now the United States, and from there to Canada.[2]

Such traditions had been forming from the time that John Milton published his tract *Areopagitica* in seventeenth-century England. Milton had successfully challenged the authority of the government with respect to the rights of individuals' freedom of assembly and speech. That document continues to be regarded as the beginning of free expression in the English-speaking world. The tradition of printing per se, was established even earlier, with the invention of a movable press by Johann Gutenberg in the mid-fifteenth century in Germany. The technology and the philosophy were joined when English colonization began in the New World in the mid-eighteenth century.

While the tradition of a free press was well-known, particularly in the New England colonies, it was not paramount in the minds of colonists—settlement was. As historians Wilfred Kesterton and Paul Rutherford[3] describe it, news sheets were born and died almost as quickly as settlements were established and moved. Nor was the tradition of a free press practised, given the authoritarian nature of rule in the new lands. As often as not, the person who started a printing press in a newly founded community served as the King's Printer, and the publication became a document of record that contained formal pronouncements by the Crown's representative in the colonies. In such an early pioneer press, characterized in large part by finan-

cial instability, the practice of free expression was seldom evident. Such free expression would not have been in keeping with the "small but steady government patronage that more often than not" kept printing enterprises alive.[4] As long as the press served as a mouthpiece for a governor's dicta, its survival was assured but a subservient press was the consequence.

Slowly, however, independence from such authoritarian restrictions became apparent, with financial support for the printing industry coming from four sources: payment by readers for issues of news sheets, even if such payment was only a pittance; advertising—rudimentary in terms of what we know advertising to be today; commercial job printing—as communities grew in size, demands for such commercial services also grew; and political party support—dependent upon the editorial attitudes and positions taken by a news sheet.

As they gained independence, the presses began to challenge policical authority. A landmark case was recorded in Canada when in 1835 Joseph Howe's Halifax newspaper the *Novascotian* accused magistrates and police of pilfering from the public purse.[5] In the ensuing libel trial, during which Howe eloquently defended his editorial right to comment publicly on violations of the public trust, a jury acquitted him of the charge. As journalism historians have pointed out, the Howe libel trial followed exactly by one hundred years a similar trial of a newspaper and its editor, John Peter

Zenger, in New York in 1734–1735. Zenger's paper, the *New York Weekly Journal,* was charged with "raising sedition" when it attacked the governor of the day for inept administration; in particular the newspaper criticized the governor for permitting French warships to spy on established military defences. In this instance as well, Zenger was acquitted and, as historians note, his defence had been based on the right of a newspaper to utter the truth.[6]

Joseph Howe, 1804–73, c. 1871. (National Archives of Canada/C 22002)

In Canada in the years preceding Confederation, there was a clear relationship between political processes and newspapers. For example politicians were often newspaper publishers or editors, as were several Fathers of Confederation, among them, George Brown, J.B.E. Dorion, D'Arcy McGee, and Edward Whelan.[7]

The tradition of political partisanship of newspapers was established in the pre-Confederation period and rival papers were identified as Tory or Grit supporters. At the same time, technological developments led to the proliferation of newspapers. The harnessing of electricity, for instance, made possible the cylinder press, and by the turn of the century newspapers were publishing in all major settlements in the country. In 1913, there were 138 daily newspapers publishing in Canada, more than ever before or since.[8]

Even at this early date it was apparent that newspaper publishing was a profitable enterprise and, as profitability increased, so did commercial competition between newspapers. A natural consequence of such profitability and competition was the trend, recognizable then and continuing into the present, towards the narrowing ownership base of Canadian newspapers and the rise of newspaper chains.

In the midst of newspaper growth and development in the country the electronic media appeared on the scene. In 1922 commercial radio station CFCF was licensed in Montreal to the Marconi Corporation of Europe, and within a decade radio stations were broadcasting in all major Canadian cities. The development of radio, however, differed from the path taken by newspapers, in that from the very first radio broadcasting was a public as well as a private enterprise. Initially the public enterprise was represented by Canadian National Railways

(CNR), a Crown corporation created from a defunct system of privately owned railroads. While public radio was established in the early 1920s to entertain passengers, CNR president Sir Henry Thornton saw the potential of radio as a unifying force in Canada and "he set out consciously to create a sense of nationhood through the medium of the Canadian National Railway service."[9]

Radio-equipped parlour observation car, CNR, 1929. (National Archives of Canada/C 26000)

This philosophical difference between public and private ownership of broadcasting, which is explored in more detail in later chapters, continues to this day. The resulting mixed public/private broadcasting system is a unique feature of Canada's broadcasting–telecommunications industry.

Experiments with television had started in the early 1920s in the United States and in Europe (the 1939 New York World's Fair had a public demonstration of television broadcasting). However, it was not until the early 1950s that the medium became popular on the North American continent. The first Canadian television stations were Crown corporations. CBFT in Montreal began telecasting on 6 September 1952 and CBLT in Toronto premiered two days later. Additional Canadian Broadcasting Corporation (CBC)-owned-and-operated stations followed quickly, as did stations that are now owned by private sector companies. In these early years of broadcasting, it should be noted that the CBC had a dual responsibility: first, as a broadcaster to provide a national service of programs and information; second, as the regulatory body over all broadcasting affairs in the country. This last responsibility was mandated to the CBC under the authority of the 1936 Broadcasting Act, the same act that created the CBC.

Television developed rapidly, and its growth was marked by the introduction of fresh ownership of the media industries. At the same time, many private companies in Canada that already owned and operated media—newspapers or radio stations, or both—were well represented in the ranks of those that were granted television licences.

It should also be pointed out that these private companies were initially granted television-operating licences on the proviso that their stations operate as CBC affiliates, that is, that they would carry a basic CBC programming service. Thus, the broadcasting strategy created in the 1950s for television emphasized the distribution to as many communities in Canada as possible of a basic national public service—in essence, a noncompetitive telecasting system.

It was in 1960 and under the authority of the regulatory body that replaced the CBC as regulator (the Board of Broadcast Governors, established under the authority of the 1958 Broadcasting Act) that privately owned second television stations were licensed in eight of Canada's largest centres. Shortly after, on 1 October 1961, these stations formed Canada's second television network, CTV, and alternative programming was introduced to Canadians.

From their inception Canadian broadcasters—both public and private—were expected to follow one guiding principle: whatever else might occur, they were obliged to produce content that would emphasize the distinctive nature of Canadian society. If this were not done, stated royal commissions and committees and sundry other reports on Canadian broadcasting, the airwaves would be flooded by content produced in the neighbouring United States.

Thus, the application of social purpose—to defend the Canadian community from acculturation by the United States—has characterized Canada's broadcasting systems from the beginning to this day. Their resolve has been unwavering and has provided the operative philosophy for most of the nation's broadcasting efforts. However, while their aim has been steadfast, it would be incorrect to suggest that the behaviour of broadcasters—both public and private—has been totally consistent with the stated philosophy. For example, U.S. television programs have been imported and slotted into Canadian prime-time schedules. This clearly goes against the stated purpose.

While the print and film industries have not been formally mandated to protect and promote the Canadian identity, they are still expected to contribute to the national identity. In effect, all media have become part of what we term a *national defensive posture*—a posture that has as its central design the production and dissemination of information that emphasizes Canadian expression and character.

While this historical overview has been brief, it has been offered to provide some insight regarding the context within which Canada's media systems have developed. There are other nonhistorical factors, however, that also need to be

Defending Canada's cultural identify. (The Beaver)

discussed in order to complete an understanding of the broader domestic context within which media have developed and continue to operate.

Geography and Population

Canada's size and population present two particular problems for mass media. Geographically, Canada is a huge country (second only to the former Soviet Union) and providing information and programming to this vast territory has been problematic and expensive. At the same time, the population of Canada is about twenty-seven million, approximately one-tenth of that of the United States. While it is true that citizens are scattered throughout this vast territory, over half of the population resides within one hundred miles of the U.S.–Canadian border. This means, of course, that Canadians are within constant reach of U.S. over-the-air broadcasting signals.

Moreover, those who live near border cities have daily access to U.S. newspapers. In a very real sense, then, Canadians are frequently exposed to a very powerful information-generating society. As a consequence we tend to be as familiar with U.S. social, cultural, and political affairs as we are with our own. Such familiarity with the American cultural environment caused Mitchell Sharp, former fed-eral minister for External Affairs, to comment at a seminar on Canadian–American relations that the problem with U.S. culture is that we treat it as our own.[10]

Regionalism

Canada's vast geography also contributes to the regionalization of the country. Sociologist Robert Brym, citing the Task Force on Canadian Unity, created in 1977, identifies factors contributing to diversity and regionalization. Primary factors are: geographical barriers; disparate levels of economic development based on the fact that extractive and manufacturing industries tend to be located in different regions of the country; ethnic distinctiveness; variations in political behaviour; and different sets of federal-provincial relationships applying to different regions of the country. Sociologists agree that the concept of regionalism means that geographic communities are distinctive because of "peculiar economic, social and cultural elements."[11] Further, Canada's uneven distribution of population (based on economic development, urbanization, and climatological factors) and differences in population gains and losses among the regions also contribute to regionalization. Generally Canada's regions are identified as the Atlantic provinces, Quebec, Ontario, the Prairies, British Columbia, and the Territories.

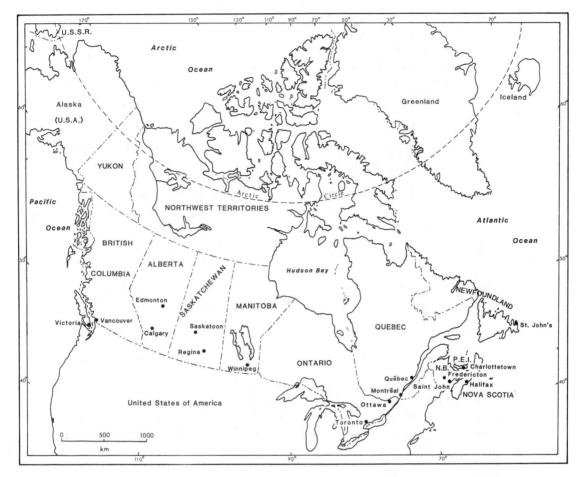

FIGURE I–I

Map of Canada

Given such regional disparities, the nationbuilding tasks of Canadian media systems become more difficult. Two facets of the problem appear to be these: First, to what extent is it possible for a national broadcasting system such as the CBC to fulfil its mandate, as defined by past Broadcasting Acts, to define a national identity and to develop national unity? Second, if regional media fulfil their community responsibilities, in the natural course of events they are likely to reflect the cultural aspirations of their own regions rather than focussing on national considerations.

In light of the current trend towards greater political power on the part of the provinces in the Canadian federal system, is it possible that the federal government has recognized the impossibility of any medium developing national unity in a society so regionalized as Canada? The fact that this specific mandate is absent from the latest Broadcasting Act could be interpreted as evidence for such a conclusion.

Historically, of course, the provincial governments in Canada have held political powers independent of the federal government, and provinces tend to use these powers in carrying out their political responsibilities in a way that often appears to be confrontational to federal authority. For example, the responsibility for education rests with the provinces, and provincial governments have used this power as an entry point into the communications area (a federal responsibility) on the basis that broadcasting is a powerful instrument of learning. While these instruments tend to have their major application within the broader concept of continuous learning, they have as well been related to the classroom setting. Out of such practices we find on the contemporary media scene organizations such as B.C. Knowledge Network, Access Alberta, Saskatchewan Communications Network, TVOntario, Radio-Québec, and Atlantic Satellite Network. Currently the question of jurisdiction over broadcasting matters is in some dispute, with provinces increasingly challenging the federal government's right to regulate educational broadcasting.

This can be seen as an example of what is referred to as the devolution of power from the federal government to the provinces, characteristic of current trends in Canadian federalism.

Linguistic and Cultural Diversity

Canada is a bilingual nation, based on a partnership of two founding immigrant cultures—French and English. At the same time, Canada exists as a multicultural society. Multiculturalism developed initially as a result of a deliberate immigration policy on the part of the federal government and secondarily due to the fact that historically there were relatively few restrictions on voluntary immigration.

The consequences of such cultural pluralism, openly encouraged by federal and provincial authorities, have been problematic. Since Canada's mass media have quite naturally behaved in a manner that is consistent with the make-up of the country's linguistic and cultural populations, the question must be raised again about the fulfillment of the Canadian identity mandate, specified for broadcasting and implicit for the print industries. Newspapers in Canada publish in at least thirty-five languages other than English and French, with approximately a half dozen of these heritage language newspapers publishing daily.[12] At the same time, in the larger communities, multilingual broadcasting abounds, and currently with cable distribution such programming is available to most of Canada's population.

The Canadian Broadcasting Corporation has always functioned as a dual language system—CBC in

English and Radio-Canada in French. However, at one point, when sentiment for Quebec separatism was growing in that province in the latter half of the 1970s, concerns were expressed in Parliament that Radio-Canada was clearly supporting separatist interests, and requests for a royal commission were made in Parliament.

Following an inquiry headed by Harry Boyle, chairman of the Canadian Radio-television and Telecommunications Commission (CRTC), it was concluded that, while some policy adjustments needed to be made concerning the working relationship between the English and French networks within the CBC, there was no need for a royal commission inquiry at that time.[13] Concerns that a separatist bias in the CBC French network contributed to the election of a Parti Québécois (PQ) government in Quebec in 1976 were quelled by the inquiry.

A problem that results from our linguistic and cultural diversity is the difficulty we have had in defining our own identity. As has been pointed out many times, it is difficult to define Canadian culture with much more accuracy than we can when we say that Canadian culture is not American culture. This problem is not likely to be eased in the future, given the rapid acceleration of technology which is characterized in large part by increasing choices of non-Canadian content available to Canadians. As will be discussed in later chapters, throughout our broadcasting history audi-

ence-rating systems have consistently pointed out that when Canadians are offered a choice we tend to prefer content produced in the United States over that produced domestically.

The regulation of media in such an environment has not been easy. In the 1980s, the Department of Communications assumed the responsibility for both communications and cultural affairs, recognizing the interrrelatedness of these components. The parliamentary committee, in this instance, became known as the Standing Committee on Communications and Culture.

In an attempt to offer greater focus to the Canadian identity mandate and to shift discussion to economic from aesthetic concerns, federal government committees and reports have taken to using the term *cultural industries*. The term is intended to include broadcasting, films, publishing, fine arts, performing arts, libraries, and museums— almost any endeavour that in one way or another creates and reflects Canadian character or conditions.

The complex set of problems faced by Canadian mass media in coping with the environment in which it has to function is portrayed in figure 1–2. The figure depicts the dilemma in which Canadian society finds itself. On the one hand, there are strong cultural, social, and economic forces that tend to drive Canada into a continental environment along with the United States. On the other hand, there is a strong inherent desire on the part

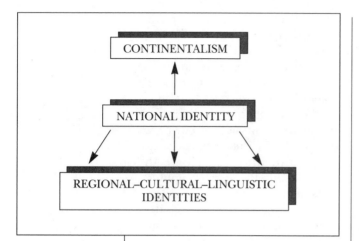

FIGURE 1–2

Factors Complicating the Creation of a Canadian National Identity

of Canadians to be clearly recognized as a people distinct from Americans. This is made more difficult by the subidentities inherent in regional, cultural, and linguistic differences. The mass media/cultural, industries at the present time find themselves at the centre of this dual directional pull.

Technological Context

Technological developments of various types have influenced mass media and have shaped the kind and design of content prepared and disseminated by the media. Gutenberg's movable press, for instance, made it possible to duplicate copies of manuscripts as well as to use highly illustrative designs in multiple copies. The introduction of electricity to printing gave rise eventually to rotary presses with multi-layout and colour capacities. The telephone and telegraph not only speeded up the movement of infor-

mation from event to media but permitted media to increase their capacity for content.

It was the post-World War II era, however, that saw the rapid reduction of time and space constraints on media content. The development of rocketry, then orbital satellites and their computerized tracking systems, miniaturization and transportability of power cells, magnetic recording tapes and other devices all followed in rapid succession. Within a fifteen-year period following World War II, media were transformed in kind as well as in their operational methods.

It is necessary at this point to explain the term *media content*. As normally used, the term refers to media product—the printed page, the audio broadcast, the television broadcast, the film for movie theatres. It is important, however, to extend this definition further, to think of content as information. In a sense the two meanings are often interchangeable because all content is information, whatever its intent.

Various definitions of *information* are available, and the term is commonly used by communications scholars, for example, when they describe current society as "the information society." Political scientist Harlan Cleveland defines information as "organized data, the raw material for specialized knowledge and generalized wisdom."[14] In this sense, and in the sense that the term is used in this text, information has a broad meaning that encompasses the words, paragraphs, pages, transmissions, media output (in whatever form) that individuals use to communicate with others. Thus, the term refers to the products of our developing media industries.

Many diverse items of technological hardware have been adapted for, or adopted by, the media industries. It is possible to categorize the hardware according to the manner in which it is used in the production or dissemination of information by the media industries. Three categories can be identified: expansion of the broadcasting spectrum and the multiplication of delivery systems; satellite distribution of content; and electronic storage, editing, and retrieval of content.

Multiplication of Distribution Delivery Systems and Programs

For many years those who regulated broadcasting did so in the safe knowledge that regulations could readily be applied and operations easily monitored because, as government reports of the 1930s and 1940s emphasized, broadcasting frequencies were a "scarce resource." In any community, for example when TV appeared on the scene in the 1950s, there existed one channel, or perhaps two. In the larger communities several stations existed, and these were limited to Very High Frequency (VHF) channels, usually numbered from two to thirteen. Such a state of affairs was generally controllable, orderly, and predictable in terms of develop-

ment. Within a decade, however, frequencies in the Ultra High Frequency (UHF) range extended the television spectrum. Channels in this spectrum are numbered fourteen to eight-two, with an upper limit yet to be determined.

Further, almost at the same time as TV stations began broadcasting, communities started to utilize radar transmission technology to bring cable television to remote areas by picking up, strengthening, then rebroadcasting signals. Thus, Community Antennae Television (CATV) distribution was developed. In Canada, the first CATV (more commonly known as cable television) was introduced on an experimental basis in London, Ontario, in 1951. Shortly after, rapid adoption of the technology took place, particularly in the Western Canadian mountain regions of Alberta and British Columbia. Expansion was rapid, especially since the coaxial cable assured quality signal reception, superior to over-the-air rebroadcasting. Cable TV distribution has continued to expand and is rapidly becoming the predominant delivery system in both Canada and the United States. In 1990, for example, 71.4 percent of Canadian households were serviced by cable.[15]

Several noteworthy consequences of such a rapid increase in the number of information distribution systems are apparent.

Content Choices

Canadians are offered multiple choices of content, so once again the nation is faced with the question

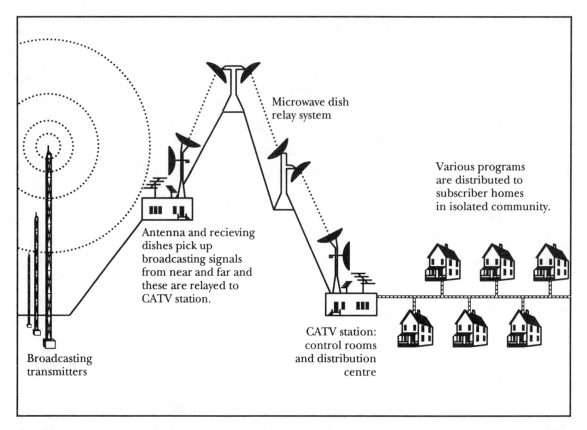

Microwave dish relay system

Various programs are distributed to subscriber homes in isolated community.

Antenna and recieving dishes pick up broadcasting signals from near and far and these are relayed to CATV station.

CATV station: control rooms and distribution centre

Broadcasting transmitters

FIGURE 1–3

CATV Distribution System

of the effectiveness of the formal and informal regulatory measures aimed at fostering national identity and unity. In the vast array of signals available, the proportion of Canadian content has been lessened.

Content Quality

The question must be raised too about the quality of content that fills the vast number of distribution systems that are available. Can we fill the number of channels available with content of quality? It is more than evident that formulaic rather than artistically designed content predominates. For example, in his lifetime, William Shake-speare wrote thirty-seven plays. Were Shakespeare alive today and writing for television, his output would barely fill out a program season for a show produced weekly.

With respect to programming, there has been a proliferation of talk shows and dramas and sitcoms with stereotypical, sensationalistic content. At the same time it is quite apparent that there is not enough "news," as conventionally defined, to fill out twenty-four hours of news programming. Thus we find in such schedules as CNN and CBC's Newsworld, a variety of talk, human interest, and current affairs features. Given the extraordinary demand for content, the traditional concept of what is news has been altered and diluted.

Economic Bases

The rapid increase in the number of delivery systems has threatened the formats and economic bases of what might be called traditional mass media, which have heretofore depended upon large audiences or numerous readers for commercial success. For example, the film industry has very quickly changed in its distribution pattern from single large theatre units to small multiplex systems. As well, the film industry has geared itself to producing and releasing film/videos for the home VCR market in addition to making films for theatrical distribution. With respect to broadcasting, economic bases are also rapidly changing. Because audiences now watch programs in small rather than large numbers, the traditional commercial pattern of delivering large audiences to advertisers is almost passé.

The future of the daily newspaper, the community newspaper, and the magazine industry is also problematic. The three industries have been considerably modified over the past decade. Readership patterns are constantly changing, given that audience attention to electronic media increases each year. Only a decade ago, scholars speculated about the "electronic newspaper." Today, the electronic newspaper is a fact, even though its format is still rudimentary. Electronic systems such as CEEFAX, the electronic news chan-nel developed by the British Broadcasting Corporation, signalled the immediate future of the electronic press. The system was quickly emulated elsewhere, and we now have electronic access to newspapers' news libraries. In Canada the best example is the *Globe and Mail's* Info Globe, accessible through telephone–computer systems.

Audience Fragmentation

Audiences today are splintered, bringing about an economic threat to conventional media, which have been functioning on a cost-per-thousand formula. For example, in 1986 the three major American television networks (CBS, NBC, and ABC) began to reshape their commercial thinking in recognition of the fact that the multiplication of distribution systems presented a threat to their commercial bases. Staff reductions were the first indicator of this trend. The networks have also asked the U.S. federal government to ease restrictions that currently limit the capacity of networks to produce their own prime-time programming. (A net effect of such relaxation of regulation would be to put the networks more in control of their own programming and to place a limit on competitive independent producers.) As well, at least two of the networks—NBC and ABC—have already made significant investments in cable television systems, a principal competitor of network schedules.[16] In effect, audiences have segmented themselves into special interest groups. The essential effect of such splintering and the development of these special interest groups is that except in some unusual circumstances, it is no longer correct to speak of "mass audiences"; it is more appropriate to describe audiences today as being "demassified."[17]

Satellite Distribution

Satellite distribution systems, while originally developed as military hardware, quickly became adapted to transmission/reflector systems by media industries. The essential characteristic of the information-based society is that more information is moved to more people at a greater speed than ever before. And tomorrow, we will move even more information at a greater speed than we do today. For extraordinary events that are of interest to global communities, audiences may number in the billions rather than millions. If one considers the acceleration of rates of travel, in the summer of 1989 space satellite *Voyager II* was sending back pictures to television audiences on Earth over distances of five billion kilometres. Travelling at the speed of light, it took a signal four and a half hours to travel from Neptune to Earth.

We are aware, as well, that insofar as surveillance is concerned (again adapting military functions to communications uses), satellites scan from outer space as would a telephoto lens. If military uses of satellite technology have allowed nations to monitor each other's military manoeuvres, commercial satellite systems can deliver information of events of any sort to television audiences. No longer is production of television programming confined to a physical plant, but initiating sources may be anywhere on the globe, or for that matter anywhere in space.

Satellite transmissions have given new meaning to the term international broadcasting. Shortwave radio transmissions have been with us since the 1920s. Most, if not all, nations on earth with a modicum of broadcasting technology are involved in broadcasting to the international community. Satellites in the 1980s have accelerated and expanded the scope of international broadcasting to include television transmission and reception.

While it may not have been the first program of its kind, in the winter of 1987, ABC in the United States initiated an international "Capital to Capital" weekly television program in co-operation with Gostelradio, the central broadcasting authority in the Soviet Union. This brief television series featured U.S. members of Congress in Washington and Politburo representatives in Moscow in live, confrontational, candid discussions. While it might be premature to suggest that Marshall McLuhan's "global village" concept has been realized, the development of communications satellites has meant a significant step towards such a reality.

Satellite transmissions have also given rise to a direct broadcast satellite (DBS) industry, whereby home-owners are able to pick up television signals from global sources with the help of home "dishes." Such transmissions bypass the need for CATV companies to pick up and retransmit such signals, as is still the current practice. DBS programming, in effect, cancels out any limiting or regulatory role that governments might have in restricting access to content. The greatest limiting factors thus far in the growth of DBS programming have been the relatively high cost of receiving dishes (averaging about three thousand dollars) and their large size (about 3.6 metres in diameter, and occasionally larger).

However, because of heavy competition within the DBS industry, both the cost and size of dishes are being reduced. Dishes are currently on the market in Western Europe that vary between thirty centimetres to sixty centimetres in diameter (about twelve inches to thirty-six inches) and in the cost range of three hundred to four hundred dollars. Given further technological developments, both price and size should continue to decrease—for example, the recent development by the British Satellite Broadcasting Company of a "squarial"—a thirty-centimetre-square aerial, which promises to make effective inroads into the current competitiveness of the industry. At stake in the immediate future for those who would use DBS systems for program transmission is the potential European market of 320 million consumers who will comprise a single market in 1992 when European trade barriers are removed.[18]

Capacities for Storage and Retrieval

The development of magnetic tape recording capabilities in the 1940s (popularized in the 1950s) revolutionized the broadcasting industry. Almost instantly, magnetic tape replaced wire recorders that had been in place for approximately a decade. As well, magnetic tape made heavy inroads into the flat disc recording industry. Henceforth, broadcasters found the days of live transmissions were over except in those instances where particular events (unusual military or terrorist actions, or natural catastrophes, for example) demanded live broadcasting.

The ability to record and retain information for future use was the obvious prime benefit of the new recording equipment. Events were recorded at remote locations and tapes were brought back to programming newsrooms for convenient scheduling. The ability to edit what had been recorded was of equal importance, and human manipulation of events became a characteristic of broadcasting as it had always been in print journalism.

But the magnetic tape recorder has had its greatest impact in the form of videocassette recording (VCR) equipment. The price of this equipment dropped in the early 1980s, bringing it within reach of the average Canadian. Statistics Canada data indicate that in May 1985, 2.1 million households (or 23 percent of total homes in the country) possessed VCRs. By 1990, this total reached sixty-six percent.[19] Because prices of the units continue to drop from year to year (given the element of strong international manufacturing competition), VCRs are quickly becoming essential and inseparable companions to television sets in the home.

Home VCRs are used in two broad ways: first as "playback" units for home video cameras and rented videos and secondly and more commonly to record programs off the air for viewing at a more convenient time. In effect, the viewer has the capacity to set his or her own media schedule.

While the question of copyright is raised with VCR recording, it is not as yet the practice for law-enforcement agencies to enter private homes to search for violation of copyright. The monitoring and enforcement tasks of such activity would be so huge and complex that it would seem impossible to institute any real controls.

What becomes clear, even from this cursory overview of VCRs, is that lifestyles have changed drastically: homes no longer are simply equipped with radios or TVs. When one looks at today's home technological instruments, we find home "information centres," where a variety of electronic instruments inter-

act with one another. It is not unusual to find "technologically advanced families"—TAFFIES—whose homes contain stereos, TVs, VCRs, answering machines, modems, and FAX machines.[20] How many such households exist is uncertain, but a ballpark estimate would be that about 15 percent.

Why Study Communication?

Why is it important to study all of these systems and developments? There are several reasons why this question and responses to it are important to students in the social sciences.

The Information Society

Economists, social psychologists, political scientists, and others recognized some time ago that societies, particularly those in the developed Northern Hemisphere, have moved well beyond the industrial age and into the "information age." Technological developments, such as those discussed earlier, offer ample evidence that such a label is appropriate.

That this is the information age is borne out by data revealing a dramatic shift over the last century in labour force distribution. As table 1–1 shows, the fastest growing area of the U.S. work force is the information, knowledge, and education sector. It is projected that, by the year 2000, two-thirds the people in the American labour force will work in this sector. Just over one hundred years ago, only 2 percent of workers were in this sector while almost 50 percent were in agriculture or extractive industries. Political scientist Harlan Cleveland uses the term the *informationization of society* to describe this phenomenon.

While the distribution of Canada's labour force differs somewhat from that found in the United States, these differences are not pronounced. For example, it is clear that given Canada's huge reservoir of natural resources, a larger percentage of our work force is committed to extractive and production industries. But the trend towards increasing employment in the information/knowledge/education industries is evident in both societies: Statistics Canada confirms that "'information workers,' who create, process, store, distribute, analyze, and otherwise handle information comprise a major portion of Canada's work force."[21]

As more of our labour force moves into the information, knowledge, and education industries, we generate more and more information to the point that the question is raised about whether we need anything like the amount of information we generate each year. Arguments have been made that we currently produce much more information than society needs, and that the gap is increasing between the amounts of information we produce and the demand and use for

TABLE 1–1					
Trends in the Distribution of the U.S. Work Force					
	1880	1920	1955	1975	2000 (est.)
Agriculture and Extractive	50%	28%	14%	4%	2%
Manufacturing, Commerce, Industry	36	53	37	29	22
Other Services	12	10	20	17	10
Information, Knowledge, Education	2	9	29	50	66

Source: Harlan Cleveland, "The Twilight of Hierarchy: Speculations on the Global Information Society," *Public Administration Review* 45 (January/February 1985): 186.

it.[22] Thus the monitoring of the changing work environment, which is having behavioural consequences in society, is essential.

Expectations of Media

The question, too, is raised in this information society about the role of our mass media/telecommunications systems. What are they doing? What should they be doing? What expectations do we have of them? Should these systems be left to their own devices of gathering, producing, and disseminating information on their own subjective bases? None of these questions has an entirely satisfactory answer.

In Canada, and in other nations, social expectations have been defined for the mass media, and media function in various ways. It is clear that media offer us varied sorts of entertainment and information in different formats, and that they give to us a representative picture of our society. In fact, we might say that everything that we do not experience directly is presented and defined for us by mass media. This is especially true of our knowledge of world news and politics.

In Canada, the United Kingdom, and the United States, post-World War II studies focussed on appropriate roles for mass media. The earliest of these, the 1948 Hutchins Commission in the U.S., reviewed the role of media with a particular focus on freedom of the press.[23] The context of such inquiries was as follows: the Second World War had ended and it was evident that mass media, particularly newspapers and radio in the 1920s and 1930s in Germany and Italy, were instruments that, in the wrong hands, could create havoc, with horrendous consequences. Thus, the role of journalism in times of conflict and in peace was being questioned. On the horizon loomed the popularization of television, a medium that predictably would become a major force on the communications scene. What about the matter of responsibility, asked the commission? Was TV to go the route of commercialized AM radio, where the driving forces were advertising and public relations industries? The central question raised by the Hutchins Commission was whether traditional laissez-faire philosophy was sufficient as a guide for media in a modern society. Were free choices in fact free? The term *social*

responsibility kept cropping up in the discussion. This new concept began to characterize Canadian media systems perhaps even more than it did American systems.

A satisfactory understanding about how mass media should be expected to function in an open democratic society is not achieved easily or quickly. There are likely to be as many positions for what media ought to be doing as there are persons who are interested in that future. Thus, the study of our social practices and needs within a framework that espouses freedom of expression for all, including the mass media, is a high priority for students of media communications.

It has been apparent since 1980 that through the United Nations Education Scientific Cultural Organization (UNESCO) pressures have mounted for mass media, wherever they might be, to function in nation-building roles. These roles stress the building of a society, rather than the welfare of individuals in these societies. Because of its importance, this subject will be discussed at greater length in the following chapter. Nevertheless, it is possible to identify summarily what mass media do in their communities. As a pioneering theoretician in communications, Harold Lasswell identified three primary functions that the media perform in a society:[24]

- "Surveillance of the environment": we recognize that the media observe our society and report to us about it. As citizens we are unable to observe most events adequately even in our own immediate communities, not to mention those larger communities (provinces, nations, global regions) to which we may belong. Mass media have equipped themselves to perform such reporting tasks.

- "Correlation of the parts of society": Media provide us with an interpretation of events which they observe and on which they report. In popular terminology, this is referred to as "mediation of reality." News stories, for example, are placed into a context through editorials, documentaries, and features of various sorts.
- "Transmission of the social heritage from one generation to the next": as mass media select their raw materials from society and prepare these materials for transmission, there is an accompanying selection and transmission of our heritage, culture, and value systems.

It is possible to add to Lasswell's typology of roles performed by communications systems.

- Media also provide economic information by serving as advertising vehicles for the industrial/manufacturing sector of society. Thus, media, at the same time as securing a financially profitable base for their organizations, serve as intermediaries between product/service producers and consumers.
- Finally, media provide entertainment—and they often do this to

the extent that the entertainment role tends to take precedence over other functions.

It is possible, of course, to observe that media perform these basic roles well or poorly—depending on our expectations. Discussions of media performance are found throughout the remainder of the book.

Dependency on Media

Increasingly, our time is spent interacting with media of one sort or another. For example, various studies have pointed out that by the time students graduate from high school, they will have spent more time watching television than they will have spent in the classroom. When we look at our ageing population, we see a society with more leisure time than ever before, and predictably much of this time will be spent with mass media. Thus, dependency upon entertainment furnished by mass media is a recognizable trend. Studies, for example, attesting to radio and television soap opera addiction are numerous. At the same time, we depend upon mass media as immediate information systems, and because we generally no longer attend town hall meetings, we depend on media to report to us the behaviour of our municipal governments, our provincial legislatures, and our federal Parliament.

Students of mass communications should therefore examine mass media not only as they serve our social and citizenship needs but also as they help to shape our aesthetics and values. According to sociologists, psychologists, and political scientists, mass media influence our behaviour as they structure our perception of society.

Media as a Political Conduit

It is clear that mass media have become the conduits for information flow between those who govern societies and those who are governed. This particular role of the mass media is a fascinating one. Few of our politicians are able to escape the scrutiny of mass media as media report to society on day-to-day events. The media version of political reality presented to us daily implies awesome power for the mass media. This is largely because media reporting of politics is accepted as real and tends to remain unexamined. It is important, therefore, that there be critical scrutiny of media as they function in a political context. Closely linked to this is a further consideration which demands constant review of media processes: media cannot only distort reality but occasionally violate the rights of individuals.

Constant monitoring of mass media is vital in a democratic community. Studies by mass media organizations themselves only go part way in fulfilling this critical need. Proper media criticism depends upon the objective observations of people who work outside the media industries, such as scholars and other citizens. As Wilbur Schramm, the noted communications scholar, often commented, one of the functions of an educational system is to help to raise a generation of critics. Let this, too, be one of the purposes of this text.

Notes

1. The 1967–68 Broadcasting Act had been faulted for its incompleteness in describing the technical instruments that fall under the jurisdiction of the act. In a proposal for a new act, the concept of cable distribution is incorporated and henceforth all instruments involved in "broadcasting receiving undertaking" fall under the jurisdiction of the Broadcasting Act, whether they are received over the air or by means of cable technology. See Canada, Ministry of Communications, *Canadian Voices Canadian Choices: A New Broadcasting Policy for Canada* (Ottawa: Supply and Services, 1988), 51.
2. See Wilfred H. Kesterton, *A History of Journalism in Canada* (Toronto: Carleton University Press, 1984), 1–5.
3. See Paul Rutherford, *The Making of the Canadian Media* (Toronto: McGraw-Hill Ryerson, 1978).
4. Kesterton, *A History of Journalism in Canada*, 2.
5. Ibid., 22.
6. Michael Emery and Edwin Emery, *The Press and America*, 6th ed. (Englewood Cliffs, NJ: Prentice-Hall, 1988), 38–44.
7. P. B. Waite, *The Life and Times of Confederation, 1864–1867: Politics, Newspapers, and the Union of British North America* (Toronto: University of Toronto Press, 1962), 5–17.

8. Kesterton, *A History of Journalism in Canada*, 64.

9. D'Arcy Marsh, *The Tragedy of Henry Thronton* (Toronto: Macmillan, 1935), 115–16, cited by Frank W. Peers, *The Politics of Canadian Broadcasting, 1920–1951* (Toronto: University of Toronto Press, 1969), 24.

10. Michell Sharp, "Can Canada Maintain a Separate Identity Beside the United States?" in *Fourth Seninar on Canadian–American Relations* (Windsor, ON: Assumption University of Windsor, 1962), 241.

11. Robert J. Brym, "An Introduction to the Regional Question in Canada," in *Regionalism in Canada*, ed. Robert J. Brym (Toronto: Irwin Publishing, 1986), 4.

12. *Canadian Advertising Rates and Data*, May 1991.

13. Canadian Radio-television and Telecommunications Commission, *Report of the Committee of Inquiry into the National Broadcasting Service 14 March 1977* (Ottawa, 1977), 71.

14. Harlan Cleveland, "The Twilight of Hierarchy: Speculations on the Global Information Society," *Public Administration Review* 45 (January/February 1985): 186.

15. Statistics Canada, *Household Facilities and Equipment 1990* (Ottawa: Supply and Services, 1990), 9.

16. Randall Rothenberg, "Advertising: 3 Networks See Declines Continuing," *New York Times*, 8 February 1989, D1, D19.

17. This phenomenon is discussed as a transition from elite to popular to specialized media. See Ralph L. Lowenstein and John C. Merrill, *Macromedia: Mission, Message and Morality* (New York: Longman, 1990), 31–38.

18. "European DBS: Off to an Unsteady but Enthusiastic Start," *Broadcasting* 117 (17 July 1989): 57.

19. Statistics Canada, *Household Facilities and Equipment 1990* (Ottawa: Supply and Services, 1990), 9. See also *Media Digest 1990/1991, Catalogue 64.202*, (Ottawa: Statistics Canada, 1989), 9.

20. William R. Oates, Shailendra Ghorpade, Jane D. Brown, "Media Technology Consumers: Demographics and Psychographics of 'TAFFIES'" (paper presented at the Annual Meeting of the Association for Education and Mass Communication, University of Oklahoma, 1986).

21. See *Canada Year Book 1990* (Ottawa: Supply and Services, 1989), 14-1. Also see David Gower, "Labour Force Trends: Canada and the United States," *Canadian Social Trends* 10 (Autumn 1988): 14–19, and "Social Inventors," *Canadian Social Trends* 16 (Spring 1990): 35.

22. Jan J. van Cuilenburg, "The Information Society: Some Trends and Implications," *European Journal of Communication* 2 (March 1987): 105.

23. *Report of the Commission on Freedom of the Press: Toward a Free and Responsible Press* (Chicago: University of Chicago Press, 1947).

24. Harold D. Lasswell, "The Structural Function of Communication in Society," in *The Process and Effects of Mass Communication*, rev. ed., ed. Wilbur Schramm and Donald F. Roberts (Chicago: University of Illinois Press, 1971), 85. See also Wilbur Schramm's detailed comments concerning Lasswell's essay in *Men, Messages, and Media: A Look at Human Communication* (New York: Harper and Row, 1973), 30–36.

C H A P T E R 2

A Framework for Comparing Mass Media Systems

Introduction

In traditional comparative studies focussing on different types of communications systems, scholars have outlined what they consider to be the major political systems and then described the media systems that were characteristic of each. In the initial theoretical formulation there were four so-called theories of the press. These were, as developed by Siebert, Peterson, and Schramm, authoritarian, communist, libertarian, and social responsibility.[1] In effect, each theory described how mass media functioned in accordance with the philosophical and political norms of the society in which they were located. The four theories marked an important conceptual development and scholars in the late 1950s and 1960s used them as a basis for comparing mass media systems. As with most theories, the four theories of the press became refined over time. Factors contributing to this refinement were continuous academic research, development of mass media them-selves, and the rapid transformation of global society, particularly the decline of colonialism in Asia, Africa, and the English-speaking Caribbean in the 1960s.

Due to the work of scholars such as John Merrill, Ralph Lowenstein, Hamid Mowlana, William Hachten, Robert Picard,[2] and others, rather than four basic systems, it is now much more accurate to speak in terms of six distinctive operative systems for media: authoritarian, communist, revolutionary, development, libertarian and social democratic. While the original four theories have been significantly refined, the underlying premise of that pioneering work, that there is a congruent relationship between a political system and the mass media system that serves it, remains unshaken. Societies foster institutions that are appropriate in terms of social needs and social desires. Institutions do not function apart from their societies, and this is what we mean when we say that there is a congruent relationship between a society and its mass media system. Thus, the comparative focus for the study of mass media involves an examination of the relationship of media to the way in which political power is organized and used—and mass media in the global community can be differentiated on the basis of that relationship.

Authoritarian Media Systems

The world has never been without authoritarian political systems, and, as the name implies, authoritarianism entails strong, undemocratic, unilateral leadership. Characteristic of such leadership is an emphasis on controlling political processes (i.e., using and keeping power) rather than on reorganizing and controlling nonpolitical elements of a society—for example, the family, religion, education, and economic concerns. These are left alone unless they infringe on or interfere with the maintenance of political control.

In such systems, expectations for mass media are no mystery. Chief among these expectations is not to offend political authority. While some conventional dictators have demanded a leadership glorification role from mass media, most are content to ensure that they personally, or their governments, are not criticized or embarrassed by media coverage. Thus censorship, in the form of self-censorship, prepublication censorship, or postpublication

retaliation, is the primary means of controlling the media in authoritarian systems.[3]

One further characteristic of mass media behaviour in authoritarian systems is worth mentioning and this becomes evident when we examine the role of the pioneer press in the colonial period in Canada, which was to disseminate and propagate dicta of the political authorities. In a real sense, as Arthur Siegel points out, the history of Canadian journalism saw its beginning in the authoritarian mold.[4] As well, Canadian history offers us a firm clue regarding the evolution of media in authoritarian societies: on occasion they may challenge or displease political authority. Bear in mind, however, that in contemporary authoritarian systems, the reporter, editor, or programmer who manages to offend the rulers is likely to be jailed, beaten, or, in some instances, even killed.[5] Thus, while there is some room in authoritarian systems for media criticism of government, precisely because the rules and expectations are not firmly fixed, it is in these systems where the practice of journalism is most hazardous. Because they are not completely controlled, media offer a powerful channel through which courageous journalists can challenge the political authorities. Harassment and victimization of media have become the earmarks of today's authoritarian societies. On occasion, a newspaper editor or publisher will overtly challenge political authority by publishing his or her newspaper with blank white spaces in place of material that has been censored. Such challenges are rare, however, and usually bring down the wrath of political authorities.

Communist Media Systems

Communist political systems are a type of dictatorship that is *totalitarian* as opposed to authoritarian. By this distinction is meant that the totality of society, including all nonpolitical institutions, becomes the focus of government attention in the exercise of power. Mass media are obviously high on the list of these nonpolitical institutions over which the government maintains control. While there have been examples of noncommunist totalitarian governments (Hitler, Mussolini, and Perón, for example), only the communist variety has achieved long-term success in maintaining power, and in light of developments over the past few years, even this is debatable.

It is possible to describe classical communist theory of the press as having its birth in the writings of Marx, developing sophistication under Lenin, and taking its characteristic operational form through the crude applications of power associated with Stalin.[6] What this means is that communism is more than just a form of government; it involves a total commitment to a way of life guided by a coherent, conflict-oriented, political philosophy. In that philosophy there is no room for the organization or operation of opposing institutions or ideologies. In this sense it is important to understand that in communist societies open choices regarding information do not exist. Thus, the mass media are seen as "serving the revolution" by performing positive tasks such as education and social mobilization. In addition to this mobilization, however, a focus of thought and action is that capitalism, as well as the accompanying freedoms associated with it, are intractable enemies of communism.

In communist systems there is no separation between government and the media in that those who manage the media and work as journalists are government employees. In effect, in communist societies there is no need for censorship because the philosophies of politicians and journalists are the same— both serve the revolutionary, unified society. Of course, not just anyone is permitted to work as a journalist. Sensitive positions, in whatever aspect of society these may be located, belong predominantly to members of the Communist Party, who also have the appropriate academic credentials. Moreover, there is a clear relationship between party loyalty and entrance into university and other programs leading to positions of authority. In Cuba, for example, entrance into the school of journalism at the University of Havana has required high scores on tests in ideology and writing, in addition to a high school average of 93 percent.[7]

While the role of the media in communist society is complex, and in the early 1990s changing rapidly, for our purposes communist media systems can be identified by three central characteristics. First, they make claims for the freedom of the press, just as in the West, except communist claims are based on the public ownership of the media: they are the voice of the people. In the West, the media are perceived in classical communist theory as functioning as servants to the elite in the class-based society. Thus, freedom of the press as an issue emerges in both communist and capitalist systems, but the existence of that freedom depends on which side of the ideological divide one stands.

Second, the communist press has a clear propagandistic role, that is to remind citizens of and to make understandable the guiding principles of their society. To some extent this is true of media wherever they function. However, the indoctrination purpose of media in communist societies is far more obvious than, for example, what we are familiar with in Canada, where alternative points of view to those held by government are usually given considerable exposure. Presidium proceedings and major addresses given by political leaders claim high priority in press coverage. In general, the media are seen as tools of the revolution.

Third, events of the day, whether internal to society or occurring elsewhere, are reported in the communist media in a mode characterized by, more than any other feature, criticism and analysis. The touchstone of the evaluation of any event is its degree of consistency with basic communist philosophy. As in Canada, communist media are considered to have a strong editorial function. The difference between the two systems, however, is marked. We expect our daily newspaper, for example, to editorialize on our governments in the fashion of classical investigative journalism, i.e., are there any conflicts of interest on the part of politicians or are there more serious abuses of the public trust? Such an extended political role for communist media simply does not exist, since revelations of such wrongdoing would serve to undermine the legitimacy of the government and thus be classified as antirevolutionary. Only when the crime committed itself is defined as antirevolutionary (as was the case with the Cuban general Arnaldo Ochoa Sanchez, involved in drug trafficking, but tried and executed for treason in the summer of 1989) would the media report on such misbehaviour.[8]

Thus far we have discussed the principles of communist media in their classical formulation and behaviour. The coming to power of Mikhail Gorbachev in the USSR in 1985 marks what was a major change from these classical principles, and a few comments about the future, although speculative, are in order.

The essential change in the Soviet Union under Gorbachev was characterized by *glasnost* and *perestroika*, defined as "openness, candidness, freedom" and "political–economic restructuring" of society, respectively. Both words have profound implications with respect to communist mass media.

There is a fundamental incompatibility between the way in which mass media function in traditional communist systems and the concept of *glasnost*. In the classical formulation control of information characterizes the entire communist society: individual choices about information do not exist. Thus, information that becomes available to citizens must undergo the analysis and criticism described earlier. It is for this reason that publications and broadcasts from outside the USSR were prevented from reaching Soviet audiences by whatever physical means possible. This kind of censorship is consistent with the principles of Marxist–Leninist unity.

A clear signal to the world, in the context of the new philosophy of *glasnost*, was offered in 1989, when the USSR announced that jamming of external radio signals would be formally halted. (These jamming measures, aimed at insulating citizens from outside information, had been in place since 1945.) We believe that the government took this step in recognition of the fact that external information can no longer be kept out. Mass media reports from abroad have continually been infiltrating communist nations. In a public opinion poll conducted after the Chernobyl nuclear accident most of the Eastern European respondents indicated that they had first heard of the incident on radio programs that originated outside the borders of their own countries and, further, they felt that foreign programs presented more reliable information than their own.[9] As well, the development of videocassette technology has permitted the infiltration of popular TV programs and films into nations where they had been forbidden. For example, the Sylvester Stallone movies, *Rambo* and *Rocky IV*, which had been banned in the Soviet Union, as were most Western films, were the most sought after on the black market by those who own videocassette players.[10]

While *glasnost* and *perestroika* and open elections represent clearly welcomed developments both within communist societies and in the global community more generally, the opening up of communist societies to both external information and competing domestic information has not come about easily given that new expectations must vie with traditional ideologies. This is true in Cuba, where Fidel Castro, in the light of *glasnost*, has recently re-emphasized the importance of orthodox communist principles.

Given the observation that media systems tend to be congruent with the norms of the societies they serve, the process of restructuring and opening communist societies will be reflected in the conduct of mass media. "Kremlinologists" and other students of communist societies might well track the progress of changes that are occurring in these systems by paying close attention to changing styles and content of mass media, particularly to the resolution of conflicts that may arise from media personnel testing the limits of what could be a new-found freedom.

Revolutionary Media Systems

In a typology of political systems, *revolutionary* implies an overt but underground activity by one political, social, and economic order aimed at overthrowing another. Revolutionary political systems are often thought of as having their origins in "people power." When citizens perceive that their human and civil rights have been removed, either formally in the law, or informally by inhumane treatment, they may rise up. In the twentieth century, in particular, revolutionary insurgencies have had their origins in the philosophy of Marxism–Leninism.

Whatever their ideological origin, revolutionary media systems are by definition transitional. They function during the time when a challenge to existing authority is being made, and because they are revolutionary, they operate outside of government supervision, control, or laws.

Popularly, this type of media has become known as the underground press. Historically, the latter might be said to have its origins in the seventeenth-century practice of pamphleteering. While pamphleteering was for the most part a normal social and literary endeavour, it was also associated with semirevolutionary activity. Underground pamphlets played a major role in the American Revolution, the most famous being *Common Sense* by Thomas Paine.

A revolutionary underground press functioned actively in Italy and Germany from the mid-1930s until the end of the Second World War, and was particularly effective in the Nazi-occupied territories of France, the Lowlands, and Scandinavia. A number of different media played a role in this underground press—newspapers, pamphlets, leaflets, posters, as well as wall graffiti. Punishments for those who prepared, distributed, or possessed such materials were severe, whether the offence occurred within the national boundaries of Italy or Germany or in the occupied lands. The central purpose of the revolutionary press was to support and keep alive a spirit of rebellion in the populace in light of impending military actions on the part of the Allied Forces that would free the societies from dictatorial rule.

Broadcasting in Europe, as on the North American continent, became popularized in the early 1920s, and both Hitler and Mussolini made active and proficient use of the new electronic medium for their massive propagandistic programs. Insofar as underground activity was concerned, the British

Broadcasting Corporation (BBC) regularly penetrated the Nazi occupation curtain with programming, and those in the occupied zones who dared, on pain of certain severe punishment if caught, tuned in to BBC broadcasts. Of particular interest were the BBC daily newscasts, which contained coded messages, recognizable only by those (usually the underground insurgent forces) for whom they were intended. Such messages referred to troop movements, arms supplies, viable sabotage targets, and instructions concerning Allied plans for the liberation of Europe. Many of these messages were offered by representatives of governments in exile, based in England. Such use of radio was an unusual form of underground revolutionary activity and served as a very valuable military instrument for propaganda and counterpropaganda.

Underground publications in the USSR and Eastern Europe flourished as well, although in a somewhat different manner. Initially, following the revolution of 1917, there was little need for an underground press activity within Russia itself. In a sense, proclaimed the early Bolsheviks, freedom had come to the country with the displacement of Tsarist rule. Nevertheless, such dissident Bolsheviks as Trotsky, even in exile, were actively engaged in writing and disseminating tracts that opposed the way in which the proletarian government was implemented. These materials were surreptitiously brought into the USSR and disseminated from hand to hand.

Not only were revolutionary tracts published, but the political activists or journalists who prepared such tracts were joined by poets, novelists, human rights activists, scholars, and artists of every sort. Collectively their commentaries reflected the life of people suffering in a police state rather than benefiting in the manner promised by the original revolution. Such publications were distributed not only in the Soviet republics but also in the West. This massive revolutionary press system became known as *samizdat*, meaning "self-published," and "published at home," or *tamizdat*, manuscripts smuggled abroad for publishing.[11] But perhaps of greater import here was that with the spread of communism into territories beyond the borders of the USSR, particularly following the partition of Europe at the end of World War II, an enlarged revolutionary press developed and flourished. Subsequently, in the 1970s and 1980s when underground publishing thrived in Eastern European nations, as many as two hundred different printing organizations published newspapers, journals of various sorts, and hundreds of books each year in Poland alone. The object of such an underground publishing system was "to create a cultural life in Poland that was independent of the nation's Communist rulers."[12]

The extent of an export revolutionary press system has been well documented, and one example will suffice. Some of the manuscripts smuggled out of the Soviet Union became best sellers in the Western world almost overnight as they caught the imagination of vast audiences worldwide. Aleksandr Solzhenitsyn's novels, among them *One Day in the Life of Ivan Denisovich* (1962) and *Cancer Ward* (1968), earned their author a Nobel Prize for literature in 1970 and a fortune in royalties. He was expelled from the Soviet Union in 1974, shortly after publication of his first volume of *The Gulag Archipelago*, which depicted the lives of resident dissidents in Soviet prisons and labour camps in the Siberian north. As an indicator of changed attitudes in the USSR, Solzhenitsyn's expulsion was rescinded and he was invited to return to his homeland.

A somewhat different sort of revolutionary press became evident on the North American continent during the Vietnam War in the 1960s and 1970s. That war (undeclared, as Western societies were reminded by this rapidly developed press) created another form of rebellious publication, which, despite its "above-ground" and open publication status, labelled itself as either the alternative press or the underground press. Initiated as a form of New Left protest against the war, and in defiant opposition to the military-industrial-arms complex in the Western world, the driving forces behind such a revolutionary press system were campus groups in the United States such as the well-

known Students for a Democratic Society. The spirit of rebellion, however, was not limited to college or university students. The banner of liberation caught the imagination of many, particularly those who were eligible for military draft in the United States. And their declared causes extended beyond opposition to the war to include elimination of poverty, social injustices, and inequities of every sort, including campaigns against the pollution of our environment.

While maintaining a firm revolutionary posture in their approach to reporting, writing, and editorializing, these newspapers also exhibited high standards of creative writing, albeit mixed with displays of pornography that even by today's more liberalized standards would offend many readers. A few of these papers have made the transition to commercial success and still publish, although in a more conventional format.

About a dozen newspapers of this revolutionary type appeared in Canada in these same years, and they imitated the revolutionary posture of their American counterparts. Successes were slight, with three or four exceptions. Of note is the Vancouver-based *Georgia Straight*, which functioned as a press organ in opposition to the established political traditions, challenging rather than reporting on the Vancouver city government. Like other underground newspapers on the continent, the *Georgia Straight* was a member of the Underground Press

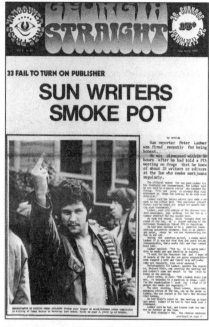

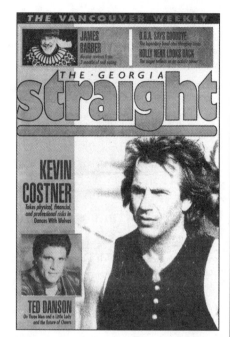

The Georgia Straight. Then and Now (Courtesy of The Georgia Straight)

Syndicate and of the Liberation News Service—wire services that fed continental and international news to their revolutionary/alternative press subscribers. A variety of charges were laid by Vancouver city police against the *Straight*, and the paper found itself hounded and harassed: in 1969 alone it faced a total of eighteen court charges.[13]

The Special Senate Committee on Mass Media reported in 1970 that several alternative/revolutionary newspapers had achieved respectable circulation figures. Among these were *Georgia Straight* (60 000); *Logos* (Montreal, 30 000); *Octopus* (Ottawa, 8000), and *Harbinger* (Toronto, 10 000).[14] The *Straight* continues to publish today as an "above-ground" community

weekly newspaper in Vancouver with a very respectable total circulation of 75 000 copies.

As the Vietnam War drew to a close, anti-establishment drives dissipated, and the underground press of the 1960s and 1970s, with its New Left drug counterculture sympathies, generally faded out of existence. Vestiges of that press were still to be found on university campuses in the late 1970s and into the 1980s. The papers that remained continued to challenge the establishment, but lacked the revolutionary, confrontational zest that was the trademark of that press in the earlier years.

To summarize, revolutionary media systems serve two primary functions. The first is to mobilize the target population against its rulers and the second is to provide information that it is denied by its rulers. The combination of the two functions give revolutionary media systems considerable power in reaching their target audience. As we examine political or military trouble spots around the globe, it is apparent that these types of media systems continue to be quite active: Southern Africa, Central America, and the Middle East all offer current examples of such media systems.

Depending on factors such as geography and the degree to which revolutionary movements actually control territory within the borders of the target state, revolutionary media facilities may have to be located outside their home state and have their content transmitted across boundaries. Whatever this configuration, revolutionary media systems are limited in duration to the time it takes either for the revolution to succeed or to fail. In the former instance, there would be a transition to another form of media system (most likely authoritarian, communist, or development), and in the latter, a kind of fading away in importance as the revolution falters.

Development Media Systems

The post-World War II period, particularly the 1960s, saw the end of the era of European imperialism/colonialism, which had provided the basis of political organization for areas such as Latin America, the Caribbean, Asia, and Africa since the 1500s. With the end of colonialism, the number of independent countries increased dramatically. The initial membership of the United Nations, when it was founded in 1945, was fifty-one, while forty years later the number stood at 159.

It is very important to understand that these newly independent countries, along with those that had had their independence for a number of years, remained economically dependent on industrialized countries. These developing countries brought to the international political arena (both in the UN and elsewhere) a radically different set of concerns from those of wealthier nations. While the United States, Great Britain, France, Canada, and the Soviet Union, for example, were caught up in the strategic competition that we have come to know as the Cold War, newly emergent and developing countries were concerned primarily with the problems of nation building and economic growth. In keeping with the previously introduced notion of congruence between political and mass media systems, it should come as no surprise that a new type of mass media system has emerged in these societies; this has been given the name *development journalism.*

This concept is a difficult one to define because it is the product of many, sometimes seemingly contradictory components.[15] It came to the scene rather unpretentiously in the early 1960s when a group of practising journalists in the Third World perceived a need to focus attention on problems of political and economic development facing their societies. They pointed out that most of the news coverage of the Third World came from the major Western wire services, Associated Press (AP), United Press International (UPI), Reuters, and Agence France Presse (AFP) and that these organizations tended to focus on events such as coups, crises, and corruption, thus presenting a distorted and negative view of these countries. The problem was further compounded by the fact that hardware systems that distribute information around the world are almost wholly owned by Western industries. Another dimension of the problem concerns the impact of Western values, as transmitted by media, on indigenous cultures. Western values, which are implicitly contained in the content of new stories, entertainment, and advertising, are generally more materialistic than those of many Third World countries. Finally, the heavy dependence that media in Third World societies experience with regard to Western suppliers inhibits development of indigenous media in every respect.

These complaints are not without foundation. The perceptions in Third World countries as to what was being reported about them have been substantiated by Western scholars.[16] Moreover the resulting negative images of these countries in the press of the developed world can result in damaging effects; for example, they can hinder the process of development, as industrialized countries can justify cutbacks in foreign aid on the grounds that such aid will do no good.

Development journalism was born as an attempt to focus attention on the successes of development in the Third World, including the building of dams and the creation of irrigation projects, schools, factories, and literacy campaigns, which were not considered "news" in the West. As the concept grew, development journalists came to see mass media as tools of nation building; hence the focus on building an indigenous communications infrastructure, which involved technology, human technical skills, human creative skills, and the creation of national media policies. In short, development journalism maintains that mass media, through the selection of content from the social environment, should reflect indigenous values appropriate to the nation-building process rather than foreign values, which may be counter-productive to nation-building strategies. These media responsibilities include providing an informational base for Third World society, offering direction to the society regarding goals and purposes, challenging Western media traditions, and developing themselves as positive utilitarian instruments.

It was inevitable that such Third World needs would become expressed in bodies such as the United Nations, particularly UNESCO. Given the majority status of Third World nations in the UN and UNESCO, a vast amount of attention was given to the expression of these needs. Through a series of UNESCO meetings in the 1970s, culminating in a report published in 1980, development journalism gained broad recognition. The title of that 1980 document (the MacBride Report) offers a description of the larger debate that followed—*Many Voices, One World: Towards a New, More Just and More Efficient World Information Order* (NWICO).[17] As it became virtually the symbol for the Third World position in the NWICO debate, development journalism, as a concept, took on particular connotations that have triggered a hostile response from Western journalists, quite incomprehensible in light of its humble origins.

The New World Information/ Communication Order took on greater definition in a UNESCO-sponsored meeting in February 1981. Proponents of the "new order" met in Paris to establish journalistic principles, which, presumably, would become the operative principles for UNESCO nations generally.[18] Major principles are as follows:

1. An international commission for the protection of journalists working in hazardous reporting situations would be established.
2. The commission would overview conditions of work for journalists on dangerous assignments outside of their home countries. The commission would also,

eventually, approach the matter of working conditions for journalists in their own countries.
3. One of the responsibilities of the commission ought to be the investigation of complaints concerning infringements of working conditions for journalists.
4. The commission would also have the opportunity to study ethics for journalism, with a view to establishing common agreements about principles of ethical behaviour.
5. As well, the commission would issue international identification cards to journalists, and it would be the only body to do so.
6. The commission should have the responsibility to evaluate whether journalists on foreign assignments conducted themselves according to accepted ethical codes.

While these principles may appear to be relatively innocuous, they are antithetical to the Western journalistic traditions that underlie a free press, as we shall see in the next section. Representatives of Western journalism were, by and large, not involved in this process, causing this group to organize a gathering of their own in Talloires, France, in May 1981. The document resulting from this meeting has become known as the Declaration of Talloires, and it enunciates in detail the principles that characterize the gathering, writing, editing, and dissemination of news in open societies (known as the Libertarian media system), which will be discussed in the following section. The so-called NWICO debate, then, is based on the fundamental disagreement between these competing media philosophies.

Development journalism, as we have described the concept, lacks precise definition. In fact, it combines noble goals of promoting economic development and national self-sufficiency with what are fairly obvious authoritarian practices with respect to journalistic freedom. We certainly are in agreement with William A. Hachten's description of development journalism as "an amorphous and curious mixture of ideas, rhetoric, influences, and grievances."[19] In one study of journalists in Chile, individuals of varying educational backgrounds, age, experience, and gender all seemed to have adopted development attitudes in addition to traditional Western attitudes. In this study, it was expected that development attitudes would supplant Western attitudes, which, clearly, they did not.[20] Thus, as Christine Ogan has suggested, it may be that there is less substance to an independent concept of development journalism than much recent writing would lead us to believe.[21]

Libertarian Media Systems

Libertarian media systems have their origins in seventeenth-century Western Europe and are associated with thinkers such as John Milton, John Locke, and, later, John Stuart Mill. The legacy of these political philosophers is immense, as their ideas underlie much of currently acceptable behaviour in the area of government–society relationships. Libertarian philosophy still prevails in our conceptions of how mass media should operate.

When Canadians complain, as we do regularly, about the narrowing ownership base of newspapers, what we decry is the reduction of forums for competing, open expression—a basic tenet of libertarian thinking. In the United States, where newspaper ownership has contracted as in Canada, the American government, in 1970, enacted the Newspaper Preservation Act. The purpose of the act was to mandate a more thorough investigation into the conditions that allow competing but financially troubled newspapers to meld under a joint operating agreement (JOA). Such agreements allowed newspapers to combine business and printing functions of both papers into one unit, while preserving competition in the news/editorial domain.

The principle underlying JOAs is that editorial policies would be independently determined by the two newspapers joined by such an agreement. Further, the JOA recognizes that preserving the editorial freedom of the two newspapers is paramount, even though the union might mean the loss of direct competition for advertising and circulation.[22]

Prior to the 1970 enactment, there were already twenty-two communities in the United States that had JOA newspapers;[23] and in each such situation, at least one of the newspapers had to be economically failing in order to qualify for antitrust exemptions. Subsequent to the 1970 act, five communities obtained JOA status for their newspapers. In the post-1970 period, however, qualification for JOA status became much more stringent and the review procedures, conducted by the Office of the Attorney General, are detailed and often lengthy.

This same notion of competing editorial voices carries over into other areas of social activity—for example, into advertising, where federal and provincial legislation is aimed at ensuring that products and product information have a fair opportunity to compete.

All of these considerations find their origin in the libertarian tradition of the "open marketplace," where the notion is that the best ideas (and presumably the best products) will prevail. In that mass media are some of the major conveyors of information, it is vitally important that there be few restrictions or constraints on the flow of that information. In the words of John Stuart Mill, in his famous essay, *On Liberty*: "If all mankind minus one were of one opinion, and only one person were of the contrary opinion, mankind would be no more justified in silencing that person, than he, if he had the power, would be justified in silencing mankind."[24] In Mill's view, there was a need to permit open expression, else if an idea held by a minority were to be silenced, we might be silencing a truth.

The legacy of this historical libertarian thinking on contemporary Western journalistic practice can be seen in the Declaration of Talloires. This meeting, which participants called the Voices of Freedom Conference, produced a statement that initially reaffirmed Article 19 of the 1948 UN Universal Declaration of Human Rights: "Everyone has the right to freedom of opinion and expression; this right includes freedom to hold opinions without interference and to seek, receive, and impart information and ideas through any media and regardless of frontiers."

Prior to their listing of principles that are inherent in the right of individuals to free expression, the journalists identified what they perceived as a central problem in the NWICO debate: governments often discourage the reporting of events that they consider to be detrimental to their nation's interest. Rather, the Western journalists emphasized the people's interests and concluded that the interests of the nation are better served by free and open reporting: "From robust public debate grows better understanding of the issues facing a nation and its peoples."[25]

The principles of the declaration can be summarized as follows:

1. Censorship, in any of its forms, should be eliminated.
2. Journalists should have unrestricted access to diverse sources of news and opinion.

3. The plurality of views in international society makes it impossible to impose an international code of ethics. Journalists in a given nation might voluntarily adopt codes, but these codes would not be imposed and monitored by governments.

4. Journalists need no special status for their protection and proposals that would control them in the name of protecting them ought to be opposed.

5. The licensing of journalists by national or international bodies should not be sanctioned.

6. Because the purpose of the press is the pursuit of the truth, any attempt to mandate responsibilities for the press would destroy its independence. The ultimate guarantee for journalistic responsibility is the free exchange of ideas.

7. The journalists also emphasized their concern about the tendency in many countries and in international bodies to put government interests above those of the individual. Rather, the declaration argues, the state should exist for the individual and therefore it has a duty to uphold individual rights.[26]

Finally, in this brief overview of the libertarian tradition the concept of self-correction needs to be mentioned. Libertarians have faith that in an open marketplace of ideas truth will win out over falsehood. Thus, restraints on the flow of information of whatever sort, except in conditions of emergency, are unnecessary.

Social Democratic Media Systems

The idea of social democratic media systems has its origins in the social responsibility model as identified in the *Four Theories of the Press*. As such, it carrries over some of the characteristics of that model, most importantly the idea that mass media cannot be depended upon to fulfill their obligations if left to function purely in an open marketplace. This is so because open marketplaces, if they can ever exist, tend to close if left on their own. Thus, while recognizing the importance of the open marketplace of ideas, social responsibility advocates believe that some degree of government intervention in the operation of mass media is mandatory.[27]

Robert Picard, who is a major proponent of an independent social democratic type of media system, sees the origins of such systems in twentieth-century Western Europe, especially where Labour and other social democratic governments have either held power or exercised considerable influence in the post-World War II period.[28] Essentially these systems have resulted in increased public ownership or public subsidy of privately owned media to ensure the presence of opposing points of view. Further there is both direct and indirect government subsidy of media content and of the performing arts.

There is a conflict between libertarian and social democratic philosophies in all Western societies. While there is agreement that governments have some role to play regarding the regulation of mass media, there is disagreement regarding the extent of such involvement.

This difference becomes apparent when one compares the degree of government subsidy of the media in Canada and the United States. In the United States there is agreement, for example, that the Public Broadcasting Corporation, the administrative body for Public Broadcasting Systems (PBS), provides an important service to the U.S. community. In fact, there is government subsidy of that service, although it is not large enough to maintain it. Therefore, despite its proven programming, public broadcasting, in order to survive, must engage in large-scale fundraising in the communities in which it operates.

In Canada, the scope of public broadcasting is far more extensive, and the CBC, a Crown corporation, is subsidized in the amount of three-quarters of its roughly one-billion-dollar-per-year budget. The remainder is raised by advertising. In the United States, PBS has not been regarded as a strong competitor to the commercial networks for audience, although PBS has become increasingly popular as audiences of the commercial networks are splintering. In Canada,

the CBC has been regarded from the day of its inception in 1936 as the "central nervous system" of Canadian broadcasting, and is the standard against which broadcasting, video and film productions are measured.

Another area in which libertarian and social democratic theories collide is in regulation of media content. The Federal Communication Commission (FCC) in the United States, while severely limited in authority by the First Amendment, has seen fit to introduce concepts such as family hour and right of reply and, on occasion, the FCC makes efforts to control excesses in areas such as violence, pornography, and advertising. Falling within the libertarian tradition, however, it is the "court" of public opinion that appears most effective in curbing these excesses.

The regulation of broadcasting content in Canada, in that it began prior to the specific recognition of freedom of speech and freedom of the press in the Charter of Rights and Freedoms contained in the Canada Act (1982), has been more widespread than it has been in the U.S. While Canadian society, in the main, has accepted a high level of government control over content, it remains to be seen whether regulations such as Canadian content quotas are found by the courts to be in conflict with the new Constitution.[29] This notwithstanding, regulation of content in Canada is so extensive as to make regulation of content in the United States seem almost nonexistent.

Insofar as the printed press is concerned, the First Amendment makes it virtually impossible to regulate content in the United States. In Canada, however, there have been strong overtures to regulate the newspaper industry, beginning with the Davey Committee in 1970. A decade later, a royal commission recommended to the federal government that a Canadian newspaper act be enacted and enforced. The general effect of such an act would have been monitoring of newspapers by communities and by the federal government.[30] The newspaper industry reacted strongly against these recommendations and they were never acted upon. Nevertheless, subsequent to the 1970 Davey Committee *Report*, the federal government did introduce Bill C-58 in 1974. This bill legislated an amendment to the Income Tax Act, the net result of which was for magazines to be considered Canadian, a minimum of 80 percent of content had to be of domestic origin. This regulation also stipulated that in order to qualify for income tax credits Canadian companies had to purchase advertising in Canadian magazines. "De-Canadianized" by this regulation were *Reader's Digest* and *Time*.[31] While there were additional ramifications of Bill C-58, at this point it is only necessary to note that Canada has introduced domestic content quotas in the magazine industry, even if such regulation has been indirect.

Thus, were we to place Canada's media system into one of the philosophies of the press described in this chapter, in our view it is clear that the behaviour of Canadian mass media is more characteristic of the social democratic model than it is of any other, including the libertarian one. It is, however, important to reiterate that strong libertarian views do prevail, especially within the newspaper industry.

Conclusion

One of the dangers of outlining characteristics of theoretical typologies is that the reader may assume that each of the systems described is mutually exclusive of the others. We must avoid such an assumption, because it is evident that no society is totally of one philosophical bent with respect to its mass media system. A revolutionary press may very well exist in an authoritarian or libertarian milieu, as may a libertarian press exist in an authoritarian milieu, albeit not likely in an open way. Because societies foster and shape their own institutions, media systems will reflect the various philosophies that are to be found within most societies.

Notes

1. Fred S. Siebert, Theodore Peterson, and Wilbur Schramm, *Four Theories of the Press* (Urbana: University of Illinois Press, 1956).
2. Ralph Lowenstein and John C. Merrill, *Macromedia: Mission, Message and Morality* (New York: Longman, 1990), 163–73; Hamid Mowlana, *Global Information and*

World Communication: New Frontiers in International Relations (New York: Longman, 1986); William A. Hachten, *The World News Prism: Changing Media, Clashing Ideology* (Ames, IA: Iowa State University Press, 1987); Robert G. Picard, *The Press and the Decline of Democracy: The Democratic Socialist Response in Public Policy* (Westport, CT: Greenwood Press, 1985).

3. Hachten, *The World News Prism*, 16–18.

4. Arthur Siegel, *Politics and the Mass Media in Canada* (Toronto: McGraw-Hill Ryerson, 1983), 85.

5. Andrew Radolf, "Violence against Journalists," *Editor and Publisher* 121 (7 January 1989): 20–21. In 1989 it was reported that "53 [journalists were] killed by violent means in the pursuit of their profession" with a caveat that the "list is almost certainly incomplete." See *Attacks on the Press 1989: A Worldwide Survey* (New York: Committee to Protect Journalists, 1990). See also Robert Carty, "The Daily Terror: Attacks on Freedom of Expression and the Rights of Journalists in Guatemala" Canadian Committee to Protect Journalists, 1991.

6. Siebert, et al., *Four Theories*, 105–16.

7. Interview with Lazara Penoñes Madan, dean of the School of Journalism, University of Havana, December 1986.

8. *Granma Weekly Review*, international edition, 2 July 1989.

9. Radio Free Europe, "East Europeans and the Chernobyl Events: Awareness, Primary Sources of Information Toward Soviet and Home Media Handling of Information," *East European Area Audience and Opinion Research* (December 1986), 8, 11.

10. Philip Taubman, "Soviet Pans 'Rocky' and 'Rambo' Films," *New York Times*, 4 January 1986, A3.

11. George Saunders, "Foreword" in *Samizdat*, ed. George Saunders (New York: Monad Press, 1974), 7. Also see David Lowe, *Russian Writing Since 1953: A Critical Survey* (New York: Ungar Publishing, 1987), 5.

12. David Rocks, "Poland's Underground Presses End Hiding 'Game,'" *Globe and Mail*, 27 March 1990, B28.

13. *Report of the Special Senate Committee on Mass Media*, vol. 3, *Good, Bad, or Simply Inevitable?* (Ottawa: Information Canada, 1970), 282.

14. Ibid., 274–76.

15. Christine Ogan, "Development Journalism/Communication: The Status of the Concept," *Gazette* 29, 1/2 (1982): 3–13.

16. Robert L. Stevenson and Richard R. Cole, *Foreign News and the "New World Information Order" Debate: Parts I and II* (Washington: U.S. International Communication Agency Report R-10-80, 1980).

17. UNESCO, *Many Voices, One World: Towards a New, More Just and Efficient World Information and Communication Order* (Paris, 1980).

18. Gunnar Garbo, *A World of Difference. The International Distribution of Information: The Media and Developing Countries*, trans. Gail Adams Kvam (Paris: Communication Documentation Centre, UNESCO, 1985), 60–61.

19. Hachten, *The World News Prism*, 30.

20. Walter C. Soderlund and Carmen Schmitt, "Development vs. Western News Values Among Chilean Journalists: Problems of Concepts and Measures" (paper presented to the Sixth Annual Intercultural/International Communication Conference, University of Miami, February 1989).

21. Ogan, "Development Journalism," 11.

22. Craig Sanders, "Aftermath of the Death of the St. Louis *Globe–Demo-*

crat: Are Failing Newspapers Still Worth Saving?" (paper presented to the Annual Meeting of the Association for Education in Journalism and Mass Communication, Portland, OR, July 1988), 3.

23. Ibid., n.32. Canada does not have legislation similar to JOA in the U.S. However, for several years, a form of JOA did exist in Vancouver where the *Province* (Southam Press) and the *Sun* (F.P. Publications) were printed in the same plant by Pacific Press, owned co-operatively by the two publishers. The arrangement ended when Southam bought out F.P. Publications. Southam currently operates Pacific Press as a wholly owned enterprise.

24. John Stuart Mill, *On Liberty*, Introduction by Russell Kirk (Chicago: Henry Regnery Company, 1955), 24.

25. "Declaration of Talloires: Voices of Freedom Conference," in *Mass Communication Review Yearbook*, vol. 3, ed. D. Charles Whitney and Ellen Wartella (Beverley Hills, CA: Sage Publications, 1982), 289.

26. Ibid., 288–91.

27. Siebert et al., *Four Theories*, 73–77.

28. Picard, *The Press and the Decline of Democracy*.

29. Robert Martin and G. Stuart Adam, *A Sourcebook of Canadian Media Law* (Ottawa: Carleton University Press, 1989), 73–74.

30. Canada, *Royal Commission on Newspapers* (Ottawa: Supply and Services, 1981).

31. Isiah Litvak and Christopher Maule, *Cultural Sovereignty: The Time and Reader's Digest Case in Canada* (New York: Praeger Publishers, 1974).

C H A P T E R 3

Introduction
    Canadian Participation in the Area of Global Communication
    Radio Canada International
    UNESCO
    Canadian Commission for UNESCO
    International Program for the Development of Communication
       (IPDC)
    CIDA and IDRC
Canadian Reporting on World Events
Convergence
    Stock Market Strategies
    Marketing Strategies
    Global Movement of Information
    Socializing Forces
    Trends with Respect to the United States
    Convergence of Ownership
    Contrary Trends

The Global Context
of Canadian
Communication

Introduction

South Africa, Israel,
China, Iraq . . .

While most Canadians have never been to one of these far-off lands, not to mention all four, we have all witnessed through the power of television, the violence and resulting tragedy that has gripped these countries over the past few years. The funeral processions in the black townships of South Africa, the stone-throwing children on the West Bank, the burning tanks and dying students in Tiananmen Square in Beijing, and dramatic air attacks on Baghdad are all a part of our reality thanks to modern systems of communication.

Furthermore, when we look at some important areas of activity in Canada, we quickly become aware that we have diplomatic, business, educational, communication, and research links with most nations on earth. With respect to mass media and communications, there are few organizations, if any, in which Canada does not have membership. These include, among many others, United Nations Education Scientific Cultural Organization (UNESCO), International Telecommunication Union (ITU), European Broadcasting Union (EBU), Asian Broadcasting Union (ABU), International Press Institute (IPI), Inter American Press Association (IAPA), International Communication Association (ICA), International Organization of Journalists (IOJ), Association for Education in Journalism and Mass Communication (AEJMC), and International Association for Mass Communication Research (IAMCR).

The number of international organizations varies according to one's definition of the term, and it is possible, using one criterion of a minimum membership of three nations, to list 24 209 such bodies. However, calculating what the *Yearbook of International Organizations* describes as "conventional" organizations of an autonomous, nonprofit, nongovernmental nature, the 1989 total was 4921.[1]

What one is obliged to conclude, and very quickly, is that in this information age no nation functions unto itself. If anything characterizes interdependency among nations, it would be that such links are increasing in number, kind, and intensity, regardless of where one looks. For example, in August 1989, Canadians learned that Radio Beijing shortwave, the information arm of the People's Republic of China, was using a CBC International rebroadcasting transmitter in Sackville, New Brunswick, to beam its programming to the North American continent. Minister of External Affairs Joe Clark, in responding to inquiries in the wake of the repression of student demonstrations, indicated that this co-operative arrangement with China had been concluded prior to the events in Tiananmen Square of June 1989. If Canadians were surprised at this particular co-operative venture, they shouldn't have been, because in the international community there are ties that bind nations together regardless of ideology. It is evident that to understand Canadian mass media and communications systems, it is increasingly important to understand the global context within which communications take place.

Canadian Participation in the Area of Global Communication
Radio Canada International

The Canadian Broadcasting Corporation (CBC) became involved in shortwave broadcasting during World War II, when in 1942 the government established the CBC International Service. At the time, the administrative arrangement called for the CBC to operate the service, while financing for the operation was arranged by Parliament under a separate granting system. Three years after approval was given, broadcasting from the transmitting site in Sackville, New Brunswick, began with programs aimed at Western European listeners. Initially broadcasts were in English, French, and German.

RCI transmitters site, Sackville, NB. (National Archives of Canada/PA 092376)

Later, the Sackville transmitter beamed rebroadcasts in twelve languages of programs originating from the International Service studios in Montreal. In 1968 the International Service became an integral part of the CBC. In 1972 the name was formally changed to Radio Canada International (RCI).[2]

International shortwave broadcasting was a development seen in many countries after the initial popularization of radio in the 1920s. It was evident in the 1930s, for example, that the British and French broadcasting systems were used as counter-propaganda tools to the Nazi broadcasts that emanated from Germany.

The Canadian shortwave system was conceived in the wartime environment, and broadcasting began about three months before the end of the war. The broadcasting structure in place was, in fact, employed in the new international struggle emerging from World War II—the Cold War. While Radio Moscow, the BBC, and the Voice of America/Radio Free Europe were the major players in this serious and prolonged period of international hostility, Radio Canada International too participated with broadcasts into Eastern Europe in Russian, Polish, Ukrainian, Hungarian, Slovak, and Czech. More recently, RCI clearly has adopted a mandate similar to that of Canada's National Film Board—"to interpret Canada abroad." To further this end, several programs have been created including "Listeners' Corner,"

which invites questions about life in Canada, and "Innovation Canada," which focusses on Canadian inventors and researchers and how their ideas and discoveries are applied to social uses. At the same time, RCI brings both Canadian news reports and current affairs programming to Canadians who live and travel abroad.

Global areas that have received programming in English include Asia, the Middle East, Latin America, Africa, Eastern Europe, Western Europe, and the United States. Most of these areas also receive French-language broadcasts. Broadcasts in languages other than English and French have included Czech, Hungarian, Russian, Slovak, Polish, Ukrainian, Arabic, Spanish, Portuguese, Japanese, and (Mandarin) Chinese.[3]

When the 1991 Broadcasting Act was being debated in Parliament in the late 1980s, and in the Committee on Communications and Culture, representatives of the CBC raised the matter concerning the administration of RCI. It might be more appropriate, they suggested, that financial and programming responsibilities for such an international service should fall under the jurisdiction of the Department of External Affairs rather than under the national broadcasting system. While budgeting for RCI has become the responsibility of External Affairs, programming continues to be a mandate of the CBC.

Budget trimming by the federal government in the early 1990s did not exclude Radio Canada International. In response to advice from the Department of External Affairs in 1991 that the RCI budget was being cut from $20 million a year to $13.5 million a year for the next five years, RCI reduced its language offerings to Russian, Ukrainian, Spanish, Arabic, and Chinese (in addition to English and French broadcasts), and cut its staff from 192 employees to 100. The future of RCI and its role in the international short-wave broadcasting community continue to be matters of debate in the Canadian Parliament.[4]

UNESCO

UNESCO was established as part of the United Nations in 1947. Canada was one of the fifty-one founding nations and has actively participated in and supported UNESCO initiatives. It was quite natural that media, communications, and telecommunications systems would fall within the scope of UNESCO interests, and UNESCO has served well as a clearing house for such interests. As well, it has served as a publication house and research organization. Even from its earliest years, those who presided over the work of UNESCO were guided by the principles of freedom of expression and freedom of the press as set forth in the previously mentioned Article 19 of the UN Universal Declaration of Human Rights.

From the beginning there were political differences within UNESCO that reflected the Cold War environment. East–West tensions carried through to the 1980s. For example, in the MacBride Report we read about the concerns over national sovereignty expressed by the Soviet member of the MacBride Commission in the context of uninvited transborder information flow. In addition to these East–West issues, UNESCO became a forum within the UN for the articulation of problems arising from North–South imbalances in areas such as economics, living conditions, and communications.

Throughout the years of Canada's participation in UNESCO, while Canadians have enjoyed a standard of living that is characteristic of First World industrialized societies, they have been sensitive to and have understood the problems related to the informational imbalances that Third World societies experience. The United States generates more information and media content than any society on the globe, and overflow information from that society as well as the information that we deliberately import have caused extreme concern in the Canadian community about acculturation processes. Such concern is similar to the complaint given voice by Third World nations regarding "media imperialism" and the impact of Western information generally.

The majority of UNESCO members were sympathetic to this preoccupation with acculturation. That majority included some Third World nations with links to the Soviet Union, combined with Third World nations that preferred to regard themselves as nonaligned with either the West or East. Western societies, in particular the United States and the United Kingdom, found themselves in the minority when concepts such as freedom of opinion and expression were being debated.[5]

In the midst of a situation where the U.S. found itself the major financial contributor to UNESCO and was experiencing overwhelming opposition to its own view of the purpose of mass media in a free society, there also arose the question of the effectiveness of the management of UNESCO. The U.S. ultimately decided to withdraw from UNESCO on 31 December 1984, giving notice a year in advance. Shortly afterwards, the United Kingdom and Singapore followed the American lead. These three countries felt that UNESCO had taken a clear anti-Western tone and, rather than defending the ideals of free thought and free expression upon which UNESCO was founded, had instead become "a comfortable home for statist, collectivist, solutions to world problems and for ideological polemics."[6]

In Canada, Joe Clark, minister for External Affairs, addressed the House of Commons on the Canadian position following the British announcement that that nation proposed to leave UNESCO at the end of 1985. While there was some pressure within the country for Canada to follow the U.S., U.K., and Singapore, Clark made the point that it would not do so. Rather, it was Canada's intention to work for reform from within UNESCO.[7]

Canadian Commission for UNESCO

While Canada has direct participation within the main body of UNESCO, the country also maintains an agency at home that performs UNESCO–Canada liaison activities. This liaison group, the Canadian Commission for UNESCO, was created in 1958 by an order-in-council. Subsequently, in 1978, a Charter of National Commissions for UNESCO was established by the UN. The function of these National Commissions is to involve member nations with programs aimed at the advancement of education, science, culture, and information. In effect, the National Commissions were intended to promote UNESCO initiatives globally.

The mandate of the Canadian Commission for UNESCO is to coordinate the organization's programs in Canada, to promote and make known such programs in the country, and to advise the government about its work. The 1988–89 *Report of the Secretary-General* indicates that the budget of the Canadian Commission for that fiscal year was $1.2 million. Because the commission is neither a direct implementation agency nor a granting agency, this sum serves primarily to offset secretariat/administration costs.[8]

While the commission concerns itself with a variety of activities in extending UNESCO programs in Canada, three in particular might be noted here. The first is an ongoing initiative known as the World Decade for Cultural Development.

During this ten-year period, which began in January 1988, Canada and other participating countries have been emphasizing and will continue to emphasize the importance of cultural values, showing that they are as significant as economic values in a society. The launch of the "World Decade for Cultural Development" was a gala concert given by the World Philharmonic Orchestra in Montreal in December 1988. The choral segment of Beethoven's Ninth Symphony was performed by choirs located in San Francisco, Geneva, and Moscow, transmitted live via satellite on three giant screens. The international dimension of this World Decade for Cultural Development was thus stressed.[9]

Second, in 1983 (World Communication Year) a Marshall McLuhan–Teleglobe Canada award was established to recognize any work or action "that will have contributed in an exceptional manner, to furthering a better understanding of the influence exerted by communications media and technology on society in general, and in particular on its cultural, artistic and scientific activities."[10] The $50 000 award, offered every two years, was established as a tribute to the memory of Marshall McLuhan by the Canadian Commission for UNESCO and by Teleglobe Canada (Canada's overseas satellite service). The award, given for the fifth time in 1991, was to British academic James Halloran. Previously the award was conferred upon Bolivian scholar and journalist Luis Ramiro Beltran (1983), Ital-

ian semioticist Umberto Eco (1985), Israeli communications sociologist Elihu Katz (1987), and French creator of audiovisual forms of expression and communications Pierre Schaeffer (1989). While the award has been placed under the permanent patronage of UNESCO, it is administered by an independent jury of five Canadians. A representative of the director-general of UNESCO sits on the jury as an observer.

A third example of UN–Canadian Commission for UNESCO activity has been the recent effort to emphasize the very serious issue of functional illiteracy. In bringing the matter to the attention of societies around the world, the forty-second session of the International Conference on Education held in Geneva pointed out that illiteracy was much more than simply the inability to read and write. As one of the discussions pointed out:

> The struggle against illiteracy is also a struggle for justice, freedom, democracy, world peace and greater equality, linked to the right of all individuals to play an economic role in the society in which they live and the recognition of the right to benefit from the advantages of development.[11]

In Canada, the Canadian Commission for UNESCO initiated a number of activities to combat illiteracy. It hosted a meeting of the International Literacy Year Advisory Group to co-ordinate literacy-year activities in this country, worked with various educational groups in preparing promotional events, and, amongst other publications and productions, prepared and sent media kits to 1145 English and French newspapers across Canada. As well, letters and posters were sent to major industries in Canada to encourage workplace literacy programs.[12]

ILY: YEAR OF OPPORTUNITY

INTERNATIONAL LITERACY YEAR

The ILY poster was designed by Zabelle Côté of Montreal. Ms. Côté explains that by placing her character on pencils she wished to convey the message that "the ability to write and read gives people a new perspective on life and the world around them."

International Program for the Development of Communication (IPDC)

Another activity of the Canadian Commission for UNESCO is the program in communications, which has recently developed a new emphasis on training people to serve in different areas of communications. It is through the International Program for the Development of Communication that such training is encouraged.

The IPDC was established as a function of UNESCO in 1984, through initiatives taken by the United States five years earlier, when a planning meeting was held to prepare a draft concerning the need to help Third World countries develop independent communication capabilities. The draft was unanimously accepted by UNESCO, and the program has been identified as having four central responsibilities.[13] First, the IPDC conducts studies of nations' communication needs and capabilities; second, it co-ordinates international communication development between nations that require assistance and those that are able to offer such assistance; third, it serves as an information clearinghouse on global information needs and resources, thus promoting an awareness of the importance of communication processes for national development; and, finally, the IPDC concerns itself with financing, in that it encourages the developed countries to underwrite communication programs in the more needy countries.

The IPDC maintains its links in Canada through the Canadian Commission for UNESCO. An example of a direct Canadian contribution is a program run by Canadian Paul Thiele, head of the Crane Library at the University of British Columbia, to expand the library services for the blind and visually impaired at Kenyatta University, Nairobi, Kenya.[14]

CIDA and IDRC

Two further Canadian involvements in international communication are worthy of note. The Canadian International Development Agency (CIDA) celebrated its twentieth year of existence in 1987–88 and currently reports to Parliament through the minister for external relations and international development. In the 1987–88 fiscal year, Canada allocated approximately $2.6 billion to international development assistance. CIDA managed about 75 percent of that amount, "with the goal of helping Third World countries to achieve self-sustaining, social and economic development." In the area of communication, an amount of $7.6 million was allotted to help Third World nations develop communication systems. This is in contrast to the contribution of $84.9 million in food aid to the global community. The 1988–89 year saw an increase of 12 percent in Canada's development assistance budget, bringing the total to $2.9 billion.[15]

The remaining 25 percent of Canadian international development money is distributed by various other government departments. Among these is the International Development Research Centre (IDRC), created by Parliament in 1970. The IDRC offers financial and professional aid in a variety of areas, one of which is communications. A unique characteristic of this Canadian body is its international, twenty-one-member board of governors, seven of whom are from developing countries. In the area of communications, the centre funds research projects, publishes informational materials, in particular a quarterly *IDRC Report* (in English, French, and Spanish), and produces documentary films. One of the organization's central concerns, fulfilled through regional offices in Bogota, Cairo, New Delhi, Nairobi, Dakar, and Singapore, is to promote co-operation between researchers in Canada and developing countries.[16]

Through these programs and others, Canada's role in the international communication community is significant. While these contributions, for the most part, have not been headline material, they have been constant and by and large effective. Through their expertise in the area of communication, Canadians have brought respect to themselves as individuals and to their country.

Canadian Reporting on World Events

What happens in the world is clearly of significance to Canadians. Although the country is not a great power with far-flung political and military interests, as an industrialized nation with a relatively small population, the Canadian economy is highly dependent on export markets. Moreover, roughly three-quarters of our foreign trade is carried on with the United States, and reciprocally, Canada is the largest trading partner of the United States. Overall, the Canadian–American trading relationship is the largest of its kind in the world. One of the consequences is that U.S. events are likely to form an important part of news reports in Canadian media.

Mass media are uniquely important in framing our understanding of world events, because most of us have relatively few independent sources from which to draw information. We depend to an extraordinary degree on the mass media for our information on, and our impressions of, world events.[17]

Given the importance of international reporting to Canadians, it is significant that over the past two decades this particular dimension of Canadian mass media has been the object of severe criticism by individual scholars, as well as by government studies. These criticisms can be summarized as follows: there is not enough international reporting, and what there is tends to be "event oriented," lacking in-depth analysis; and not only is news about the United States given undue prominence in Canadian reporting, news concerning other regions of the world is reported largely by American international wire services (for example AP), leading to an American perspective on world events.[18]

How "good" or how "bad" is Canadian international reporting?

It is clear that we have to be careful when we talk about "quality" of media product. We cannot assume that a report about an event in Asia or Europe written by a Canadian is somehow journalistically superior to a story on the same event prepared by an American reporter. However, in that it is objectively clear that, on a number of global issues, Canada has a set of concerns that are different from those of the United States, we see the news events reported through a Canadian reportorial value system as constituting a societal benefit. Moreover, the use of U.S.-reporter-originated stories in Canadian media creates a particular problem, as the Special Senate Committee on Mass Media in Canada reported in 1970:

> [The U.S. journalist] writes from a background of American experience and American national interest, which are not the Canadian experience and the Canadian interest. He uses American illustrations which are not Canadian illustrations, and he draws on a literature, a history, and a political tradition which are his and not ours.[19]

It appears to us that while weaknesses in Canadian international reporting do exist, and are documented in the research literature, over the past ten years there has been a noticeable improvement in this area of reporting and a new assessment needs to be made. Several research contributions attest to changes, and it is fair to say that this research has been triggered by the kinds of criticisms cited previously.

Taken as a whole, this research indicates that a change in awareness on the part of media practitioners of the importance of international news has occurred, with a resultant change in practice and content.

First, it is important to point out that Canadian international reporting in the past clearly has been deficient, particularly if compared with American reporting. For example, in a comparative study of the *New York Times* and the *Globe and Mail* coverage of Cuba in 1953 and 1956 (both key years leading up to the Cuban Revolution in 1959), 93 percent of the total number of news items appeared in the *New York Times*, as opposed to 7 percent in the *Globe and Mail.* Fidel Castro was not even mentioned by name in the 1953 and 1956 *Globe and Mail* sample.[20] A comparison of coverage of the Nicaraguan Revolution in 1978, 1979, and 1980 in three leading American and three leading Canadian newspapers showed that the ratio of coverage was 64 percent American to 36 percent Canadian. This ratio, approximately two-thirds to one-third, is typical of American and Canadian coverage of events in Latin America. This is not unreasonable: we should point out that there are many reasons—political, economic, ideological—why the U.S. media generally give more coverage to Latin America than do Canadian newspapers.

The figures are quite different for events in the Caribbean: the Grenadian election of 1984 produced roughly equal coverage in a sample of six American and six Canadian newspapers, and in the Haitian election crisis of 1987–88, Canadian press coverage actually exceeded that of the United States (53 percent to 47 percent).[21] While there are reasons for the greater focus of Canadian newspapers on the Caribbean region (Commonwealth connections and common languages), international coverage based on quantity clearly has improved. This is so particularly if we keep in mind that included in the American sample of newspapers were the *New York Times*, the *Washington Post*, and the *Los Angeles Times*, all large papers with global reputations in international reporting. Moreover, with respect to commentary (editorials and feature columns), it was not evident that Canadian papers were deficient in comparison with their American counterparts.

An area of continuing concern, however, is the extent to which Canadian international reporting by Canadian Press (CP) is dependent on U.S. wire services for its content. A report for the 1981 Royal Commission on Newspapers pointed out that two-thirds of Canadian foreign news focussed on the U.S. Moreover, in terms of overall coverage of the world, Canadian Press was credited with less than a fifth. "Nearly three-quarters of the [international] Datafile emanated from [American-based] Associated Press."[22] Nevertheless, the fact that CP has the opportunity to rewrite and edit the foreign news reports that it receives, even if it does not solve the problem of American bias, at least introduces a Canadian dimension.[23] As well, it has become evident that large Canadian media organizations have expressed a greater interest in the global community as they have increased the number of their foreign news bureaus.[24]

Further evidence of change is seen in the results of a 1988 survey of Canadian daily newspaper editors, eliciting their evaluations of Canadian international reporting. Responses by editors to the question "How would you rate Canadian newspaper coverage of international news in terms of amount, quality, depth, range and objectivity?" showed that less than a quarter deemed performance as "less than satisfactory." Moreover, 57 percent responded that Canadian papers were doing a "good job," while 22 percent rated coverage as "very good" to "excellent." When asked to assess trends in such coverage based on the same criteria, 49 percent believed quality had remained the same and 51 percent felt that it had improved. Not a single editor felt that it had declined. Among the editors of the country's largest newspapers, fully 92 percent considered that improvement had taken place over the past five years.[25]

In the same study, on a question specifically aimed at ascertaining the impact of American sources on Canadian reporting, the editors were asked to rate the importance of this problem on a 1 to 10 scale (where 1 represented "frivolous" and 10 represented "very serious"). The mean score was 6.9, indicating that they considered the problem to be quite serious. Indeed, in response to the question "What single thing can be done to improve the quality of Canadian international reporting?" variations to the statement "get more Canadians into the field to report the news" overwhelmed all others.

Data for television are not as readily available, as fewer studies compare Canadian and U.S. reporting on this medium. However, a study conducted in 1985 by the authors indicated some interesting relationships. On CBC's "The National," 48 percent of stories focussed on Canada, 15 percent on the United States, and 37 percent on international material excluding the U.S. For CTV network news, the analogous figures were 53 percent, 19 percent, and 28 percent. The three major American networks (ABC, CBS, and NBC), by contrast, featured virtually no stories about Canada. Approximately two-thirds of stories dealt with events in the United States, while one-third were international. Within the international category, armed conflict, terrorism, and riots tended to attract TV coverage in both countries. The American stations tended to concentrate on the Soviet Union and areas of the world where their own political and military interests were at stake. Conversely, Canadian international coverage was more broadly focussed.[26]

Convergence

While we have been discussing the Canadian impact on the international community and the impact of the international community, as filtered through the mass media, on Canada, it is impossible to ignore a third theme—the very real possibility that the global community is being subjected to common socializing forces as information moves from one society to another. Early in his career, Marshall McLuhan predicted such a possibility, terming the phenomenon the *global village*. It is now evident that with respect to ownership, distances are largely irrelevant in the global community, and that a particular owner can be active in business operations in many different countries (see chapter 13). But, in addition to the ownership dimension, there are other ways in which global communities are coming together.

Since the early 1980s business and public administration journals have been featuring articles that focus on the possibility of advertising–marketing standardization by multinational corporations. In effect, standardization implies integration or convergence of marketing practices, rather than expensive diversification from one national market to another. Implicit in this view is the perception that people, their behaviour, and their societies are noticeably converging; that is, beginning to resemble each other more closely.

It is not our purpose here to take sides in the ongoing debate on this issue, rather it is to offer some insights into the types of arguments that are being presented about these convergences. On occasion one hears such arguments described as "convergence theories." We do not propose to introduce a new theoretical approach to this facet of international communication, but it is important to identify the major factors that are seen as leading to this phenomenon.

Stock Market Strategies

Global stock market strategies have been integrated for a number of years, and it is clear that stock markets interact with one another—in New York, London, Bonn, Tokyo, Toronto, Paris, and Hong Kong. In any market fluctuation, one market seems to hold its breath awaiting to see how another, thousands of miles away, reacts to some business event. Constant, twenty-four-hour computer links now permit buyers and sellers of stocks to act in the market of any nation on the globe as readily as they can act in their own. There is little doubt that such interaction offers justification to any discussion of global business and economic convergence.

Marketing Strategies

More evidence of convergence is offered in the examples of international trade and marketing. The marketing of products through multinational corporations has proliferated globally, particularly since 1945. Many nations, including

Canada, have accepted, for example, well-known products such as soft drinks, blue jeans, and cameras, as if they were their own. One nation using the products produced in another is a daily and accepted way of life in the global community. Given the trend towards greater economic integration, this international movement of products should continue to accelerate. Since most products are likely to bear the imprint of the culture in which they were produced, popularization of particular products, therefore, also suggests the potential for the popularization of different cultural values.

At the same time one can look at the already well-established cross-national manufacturing of automobiles. Corporate cross-ownership began over a decade ago, when North American automobile manufacturers became corporate associates of auto manufacturers in Europe and Asia. While the vehicles we drive on Canadian highways might well be wholly manufactured in Canada or in the United States, it becomes increasingly apparent that our automobiles may be designed in Germany, assembled in Mexico, with parts manufactured in Japan and Korea, but marketed by dealerships in our own communities.

Global Movement of Information

Global movement of information has been discussed earlier, but the topic must be re-emphasized here. Satellite distribution of news of events from one society to another has been reducing whatever space or time barriers existed earlier. Transmission of a news event from the United Kingdom or France to the colonies at the time of the pioneer press was often measured in months, rather than at the speed of light. The multiplication of such TV "studios" globally has brought the world much closer together in terms of the knowledge we all have regarding other societies. In the same way that communication systems have brought us closer together internationally, so too have developments in transportation. Air travel from New York to London via the Concorde, for example, is about four hours. Even normal subsonic air travel permits a company's general manager to visit offices or plants around the world within a relatively short period of time. As well, in the business world, teleconferencing permits people to use a combination of telephones, satellites, television, and computers to "meet" with their counterparts regardless of where their offices are located. Computerized facsimile (fax) transmissions have had the result of moving "mail" from office to office, regardless of where they are, without recourse to a postal system. Some technological developments currently underway in the areas discussed above will have the effect of reducing constrictions of space and time even more.

Socializing Forces

Societies around the world are beginning to resemble each other in terms of urbanization, aging, standards of living, changing profiles of work forces, and increasing access to mass media. There is also evidence of convergence at the point of production of cultural products. The production of the TV miniseries "Marco Polo" in 1982, for example, involved teamwork from individuals and organizations in the U.S., Italy, Japan, the U.K., and the People's Republic of China.[27] In April 1989, an international program, "World Music Video Awards," originating in Toronto, included live performances from Toronto, London, New York, Munich, and Moscow. The producer of this program considered it to be the single largest commercial live TV event ever mounted and described the event as "something for everyone who understands music as a common international language."[28]

Marketing journals also argue that prior to television, in the early years of the entertainment industry, film stars from Hollywood, in particular, were adored and their films were followed anywhere in the world they were shown. The stars of Hollywood, given the absence of a film industry in Canada, were Canada's stars as well; indeed some, such as silent-screen legend Mary Pickford, were Canadian born. This same phenomenon was repeated in many global communities. The impact of the Hollywood film industry, and later of U.S. television programming, was to contribute to a type of cultural convergence.

Trends with Respect to the United States

At this point in our discussion about convergence in the global community, it is quite appropriate to respond to questions that are likely to be uppermost in the readers' minds: What about the United States? Is the U.S. a part of this phenomenon as well? Does the product of the giant U.S. film–telefilm production industry continue to dominate the foreign marketplace as it has over the past half century?

While it is true that the U.S. film and entertainment industries have been dominant in the global community, there is some evidence that this dominance is lessening. Other countries have gained production expertise, accelerated by the rapid growth of television since the 1950s, and have intervened in the global marketplace to modify significantly the earlier U.S. dominance.

For example, one may look to the advertising industry, perhaps the most pervasive of all cultural

TABLE 3–1
The Global Advertising Market

	Overall Global Advertising Expenditures (in billions) $	U.S. Share (in billions) $	U.S. Share (in %)
1960	18	12	66
1970	35	20	57
1980	110	55	50
2000 (projected)	780	320	41

Source: Table is compiled from data in Robert J. Coen, "Vast U.S. and Worldwide Ad Expenditures Expected," *Advertising Age* 51 (13 November 1980), 10-16.

industries insofar as it influences society's tastes, values, fads, and lifestyles through sophisticated persuasive messages. The U.S. influence is noticeably decreasing in the global community, and this may be identified in two ways.

First, in terms of the global ranking of advertising agencies in dollar volume of business conducted, for at least the past decade, Dentsu Advertising of Tokyo has headed the listing of global agencies, with Saatchi and Saatchi from the United Kingdom in second place, and Young and Rubicam of the United States in third.[29] Prior to the 1990s U.S. agencies dominated in terms of dollar volume of advertising. Second, measured by expenditures of funds in the global marketplace by multinational corporations, U.S.-based companies continue to rank first. However, their global share is decreasing. Table 3–1 identifies this change.

Furthermore, corporate takeovers of American feature film and television program production by non-U.S. corporations has suddenly changed the production industry. In December 1990, Matsushita Electric Industrial Company of Japan acquired MCA (Music Corporation of America) for $6.13 billion. (MCA owns the movie studio that produced *Jaws* and *E.T.*) Earlier, in the 1980s, Rupert Murdoch (a media baron who operates on three continents) purchased Twentieth Century-Fox Corporation; Sony Corporation of Japan acquired the holdings of Columbia Pictures and Columbia Records; France's Pathé

Communications purchased MGM/ United Artists Communications.[30] Of the latest takeover of MCA by Matsushita, the *Globe and Mail* correspondent in Tokyo indicated that a survey conducted in the U.S. revealed that 63 percent of respondents felt that the takeover would lead to Japanese "cultural control of the U.S. industry."[31]

While it is still too early to assess what the cultural impact of these takeovers of U.S.-owned companies will ultimately be, it is evident that at least boardroom strategies of these companies will undergo changes. At the same time, it is also clear that the impact of the United States on the global community of these powerful production companies will have lessened.

It has become evident, as well, that as coproduction between content producers in various nations has been found to be mutually beneficial to all of the participants, the U.S. film–television production industry has begun to lose the exclusivity it has held for decades with respect to production quality and product distribution. "Coproduction" is the process whereby producers from two or more nations join forces, talents, and resources, to produce marketable television content. The September 1985 issue of *Telecommunication Policy* notes that "the days of little or no competition have ended for U.S. [TV programming] companies. In recent years a dozen nations ranging from Brazil and Mexico to the UK, Italy, and Australia, have gone into the telefilm export markets throughout the world."[32]

At the same time as the United States has had to face such competition, it has had to contend with another development: countries that previously bought U.S. telefilm product have introduced quota systems to limit foreign content. In Canada and Australia, for example, a limit on nondomestic TV product is 40 percent, in France it is 12 percent, and in the U.K. 14 percent.[33] There are several reasons for such restrictions on foreign content, but in the case of Canada two stand out: first, domestic production initiatives have been stifled, given the ready and relatively inexpensive availability of U.S. product; second, the absence of domestic content in the face of the abundance of U.S. content introduced a very real threat to political, social, and cultural identity.

In summary, significant changes have occurred in the global marketplace of film and television products: the television industry has come of age globally; the trend towards international coproduction has increased; the change in the U.S. from its earlier exporting role to its current position of accepting increasingly more non-U.S. product for its media systems is apparent; and the installation of protective barriers towards U.S.-originated product has had the overall result of lessening the impact of the U.S. entertainment industry on the global community. As well, with the popular advent of international coproduction, it is possible that "this process might accentuate the internationalization of television programming."[34]

Convergence of Ownership

The matter of mass media ownership is examined in detail in later chapters. However, in this discussion of global convergences, some reference to trends in media ownership is necessary.

What was speculation in the 1950s and 1960s about concentration—that, theoretically, all information and entertainment media, globally, could pass into a few hands—is today a reality. Anthony Smith, president of Magdalen College, Oxford, offers the following explanation for the globalization of media ownership:

> Publishers want to be in a position to exploit a work of talent across the whole media landscape; they have come to fear the consequences of being excluded from an audience if they do not have a finger in every kind of media pie. Furthermore, it is becoming easier in technological terms to become involved in a wider range of media. Transitional media empires are thus coming into being to exploit new opportunities and as a protection against possible loss of opportunity. Newspapers, film businesses, radio, television and publishing are passing into the same institutional hands.[35]

What form such globalization of ownership will eventually take is anyone's guess. The point to be made here is that the extremely powerful socializing force of ownership is becoming apparent. Theoretically, at least, similarity rather than diversity of content is likely to be the result.

Contrary Trends

At the same time that evidence confirms a general process of international convergence, one can also make an argument for growing cultural specificity and international divergence. Even though one might be tempted to conclude that the global village has arrived, such a conclusion might be premature.

While problems associated with cultural particularism were most vivid in the USSR, where republics have achieved cultural and political autonomy, Canadians need look no further than to their own situation for confirmation of the strength of cultural and linguistic differences. In spite of the defeat of the separatist option in the referendum in 1980, a separate Quebec identity is as evident today, and perhaps even stronger than it ever was.

Further evidence of the distinctiveness of Quebec culture comes from the business–marketing community. While considerable commonality of tastes exists in Canada, clear Francophone preferences for products and the way they are merchandized and advertised are apparent. For instance, French Canadians are more likely to use premium-priced products and generally spend more money than do Anglo-Canadians on clothes, personal care

items, alcohol, tobacco, and cultural activities.[36] There are differences (albeit to a lesser extent) evident in western and maritime regions of the country as well. Certain members of the business community maintain that the successful marketing of a product depends on the marketer's ability to portray that product in a manner that uniquely reflects the characteristics of the society in which that product is to be purchased and used.

Within the broad study of communication the recognition of cultural specificity and its effects on communication are explored under the subfield of intercultural communication. One of the characteristics of intercultural communication is that culture is not necessarily defined by national boundaries. Rather, cultural values and aspirations often tend to form much stronger identities than those that result from a definition of a national boundary. In Canada it is evident that within the national boundary, there are several distinct cultural groups. In addition to the traditional French, English, and other heritage language groups, the First Nation of aboriginal peoples is emerging as a strong political force in the 1990s. At the same time, the study of intercultural communication reveals that individuals and groups, wherever they may be, share certain universal emotions such as happiness, fear, anger, and disgust. Some TV commercials try to take advantage of such perceived common symbolic representations (for example, Coca Cola's "global harmony" commercial and the "united colours of Benetton" ads.

While acknowledging that, in many ways, peoples in the world have much in common and that the extent of this commonality is increasing, it is important for us in one of the most affluent and comfortable societies on earth to realize that it is dangerous to assume that other societies are mirror images of our own. There are obvious questions raised in a discussion of convergence regarding whose cultural values are being represented in mass media product and the effects of *dominant* cultures on *subordinate* cultures (i.e., "media imperialism"). The reality is that a number of Third World societies are reacting strongly to a process of convergence wherein their cultural values are perceived as being destroyed. It is virtually axiomatic that a perceived threat to such fundamental values such as language, religion, lifestyle (i.e., culture in its broadest manifestations) will provoke defensive or even rebellious counteractions. When trying to understand the world as it is, it is not very helpful to project our own value system onto that world and it is not always possible to interpret events in other parts of the world through *our* own standards of behaviour and beliefs. The problem of understanding the global context for the study of communications is much more complex and demands study and reflection. Our purpose here has been to sketch out the complexity of that problem and to identify approaches of study that might be taken in the future.

Notes

1. See *Yearbook of International Organizations 1989/90*, vol. 1 (New York: K.G. Saur, 1989/1990) appendix 7, table 1. Another estimate, published a year earlier, identified some 400 intergovernmental organizations, 4000 international nongovernmental organizations, and a further 4000 business international nongovernmental organizations, noting that the number of such organizations is growing as is the membership of each organization. See Paul Taylor, ed., *International Institutions at Work* (New York: St. Martin's Press, 1988), 7.
2. Canadian Broadcasting Corporation, *A Brief History of the CBC* (Ottawa: CBC, 1976), 12.
3. Radio Canada International, *Program Schedule 1990–1991* (Montreal, 1990), 2–13.
4. Stephen Godfrey, "RCI Slashed by Nearly Half," *Globe and Mail*, 23 March 1991, C1.
5. See the volume of *Journal of Communication* (34 (August 1984)) entitled "Ferment in the Field," which in its entirety is devoted to this controversy.
6. William G. Harley, "Memorandum," *Journal of Communication* 34 (August 1984): 89–92.
7. "Clark Promises to Keep Canada in U.N. Agency," *Toronto Star*, 4 December 1984, A9.
8. Canadian Commission for UNESCO, *Report of the Secretary-General, 1988–1989* (Ottawa, 1989), 15.

9. Ibid., 39.

10. Louis Patenaude, memorandum and accompanying brochure, "McLuhan Teleglobe Canada Award 1991" (Ottawa: Canadian Commission for UNESCO, 20 December 1990).

11. *Canadian Commission for UNESCO Bulletin* (Ottawa: Canadian Commission for UNESCO, 13 February 1991), 14.

12. Ibid., 10.

13. Gunnar Garbo, "A World of Difference: The International Distribution of Information: The Media and Developing Countries" (Paris: UNESCO, 1985), 81–82.

14. Canadian Commission for UNESCO, *Report*, 43.

15. Canadian International Development Agency, *CIDA Annual Report 1987–1988* (Ottawa: Supply and Services, 1989), 16. Also see *CIDA Annual Report 1988–1989* (Ottawa: Supply and Services, 1990), 65.

16. *IDRC Annual Report 1987–1988* (Ottawa: IDRC, 1988), 3, 15.

17. Tod Gitlin, *The Whole World Is Watching* (Berkeley: University of California Press, 1980), 2.

18. In addition to the Reports of the Special Senate Committee on Mass Media (1970) and the Royal Commission on Newspapers (1981), see Denis Stairs, "The Press and Foreign Policy in Canada," *International Journal* 31 (Spring 1976), and T. Joseph Scanlon, "Canada Sees the World through U.S. Eyes: One Case in Cultural Domination," *Canadian Forum* 54 (September 1974): 34–39.

19. Canada, Senate, *Report of the Special Senate Committee on Mass Media: The Uncertain Mirror*, vol. 1 (Ottawa: Information Canada, 1970), 233.

20. W.C. Soderlund, "Western Press Coverage of Fidel Castro: The Early Years, 1953–1956" (paper presented at the Conference "Thirty Years of the Cuban Revolution: An Assessment," Halifax, November 1989).

21. W.C. Soderlund, "Press Images of the Nicaraguan Revolution, 1978–1980: A Canadian–American Comparison" (paper presented at the 7th Annual Intercultural/International Communication Conference, University of Miami, February 1990); and W.C. Soderlund and R.C. Nelson, "Canadian and American Press Coverage of the Haitian Election Crisis" in *Mass Media and the Caribbean*, ed. S.H. Surlin and W.C. Soderlund (New York: Gordon and Breach, 1990).

22. Carman Cumming, Mario Cardinal, Peter Johansen, *Canadian News Services, Research Studies on the Newspaper Industry for the Royal Commission on Newspapers* (Ottawa: Supply and Services, 1981), 36–37.

23. Vince Rice, "The 'Canadianization' Process: Editing Inflowing International Stories from Foreign Sources" (unpublished paper, School of Journalism, University of Western Ontario, 1988).

24. Interview with Norman Webster, editor-in-chief, *Globe and Mail*, November 1986.

25. W.C. Soderlund, R.M. Krause, R.G. Price, "Canadian Daily Newspaper Editors' Evaluation of International Reporting," *Canadian Journal of Communication* 16, 1 (1991): 5–18.

26. S.H. Surlin, W.I. Romanow, W.C. Soderlund, "TV Network News: A Canadian-American Comparison," *American Review of Canadian Studies* 18 (Winter 1988): 469–72.

27. Jean-Luc Renaud and Barry R. Litman, "Changing Dynamics of the Overseas Marketplace for TV Programming: The Rise of International Co-Production," *Telecommu-*

nications Policy 9 (September 1985): 257.

28. Gregg Quill, "Much Music's Video Awards, A Monster Bash," *Toronto Star,* 9 April 1989, C1.

29. "Top 100 Agencies Worldwide by Gross Income," *Advertising Age* 61 (24 December 1990): 16.

30. John McManus, "MCA Deal Could Aid Fin-Syn Fight," *Advertising Age* 61 (3 December 1990): 10.

31. Edith Terry, "The Samurai Take Hollywood," *Globe and Mail,* 12 December 1990, A13.

32. Renaud and Litman, "Changing Dynamics of the Overseas Marketplace," 256.

33. Ibid.

34. Ibid., 261.

35. Anthony Smith, "Media Globalism in the Age of Consumer Sovereignty," *Gannett Center Journal* 4 (Fall 1990): 8–9.

36. John S. Wright, Willis L. Winter, Sherilyn K. Zeigler, P. Noel O'Dea, *Advertising, First Canadian Edition* (Toronto: McGraw-Hill Ryerson, 1984), 364–65.

THE BEATLES: Paul, John, George and Ringo in the early days

Remaining Beatles' reunion creates mixed feelings

The remaining members of the Beatles have reportedly agreed to a reunion of sorts, but it has created a peculiar ambivalence: Excitement from fans who weren't even born when the Beatles broke up, and trepidation from Baby Boomers who don't want to soil the memories of a sacred symbol. **D11**

C H A P T E R   4

Theoretical Approaches to Communication

Introduction

While communication theorists can trace their roots to classical logic and rhetoric (Plato and Aristotle) to identify the bases of both the art and the science of human verbal and nonverbal interaction, modern theorists tend to take their cues from Harold Lasswell's well-known paradigm of "Who says what, in which channel, to whom, with what effect."[1] As Lasswell's concept of communication served theorists in the 1940s, it serves equally well to ground our discussion of communication theory in today's context.

Nevertheless, it should be made clear that while we have chosen the Laswellian paradigm as a means to study communication theory, other approaches to the field fall well outside the paradigm. For example, the study of language systems and their symbolic representations, as well as the complexities of human interactions, are dominant areas of ongoing research. However, the approach taken here seems most useful insofar as it provides a man-ageable starting point to a complex field of study that crosses a number of disciplines.[2]

From Lasswell's paradigm it is possible to sketch a few basic definitions. A communication act is the transfer of information, mutually understood by the *sender* and the *receiver*. Although such a definition appears to be simplistic, it presupposes the existence of *contexts*, or conditions of commonality between the two participants. Wilbur Schramm identifies these similar contexts for senders and receivers as *life spaces*.[3] For Schramm, a life space is defined by language, values, cultural or social conditions, or any characteristic that identifies the lifestyles of individuals. As figure 4–1 illustrates, when life spaces of two individuals overlap (in that common conditions exist) there is a greater probability that communication will take place.

Thus, the basic condition of the communication act and that which governs its effectiveness is the degree to which the sender and receiver share common characteristics. It is in this sense that some

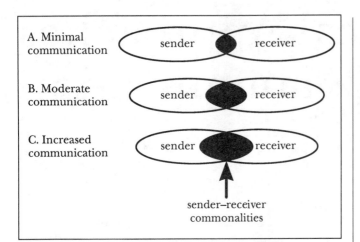

FIGURE 4-1

Conceptualizing the Effectiveness of Communication

(state religion and social class) and therefore we will miss some of the film's meaning. Communication is not as complete as it would be for a Swede viewing the film in Stockholm.

The film analogy leads us into a discussion of *mass communication*, a term that has been refined over the past several decades due to dramatic changes in the mass media industries. It is now common to speak of *segmented mass communication*, or *narrowcasting*. This term does not refer to any particular technology, but rather to the nature of the audience. Instead of being perceived as an undifferentiated mass, audiences are now perceived as consisting of smaller groups of people who share certain characteristics and preferences. In today's society, with a multiplicity of competitive media, audiences seek out the media and media content that display life spaces with which they are familiar. Moreover, entrepreneurial enterprises quite frequently identify such groups, and media (magazines or FM radio stations, for instance) are shaped to serve them. While it is true that there are still many events with which large, undifferentiated audiences identify (World Cup Soccer and the Olympic Games, for example), it appears that this phenomenon is not as great as it was when people had fewer alternatives in terms of media available to them.

Finally, in looking at definitions, interpersonal communication occurs when the participants in the communication act are both in the same place. When we speak of mass

theorists insist that there can never be total communication, since a complete overlap of life spaces is never likely to occur, given that all people are to some extent different.

An analogy can further explain the difficulties inherent in the communication act. Imagine, first of all, that you are watching a movie produced in Sweden, for example, with all the symbols of Swedish society, including language, contained in that movie. With no English subtitles, and unless we have some familiarity with Swedish culture and its symbols, we are not likely to grasp much from the movie beyond basic human emotions, such as anger, fear, affection, that we share as human beings everywhere. Imagine now that we view the same movie, this time with subtitles. The subtitles enable us to follow the story line and interactions of the actors more clearly, but not as well as we might want to. Even if the dialogue has been dubbed into English, we will not understand many of the nuances unique to Swedish culture communication or, more properly now, segmented mass communication, we refer to a situation where (1) sender and receiver are distant; (2) they come together through the intervention of some organizational structure combined with its technology, whether that be print, radio, TV, or film; and (3) the message transmitted is aimed at a specific group of anonymous receivers. Although segmented mass communication often attempts to simulate the interpersonal mode, the very fact that senders and receivers are at a distance and separated often by time as well as space results in such technological simulation failing to capture the full range and potential of detailed action and interaction that normally go on between two persons or in a person-to-group context.

The Evolution of Mass Communication Theories

The coincidence of the development of radio technology and totalitarian political systems in Europe that used this technology with great effectiveness set the context for modern attempts to understand the communication process. While through the ages the study of rhetoric and debate was popular in universities, and indeed is still contained in curricula such as speech–

communications and/or philosophy, our interest here focusses on communication theories as these have been developed since the popularization of electronic media in the 1920s.

The Direct Effects Theory

The interpersonal communication model, as we have attributed it to Wilbur Schramm, has not always dominated the thinking of communication theorists. An early theory of mass communication, which was developed within the discipline of sociology in Europe, can be identified as the theory of direct effects, or, more colloquially, as the *shotgun, transportation,* or *hypodermic needle model.* This approach to communication implies that an individual sender could project messages through broadcasting or extensive public address systems to a group resulting in a homogeneous and convincing effect. Historically, we are reminded that Benito Mussolini and Adolph Hitler, in the early 1930s, achieved stunning success through such techniques. Working in the light of these experiences, communication theorists saw the sender and the mass media of communication as all-powerful, with the audiences or receivers as largely powerless to defend themselves against the messages delivered by new technology.

In describing the parts of this model, we recognize the sender, the receiver, the medium, and the message. However, we note the absence of *feedback.* Feedback is not

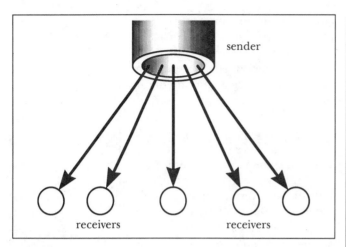
sender

receivers   receivers

FIGURE 4–2

The Shotgun Model

of Communication

a necessary component of the communication paradigm, in that communication can occur without it. Still, it does increase the probability of more successful communication. Senders, in both interpersonal and mass communications modes, depend upon feedback for guidance as to whether their messages are being understood or at least received. As well, senders are advised as to how to produce more effective successive messages. Thus, ideally, the communication act entails an element of reciprocity. It should be pointed out here that the very acts of compliance on the part of audiences of the 1930s to suggestions contained in Fascist and Nazi broadcasting were in fact evidence of a crude feedback process. Nevertheless, as historians remind us, such compliance much of the time was the result of coercion. Such behaviour is not congruent with legitimate persuasion or communication processes. This theory provided the basis under which propaganda was studied during

World War II. A specific discussion of propaganda follows later in this chapter.

Filter Models of Communication

As communication became more intensively and scientifically studied during World War II and following, it became apparent to researchers that senders could not in fact assume that receivers of their messages would behave as a single-minded, single-experience unit. While some common group characteristics are always evident when individuals gather, and while in some instances the behaviour of a group will be reflected in the behaviour of individuals, each member of society is a unique individual with his or her own set of experiences, aspirations, and values. These distinguishing characteristics act in effect as filters through which the message transmitted through a medium of mass communication must pass. We now know that some messages pass through these filters virtually unchanged, some are rejected outright, while others are only partially absorbed or altered in meaning. Descriptions of such communication processes have been made, and thus we have in the literature such terms as *selective attention, selective perception,* and *selective retention*—all key components of the filter model of communication.[4]

Selective attention means that the individual takes information from the environment according to his or her own psycho-sociological predispositions. Selective perception means that as we take information from the environment, we give it our own unique interpretation or "spin," again, according to our own unique predispositions. Selective retention means that we are more likely to recall events that are congruent with our predispositions. In short, the filter model reduces significantly the power of the sender in the mass communication process. Such earlier theories, then, about the sender being in control of his or her audience—the shotgun model—have become largely discredited. We use the term *largely* advisedly because under certain conditions magnetic and powerful personalities, using well-produced messages, are capable of swaying mass audiences. However, the instances of such acts of persuasion require unique conditions and their occurrences today are rare.

The Two-Step Flow Theory

Studies of mass communication took on considerable depth when mass and interpersonal modes of communication were connected theoretically. In one noted instance, such a link was convincingly made and recorded in *The People's Choice*, published in 1944 by Professors Paul Lazarsfeld, Bernard Berelson, and Hazel Gaudet.[5] In this landmark study, the trio of scholars noted, as they studied voter behaviour in the 1940 American presidential election, that the effect of mass media on decisions for

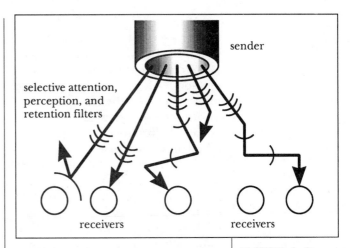

selective attention, perception, and retention filters

sender

receivers   receivers

FIGURE 4–3
The Filter Model of Communication

whom to vote did not appear to be as powerful as theories of the time led them to expect. Rather their data pointed to individuals, such as friends, family, and co-workers, being as influential as mass media, if not more so, in terms of how voters arrived at their decisions. From these observations the scholars concluded that information was dispersed from sender to receiver in a *two-step flow process*.

Key to understanding this theory was the identification of significant personal characteristics among those involved in the information flow, especially those that scholars labelled *opinion leaders*. Opinion leaders have the following characteristics: they spend more time with mass media than do their colleagues; they are unusually knowledgeable in identified areas; at the same time they are similar demographically to the group that they influence.

From this theoretical contribution we learn that receivers not only get information directly from mass media but get this information through second-step interpersonal channels of communication as well. Of particular significance is that opinion leaders not only pass along information but they interpret that information as they pass it along. Finally, as we move from group to group, different persons fill the role of opinion leaders. As the two-step flow theory has evolved over time, it has become clear that opinion leaders themselves often have opinion leaders. Thus, while dispersal of information through this combination of mass/interpersonal modes of communication continues to be referred to as the two-step flow theory, it really involves more that just two steps. As well, information dispersal studies have extended beyond the realm of voter behaviour examined by Lazarsfeld and his colleagues. For example, a broad range of research was triggered for scholars who applied these concepts to marketing and consumer behaviour research.

Critical Theory

Over the past decade or so an approach to understanding communication processes in society, referred to as critical theory, has been associated with the work of such European scholars as Antonio Gramsci, Jurgen Habermas, and Stuart Hall, and has had a major influence on North American communication theory, particularly in Canada.

Critical theory is based on a neo-Marxist interpretation of society in which social class divisions and social power relationships are essential components. Crucial to this theory is the concept of the hegemony of the ideology of the dominant class, i.e., the ruling capitalist class. This class exercises both overt and covert control over subordinate and powerless groups in society through a number of institutions, be they economic, social, political, or cultural.

With respect to communications, economic control is relatively simple. Theorists hold that those who own the instruments of mass media (newspapers, radio and TV stations) exercise control over the content appearing in those media, and that content legitimizes the continuation of the existing system of social dominance. (We will discuss a number of important questions regarding media ownership in chapters 12 and 13.) Social control, and how it is achieved and maintained through the mass media is far more complex. Key to understanding this process is the concept of symbolic manipulation, whereby those in control of producing mass media content encode into that content political and social values that support the existing social order. For example, if upward mobility in society is related to education, it is possible to explain the plight of disadvantaged groups in terms of lack of education, while not addressing questions of differential access to education. Much of the research done in the area of critical theory has focussed on the process of "decoding" media content by sub-ordinate groups. This area of research, known as *constructionist* theory, will be discussed in greater detail later in this chapter.

In general, critical theory assumes an unjust society that is maintained in part by deliberate manipulation of symbols through the mass media. It is the role of the communication researcher to lay bare the unequal power relationships in society and to demonstrate how mass media are used to preserve the dominant ideology, thereby undermining this important method of social control.

In a discussion of the evolution of mass communication theories, critical theory at the same time points to the power of elites in maintaining social control through the mass media and to the different interpretations, or *readings*, that various social classes or ethnic groups give to mass media messages. It is unclear, therefore, whether critical theory comes down on the side of the shotgun model, stressing the power of mass media, or on the more limited effects model of mass media, as suggested by the filter and two-step flow models. Whatever the answer, in the critical theory approach, mass media are seen as ideologically charged in that they transmit a view of the world in news programming or cultural values in entertainment programming and advertising that reinforces a set of power relationships wherein some groups gain a privileged position and some become disadvantaged.

Medium-Related Theories of Communication

Keeping in mind the communication act and exploring Lasswell's paradigm further, the medium that links the sender and the receiver has been the subject of considerable research, and with good reason. Information that is sent through radio, the newspaper, or television does not emerge identically from medium to medium. Indeed, one news story distributed through the three types of media might well result in three quite different stories, both in terms of how they are constructed and how we perceive them. We have all studied poetry and composition and can doubtless recall that poetry has both content and form and that form often gives meaning to content. Odes are different from rhyming couplets, and by the very nature of their style evoke different responses. Thus, Marshall McLuhan, as a former English literature scholar, discusses the impact of form on content in his *Understanding Media.* He points out that there is obviously more meaning to a message than is suggested by its content and that as we change format or medium of message transmission, the consequent message is likely to bear the imprint of the medium through which it passes.

For example, McLuhan emphasizes that different media demand

differing degrees of participation from their audiences: some media require considerable involvement for message completion; others require considerably less.[6] Thus, as the participatory roles of audiences change according to which medium they select for information or entertainment so will their understanding of messages offered by the media.

As well, McLuhan underlines that media are endowed with different *grammars* by virtue of their technological makeup. The grammar of print, for example, is its typography—style of font, size, spacing, assembly of type. When students were exposed to the same message delivered through different media (a live lecture, radio, print, and television), subsequent tests revealed that television and radio were more effective in transmitting content than were lecture and print.[7]

Marshall McLuhan, 1911–80, c. 1977 (Juster/ Montreal Star/National Archives of Canada/ PA 133299)

The appropriate study of content, then, McLuhan emphasizes, should include the study of pertinent medium characteristics as well as the cultural environment within which media function.[8]

This is an appropriate place to comment on a Canadian colleague of McLuhan, who came to an examination of communication processes late in his career, roughly at the same time as McLuhan. Harold Innis, who approached communication from the perspective of political economy, stresses the impact of technology on modern society.[9] References to Innis in the literature often link him to the term *technological determinism*. It is possible to look on both McLuhan and Innis as concentrating on medium-oriented theory but from different perspectives and social/cultural dimensions.

There is always danger of oversimplifying the complex work of these two scholars. McLuhan's emphasis was on message systems (i.e., the relationship between form, content, and environment). Innis's work, more reflective of his training, covers the component parts of society in a broader framework. The behaviour of social units, the economy, the communication system, the transportation system, are based on technological concepts that are interrelated. These technological systems affect, or more properly determine, societal directions and social relationships. For example, when Innis describes the economic history of the fur trade, he focusses on technologies and distances as factors that affect the direction and

Harold A. Innis, 1894–1952 (National Archives of Canada/C 19694)

amount of information flow. In this sense, his work becomes the basis for communication theories relating to information movement.

Innis stresses that information moves from the core to the periphery, from the large city to the small town (or in his terminology, *the hinterland*),[10] rather than the other way around. He also discusses *weighted* relationships as factors in information movement. By weighted he means that the powerful economic community generates more information than does the weaker one. Information is likely to flow from the home country to the colony in greater volume than in the opposite direction.

While it is difficult to accommodate all of their major theoretical

contributions, our intent here has been to acknowledge the work of two outstanding Canadian scholars of world repute, who have contributed immeasurably to our understanding of communication and communications systems.

Gatekeeping Theory

It is possible to make a link between McLuhan's assertion that "the medium is the message" and a body of theory that serves as a primary base for the study of mass communication—namely, *gatekeeping theory*. In effect this branch of theory describes the process by which some information is selected from the environment for transmission by the mass media while other information is not.

The term was initially coined by Kurt Lewin, a German sociologist who described the means by which food was marketed and then found its way into consumers' hands.[11] Essentially, said Lewin, each shopper is a gatekeeper who selects products differently than others. For example, if three people are sent to the supermarket to buy ice cream, each is likely to buy the flavour that he or she prefers.

The gatekeeping analogy came into mass communication literature through a study by David Manning White in which he investigated how wire service copy was handled in a typical newsroom.[12] From White's study, as well as from others that quickly followed it, we can describe gatekeeping as having two characteristics. First imagine a physical gate controlled by an individual who either closes it, opens it somewhat, or opens it fully, thus permitting no information, some information, or a lot of information to pass through the gate. There is a quantitative dimension to gatekeeping then, insofar as the volume of information is affected by the person controlling the gate. There is also a qualitative aspect to the process in that the information that passes through the gate is likely to take on some of the orientations of the gatekeeper. For example if the day editor and the night editor of a daily newspaper are of different backgrounds, the news that they choose to publish is likely to differ in predictable ways.

Gatekeeping theory, then, focusses on those who are in a position to control the content of mass media, namely, editors, reporters, and producers. While most research focusses on human beings as occupying the role of gatekeeper, external events, such as financial conditions and legal constraints, can also control or modify information. For example budget restrictions will directly affect the quantity as well as quality of news coverage provided to a particular community. Likewise, a quota system for broadcasting station content, such as the regulations that we have in Canada, affect the balance of items in a program schedule for radio or television.

In summary, gatekeeping theory alerts us to the reality that not everything that happens in the world gets reported by the mass media. What does get reported is not the result of luck or accident, but rather is the product of conscious or unconscious decisions by persons involved in the news processes, as well as technological and other constraints.

Agenda-Setting Theory

Our discussion of gatekeeping, that process of selecting content for mass media, leads us directly to a discussion of another medium-centred

FIGURE 4–4

The Relationship Between Gatekeeping and Agenda Setting

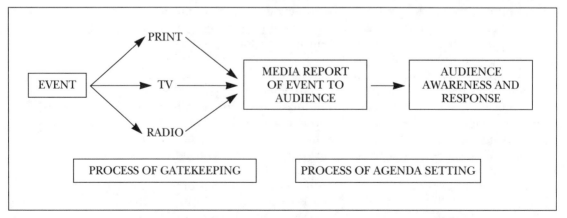

Source: W.C. Soderlund, W.I. Romanow, E.D. Briggs, R.H. Wagenberg, *Media and Elections in Canada* (Toronto: Holt, Rinehart and Winston, 1984), 31. (Reproduced by courtesy of the publisher)

theory, that of *agenda setting*. While gatekeeping concentrates on the movement of news from an event to its eventual reporting by mass media, agenda setting focusses on the way in which mass media reporting affects those in the audience who read, see, or hear it. Agenda setting has been identified as possibly the most important effect of mass communication: it mentally orders and organizes the world for viewers, readers, and listeners.[13]

The word *agenda*, as readers will readily recognize, derives from the schedule of activities that groups have agreed to follow as they go about their meetings. In the same way that the listing of items on an agenda has been selected as important to the organization concerned, the items selected by an editor for his or her newspaper from the list of problems facing a community are considered to be the important issues that face that community. The first characteristic of the agenda-setting process is that the items that have been selected by editors are, by their very selection, given heightened prominence. A second characteristic of agenda setting is that, while mass media establish agendas, we in society as well have to make decisions regarding what is important to our lives. Not surprisingly, studies that compare media agendas to our own find that there is a strong relationship between the two: that is, our personal agendas tend to reflect those agendas chosen by the media. Thus, the salience of particular issues, for example, famine in Ethiopia, politi-

cal change in Eastern Europe or Central America, or the Gulf War, not to mention domestic issues such as federal–provincial relations, unemployment, social unrest, and environmental degradation is highlighted in our own consciousness by the relative amount of media attention these items receive.[14]

This leads to the obvious question of cause and effect. Some media theorists insist that when we are exposed to media agendas, we are advised only what to think *about*, rather than *what* to think.[15] For example, media coverage of a controversial topic such as abortion will serve to raise the public's consciousness regarding the issue but is not likely to change beliefs regarding its acceptability. Scholars also argue, equally convincingly,[16] that as Walter Lippman astutely pointed out in his 1924 volume, *Public Opinion*, the "pictures in our heads" regarding the world around us are gleaned from the mass media.[17] George Gerbner's *cultivation theory*, which takes the position that as we absorb information from mass media our views of the world are shaped accordingly, supports Lippman's notion that we develop our "what-to-think-about" agendas from mass media.[18]

Gerbner's cultivation theory has been applied to the relationship between the depiction of violence in the mass media and violence levels in society. The Ontario Royal Commission on Violence in the Communications Industry (1976) had organized its inquiry around three general questions:

Does media presented violence significantly increase the probability of disruptive, destructive or aggressive behaviour . . . in individuals and subsequently in society as a whole?

What are the conditions under which aggressive effects are obtained?

What are the means by which potentially or actually harmful influences of the media on society can reliably be reduced?

The commission's findings were that while direct effects are difficult to document, "it is now fairly clear that, in addition to the often recognized causes, one of the major causes of violence is the depiction of violence in the communications media."[19]

To the present, the perceived relationship between media violence and societal violence has not changed. As the royal commission reported, the media continue to be attracted to reporting acts of violence resulting in a constant flow of information regarding violence. It is also clear that violence has become a popular entertainment mode and that there is a high degree of audience interest in violence. Gerbner reports that exposure to violence on television correlates with higher levels of audience insecurity, mistrust, and anxiety. This is not surprising in that "humankind may have had more bloodthirsty eras but none as filled with images of violence as the present. We are awash in a tide of violent representations the world has never seen. There is no escape from the massive infusion of colorful mayhem into the homes and cultural life of ever larger areas of the world."[20]

Who Sets the Agenda: News Makers or Media?

While gatekeeping theory suggests that by selecting information from the environment, media institutions in effect set the agenda, there is an alternative explanation that focusses attention on the relationship between news makers and mass media organizations that report on their activities.[21]

In work on media coverage of the 1979, 1980, and 1984 Canadian federal elections, two main results were apparent. First, politicians or political parties were able to identify and give prominence to issues as they saw them benefiting their particular campaigns. The media readily picked up their cues about what was important in the campaigns from the political parties and faithfully wrote about them.[22] Second, as various media selected issues from the electoral informational environment, there was very little difference between types of media with respect to issues which were given attention. In the 1979 campaign, for example, the leading issues in terms of frequency of mention in radio and television coverage were leadership, national unity, inflation, unemployment, and Quebec separatism; the newspaper list consisted of leadership, national unity, Quebec separatism, inflation, and federal–provincial relations.[23]

The conclusion that news makers to a large extent set the media agenda of electoral items with tacit acceptance by the media has been corroborated by Richard V. Ericson and his colleagues. They examined the relationship between news sources and reporters in such diverse areas as courts, law enforcement, day-to-day politics, and private industry. According to this study,

> Convergence is evident at the institutional level. The media elite is not separate from the elites who control many of the government and corporate bureaucracies that are reported on. . . . They interlock with these organizations in ownership, management participation, and social participation, sustaining an elite culture that circumscribes the ability of the news media to be analytically detached from the elite persons and organizations they report on.[24]

Research continues to establish, more and more convincingly, that social relationships are effective instruments in establishing a community's informational environment.[25] Often that environment may be limited quantitatively and qualitatively by the set of social relationships that link the institutions that make news with those that report it.

In this chicken and egg argument, it is apparent that a vast amount of research is still needed. The very best that can be concluded at the moment is that the interactive process between news makers and mass media is a symbiotic one, whereby they depend one upon the other.

Message-Related Theories

Agenda setting leads naturally to a discussion of messages that mass media generate and disseminate. These messages become *symbolic representations* of social reality as perceived and disseminated by the mass media. While there is a real world, few of us are able to see it in its totality and are forced to rely on media representations of the world in arriving at our understanding of it.

In formal studies of rhetoric (the organization and delivery of messages initially in oratorical contexts) the categories of informing, entertaining, and persuading are used to classify strategies and effects. Rhetoricians would argue that such categorization has a practical value with respect to message construction, but are likely to point out that all messages are inherently persuasive. When discussing the goals of rhetoric, A. Craig Baird emphasizes that the aim "has been and still is chiefly to influence an audience to think, feel, and act in harmony with the communicative purposes of the speaker or writer."[26] It becomes difficult to separate language that may have as its focus entertainment, information, or persuasion. For example, stand-up comedians might identify a particular truth about a politician, and in relating that truth in a way calculated to entertain their audiences, may also introduce an element of persuasion regarding that politician, even though that may not have been the intent. Studies of media messages have tended to focus on strategies employed by persuaders and propagandists. In understanding their strategies, we are likely to understand their motivation.

Persuasion Processes

Psychologists, sociologists, and communications scholars generally agree that there are four broad categories of activities that have an impact on us as we make our daily decisions. First, we make decisions as individuals. From the day of our birth, we develop a perspective on the world that is unique. That uniqueness stems from our life experiences, which result in individual synthesis. Our personality is a prime agent in choosing or rejecting options.

Second, our capacity to make decisions is modified by our communal cultural environment. Our racial and ethnic groups, our language, the cultural values it carries, our families, our religion, our education, and our peers are often very powerful influences in our acceptance or rejection of social concepts.

A third element in our daily decision-making is measured by demographics and is related to groups to which we belong based on such categories as sex, income, occupation, education, or age. Further, sociologists and psychologists point out that we are affected by our membership in specific social groups: (a) the groups to which we choose to belong—athletic/sports organiza-

tions, stamp-collecting clubs, sororities or fraternities; (b) the groups to which we aspire to belong, but for either lack of qualifications or limitations of some sort, we have not joined; and (c) the groups we clearly avoid. In effect, then, social relationships not only represent a personal interaction with others who have an influence on us, but often include social groups that may have an effect on our decisions.[27]

The fourth source of impact on our daily decisions are influences that flow from the mass media and cultural industries more generally. These influences may be measured in various ways. For example, Neil Postman, in what he calls the "television curriculum," indicates that by the time today's student completes high school, that student will have spent 12 000 hours in the classroom. At the same time, he or she is likely to have spent 15 000 hours watching television. Postman's point is that in a comparison between the two "curricula" (the classroom and television), the television curriculum, for a variety of reasons, is often the most attractive, enticing, and meaningful.[28] What must be added here is that in addition to those 15 000 hours spent watching television, these students will also have spent countless hours listening to radio, Walkmans, records, and CDs. They will also have viewed countless movies and read hundreds of magazines and newspapers.

When we look at how we are persuaded to think or behave in a particular manner, it becomes further apparent that mass media are becoming increasingly influential over our lives in four ways. First, if our beliefs are relatively complete and extensive, new information would produce no changes. Second, messages received from mass media provide a stamp of approval for beliefs that we already have. Third, if we hold weak beliefs or have none on a subject, mass media messages might well provide beliefs. Finally, as we receive new information related to previous beliefs, but which provides an alternative view, it is possible that our beliefs might change.[29]

Message Construction

We live with persuasion every day—for example, with commercial advertising, with information from institutions and governments—because argumentation and persuasion are fundamental to the sort of social environment in which Canadians prefer to live.

We are a pluralistic rather than an autocratic society. We permit our citizens various freedoms to choose their own patterns of thought and behaviour. As well, individuals unite into interest groups, political parties, and social groups, and such groups vie for our attention and support. What is important, then, in determining to which group or to which pattern of thought we might want to turn, is to understand principles of persuasion, and to understand messages is

to arm oneself against abuses, since the dividing line between legitimate persuasion and propaganda (in a pejorative sense) is often obscure.

Persuasive messages that originate from a commercial corporation selling its products, a political party asking for support, or even from a sophisticated propaganda ministry such as we saw in operation from the mid-1930s to the mid-1940s in Fascist Italy and Nazi Germany, essentially follow a similar format.

Earlier we discussed the contribution of Wilbur Schramm to communication theory. Schramm, as well, wrote about message properties that enhance effectiveness.[30] First, a message must catch the attention of the receiver; second, it must be understood in similar ways by both sender and receiver; and third, messages should be related to a receiver's lifestyle and should as well be aimed at particular needs.

It was after the Second World War when communication theories began to develop rapidly and when the advertising industry mushroomed as a consequence of peacetime industrial rebuilding that theorizing about effective messages became part of the communications literature.

Taking Schramm's models as a beginning, many scholars and advertising practitioners contributed to theory building. Perhaps the best known model, designed in a marketing context, was that of Robert J. Lavidge and Gary A. Steiner. Their hierarchy of effects

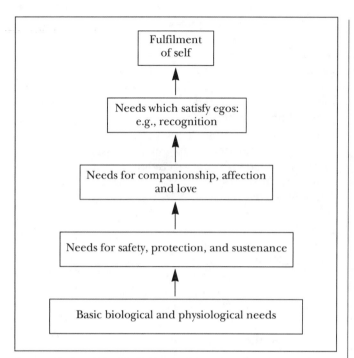

Fulfilment
of self

↑

Needs which satisfy egos:
e.g., recognition

↑

Needs for companionship, affection
and love

↑

Needs for safety, protection, and sustenance

↑

Basic biological and physiological needs

Source: Abraham H. Maslow, "A Theory of Human Motivation," *Psychological Review* 50 (1943): 370–96.

FIGURE 4–5

Maslow's Hierarchical Structure of Needs Applied to Message Targeting

With respect to the identification of needs and satisfaction of those needs, reference is frequently made to psychologist Abraham Maslow's well-known hierarchical model of human needs. (See figure 4–5.) The essence of Maslow's model is that before spiritual or social fulfilment is possible our basic biological needs must be met—our needs for shelter and food, for example. A message properly designed for a specific audience, then, would have a particular needs level of Maslow's hierarchy in mind.

What becomes clear as we study persuasive message formats is that the practice of persuasion and propaganda utilize similar formats but differ with respect to ends.

The Propagandist's Strategy

model continues to be used by advertising copywriters and those who practice the craft of persuasive writing. In their 1961 article in the *Journal of Marketing*, Lavidge and Steiner indicate that there is a natural flow as consumers move through a decision-making process: awareness; knowledge; liking; preference; conviction; and purchase.[31] The above model is often compressed by advertising copywriters into a five-step process: catching the attention of would-be audiences; identifying a particular problem or need; identifying an appropriate solution to that problem; offering evidence that the solution will work; and finally, identifying some action to be taken by receivers of messages.

While there are many publications about propaganda, and one might refer to a number of theorists who have contributed pertinent literature, contemporary studies of this subject find their bases in the work of the French philosopher Jacques Ellul.[32]

Throughout his writings Ellul focusses on strategies employed by propagandists, but in essence distinguishes propagandists from legitimate persuaders as those who deliberately distort reality with a view towards shaping individual or group thinking and behaviour. From Ellul's writings, it is possible to identify some bases of the propaganda process. First, the propagandist is not likely to create outright falsehoods, unless those are needed as adornments. The propagandist, rather, identifies a reality in society, thus giving the message initial credence, and then distorts that reality. Second, the propagandist does not work by accident—his or her behaviour is planned and deliberate. Third, the propagandist engages in distortion and deception in a manner that is self-serving—that is, the propagandist is interested in gaining support for his or her point of view. Finally, in modern propaganda, Ellul emphasizes that support should become manifest in action—either overt mobilization for action or full approval for action. For Ellul, propaganda is not simply a matter of public opinion; to be effective, it must move beyond that to appropriate behaviour itself.

It is important at this point to indicate the difference between propaganda and education. In style, both are intended to provide information. The successful teacher, however, will, in a non-self-serving and objective manner, encourage students to think for themselves so that they can arrive at their own conclusions about truth. The propagandist, on the other hand, has a predetermined version of a truth, and it is that predetermined version that receivers are expected to arrive at and act upon. Our purpose in introducing this brief discussion about persuasion and propaganda is to point out that our world contains strong elements of both. It is our responsibility, as individuals in a free and open society, to learn to distinguish between the two.

Receiver-Related Theories

Historically, communications theories have focussed on senders and messages. However, over the past two decades, scholars have turned their attention to the receiver in the communication process, and such receiver-oriented theories present a different perspective regarding the locus of power within the communication process.

Uses and Gratifications Theory

There were several initiators of the uses and gratifications approach to the study of effects of mass media on audiences. Central among these were Elihu Katz, Paul Lazarsfeld, and Bernard Berelson, who in the late 1950s and early 1960s focussed their research on uses that people made of mass media.[33] Such uses, they concluded, were conscious and deliberate rather than accidental. In 1969, these initiatives found focus in studies on mass media and politics by Jay G. Blumler and Denis McQuail.[34] Their research examined the reasons people chose to view television to gain information about political processes.

Audiences not only select information consciously and deliberately but also select the type of media that will bring them this information: they are active rather than passive receivers. Audiences select information in a manner designed to satisfy particular and personal needs: thus, media consumption is personally motivated. As one scholar has observed, we select information from the environment so as to provide ourselves with "systems maintenance," that is, information which enhances our well-being and satisfaction.[35]

Narcotizing Dysfunction

The term *narcotizing dysfunction* came into the literature in a 1948 article by Robert Merton and Paul Lazarsfeld, where the authors describe the situation in which mass media exposure could possibly serve as an excuse for nonaction on a given issue. Later, Kaarle Nordenstreng expanded the concept to include the possibility that while individuals may read, listen, and watch mass media, they in effect get little in the way of lasting information from their efforts.[36] In support of this phenomenon, an October 1989 public opinion poll conducted for the *Globe and Mail* and the CBC revealed that 63 percent of Canadians indicated that they had firm advice to offer the federal government regarding what action should be taken with regard to federal–provincial discussions on the constitution (the Meech Lake Accord). However, when pressed in the interview, 67 percent admitted that they knew "little or nothing" about the issue.[37]

Speculation about the frequency with which these noninformed public opinions might be occurring is disquieting. The thought that governments may be elected on the basis of uninformed voting is particularly troubling.

The uses and gratifications approach to studying media effects has proven to be a most useful avenue of research. Year after year, the horizons of uses and gratifications research are expanded. Such "effects" studies in the 1980s, for example, stressed the need to address (a) the relationship of audiences to new media technologies (CATV, VCRs, videotexts); (b) the processes of social change with respect to audience media behaviour; (c) the impact with which changes in society (political and economic, for instance) affect the functioning of mass media; and finally (d) the relationship between media usage and a broad range of activities related to aggression and violence in society.[38]

Diffusion of Innovative Ideas

While the two-step flow model continues to present a valid overview regarding how ideas are spread in a society, clearly it is inadequate as a full explanation. As indicated previously, the two-step pattern is, indeed, a multistep process. Further, studies concerning the roles of opinion leaders in such a model have suggested that these opinion leaders may be less influential than is credited in the two-step flow model.[39]

Concurrent with research about the two-step flow model have been studies of a broader scope, which relate more generally to the impact mass media have in bringing about changes in society.

Such studies have focussed on how ideas for change have become adopted by society, and have become identified as *innovation diffusion*—that is, the spreading of new ideas.

Foremost among researchers in the area of innovation diffusion has been Everett Rogers. He presents a five-step model of the process through which individuals move as they (1) gain knowledge of an innovation; (2) form attitudes about it (become persuaded); (3) make decisions regarding adoption or rejection; (4) implement the decision; and (5) confirm the decision. *Diffusion of Innovations*, first published in 1962, is Rogers' landmark contribution to the field in which he further indicates that the rate of adoption of ideas will be related to several factors: advantages perceived by receivers of a new idea; compatibility of the new idea to the psychological state of the receivers; complexity or ease of understanding the idea; the possibility of trying out or testing a new idea and determining whether the idea has a "fit" with the receiver; and the opportunity to observe the results of the new idea on others in society.[40] The more favourable new ideas are to the personality of the receiver the greater will be the ease with which the receiver is able to gain understanding and appreciation of the new ideas, and the more likely these ideas will be adopted. It is in this sense that mass media are able to play effective roles in introducing and bringing about social change.

Constructionist Theory

The latest receiver-oriented theory to gain credibility is what is known as either *constructionist* or *interactionist theory*. This theory deals with the interaction between media *texts*, or messages, and the social environment within which the audience exists. As explained by James A. Anderson, "interactionist or constructionist notions of meaning hold that content is only one part in a process of meaning construction. The other parts are the communicants and the contexts in which the communication takes place. Content does not deliver meaning; rather meaning is constructed from content by the individual operating in some context vis-à-vis that content."[41] Research has documented multiple interpretations, or readings, of a single text by audience members.[42] In particular, television programs "invite negotiating and permit different readings."[43]

The major difference between constructionist theory and the filter model discussed earlier (selective perception) is that constructionist theory holds that large subgroups in society (e.g., those determined by class, language, ethnicity, or nationality) share common filters. Therefore, these groups will have a propensity to read a particular message similarly, in spite of idiosyncratic differences between people within these groups.

Thus, what is important in understanding the meaning accorded to messages are individual personality states as well as the cultural context of the receiver—and these are uniquely different, not only from person to person, but from society to society. It is worth noting here that constructionists extend Wilbur Schramm's idea of the importance of contexts of receivers and senders in ensuring understanding in communication. In particular, they add to the theory by indicating that the receiver's social context is an important factor in interpreting messages. Consequently, if Canadians and Jamaicans, for example, watch an American television program ostensibly for entertainment, they are likely to come away from the experience with different interpretations of messages contained therein, despite the identical programming and their equal fluency in English.[44]

Conclusion

Communication involves a number of components, which we have identified as sender, medium, messages, receiver, and feedback, and the purpose of this chapter has been to examine how scholars have theorized about the interaction of these components during the process of communication. At the same time, it must be underlined that while we have emphasized particular theorists and theories, these theories are constantly undergoing retesting, reevaluation, and modification. Our purpose here has not been to review the entire field of communication theory, for such a task properly done would be the subject of a book in itself. Nevertheless, contemporary research in communication theory, by and large, does have its origins in the Lasswellian paradigm. While individual theorists have tended to focus on one or perhaps two components of the communication process, it should be clear that all components are important in understanding communication and that single-focus theories, while perhaps accurate with respect to the aspect of communication which they address, do not fully explain the complexity of modern mass communication.

The development of communication theory has not been the exclusive preserve of any one nation. Rather, theory development has been characterized by an accumulation of knowledge whereby scholars in one society often base their research on ideas developed in another. Wherever one goes in academic environs, for example, the same theorists and their theories, whatever their nationality, are commonly understood by all. The development of communication theory serves, then, as one example of international convergence (as discussed in the previous chapter) on the part of the academic community.

Notes

1. Harold D. Lasswell, "The Structure and Function of Communication in Society," in *The Communication of Ideas*, ed. Lyman Bryson (New York: Harper and Bros., 1948), 37–51.
2. For students who wish to pursue theoretical studies in communication at greater length, we recom-

mend Melvin L. DeFleur and Sandra Ball-Rokeach, *Theories of Mass Communication*, 4th ed. (New York: Longman, 1982) and Stephen W. Littlejohn, *Theories of Communication*, 3rd ed. (Belmont, CA: Wadsworth, 1989).

3. Wilbur Schramm, *Men, Messages, and Media: A Look at Human Communication* (New York: Harper and Row, 1973), 43.

4. Joseph T. Klapper, *The Effects of Mass Communication* (New York: The Free Press, 1960), 22.

5. Paul Lazarsfeld, Bernard Berelson, and Hazel Gaudet, *The People's Choice: How the Voter Makes Up His Mind in a Presidential Campaign* (New York: Columbia University Press, 1944), 150–58.

6. Marshall McLuhan, *Understanding Media: The Extensions of Man* (New York: New American Library, 1964), 36.

7. Ibid., 271.

8. Ibid., 26.

9. See especially, Harold A. Innis, *Empire and Communications* (Victoria, BC: Porcepic, 1986) and *The Bias of Communication* (Toronto: University of Toronto Press, 1951).

10. Harold A. Innis, *The Fur Trade in Canada: An Introduction to Canadian Economic History*, rev. ed. (Toronto: University of Toronto Press, 1970).

11. Kurt Lewin, "Psychological Ecology," in *Field Theory in Social Sciences*, ed. Dorwin Cartwright (New York: Harper and Bros., 1951): 174–77.

12. David Manning White, "The Gatekeeper: A Study in the Selection of News," *Journalism Quarterly* 27 (Fall 1950): 384.

13. Maxwell E. McCombs and Donald L. Shaw,"The Agenda-Setting Function of Mass Media," *Public Opinion Quarterly* 36 (Summer 1972): 176–87.

14. Michael B. Salwen, "Effect of Accumulation of Coverage on Issue Salience in Agenda-Setting," *Journalism Quarterly* 65 (Spring 1988): 100–6.

15. Bernard Cohen, *The Press and Foreign Policy* (Princeton: Princeton University Press, 1963), 13.

16. George Gerbner, Larry Gross, Michael Morgan, Nancy Signorielli, "The 'Mainstreaming' of America: Violence Profile No. 11," *Journal of Communication* 30 (Summer 1980): 10–29.

17. Walter Lippman, *Public Opinion* (New York: The Free Press, 1965): 3–20.

18. Gerbner et al., "Mainstreaming," 14–15.

19. Ontario, *Report of the Royal Commission on Violence in the Communications Industry*, vol. 1 (Toronto: Queen's Printer for Ontario, 1976), 144.

20. George Gerbner, "Violence and Terror in and by Media" (paper presented at the conference "Media and Crisis," Université Laval, October 1990), 6.

21. For an extended discussion, see David Taras, *The Newsmakers: The Media's Influence on Canadian Politics* (Toronto: Nelson, 1990).

22. Walter C. Soderlund, Walter I. Romanow, Ronald H. Wagenberg, E. Donald Briggs, *Media and Elections in Canada* (Toronto: Holt, Rinehart and Winston, 1984), 71–72; 93–94.

23. Ibid., 62, 83.

24. Richard V. Ericson, Patricia M. Baranek, Janet B.L. Chan, *Negotiating Control: A Study of News Sources* (Toronto: University of Toronto Press, 1989), 5.

25. Dan Berkowitz, "TV News Sources and News Channels: A Study in Agenda-Building," *Journalism Quarterly* 64 (Autumn 1987): 508–13.

26. See A. Craig Baird, *Rhetoric: A Philosophical Inquiry* (New York: The

Ronald Press Company, 1965), 10. Such discussions as are offered on the purposes of rhetoric are consistently Aristotelian. See *The Rhetoric of Aristotle*, trans. Lane Cooper (Englewood Cliffs, NJ: Prentice-Hall, 1932), 7.

27. The above discussion is based on ideas contained in Erwin P. Bettinghaus, *Persuasive Communication*, 3rd. ed. (Toronto: Holt, Rinehart and Winston, 1980), 70–87. Also see Shearon A. Lowery and Melvin L. DeFleur, *Milestones in Mass Communication Research*, 2nd ed. (New York: Longman, 1988), 22–28.

28. Neil Postman, "The First Curriculum: Comparing School and Television," *Phi Delta Kappan* 61 (November 1979): 163–68.

29. Bettinghaus, *Persuasive Communication*, 24–27.

30. Schramm, *Men, Messages and Media*, 43. See also the revised edition, Wilbur Schramm and William E. Porter, *Men, Women, Messages and Media: Understanding Human Communication* (New York: Harper and Row, 1982), 56–71.

31. Robert J. Lavidge and Gary A. Steiner, "A Model for Predictive Measurements of Advertising Effectiveness," *Journal of Marketing* 25 (October 1961): 61.

32. Jacques Ellul, *Propaganda: The Formation of Men's Attitudes* (New York: Alfred A. Knopf, 1965), 3–87.

33. Elihu Katz and Paul F. Lazarsfeld, *Personal Influence: The Part Played by People in the Flow of Mass Communications* (Glencoe, IL: The Free Press, 1955); Jay G. Blumler and Elihu Katz, eds., *The Uses of Mass Communications: Current Perspectives on Gratifications Research* (Beverly Hills: Sage Publications, 1974); and Bernard Berelson, "What 'Missing' the Newspaper Means," in *Communications Research 1948–1949*, ed.

Paul F. Lazarsfeld and Frank Stanton (New York: Harper and Brothers, 1949): 111–29.

34. Jay. G. Blumler and Denis McQuail, *Television in Politics: Its Uses and Influence* (Chicago: University of Chicago Press, 1969). Also see, Elihu Katz, Jay G. Blumler, and Michael Gurevich, "Utilization of Mass Communication by the Individual," in *The Uses of Mass Communications: Current Perspectives on Gratifications Research*, ed. Jay G. Blumler and Elihu Katz (Beverly Hills: Sage Publications, 1974), 19–32.

35. Elihu Katz, "The Uses of Becker, Blumler, and Swanson," *Communication Research* 6 (January 1979): 77.

36. For a discussion on narcotizing dysfunction, see David Morley, "The Construction of Everyday Life: Political Communication and Domestic Media," in *New Directions in Political Communication*, ed. David L. Swanson and Dan Nimmo (Newbury Park, CA: Sage, 1990), 123–25.

37. Christopher Waddell, "Meech Lake Accord Generating Little Support, Survey Finds," *Globe and Mail*, 23 October 1989, A1, A11.

38. Karl Erik Rosengren, Lawrence A. Wenner, and Philip Palmgren, "Uses and Gratifications Research: The Past Ten Years," in *Media Gratifications Research: Current Perspectives*, ed. Karl Erik Rosengren et al. (Beverly Hills: Sage Publications, 1985), 11–37.

39. Schramm and Porter, *Men, Women, Messages, and Media*, 112.

40. Everett M. Rogers, *Diffusion of Innovations*, 3rd ed. (New York: The Free Press, 1983), 163–65; 232–34. See also, Everett M. Rogers and F. Floyd Shoemaker, *Communication of Innovations: A Cross-Cultural Approach*, 2nd ed. (New York: The Free Press, 1971).

41. James A. Anderson, *Communication Research: Issues and Methods* (New York: McGraw-Hill, 1987), 68.

42. James A. Anderson and Robert Avery, "The Concept of Effects: Recognizing Our Personal Judgments," *Journal of Broadcasting and Electronic Media* 32 (Summer 1988): 359–72 and S. Livingstone, "Interpretive Viewers and Structures Programs," *Communication Research* 16 (February 1989): 25–37.

43. Tamar Leibes, "Cultural Differences in Retelling of Television Fiction," *Critical Studies in Mass Communication* 16 (December 1988): 278.

44. Stuart H. Surlin, "Caribbean Cultural Identification, Cultural Consciousness and Mass Media Imperialism," in *Mass Media and the Caribbean*, ed. S.H. Surlin and W.C. Soderlund (New York: Gordon and Breach, 1990), 299–317.

C H A P T E R 5

Canadian Audiences and Their Mass Media

Introduction

When we talk about audiences, we are talking about you—as viewers, listeners, readers, and participants in the communication process. And one thing that we all have in common is that we are all very experienced and adept in these roles.

While it may not have been apparent to you at the time, you began functioning as part of an audience when you were preschoolers, watching programs such as "Mr. Dress Up," "Mister Rogers," and "Sesame Street," in addition to innumerable Saturday morning cartoons. In fact, you have been *measured* as a member of media audiences since the time you were two. Media broadcast rating systems, for example, group young television viewers in categories of age two to twelve, and teens. Thus, you have been part of this mass media audience for virtually all of your lives, and as you have switched channels to watch your favourite program, you have participated in a democratic process of sorts. As you have chosen to view one program instead of another, or read one newspaper or magazine rather than another, you and others like you have signalled your choices to the media industries. Because the economic bases of mass media are directly related to the numbers who listen to, view, or read their product, media executives are more than willing to respond to your preferences. At the same time as this democratic process functions, the media take particular initiatives on their own. For example, they produce programs that they consider to be commercially marketable and important to you as audiences and as citizens in terms of entertainment and information. Your choice operates, then, within the constraints of extant programming, much of which is very similar in the first place. However, there is most certainly an interactive process between you and the mass media in terms of your wants and needs.

At the same time, the massive technological developments that have been made in the media industries have inevitably brought about change in the competitive relationship between various media. As Canadians became attracted to television very quickly in the 1950s, audiences for the radio and film industries began to shrink: the result was that these latter industries needed to change to compensate for the new competition from television. But even in the context of such changes, where media have caused change, these changes have been brought about according to shifts in audience preferences.

The Electronic Media and Their Audiences

Radio and television penetration into Canadian households has been virtually complete for several years, with radio penetration in the 99 percent–plus and television in the 98 percent–plus categories. In 1989 Canadians watched an average of 23.4 hours of television per week, a decline from a high of 24.3 hours per week in 1984. In terms of programming, as has been the case since TV first appeared on the scene, Canadian viewing preference overall continues to be for foreign programming predominantly from the United States. In 1987 the latter accounted for 64 percent of all viewing time. The most popular type of program in Canada was drama

(movies, dramatic and comedy series, soap operas, action-adventure series), followed in descending order by news and public affairs, variety/game shows, and sports. Drama programs represented about one third of all viewing time, and of this, 28.8 percent was of foreign programs, while 4.2 percent was of Canadian programs. In 1989, in this same genre, Canadian programs accounted for just less than a third of francophone viewing, while among anglophones only one hour in twenty was spent watching a Canadian show.[1]

Community Antennae Television (CATV), one of the few remaining monopoly media industries in Canada, increases penetration into Canadian homes slightly each year, with penetration now standing at just over 70 percent. Table 5–1 identifies cable television usage in Canada.

Cable TV penetration in Canada is about 25 percent greater than current cable penetration in the United States. There is one primary reason for the higher rates of cable usage in Canada. In the developmental phase of CATV, the technology became popular in Canada chiefly because it offered quality-picture access to American television programming. Over-the-air transmission of "Gunsmoke," for example, may have been fuzzy in regions not immediately adjacent to the border, but cable transmission was nearly perfect. As well, while U.S. TV content was available in Canada, Canadian TV stations or networks were limited in the amount they could purchase. Initially in 1960, foreign content was limited to 45 percent and this was reduced to 40 percent in 1970 and has remained at that level. Cable represented access to the three major American networks, and it was that access that has caused cable usage to be considerably higher in Canada than in the United States. Cable usage in the United States developed primarily as a convenience that allowed more signals in the home than the immediate community could provide, and, as well, it meant picture quality improvement of signals brought in from a distance. But the United States has been, from the very beginning of TV in the 1950s to the 1980s, a very low importer of foreign programs. While in the past decade there have been increases in the number of imported programs in the United States, in Canada the situation has been different: Canadians have imported heavily from the very beginning.

Audiences as Readers

With the rapid expansion of electronic media choices, it is to be expected that Canadians will spend less time reading and more time watching television or listening to the radio. Newspaper circulation has held its own over the last decade, and in some parts of the country it has actually increased.

TABLE 5–1	
CATV Penetration in Canadian Homes*	
1968[a]	13.2%
1980[a]	54.0%
1984[b]	60.8%
1987[c]	67.2%
1989[d]	70.8%
1990[e]	71.4%

*Penetration of cable TV just in areas where the service is available would be near 80 percent. Data in table 5–1 are computed for all Canadian homes.

Sources: [a] *The Canadian Year Book 1985* (Ottawa: Supply and Services, 1985), 450.
[b] Canada, Department of Communication, *Report of the Taskforce on Broadcasting Policy* (Ottawa: Supply and Services, 1986), 553.
[c] Statistics Canada, *Household Facilities and Equipment 1984* (Catalogue 64-202) (Ottawa. 1989), 9.
[d] *The Canadian Yearbook 1990* (Ottawa: Supply and Services, 1989), 15–31.
[e] Statistics Canada, *Household Facilities and Equipment 1990* (Ottawa: Supply and Services, 1990), 9.

Readership, however, as distinct from circulation, is also undergoing changes, and some studies indicate that it is on the decline.

A general social survey conducted by Statistics Canada in 1986 found that leisure time for Canadians amounted to five and a half hours per day. Of that time, 190 minutes were allocated to media/communication activities, and 87 percent of the population, fifteen years and over, was involved in such activities daily. Of those 190 minutes, television alone accounted for 140 minutes a day. While those who read magazines and books spent a sizeable amount of time doing so (up to one hundred minutes a day), the national participation rate in these activities was only 16 percent. Of those who read newspapers daily (up to sixty minutes per day), the national participation rate stood at 18 percent.[2]

Canadians as Film Patrons

Film attendance has been severely affected by the broadcast industry—by television initially and subsequently by cable TV. Attendance at cinemas has dropped from the 1950s, and the number of motion picture theatres in Canada has declined accordingly. In the early 1950s, before television was popularized, nearly 250 million movie tickets were sold annually, representing about seventeen movie attendances per person per year. In 1985, fewer than 75 million tickets were sold to movie goers and this represents less than three movie visits per person per year. In this same period, movie theatres declined in number from 1950 in 1955 to 788 in 1985.[3]

Canadians as Patrons of the Arts

In Canada, concerns about mass media and national identity have been evident since at least the early 1920s. Prior to that time, such concerns focussed on Canadian art, literature, and the performing arts, which continue to flourish today. To what extent Canadians have attended these artistic performances or displays is of immediate interest here.

In 1987, 36 000 public performances were given by 317 performing arts companies in Canada. Audiences for these performances totalled over 13 million persons. In comparison to the previous year, 1987 represented a 4 percent increase in performances and an audience increase of over 8 percent. Performing arts companies offered live theatre, opera, music, and dance productions. Of the totals cited above, theatre performances represented 84 percent of performances and attracted 62 percent of the audiences. Revenues gained by these performing groups represented a total of about $265 million, about half of which was in the form of grants from federal (38 percent), provincial (28 percent), and municipal (8 percent) agencies as well as from private donations. A review of statistics for the year 1988 reveals very few changes from the above data.[4]

The Dominant Medium: Television

But it is with respect to electronic media that audiences, globally and domestically, have been most affected. And, as these media and their programs have penetrated communities, audience interests have broadened in immeasurable ways. For example, Saskatonians and Edmontonians view Detroit, Michigan, local newscasts with nearly the same frequency as they do their own community-produced telecasts. Given satellite-to-cable distribution of Detroit TV stations to Canada, Detroit sports fans abound in Canada. Television viewing data for 1988 confirm a Canadian preference for foreign programs:

- of all television *programs* watched, 37.8 percent were Canadian and 62.2 percent foreign;
- of all *channels* viewed, 78.2 percent were Canadian and 21.8 percent were foreign; however, even on Canadian channels, there was more foreign-produced programming viewed by Canadians than there was Canadian programming viewed.

Thus, even though more programming was received via Canadian TV channels, this programming was not necessarily Canadian in origin.

When data on Francophone viewing are examined separately, on all television channels viewed, 64.4 percent of the programs were Canadian (the popularity of French-language programs is evident) and 35.6 percent were foreign. As well, over Canadian channels, 64 percent of the programs were Canadian and 30.1 percent were foreign. However, when data for Anglophone viewing habits are examined (Anglophones represent approximately 21 million of the national population of 27 million persons) results point emphatically to a preference for foreign programs:

- of all programs viewed by Anglophones, 26.8 percent were Canadian while 73.2 percent were foreign;
- of all programs viewed on Canadian channels by Anglophones, 26.6 percent were Canadian and 45 percent were foreign.

By far the most popular category of Canadian programs was news and public affairs (24.6 percent Francophone and 15.9 percent Anglophone viewing time); and the most popular category of foreign program was drama/comedy (25 percent Francophone and 44.3 percent of Anglophone viewing time). These data appear to be relatively consistent over the past few years.[5]

To what extent such divided loyalties between domestic and foreign programs are likely to affect the Canadian psyche is unknown. What seems plausible, however, is that, "we are what we see." And given the rapidly expanding distribution of mainly foreign broadcasting programming available to Canadians, these viewing loyalties are going to be tested more severely than ever before.

Literacy and Illiteracy

As media audiences, we become bound to the technologies with which we interact regularly—and we have become able users of much of that technological hardware. As data attest, television has become our favourite medium.[6] As proof one can point to the fact that television has rapidly been overtaking the daily newspaper as the most popular advertising medium.[7] This is not surprising, since understanding television messages is an easy, relatively passive task: no training is required for television viewing, as is the case for reading. Reading demands a much greater imaginative effort on the reader's part. Television, much less demanding, presents us with a series of visual images that most of the time are readily recognizable by anyone, anywhere.

The broad movement of audiences away from the written word and towards broadcasting media may be underscored by illiteracy figures in various parts of the globe. In 1980, the director general of UNESCO indicated that the number of illiterate persons in the world would probably reach a thousand million before the end of the century.[8] A subsequent UNESCO report of January 1990 indicated that as of 1985 there were an estimated 889 million illiterate adults in the world. The report also indicated that poverty and underdevel-

opment are related to illiteracy— evident from the fact that 98 percent of the world's illiterate persons live in developing countries.[9]

While it is understandable that developing societies would be characterized by high rates of illiteracy, we should look at the problem in our own society. We consider ourselves in Canada to be a progressive, advanced, and industrialized nation. However, the 1987 Southam News study of illiteracy is a stunning reminder that about a quarter of our population is unable to perform very basic alphanumeric skills.[10] When the yardstick of incompleted grade school attendance is used to measure illiteracy, the results are as follows: five million Canadians cannot read, write, or use numbers well enough to meet the demands of today's society. When specific tests

TABLE 5–2
Measures of Functional Illiteracy

percent having difficulty

category	0	10	20	30	40	50	60	70
reading directions on medicine bottles		10%						
getting facts right in newspaper articles			20%					
figuring correct tip on a restaurant bill					40%			
using bus schedules						50%		
interpreting correctly a section of the Charter of Rights and Freedoms							60%	

Source: *Windsor Star,* 12 September 1987, A12.

were given to subjects in the Southam News study, literacy weaknesses were identified. Table 5–2 indicates the results.

The problem of illiteracy in Canada is not confined to what might be considered remote regions. For example, the Southam study indicated that in Ottawa, the nation's capital, the illiteracy level is 23 percent, which is almost identical to the national rate of 24 percent. A more recent investigation conducted by Statistics Canada in the fall of 1989 identified a new group of Canadians who are at risk of becoming functionally illiterate.[11] Although members of this group, numbering 22 percent of the Canadian population, are able to carry out simple reading tasks such as correctly reading the prescribed dosage on a medicine bottle, they try to avoid reading. According to the study, such avoidance is likely to result in illiteracy.

Some inroads appear to have been made regarding illiteracy in developing nations: while the number of illiterate persons continues to rise from year to year, the percentage of such persons in a growing global population appears to be declining. At the same time, a new awareness of the problem has been reached in Canada. For example, provincial ministers of education, with assistance from the federal government, have instituted financial aid and other support systems to Canadian communities to combat illiteracy. And, for at least a decade, public libraries in Canada have been conducting programs to help illiterate persons learn to read. Nev-

ertheless, there is no question that extant illiteracy, combined with the increasing popularity of television, is creating behavioural patterns that are different from those we have become accustomed to in the past. Learning through cognitive processes associated with reading is decreasing, while learning through affective-sensory processes associated with television is increasing. What this change means for the future is open to speculation, but we anticipate the rise of an audiovisual literacy, with its own rules of *grammar* that will permit individuals to interact with one another.

Participation and Interaction with Mass Media

Our viewing, listening, and reading choices are our instructions to those who produce and distribute content that we want more of the same. As well, should we be recognized by demographers as belonging to a sufficiently large group, with roughly similar demographic or psychographic (needs, lifestyles, for example) characteristics, some enterprising media owner might design new content or format to match the characteristics we demonstrate. Such behaviour is typical of today's magazine industry—the moment some need is perceived, it seems a new magazine appears on the scene to fill it.

We help to shape the media in other ways. It is clear that as we respond to advertising messages that the media present to us, we contribute to the coffers of the media industries. With the exception of the CBC—a Crown corporation—and of provincially owned broadcasting outlets, media depend almost entirely upon revenues that they generate from selling advertising space or time. Should we, for whatever reason, overtly or accidentally, cease to purchase advertised products or services, the media would quickly feel the result. A case in point is the recent threat to boycott accounts whose products are advertised in programs that demonstrate gratuitous amounts of violence or pornography. Community consumer groups in the United States, in the spring and summer of 1989, sent just such a clear message to the ABC television network sponsors of "Crimes of Passion." Advertisers quickly dropped their sponsorship of the program, and ABC responded by withdrawing the program.[12]

Interestingly, network executives indicate that advertisers' have withdrawn from certain programs because they perceive heightened concern in American society about

---

BOX 5–1

"Crimes of Passion II"

"Crimes of Passion II" was scheduled for telecasting by the ABC television network in the spring of 1989. The episode was commissioned by ABC on the basis of a reasonable rating of 13.2 percent gained by "Crimes of Passion I." On the basis of viewer complaints and advertiser withdrawal, the sequel was cancelled by the network. Reporter Bill Carter of the *New York Times* reported that the cancelled prime-time program had contained: two stabbings, a shooting, as well as an incident in which a man sets fire to his wife.

The *New York Times* also reported that viewer complaints led the following network advertisers to cancel commercials on selected programs on the three U.S. networks in the spring of 1989:

- Domino's Pizza
- Chrysler Corporation
- Coca-Cola
- McDonald's
- General Mills
- Campbells Soup
- Ralston-Purina
- Sears
- Mennen

Source: *New York Times*, 23 April 1989 and 3 May 1989.

the vulnerability of children to drugs and violence. There seems to be clear public hostility to sensationalized sex and violence. The ready availability of video recording equipment has made it possible for monitoring groups to record and study programs in detail and to report on excesses.[13]

As audiences, we also regularly provide mass media with content. We write letters to newspaper editors, we participate in talk shows, and we help to fill the community channel of each cable company in the country.

Audiences also have an important citizenship role to perform with respect to the mass media. We actually help to regulate the media in several ways. This may be illustrated by the following incident. Parents and other concerned individuals in the 1960s complained to politicians and to the Canadian Radio-television Telecommunications Commission (CRTC) about toy commercials that enticed children into asking their parents to buy particular toys. The CRTC responded by appealing to broadcasters, through the Canadian Association of Broadcasters (CAB), to self-regulate any abuses. The broadcasters agreed, and for a year or two their close monitoring of toy commercials worked adequately. Slowly, however, the monitoring process fell off, and these commercials were once again produced in the same manner as before. Parents complained again, and this time the CRTC indicated that observance of the Code of Advertising to Children, which included guidelines on advertising of toys, would become a condition of licence for broadcasters.[14]

This kind of interaction between the media and the public continues to operate. Broadcasters have instituted complaint-receiving procedures so that they can keep in touch with their audiences. Canadian newspapers also quite often run advertisements advising readers that they may write in about any ads in the papers that they find problematic. In effect, systems to accommodate complaints have become integral features of mass media behaviour.

Citizens also help to regulate the media through consumer groups. The Canadian Association of Consumers (CAC), for example, is a social monitoring group which receives some federal funding to maintain offices around the country. This funding, while not always as much as CAC might prefer, comes from the federal Ministry of Consumer and Corporate Affairs. Amongst its varied activities, the CAC on occasion submits feedback from its members and often forwards briefs on events that affect consumers to Canadian networks, newspapers, magazine publishers, and the CRTC. In addition to consumer associations, citizens have formed other media-monitoring groups, such as the successful Media-Watch and the Toronto-based Canadian Women in Radio and Television. These organizations have been praised by the CRTC for their contributions to policies concerning the employment of women in media and the depiction of women in broadcast programming. Although such monitoring groups have not grown on the same scale as they have in the United States, it is clear that they are gaining popularity.

FOR A BETTER REFLECTION OF US

ÉVALUATION-MÉDIAS
MEDIAWATCH

◆ EDUCATIONAL WORKSHOPS
   AND RESOURCES

◆ COMMUNICATIONS RESEARCH

◆ FACILITATING PUBLIC ADVOCACY

◆ LOBBYING FOR EQUALITY
   IN BROADCAST LEGISLATION

◆ PROMOTING CHANGE
   IN MEDIA INDUSTRIES

MediaWatch uses education, organizing, and lobbying to eliminate sexism in the media.

As well, in regulation of the broadcast media, the federal government has made it compulsory for such bodies as the CRTC to hold public hearings on certain policy matters. In the instances of issuing a licence or the suspension or revocation of a licence, the CRTC is obliged to hold such hearings and to solicit public comment. Advertisements in newspapers and in the broadcasting media concerned inform the public of these hearings. To make it easier for people to participate, the CRTC schedules these hearings in convenient locations across the country. Citizens may oppose or support a particular licence application and may do so in person or through letters or formally prepared briefs.

Finally, as citizens in different communities, we are invited to sit on committees, boards, and councils, where we help to pass judgement on the mass media and their policies. Since 1970, when they were first recommended by the Special Senate Committee on Mass Media (the Davey Committee), press councils have become popular means of adjudicating complaints against the media. (These councils exist at both the municipal and the provincial level.) Participation on such councils is crucial to their deliberations. At the national level, citizen participation can be seen in the CRTC, where six of the nineteen members are members of the public who have been chosen to represent various regions of the country. While they sit as part-time members, they function with the full authority of the Broadcasting Act and perform duties as expressed in the act.

Conclusion

As content consumers, we make our wants and needs known to media producers in what we have described as a democratic process. Just as that democratic process works with respect to media content, audiences also participate in policy-making and regulation. Our role goes considerably beyond that of passive receivers of content.

There seems to be a paradox in our double behavioural roles as audiences and regulators. Dr. Andrew Stewart, chairman of the first independent regulatory body for broadcasting in Canada, once privately commented that there was a lack of congruence between what people wanted and what they watched. As citizens, he observed, we demanded Canadian theatre, music, and ballet, but as viewers, too often, when we went home, we watched a U.S. TV show. Dr. Stewart's observation correctly identified Canadian audiences' behaviour—consistent to this day—that when offered a choice most of the time Canadians prefer to watch non-Canadian TV programming.

One of the characteristics of a democratic process is that sometimes the decisions we make benefit a community and on other occasions when we fail to take action, our communities may be harmed. As media-monitoring groups have pointed out, it is not necessarily the case that simply because a program gets an audience that that program is appropriate for society. They point out further that when we fail to take action in monitoring and reporting what we consider to be unacceptable programs, we are in fact surrendering to content producers the power to set the values for our society. If we are unhappy with the quality of mass media product presently available to us, we cannot lay the full blame for it on producers or the government. We, as audiences and as citizens, must accept at least part of the responsibility.

Notes

1. Anthony Young, "Television Viewing," *Canadian Social Trends* 14 (Autumn 1989): 14. Also see Statistics Canada, *Television Viewing 1989 Culture Statistics* (Ottawa: Supply and Services, 1991), 7.
2. Statistics Canada, General Social Survey, *Preliminary Data Cycle 2: Time Use and Social Mobility Models* (Ottawa, 1989), tables 1 and 4.
3. Carol Strike, "The Film Industry in Canada," *Canadian Social Trends* 9 (Summer 1988): 14–16.
4. Statistics Canada, *Performing Arts 1987: Culture Statistics* (Ottawa: Supply and Services, 1990), 7. Also see Statistics Canada, *Performing Arts 1988: Culture Statistics* (Ottawa: Supply and Services, 1990), 5.
5. Statistics Canada, *Television Viewing in Canada 1988: Cultural Statistics* (Ottawa: Supply and Services, 1990), 12–13. In the calculations of programs, only eleven categories of programming were included, thus, in some instances totals were less than 100 percent.
6. For example, in 1970, in response to the question "Which medium is

most influential on thought and lifestyle?" 66 percent of Canadians chose television. (Canada, Senate, *Special Senate Committee on Mass Media*, vol. 3 (Ottawa: Information Canada, 1970), 857.) A decade later, in response to the question "Which medium do you find 'most believable'?" 54 percent of Canadians chose television and in response to the question as to which medium was "most influential," 67 percent picked television. (Leonard Kubas et al., *Newspapers and Their Readers*, Royal Commission on Newspapers Research Publications, vol. 1 (Ottawa: Supply and Services, 1981), 27.) Data about U.S. attitudes concerning the relative credibility of media, tracked from 1959 to 1978, show the percentage of Americans believing television to be the "most believable" medium increasing from 29 percent to 47 percent. In the same period, the percentage citing newspapers as "most believable" fell from 32 percent to 23 percent. (Burns W. Roper, *Public Perceptions of Television and Other Mass Media: A Twenty-Year Review* (New York: Roper Organization Inc., 1979), 4.)

7. Maclean Hunter Research Bureau, *A Report on Advertising Revenues in Canada* (Toronto: Maclean Hunter, 1987), 7.

8. Amadou-Mahtar M'Bow, *UNESCO and the Solidarity of Nations: Building the Future* (Paris: The UNESCO Press, 1980), 158. In 1989, UN illiteracy predictions were somewhat reduced. They are now estimated at 912 million by the turn of the century. See "World Illiteracy on Rise, Experts Say," *Globe and Mail*, 9 September 1989, A7.

9. "The Challenge of Literacy: National Library of Canada Improving Access to Information," *Feliciter* 36 (March 1990): 19.

10. Peter Calamai, "5 Million of Us Can't Read," *Windsor Star*, 12 September 1987, A12.

11. Vivian Smith, "4 Million Adults 'At Risk' of Illiteracy, Study Says," *Globe and Mail*, 1 June 1990, A4.

12. Bill Carter, "ABC Cancels Crime Show That Fails to Get Any Ads," *New York Times*, 3 May 1989, D21.

13. Bill Carter, "TV Sponsors Heed Viewers Who Find Shows Too Racy," *New York Times*, 23 April 1989, A1.

14. The Canadian Association of Broadcasters, *The Broadcast Code for Advertising to Children* (Ottawa, 1988), 1; and Canada, CRTC, *Annual Report 1987–88* (Ottawa, 1988), 26.

The Mass Media Industries

C H A P T E R 6

Print Media

Introduction

In the preface, we indicated that this book focusses on mass media as they have developed and presently function in Canadian society. As we begin an examination of specific media, it is worth keeping in mind that societies expect media to behave in certain ways. Canadians want them to help create a society that is distinctly different in political, economic, and social terms from the neighbouring United States.

While such a function has been formally defined for the nation's broadcasting system, the cultural mandate for print industries is less specific. However, as we shall demonstrate in this chapter, it is clearly there.

Although the publishing industry has not been subjected to as many formal studies (i.e., royal commissions and committees) as has broadcasting, it has, nevertheless, been the object of intense scrutiny with respect to purposes, ownership, and quality of its products. Several of these studies are important in

understanding the historical evolution of these issues, for example the 1951 Royal Commission on National Development in the Arts, Letters, and Sciences (the Massey Commission), and the 1961 Royal Commission on Publications (the O'Leary Commission). Two subsequent studies, however, stand out more prominently in terms of drawing attention to the roles of a free press in an open society and Canada's expectations of its print media. The latter were reports of the 1970 Special Senate Committee on Mass Media (the Davey Committee)[1], and the 1981 Royal Commission on Newspapers (the Kent Commission).[2]

The Davey Committee Report (1970)

The rationale for the establishment of the Special Committee in 1969 was offered by Senator Keith Davey, committee chair, as follows:

It occurred to me that there had never been a national accounting for the media. Most people agreed that freedom of the press assumes responsibility, but few had really stopped to assess that responsibility. It also occurred to me that Parliament might be the ideal instrument through which the people of Canada could determine whether they have the press they need or simply the press they deserve.[3]

The three-volume report prepared by Davey and his colleagues made a number of recommendations, among which were the following. First, it was important, the committee felt, to establish regional and national press councils, much in the manner of the British Press Council, a body concerned with journalistic ethics and standards. When established in 1953, the British Council was composed of journalists and publishers. Later, lay members were included in the council. The Davey Committee felt, in offering the recommendation for press councils, that confidence in the Canadian press had in fact declined, and that curbs on the concentration of media ownership were needed. In effect, this system of press councils, according to the committee's rationale, would function as a watchdog on behalf of press freedom in the country. Subsequently, on their own initiative, newspapers, and in some instances other media, formed or joined community or regional press councils. As in the United Kingdom, these councils included representatives from media and the communities they served. While their numbers as yet are not large, and while a National Press Council as envisioned by the Davey Committee has not yet come about, the principle of a

Report of the Special Senate Committee on Mass Media, 1970. (Senate of Canada, Reprinted with permission)

BOX 6–1

Windsor Media Council

The Windsor Press Council (since 1987, the Windsor Media Council) was the first community press council set up in Canada following the Davey Committee's hearings.

Preamble

The Windsor Media Council, like other press councils in Canada and abroad, exists because its newsprint and electronic media members recognize that fairness in delivery of information to the public is a fundamental responsibility.

Although the Windsor Media Council acts independently of its media participants, it vigorously defends both the independence of the press and electronic media, as well as full freedom of public expression.

Objectives

1. To preserve the established freedom of the media on behalf of both the public and the media.
2. To serve as a medium of understanding between the public and the media.
3. To promote the highest standards of professional ethics in the gathering and dissemination of news.
4. To encourage the highest ethical and professional standards of journalism, advertising practices, reporting, and broadcasting.
5. To consider specific, unsatisfied complaints from the public about the conduct of the media in the gathering, publication, or broadcasting of news, opinions, and advertising; to consider specific complaints from members of the media about the conduct of individuals and organizations towards the media; and to report publicly on action taken.
6. To review and report on attempts to restrict access to information of public interest.
7. To make representations to governments and other bodies on matters relating to the purposes of the council.
8. To publish periodic reports recording the work of the council.

Source: Windsor Media Council, By-Law No. 1 (revised November 1987).

community overseeing the behaviour of its own media has been established as a consequence of the work of the Special Senate Committee.

Second, the committee recommended that the government establish a Publications Development Loan Fund. The objective of this fund was to create a "Volkswagen press," which would make money available to potential newspaper and magazine publishers to permit them to publish, on a minimal level, alternative editorial positions in communities where newspaper competition did not exist.

The model for such a loan fund was an act that had been passed earlier by Parliament to promote the establishment of a feature film industry in Canada, the Canadian Film Development Corporation Act, 1966–67. It was intended that, like the film development corporation, the fund would function as a federal corporation. While some efforts were made to foster an alternative press system with the aid of government funding, this recommendation for a Publications Development Loan Fund has made no impact in terms of ownership and industrial development trends.

Third, the committee took note of an idea that had been discussed earlier by the O'Leary Commission with respect to the magazine industry. As the Davey Committee described it: "Magazines constitute the only national press we possess in Canada. Magazines add a journalistic dimension which no other media can provide. . . . Magazines, in a different way from any other medium, can help foster in Canadians a sense of themselves."[4] With such a mission, it was important, the committee argued, that Canadian magazines be protected from popular magazines from the United States, which were outselling many times over the Canadian publications. For example, at the time the Committee made its study, Canadians were spending twice as much on U.S. comic books and *Playboy* as they were on Canada's top seventeen magazines taken together.

An equally important concern of the committee was that Canadian magazines were being hurt financially with respect to advertising revenue. *Time* and *Reader's Digest*, publishing in Canada at the time with only token Canadian editorial content, received more than half of all magazine advertising money spent in the country. Such a condition, the committee insisted, needed to be changed, and it recommended that *Time* and *Reader's Digest* be stripped of what was considered to be an unfair competitive advantage. This recommendation, while not acted on at the time, brought about legislation in 1977 that resulted in the modification of the Income Tax Act. This legislation, known as Bill C-58, in effect demanded majority Canadian content as well as majority Canadian ownership of any publications in which Canadian advertisers placed their advertising and expected to assign those advertising costs as regular business expenses.

The effect of the legislation was twofold: (a) Canadian advertisers,

BOX 6-2

What Makes a Publication Canadian

(a) "Canadian Issue" means,
   (i) in relation to a newspaper, an issue, including a special issue,
      (A) the type of which, other than the type for advertisements or features, is set in Canada,
      (B) the whole of which, exclusive of any comics supplement, is printed in Canada,
      (C) that is edited in Canada by individuals resident in Canada, and
      (D) that is published in Canada, and
   (ii) in relation to a periodical, an issue, including a special issue,
      (A) the type of which, other than the type for advertisements, is set in Canada,
      (B) that is printed in Canada,
      (C) that is edited in Canada by individuals resident in Canada, and
      (D) that is published in Canada, but does not include an issue of a periodical
      (E) that is produced or published under a licence granted by a person who produces or publishes issues of a periodical that are printed, edited or published outside of Canada, or
      (F) the contents of which, excluding advertisements, are substantially the same* as the contents of one or more issues of one or more periodicals, that was or were printed, edited or published outside Canada

*"substantially the same" means more than 20% the same

In addition, the act specifies that, in order for businesses to claim their advertising expenditures in publications as expenses, the publications in which their advertisements appear would have to qualify as Canadian in terms of *ownership*. Canadian ownership would be gained by meeting one or more of the following conditions: if the single owner of the publication is a Canadian citizen; in a partnership, if three-quarters of members are Canadian citizens and at least three-quarters of value of the property held by the partnership is owned by Canadian citizens; in cases of corporate ownership, if the chairperson and at least three-quarters of the directors are Canadian citizens and at least three-quarters of the share capital and three-quarters of the shares that have voting rights are owned by Canadian citizens.

Source: *Canadian Income Tax Act with Income Tax Regulations Consolidated* to 22 September 1988 Sections 19 (5) (a) and (b) (Don Mills: Commerce Clearing House, 1988), 36 533–36.

so as to gain the income tax benefits of business expenses, shifted their budgets from *Time* and *Reader's Digest* to Canadian magazines, although some advertisers felt that if they could not advertise in the extremely popular *Time* and *Reader's Digest* they preferred to move their advertising budgets from magazines to other types of media; (b) the amendment to the Income Tax Act has proven to be an indirect method whereby Canadian print media—newspapers as well as magazines—have remained in Canadian hands. The Davey Committee's recommendations, once implemented, achieved their original intent in this area—the protection of the Canadian magazine industry.[5]

The Davey Committee also made specific recommendations regarding concentration of ownership of mass media, and expressed its concern about the fact that there were only seven cities in the country in which newspaper competition continued. In commenting on the matter of concentration, the committee stated that "All transactions that increase concentration of ownership in the mass media are undesirable and contrary to the public interest—unless shown to be otherwise."[6] The committee emphasized that while it was not recommending retroactive legislation to undo existing levels of concentration, the quotation cited above would serve as the operative principle for a federal body that would thereafter approve or deny applications for takeovers or mergers or changes of ownership that would result in a further concentration of ownership. That regulatory body, which would have been known as the Press Ownership Review Board, was never created due to lack of government response in the form of legislation.

The Kent Commission Report (1981)

A decade later, in August 1980, the *Winnipeg Tribune* and the *Ottawa Journal* were closed by their respective owners, Southam Press and Thomson Newspapers, leaving each company in a monopoly position in the two cities. The newspapers that remained were the *Winnipeg Free Press* (Thomson) and the Ottawa *Citizen* (Southam). The federal government at the time responded to what appeared to be a clear act of collusion on the part of the two publishing companies,[7] and established a Royal Commission on Newspapers (the Kent Commission).

The report of that commission, in its foreword, expressed the degree of concern felt in the country:

This Commission was born out of shock and trauma. . . . Journalists and other employees of the two newspapers were stunned. Readers were angry. Thoughtful people throughout the country became seriously concerned, for the demise of the *Journal* and the *Tribune* was merely the culmination of a series of takeovers and "rationalizations" that have changed the face and nature of the press in Canada.[8]

The commission moved quickly and initiated research studies throughout the country, travelled the nation as it held public hearings, and received hundreds of briefs and letters from industry representatives and the general public. Over three hundred people appeared before the commission, which completed its report within a year of its formation. Its recommendations were many, and were brought together in its foremost proposal to the government—to enact legislation that would result in a Canadian Newspaper Act. In effect, this act would function in the manner of the Canadian Broadcasting Act, i.e., it would provide for a regulatory body for the newspaper industry.

The recommendations of the royal commission may be categorized under the following headings, which identify the central concerns of the commission: (a) rules of ownership, (b) concentration of ownership, (c) freedom of editorial expression, and (d) quality of journalism.

Rules of Ownership

In the first instance, ownership of newspapers was to be controlled by the following rules: newspaper ownership would be limited to five daily newspapers; circulation controlled by any one owner would not exceed 5 percent of the total circulation of all newspapers in Canada; if multi-

ple newspapers were owned by any single owner, these would need to be at least five hundred kilometres apart.

Concentration of Ownership

In further confronting the matter of concentration of ownership, the Kent Commission introduced the concept of divestment, i.e., a reduction in the existing levels of concentration. Specific recommendations for divestiture, to break up what the commission considered to be monopolies, were introduced for publishers in the provinces of New Brunswick, Saskatchewan, and Newfoundland where concentration of ownership was especially prominent. The commission also focussed particular attention on concentration of ownership in Thomson newspapers because of its large holdings in Canada. A choice under the Newspaper Act would be offered to Thomson for reducing its share of ownership by selling off either the forty newspapers that it held across the country or selling the *Globe and Mail,* a newspaper that was rapidly gaining national circulation through satellite printing. This latter recommendation regarding Thomson holdings served as an example of the problem of concentration of ownership, which the commission in its report identified as "too much power in too few hands."[9] Further measures of divestiture would also be imposed upon multimedia owners, whose different types of media outlets either published or broadcast in the same community.

Editorial Freedom

With respect to the issue of editorial freedom, the commission's central concern was that those who owned newspapers too often interfered in the affairs of the newsroom. Research on this matter has been contradictory. For example, in studies done of Canadian newspapers owned by the same chain it was found that these papers were editorially diverse.[10] At the same time, however, studies indicate that even if a newspaper owner/publisher never enters the newsroom, his or her presence is felt by employees who often attempt to conform to political attitudes that they perceive (rightly or wrongly) as belonging to the owner/publisher.[11]

The commission introduced several measures to offer journalists freedom from interference on the part of vested ownership interests. In the situation of a chain ownership, the editor-in-chief would be obliged to submit an annual report on the question of editorial independence. This report would then be published in his or her newspaper. There would also be in a community in which a chain newspaper published an Editorial Advisory Committee, which would function in two ways. First, it would review the annual report by the editor; second, it would itself report annually to a National Press Rights Panel (that panel would be appointed by

the federal cabinet). Finally, in such a chain of command, the Press Rights Panel would report on the behaviour of newspapers across the country to Parliament through the Ministry of Justice.

Quality of Journalism

The Kent Commission expressed its concern with the quality of journalism in Canadian newspapers as the Davey Comittee had a decade earlier. In both the committee and the commission, deliberations focussed on what was often found to be characteristic of large conglomerate ownership—the overriding interest in profitability. To counteract a perceived decline in the quality of Canadian journalism, the royal commission recommended that where newspapers assumed an initiative to spend more than the industry average on editorial expenses, tax credits should be offered to that newspaper as an incentive. At the same time, the commission recommended that the Newspaper Act should include a tax incentive for the Canadian Press (CP) wire service co-operative. This particular incentive would be offered to expand and improve the reporting of international news by Canadians.

Subsequently, the recommendations of the commission were presented to Parliament in the form of a Newspaper Act in May 1982. The whole matter was hotly debated in Parliament, because some sectors of the Canadian community believed that such an act would constitute a direct violation of freedom of the press. On the other hand, the government supported the bill, arguing that regulation would benefit the newspaper industry as it had the broadcasting industry. The same argument had been made by the Davey Committee twelve years earlier.

It is not known what the impact of a Canadian Newspaper Act would have been. Before debate on the bill was concluded, Parliament was dissolved, and a federal election was held in 1984, which resulted in a Progressive Conservative government under Brian Mulroney. The bill died on the order paper and was not resurrected.

We have, in discussing the two reports, included material pointing out the nature of the problems needing attention, but the question of possible negative consequences of newspaper regulation needs to be addressed as well. At the time of the presentation of the report of the Kent Commission, Professor Arthur Siegel commented on some of the dangers inherent in its recommendations:

> The control and supervisory process recommended by the Kent Commission could become a constraining influence. The idea of committees at both the local and national levels second-guessing journalistic decisions in hindsight of latter developments is likely to lead to a pallid product in which avoidance of controversy could become a major consideration in the information presentation process. This situation carries dangers of psychological self-censorship.[12]

Report of the Royal Commission on Newspapers and research volumes (1981). (Privy Council Office/Reproduced with permission of the Minister of Supply and Services Canada, 1991.)

Nevertheless, in pointing out such a danger Professor Siegel does not discount the increasingly difficult problems for Canadian society that are presented by unabated concentration of newspaper ownership. It is in this sense that he believes the commission performed "laudable service" in focussing public attention on the essential problem and implications of concentration of ownership. It is up to Canadians to decide whether the proposed regulatory medicine would have been worse than the disease.

Status of the Industry

The Daily Press Newspapers

For the past half dozen years, the number of newspapers publishing in Canada has been fairly consistent: between 105 and 115. Likewise, circulation appears to have been relatively constant: 5 534 000 in 1978 to 5 640 580 in 1991.[13] Where there have been circulation increases, these have occurred in the English-language press, mainly in the large cities. In fact, there has been a slight decline in circulation in the French-language press.[14] While circulation has generally held its own, it is apparent that Canadians spend less time reading the daily newspaper than they do listening to radio or watching television.[15] As is evident from data in table 6–1, daily newspapers tend to be concentrated in the

provinces of Ontario (forty-five), British Columbia (seventeen), and Quebec (eleven). Although British Columbia has many more newspapers than Quebec, Quebec has nearly twice the circulation.

The Nondaily Press

There is abundant evidence that nondaily newspapers, more popularly known as "community newspapers," have experienced recent growth. Between 1983 and 1986, the number of newspapers grew from 1154 to 1295 and, correspondingly, circulation increased over the same period from 12 348 000 to 16 255 000.[16] What has always characterized the community press has been its strong emphasis on local content.

The consequence of this orientation has been a strong, loyal readership. The Canadian Community Newspapers Association (CCNA) has taken note of this readership loyalty in its marketing of the community press. As well, package-selling strategies (selling advertising as a group rather than as individual newspapers) have proven to be a successful technique for raising revenue. For a comparatively low cost ($913) an advertiser is able to buy a classified advertisement in nearly 700 community newspapers.[17] Moreover, it is apparent that community newspapers attract an audience that is substantially different from that of daily newspapers: among English-speaking, adult Canadians, about 40 percent of

TABLE 6–1
Number of Daily Newspapers and Circulation by Province

Province	Number of Dailies	%	Circulation (Daily)	%
Newfoundland	2	1.8	54 313	.9
Prince Edward Island	3	2.7	35 739	.6
Nova Scotia	7	6.4	222 942	3.9
New Brunswick	5	4.5	150 348	2.6
Quebec	11	10.0	1 101 632	19.5
Ontario	45	41.2	2 508 151	44.4
Manitoba	5	4.5	245 012	4.3
Saskatchewan	4	3.6	153 480	2.7
Alberta	9	8.2	541 673	9.6
British Columbia	17	15.5	623 881	11.0
Yukon	1	0.9	3 409	0.06
Total	109	99.3%	5 640 580	99.5%

Source: Compiled from data contained in *Canadian Advertising Rates and Data*, August 1991.

community newspaper readers do not read daily newspapers.[18]

Heritage Language Nondaily Newspapers

The so-called *ethnic*, or *heritage, press* in Canada has grown and developed in an interesting way. When representatives of that group of newspapers appeared before the Davey Committee in 1970, they indicated that their newspapers, which were in languages other than English and French, fulfilled two primary functions: (1) to report to readers on events occurring in the homelands, and (2) to play a strong citizenship role, in bringing significant Canadian events to the attention of readers. As the Davey Committee pointed out, there existed the possibility of contradictory objectives, since a successful program of socialization or integration might well deflect readers' interest from their cultural heritage.[19]

At the same time, it should be noted that data show that immigrant groups lose their ability to read the heritage language to the point where less than 1 percent of third-generation citizens are literate in the heritage language.[20] Thus this press is likely to be a transitional phenomenon. In fact, a number of heritage language newspapers publish in both the heritage language and in English.

Trends in Newspapers

Several trends are evident in the newspaper industry and these should be noted.

TABLE 6-2
Heritage Language Newspapers, by Province and Language of Publication*

Heritage Language	Atlantic Canada	Quebec	Ontario	West and NWT	Total
Chinese			3	4	7
Croat/Slovenian			3	2	5
Dutch			2	2	4
German			2	4	6
Greek		3	3	1	7
Hungarian			5		5
Italian		6	10	5	21
Jewish		1	1	3	5
Punjabi			1	4	5
Ukranian			6	5	11
Urdu			5		5
Other (fewer than 4 papers)	1	3	29	7	40
Total	1	13	70	37	121

* These 121 papers represent a total of thirty-five different cultural language groups. Frequency of publication varies.

Source: Compiled from data in *Canadian Advertising Rates and Data*, May 1991.

Declining Readership

The newspaper industry in both Canada and the United States has expressed concern about the declining number of people reading newspapers. First, as more time is spent by people watching television, time spent reading newspapers has been dropping. Second, as we pointed out in chapter 5, in 1987, Southam News reported what educators had suspected for years, that up to 25 percent of the Canadian population is functionally illiterate. Third, when young people are compared to the current population aged forty and above, there is a marked drop in newspaper readership among the young group.

While the research literature makes no direct U.S.–Canadian comparisons of newspaper circulation and readers, general trends concerning readers, audiences, and their media do not appear to differ greatly in the two nations. For example, studies that show that TV is a prime source of news, with newspapers rated second, hold true for both countries. In the same vein, studies indicating which media are "most believable" (TV), "most influential" (TV), and "most fair and unbiased" (TV) produce similar results in both nations. As well, current studies that examine readership trends discuss these in terms of a newspaper industry "troubled by readership drop-offs" rather than as distinct Canadian problems.[21] Despite facelifting changes that Canadian newspapers have been making (bold graphics, more colour, shorter articles—in the style of the successful *USA Today*), a major Canadian newspaper publisher admitted "We're facing the same issue which most newspapers are, which is a decline in circulation, certainly a decline in the household penetration of newspapers." Newspapers are finding it increasingly difficult "to land new readers or to hold on to old ones."[22]

The 1970 *Report of the Special Senate Committee on Mass Media* indicated that Canadians spent, on an average, thirty-one minutes daily reading a newspaper.[23] The 1981 *Report of the Royal Commission on Newspapers* stated that almost 80 percent of Canadian adults read a daily newspaper during the course of a week and that 69 percent of adults tended to be "heavy" newspaper readers, i.e., they read five issues or more per week. In total time, Canadians spent on an average fifty-three minutes reading weekday papers and sixty-six minutes on weekends.[24] In calculating aggregate (weekday and weekend) per capita circulation, along with household penetration, the following becomes apparent.

The telling figures in table 6–3 are those that reveal household penetration: in effect, while circulation has risen in the two-decade period, this increase has not kept

TABLE 6–3 Declining Household Penetration	1970[a]	1980[b]	1990[c]
Aggregate newspaper circulation per week (in millions)	27.8	32.4	37.3
per capita newspaper circulation per week	1.29	1.33	1.40
household penetration	4.62	4.22	3.85

Sources: [a] Leonard Kubas et al., *Newspapers and their Readers: Research Studies on the Newspaper Industry* (Ottawa: Supply and Services, 1981), 95.
[b] Ibid., 102.
[c] Research Office of the Canadian Daily Newspaper Publishers Association (August 1990) and Statistics Canada, *Projections of Households and Families for Canada, Provinces and Territories* (Ottawa: Supply and Services, 1990), 53.

up with household growth. The result is that newspaper consumption per household is dropping off.

The pattern is similar in the U.S. where circulation per thousand fell by 34 percent between 1946 and 1990.[25] And, for the people who read the newspaper daily, from 1967 to 1988, the drop-off was from 73 percent to 51 percent. The decline, according to Robert L. Stevenson, is slow, steady, "and apparently irreversible. . . . In theory, at some point in the 21st century, daily readership could drop to zero."[26]

In a seminar conducted by the Canadian Daily Newspaper Publishers Association in the summer of 1990, a newspaper readership consultant with sixteen years experience in both Canada and the U.S. categorized newspaper readers as follows:

• 20 percent are nonreaders, who might occasionally glance at a headline;

- 40 percent are described as "mass-market" readers, who, while receiving the paper daily, basically look at headlines and pictures, and if something strikes their fancy, they read it;
- 30 percent are "specialists" who read a paper every day for specific information;
- 10 percent are "Sunday-only" readers who get most of their news from TV, but play "catch up" with the fat weekend papers.

Reasons why people say they do not read newspapers are interesting to examine: 39 percent have no time, 21 percent prefer broadcast news, while 19 percent find newspapers boring and difficult. "Nonreaders," the consultant summed up for the CDNPA seminar, "don't find fault with what you're doing, they just find it irrelevant."[27] Demographic analyses add further concern for newspaper publishers as "nowhere are the swelling ranks [of nonreaders] more problematic to the future of the newspaper industry than among the teenage population."[28]

The Electronic Newspaper

The so-called *electronic newspaper* is well off the drawing board and is a reality, even though the popularization of this new medium has not yet occurred. The term electronic newspaper has been in the language for well over a decade, and refers to facsimile transmission of electronically produced data on a television screen. Several competing systems have been available in the United Kingdom, with the British Broadcasting Corporation–produced CEEFAX, one of the earliest to be marketed. The overall implication is that the traditional newspaper, printed and delivered to your doorstep, is a gradually disappearing phenomenon. In addition, we have witnessed the development of systems for computer access to newspaper files, currently available in public and university libraries across the country. The earliest and still the leader in the field is the *Globe and Mail's* Info Globe on-line historical access system, which was mentioned briefly in chapter 1. While systems such as Info Globe give us access to information generated in the past, they are clear forerunners of future technological developments, where on a daily basis, we will soon be able to identify and, through phone access, indicate news theme preferences and have a customized newspaper prepared and presented to us electronically. This phenomenon can be compared to developments in broadcasting, which have led to "narrowcasting," or broadcasting aimed at special interest groups.

Distribution

A third trend is also evident with respect to newspaper distribution. The *Globe and Mail*, which for a number of years has billed itself as Canada's "National Newspaper," has become that in reality through the use of satellite technology. Today there are few communities in Canada that do not receive the *Globe and Mail*. It is currently printed and distributed, as is the American *USA Today,* in multiple locations in the country. To reflect its national distribution, studies have shown that the content of the newspaper has shifted in focus from Toronto to the nation.[29]

In an attempt to keep up their circulation, newspapers have also tended to ship copies to communities other than the one in which they publish. For example, the *London Free Press* ships to an increasingly wider community. It is possible to look at this trend by examining the situation in Windsor, Ontario. On weekdays, Windsorites have access to the *Windsor Star,* the *Globe and Mail,* the *Financial Post,* the *London Free Press,* and on weekends, the *Toronto Star.* In addition, Windsor newspaper readers have daily access to the *Detroit Free Press,* the *Detroit News,* the *New York Times,* and *USA Today.* To what extent this attempt to maintain such wide circulation will continue is anyone's guess, but the phenomenon is becoming more widespread in Canadian cities.

The Tabloid Press

The daily tabloid press is now firmly established on the Canadian newspaper scene. Whether this is a consequence of imitating the U.K.'s tabloid press remains open to debate. Characteristic of large cities, tabloids are said to have had their origin as commuters' newspapers, because of their smaller size and ease of folding in subways, buses, and trains. But it is the content of the tabloid press that makes it distinctive—in a word, the tabloid press is sensation-alistic; and is characterized by "sex-ploitation," overdramatization of events, lack of analysis, and a generous use of photos.

Magazines

While the 1951 O'Leary Commission dwelt on the threats to the Canadian magazine industry, it was the Davey Committee *Report* of 1970 that focussed popular attention on such threats. The committee believed that Canadian magazines, more than any other media, could foster in the population a sensitivity to being Canadian. There is indeed merit in such a belief, for magazines are recognized as a highly personalized medium, as advertisers will readily attest. "In terms of cultural survival," said the committee *Report,* "magazines could potentially be as important as railroads, airlines, national broadcasting and national hockey leagues."[30] It is entirely possible that the importance of magazines is even greater today, given the decreasing importance of other national links (e.g., railroads) cited in the 1970 Davey Committee *Report.*

The key event in the recent history of the Canadian magazine industry was the passage of Bill C-58. The protection offered the industry by this legislation has been crucial. It is questionable whether many Canadian magazines, *Maclean's* and *Saturday Night* included, would have survived without the large measure of federal protection this legislation afforded them. In addition to the provisions aimed at preventing advertising money leaving the country, Bill C-58 also protected the industry from takeovers by non-Canadians. But equally as important as a protective measure has been the federal government's offer of subsidies, which currently permit Canadian publishers to mail their product at a fraction of the cost charged non-Canadian publications. There have been two reasons for such postal subsidies: first, to reduce the inordinately high cost of distributing magazines over a large geographical area; and second, to help the industry withstand the high level of competition from the U.S. magazine industry. These subsidies have been in effect for over one hundred years. This notwithstanding, the matter of postal subsidy is of continual concern to the industry. A spokesperson for the Canadian Periodical Publishers Association commented, "Cheap postal rates are a pivotal part of an intelligent, long-term strategy to build a Canadian magazine industry. The strategy has been amazingly successful—we have twice as many magazines as we did 20 years ago."[31] Nevertheless, as part of its deficit reduction policy, the federal government, in June 1990, announced an overhaul of its postal subsidy program for Canadian publications—magazines, newspapers, and books. The subsidy program, valued at $220 million per year, was changed to permit Canadian-paid subscription publications to receive direct grants in lieu of previous postal subsidies, and at the same time, non-Canadian publications were cut off from whatever postal subsidies they had been receiving from Canadian taxpayers. In responding to these changes, the president of the Canadian Magazine Publishers Association praised the government for its removal of subsidies to foreign magazines: "for the post free-trade atmosphere, this is a gutsy decision and one we applaud."[32] The program, with several phases, was begun in April 1991.

Magazines in both Canada and the United States tend to be categorized according to four criteria: their size, mode of distribution, frequency of publication, and content.[33] It is the fourth criterion that concerns us. Type of editorial content falls into four broad categories. By far the largest is the business or trade magazine, which is aimed primarily at industries and their employees—for example, *Landscape Trends, Pensions and Benefits, Canadian Insurance*, and *Industrial Product Ideas*. The second category is the consumer magazine, and examples of this type are *Maclean's, Chatelaine, Reader's Digest*, and *Canadian Geographic*. Farm publications constitute the third category, examples being *The Union Farmer, Western Producer, Le producteur Agricole*, and *Hog Quarterly*. The fourth category is the religious/ scholarly, examples of which are *Atlantic Baptist, Diocesan Times, Canadian Journal of Communications*, and the *Canadian Journal of Political Science*.

Depending on the criteria one uses for deciding what constitutes a magazine, there are no less than 1018 and probably no more than 1300 magazines in the country.[34] Also the numbers fluctuate continually, since a characteristic of the industry is that titles "drop in" and "drop out" with considerable frequency. This fluctuation is a result of changes brought about by the high level of specialization entailed in the targeting of special interest groups.

The industry is extremely sensitive to demographic and sociographic changes in the population. For example, over the past eight years, up to thirty magazines have appeared that are targeted at the Canadian senior citizen. In the 1980s, publishing entrepreneurs quickly recognized that a large percentage of the population was aging and began to aim magazines at that group. In *Canadian Advertising Rates and Data*, the media industry's fact book, we note the following: in 1983, no category for seniors' magazines is listed in the classification index. In 1984, "senior citizen" first began appearing in the consumer magazine index as a separate category with three publications—*Age d'Or Vie Nouvelle* (Quebec), *Discovery for Seniors & 50 Plus* (Ontario), and *The Elder Statesman* (British Columbia). By 1987 there were sixteen such publications listed; in 1991 there were twenty-eight.[35] Such a rapid growth in the number of these magazines has introduced an element of serious competition in the industry. In such an environment, some magazines are likely to fail and drop out, others will persist and prosper.

The magazine industry today is vastly different from what it was twenty-five years ago. The current pattern of highly specialized readership is considerably different from the broad, general-interest approach of earlier publications. As well, today much of the industry operates under the concept of *controlled circulation*, which means that a magazine is offered free to selected readers. The publisher gains profit from advertisements placed in the publication, with an obvious match made between the messages of advertisements and the needs and interests of readers, whose names appear on selective lists compiled by professional researchers.

The magazine industry also faces a large measure of competition from other media. Cable TV and weekend newspapers, in particular, have absorbed the photo essay and feature news reports, which were the staples of magazines twenty-five years ago. At the same time, the publishing industry in general has experienced a drop in advertising revenues, due to the recent rapid development of direct marketing strategies. A typical news story headline describes the sense of threat that magazines face in this regard: "Magazines fight for life as ad revenues weaken."[36]

The Canadian magazine industry has recently become engaged in the following activities in an effort to maintain circulation numbers: price discounts (via clearing houses that represent publishing groups or their products, often with the attraction of "winning millions");

package selling (buy one, get several others without additional payment); and controlled circulation.

With respect to this last activity, it is important to outline a distribution strategy devised by the *Globe and Mail*, a Thomson-owned newspaper. Beginning in 1984, the *Globe and Mail* began issuing the *Report on Business Magazine* as an insert in the regular paper. Subsequently, the paper extended the practice by adding additional magazines, up to a total of seven (with some regional variation). The change, "the first bright newspaper idea in 30 years," stated Peter Desbarats, "is simple: to make the *Globe* a more effective advertising vehicle and to bolster the *Globe's* national circulation."[37] Certainly, it is a bold strategy and, from the sidelines, it appears to be equally aimed at promoting magazines, which might have difficulty functioning independently of such alliances as they have with the *Globe.* While some of these magazines have been downsized and some have disappeared, the practice of inserting magazines into daily newspapers continues. For example, in the spring of 1991, *Saturday Night,* Canada's oldest magazine, made an arrangement with Southam News to distribute the magazine free to readers of five major Southam newspapers. Such distribution would raise the magazine's circulation from under 130 000 to over 400 000 and thus would make it a more attractive advertising vehicle than it currently is.[38] And, in the fall of 1991, the magazine was distributed within the *Globe and Mail* to the newspaper's subscribers in the Toronto market.

To what extent the Canadian magazine industry is likely to defend Canadian culture in the way that the Davey Committee indicated is questionable, although it is possible that a few magazines such as *Maclean's* and *Saturday Night* continue to "foster in Canadians a sense of themselves" as the committee believed they would. Apart from that consideration, however, the magazine industry faces constant, unrelenting competition and threats to survival.

Books

Within the context of concern for national identity, the book publishing industry in Canada has raised particular questions. One such question pertains to the perspectives of writers of textbooks. Their point of view is important because writers bring into their work, not only their own individual experiences, aspirations, and ideals, but those of the places they write from as well. It is desirable, in terms of creating a national culture, that Canadians be the writers of Canadian textbooks. As the introduction to the O'Leary Royal Commission commented on this question: "Only a truly Canadian printing press, one with a 'feel' of Canada and directly responsible to Canada, can give us the critical analysis, the informed discourse and dialogue which are indispensable in a sovereign society."[39]

A second concern is the threat to Canadian ownership presented by publishers in the United States and

Great Britain. The development of an economically sound, indigenous industry is "an essential condition to the existence of a Canadian literature," according to the Massey Commission.[40] Canadians have therefore expected a protective stance from their governments concerning book publishing.

Books are generally classified into three categories: textbooks (elementary, secondary, and postsecondary levels), trade books (fiction and nonfiction books, normally of a popular nature), and reference/professional books (dictionaries, atlases, and encyclopedias as well as books that are aimed at particular professions and trades).

The overall book market in Canada comprises books published by Canadian publishers for sale in Canada as well as books imported into Canada. Net sales of all books from 1981–82 to 1989–90 ranged from $720 million to $1.4 billion. Data in table 6–4 show relevant changes as well as the percentages of sales accounted for by ownership of firms publishing in Canada. With the exception of 1986–87, the data show a trend to greater sales by Canadian-controlled firms.

Data in table 6–5, which show the numbers in various book categories published by Canadian-controlled and foreign-controlled firms in both languages, indicate some interesting differences. In English, Canadian-controlled firms dominated in publication of trade and reference books, while the foreign-controlled firms published the majority of textbooks. On the French-language

TABLE 6–4

Total Net Sales, by Canadian-Controlled* and Foreign-Controlled Firms (in millions)

Year	Canadian Controlled	Foreign Controlled	Total
1981–82	$358 478 (49.7%)	$362 254 (50.3%)	$720 732
1984–85	$451 239 (49.4%)	$462 542 (50.6%)	$913 781
1985–86	$514 062 (52%)	$474 534 (48%)	$988 596
1986–87	$395 436 (43.2%)	$520 339 (56.8%)	$915 774
1989–90	$835 624 (59%)	$579 678 (41%)	$1 415 302

* Control does not imply 100% Canadian ownership.

Source: Compiled from data in *Book Publishing in Canada: Culture Statistics* (Ottawa: Supply and Services, 1982 to 1990).

TABLE 6–5

Number of Book Titles Published, by Canadian vs. Foreign Control, by French and English

	Eng. Lang. Canadian	Eng. Lang. Foreign
textbooks	3 959	6 334
trade books	12 952	5 240
scholarly/reference books	6 068	1 129

	Fr. Lang. Canadian	Fr. Lang. Foreign
textbooks	4 916	1 481
trade books	9 236	65
scholarly/reference books	3 100	—

Source: Compiled from data in *Book Publishing 1988-89: Culture Statistics* (Ottawa: Supply and Services Canada, 1989), 14–17.

side, Canadian-controlled firms dominate in the publication of all categories of books. In terms of authorship, and regardless of whether the firm was Canadian or foreign controlled, Statistics Canada indicates that Canadian authorship predominates: 57 percent of books published in Canada in 1984–85 were written by Canadian authors, while in 1987–88, this figure had risen to 73 percent. Canadian authors tended to write for Canadian-controlled companies (81 percent).[41] Thus ownership or control of publishing does appear related to Canadians appearing in print.

Ownership

The 1980s were characterized by several intercorporate take-overs, mergers and the like. The publishing industry overall, and the Canadian book publishing industry in particular, were not exempt from such business practices. The nations that were active on the Canadian scene were primarily the United States, Great Britain, France, Germany, and Japan. Because of their complexity and volume of activity, links in conglomerate ownership are often difficult to trace.

Canada's federal and provincial governments have been mindful about the inherent value of book publishing and of the corporate ownership practices that could readily undermine Canadian control of the industry. The government response to this problem has been evident in two ways. First, direct subsidies have been provided to the industry, and second, policies have been implemented concerning foreign ownership. With respect to subsidies, in 1989–90, 193 publishing firms received a total of $22 032 000 in direct aid, just over two-thirds of this coming from federal sources.[42]

Policies concerning the question of ownership in publishing generally reflect those that Canada has crafted to deal with the problem in other media industries. In 1985 in Baie Comeau, Quebec, the federal government introduced a policy that intended, while not prohibiting acquisition and investment by non-Canadian firms, to keep decision making in Canadian hands. This was felt necessary particularly in a time of increasing business expenditures at the international level and in light of "the homogeneity that will necessarily accompany economic globalization."[43]

But the attempt to enact and enforce firm guidelines to ensure that Canadians have a satisfactory measure of ownership and control of their book publishing industry appears to have failed. That set of guidelines, known as the Baie Comeau Policy, has had two major provisions: (1) no new foreign-controlled companies were to be allowed into Canada, either in publishing or in distribution, and (2) if a Canadian publisher were sold to foreign interests as a part of a larger transaction, 51 percent of the company would have to be sold to Canadians at fair market value within two years.

An analyst of the policy claims it was based on two assumptions: (1)

Canadian publishers would have the capital necessary to buy companies coming up for sale, and (2) foreign companies would play by the rules. Neither of these assumptions proved to be correct.[44] In spite of numerous opportunities to apply the policy, right from the beginning large foreign-controlled companies lobbied the Canadian government to have their own particular cases exempted from the established rules. To its discredit, the government wavered and the door was open to other circumventions. Also, the disparities in size and financial clout between a relatively small Canadian publishing industry and vast multinational corporations made even those cases where the policy was applied open to suspicion as to whether Canadians truly controlled policy. Finally, since the Baie Comeau policy lacks the force of law, it is seen as unworkable. Little continuing support is envisioned for the Baie Comeau policy by a government committed to free trade with the United States. The policy is likely to be replaced by a system of subsidies and tax credits to Canadian-owned firms, so as to aid them in maintaining ownership of and in operating their publishing companies.[45]

Such government policy to Canadianize the book publishing industry has not been acceptable to some U.S.-based media companies. For example, mergers of U.S. companies, if ownership changes of Canadian properties are involved, can mean the mandated sale of 51 percent ownership of the Canadian companies. Such Canadian involvement, even though minimal in terms of dollars, has been interpreted as an unfair trade practice. At a congressional hearing discussing conglomerate mergers, Representative John Dingell of Michigan offered the following unflattering assessment of the practice: "In plain and simple language, it appears to be nothing more or less than extortion disguised as Canadian cultural nationalism."[46] The Canadian policy raised the possibility of "mirror" U.S. legislation aimed at controlling Canadian ownership of U.S. media. Should such retaliation occur, several Canadian companies would be affected, such as Thomson Newspapers (which owns over 100 newspapers in the U.S.), Hollinger Inc., and Maclean Hunter, among others.[47]

Conclusion

From the observations made in this chapter regarding Canadian print media, some concluding comments are in order. First, as we shall discuss in the following chapter, broadcasting has been the instrument most directly regulated by the government in support of national cultural aspirations. The print industries have been less directly impacted by similar legislation. Nevertheless, through such protective policies as postal subsidies, incentives to keep advertising money in the country, the ownership clause control in Bill C-58, and direct subsidies to periodical and book publishers, we find a less planned, less direct harnessing of the print industries to serve Canada's cultural needs. To what extent such a cultural role will be fulfilled successfully cannot be determined with any degree of accuracy, especially with continuing proposals in the early 1990s for expanded free trade.

Second, the media industries overall are characterized by massive changes resulting primarily from technological invention and innovation. When media function with an awareness of technological change, these media are more likely to adapt and persevere. Thus change, not rigidity, will have to be recognized as essential, not only by the industries themselves, but by those who legislate for the industries as well as consumers of media product. If this is not done, the print industry will become a sort of living museum of life in a past age.

Notes

1. Canada, Senate, *Report of the Special Senate Committee on Mass Media* (Ottawa: Information Canada, 1970), hereafter referred to as the Davey Committee.
2. Canada, *Royal Commission on Newspapers* (Ottawa: Supply and Services, 1981), hereafter referred to as the Kent Commission.
3. Davey Committee, *Report*, vol. 1, "The Uncertain Mirror," vii.
4. Davey Committee, *Report*, vol. 1, 153.
5. Shortly after passage of Bill C-58, *Reader's Digest* complied with the demands of the legislation by increasing its Canadian content and ownership. *Time*, on the other hand, abandoned its Canadian publication, claiming that the legislation was direct government intrusion into editorial matters. The magazine, however, subsequently returned to Canada and has attracted advertising accounts in spite of the increased costs of such advertising. For details on this issue see, Isaiah Litvak and Christopher Maule, *Cultural Sovereignty: The Time and Reader's Digest Case in Canada* (New York: Praeger Publishers, 1974).
6. Davey Committee, *Report*, vol. 1, 71
7. The two companies were charged under the Combines Investigation Act, brought to trial and acquitted.
8. The Kent Commission, *Report*, XI.
9. Ibid., 220.
10. W.C. Soderlund, W.I. Romanow, R.H. Wagenberg, and E.D. Briggs, *Media and Elections in Canada* (Toronto: Holt, Rinehart and Winston, 1984), 90–91.
11. Joe Fox, "Social Influences on Decision-Making in the *Toronto Star* Newsroom" (M.A. thesis, Department of Communication Studies, University of Windsor, 1988).
12. Arthur Siegel, *Politics and the Media in Canada* (Toronto: McGraw-Hill Ryerson, 1983), 150.
13. In collecting these data the following sources were consulted: *Canadian Advertising Rates and Data* (August 1991); Peter Desbarats, *Guide to Canadian News Media* (Toronto: Harcourt Brace Jovanovich, 1990), 57–62; Wilfred Kesterton and Roger Bird, "The Press in Canada: A Historical Overview," in *Communications in Canadian Society*, ed. Benjamin Singer (Scarborough, ON: Nelson Canada, 1991), 29–49.
14. Ibid.
15. Ted Wannell and Craig McKie, "Expanding the Choices," *Canadian Social Trends* 1 (Summer 1986): 17.

16. *Canada Year Book 1990*, 14–17.

17. *Community Markets Canada 1990* (Toronto: Canadian Community Newspaper Association, 1990), 25.

18. *CCNA Publisher* 71 (January/February 1990): 12.

19. Davey Committee, *Report*, vol. 1, 179.

20. K.G. O'Bryan, J.G. Reitz, O.M. Kuploska, *Non-Official Languages: A Study in Canadian Multiculturalism* (Ottawa: Supply and Services, 1976), 46, table 4.5.

21. Brian Millner, "Newspapers Fight for Readers," *Globe and Mail*, 9 July 1990, B1.

22. Ibid., B2.

23. Canada, Senate, *Report of the Special Senate Committee on Mass Media*, vol. 3, *Good, Bad, or Simply Inevitable* (Ottawa: Information Canada, 1970), 128.

24. *Royal Commission on Newspapers*, 11–13.

25. Robert L. Stevenson, "The Disappearing Newspaper Reader" (paper presented at the Annual Meeting of the Association for Education in Journalism and Mass Communication, MN, August 1990.)

26. Ibid.; and Philip Meyer, *The Newspaper Survival Game: An Editor's Guide to Marketing Research* (Bloomington, IN: Indiana University Press, 1986), 98.

27. Stan Sutter, "Non-readers Uneducated Slobs? Nonsense," *Marketing* 95 (4 June 1990): 14.

28. Cathy J. Cobb-Walgren, "Why Teenagers Do Not 'Read All About It,'" *Journalism Quarterly* 67 (Summer 1990): 347.

29. W.I. Romanow and W.C. Soderlund, "Thomson Newspapers' Acquisition of the *Globe and Mail*: A Case Study of Content Change," *Gazette* 41, 1 (1988): 5–17.

30. Davey Committee, *Report*, vol. 1, 153.

31. Catherine Keachie, executive director, Canadian Periodical Publishers Association, "Magazine Postal Subsidy Is Vital" (letter to the editor), *Globe and Mail*, 22 July 1989, D7.

32. John Partridge, "Grants Replace Publisher Postal Subsidy," *Globe and Mail*, 28 June 1990, B1, B2. Also see, Stan Sutter, "Publications Lose Postal Subsidy: No More Second-Class," *Marketing* 95 (8 January 1990): 4.

33. John S. Wright, Willis L. Winter, Sherilyn K. Zeigler, P. Noel O'Dea, *Advertising, First Canadian Edition* (Toronto: McGraw-Hill Ryerson, 1984), 274–76.

34. *Gale Directory of Publications* (Detroit: Gale Research Inc., 1989), vii; and *Canadian Advertising Rates and Data* (January 1990).

35. *Canadian Advertising Rates and Data* (June 1991).

36. *Toronto Star*, 27 January 1990, C1.

37. Peter Desbarats, "Gamble at *The Globe*," *Canadian Business* 62 (December 1989): 74.

38. John Partridge, "Magazine Revamps Distribution Plans," *Globe and Mail*, 14 May 1991, C1.

39. Canada, *Report of the Royal Commission on Publications* (Ottawa: Queen's Printer, 1961), 2.

40. Canada, *Report of the Royal Commission of National Development in the Arts, Letters and Science, 1949–1951* (Ottawa: King's Printer, 1951), 231.

41. *Book Publishing 1988–89: Culture Statistics* (Ottawa: Supply and Services, 1990), 16–20.

42. Ibid., 51.

43. Diana Sheperd, "Masse Vows Support for Baie Comeau," *Quill & Quire* 55 (April 1989): 4.

44. Roy MacSkimming, "Sunset Over Baie Comeau," *Quill & Quire* 56 (July 1990): 10–11.

45. Ibid.

46. Terrance Wills, "Ottawa's Publishing Policy Finds Foes in Washington," *Toronto Star*, 29 April 1989, C4.

47. Ibid.

C H A P T E R 7

Broadcasting

Introduction

While Canadians have expected the print media to contribute to the development of a distinct national identity, their expectations of radio and television in this regard have been even greater. They have, in fact, formally mandated these last to promote and preserve the national identity. As in other societies, broadcasting has been dynamic in terms of its growth. From the earliest years of the 1920s, when it was clear that the new medium of radio possessed the capacity to attract listeners and to become a part of their daily lives, parliamentarians began to express concerns about it, since it appeared to function chiefly to import programming from the United States. This imported content, which typified programming on Canadian radio stations (some of the early stations were in fact directly affiliated with U.S. networks), could serve only, went the argument, to supplant the Canadian cultural identity.

Experimentation in radio transmission had been underway for several decades prior to the turn of the century. The most notable experiments were those conducted by Guglielmo Marconi, who in 1901 received the first transatlantic spoken signal at St. John's, Newfoundland. Marconi's experiments, as well as those in the U.S. and Western Europe, clearly presaged the development of popularized radio broadcasting. The Marconi Company of Canada was awarded Canada's first broadcasting licence, WXA in Montreal in 1919. The station soon changed its call letters to CFCF, under which it broadcasts today. From 1922 onwards, licences for commercial stations were granted by the federal government and, before the decade was out, Canada boasted its own domestic broadcasting industry, consisting of both public and private sectors. The focus during this early period was growth and development, and historians note that little attention was paid to what sort of broadcasting

First wireless transmission across the Atlantic, 12 December 1901. Marconi and his instrument inside Cabot Tower, Signal Hill, St. John's, Newfoundland. (National Archives of Canada/C 5945)

service Canadians preferred, in terms of programming and purpose.[1]

It was in 1929, fully seven years after the introduction of commercial radio, in the midst of parliamentary debates regarding how the domestic broadcasting industry should develop with respect to ownership—private or public—that Canada's first Royal Commission on Broadcasting enunciated a principle that has been the basis of the industry's operation to this day. That commission (the Aird Commission, named after its chairman, Sir John Aird) stressed that the destiny of Canada depended upon the ability and willingness to control and utilize internal communications for Canadian purposes.[2]

Thus, Canadian broadcasting, from its infancy, has developed and has continued to function to this day under dual pressures: first, the vying for prominence between the public and private sectors; and second, the mandate to protect and enhance the national identity. In the first instance, broadcasting ownership was characterized by a public sector organized under the auspices of the Canadian National Railways and a private sector, which was characterized by unregulated growth of individual enterprises emphasizing U.S. programming. The dilemma inherent in this situation, as noted in a report to Parliament in 1932, was that "broadcasting, while too important to be left to private enterprise, is nevertheless too sensitive to be brought fully into the machinery of the state. . . ."[3] This ownership dilemma continues to set the context within which broadcasting, its regulation, and its place in a free society are debated.

In the second instance, broadcasting has had a clear mandate to promote a national identity, to prevent foreign acculturation, and to develop broadcasting content that would give expression to a national consciousness. These two considerations, ownership and purpose, have been focal points for policy, regulation, and legal measures taken with respect to the broadcasting industry.

Structure of the Industry

The term *infrastructure* is often used in broadcasting literature to describe the various parts of the industry: broadcasting stations and networks; cable and satellite distribution systems; technology and research; pro-

TABLE 7–1
Public Broadcasting: Canadian Broadcasting Corporation-Owned-and-Operated Stations

TV	1977	1979	1982	1985	1990
English	17	17	17	18	18
French	9	10	10	13	13
TOTAL	26	27	27	31	31

Radio	1977		1979		1982		1985		1990	
					Mono	Stereo	Mono	Stereo	Mono	Stereo
	AM	FM	AM	FM	AM/FM	FM	AM/FM	FM	AM/FM	FM
English	26	8	28	14	31	14	31	16	33	10
French	12	4	14	5	14	6	15	6	16	6
TOTAL	38	12	42	19	45	20	46	22	49	16

Source: Compiled from data in Canadian Broadcasting Corporation, *Annual Reports*: 1976–77, 1978–79, 1981–82, 1984–85, 1989–90.

gramming and production; talent and personnel; regulations and regulating agencies. It also includes educational institutions that study mass media systems and offer courses about them. The term then is broadly inclusive.

The industry has three sectors defined by ownership: public, private, and community

The Public Sector

The public sector includes all systems under the direct aegis of the Canadian government, usually in the form of Crown corporations. The Canadian Broadcasting Corporation and the Canadian Radio Broadcasting Commission before it have been and are such institutions. The model for public broadcasting in Canada was established early and was based on the belief that our country, as huge as it is, could only

be served properly by public ownership. The Aird Commission of 1929, having studied several European nations, indicated in its report that the British Broadcasting Corporation system, in terms of ownership and control, was a system that we could well adopt for ourselves. We find in parliamentary debates of the period, Conservative Prime Minister R.B. Bennett indicating his own persuasion in the matter: "No other scheme than that of public ownership can ensure to the people of this country, without regard to class or place, equal enjoyment of radio broadcasting."[4]

The prime minister's statement was consistent with beliefs held by many Canadians that private enterprise, operating on the profit motive, would neither venture into nor serve noncommercially viable or remote areas. In particular, the Canadian Radio League, which was established in the fall of 1930 and attracted members over a wide political spectrum, was from its beginnings a strong advocate of public broadcasting.

The Private Sector

The principle of private ownership was established in the United States early in the history of broadcasting. It developed rapidly, mainly in the urban areas, where competition between stations and networks flourished. The early pattern of Canadian radio ownership followed the American experience closely, as it was quickly evident that promises of profitability were real. At the same time, there was another attractive argument for private ownership: the principle of avoiding a public monopoly in broadcasting. Arguments by private broadcasters in opposition to a government monopoly in an industry where

TABLE 7-2

Private Broadcasting: Privately Owned Originating Broadcasting Stations

	1977	1982	1988	1989	1990
TV					
CBC affiliates	32	32	37	33	29
Independent	10	13	13	13	14
Quatre Saisons	—	—	4	7	7
TVA	4	6	10	10	10
CTV	25	26	28	28	26
Global	—	1	1	1	1
Ethnic	—	—	1	1	1
TOTAL	71	78	94	93	88
AM					
CBC affiliates	94	82	18	14	15
Independent	245	273	307	313	315
Ethnic	—	0	6	6	6
TOTAL	339	355	331	333	336
FM					
CBC affiliates	—	1	9	7	6
Independent	115	175	151	150	154
Ethnic	—	—	2	2	2
TOTAL	115	176	162	159	162

Source: Compiled from data in CRTC *Annual Reports*: 1976–77; 1981–82; 1987–88; 1988–89; 1989–90.

freedom of expression was proving to be as important as it was in newspapers of the day were expressed through the Canadian Association of Broadcasters (CAB). This organization, from its founding in 1926, represented the interests of private broadcasters.[5]

The CAB, which has head offices in Ottawa, has functioned as an effective lobby group on behalf of the private sector of the industry from its inception to this day. It has concerned itself with matters such as government policy, regulation, and the direction in which the industry is headed.

Community Broadcasting

Community broadcasting, the third type of ownership found in the industry, is characterized by communal, nonprofit ownership of broadcasting stations. This type of broadcasting has developed in a manner that has been complementary to the larger industry. For example, it has served communities in remote areas and has catered to community special interests. The data in table 7–3 present the current statistics relating to this type of broadcasting ownership.

Public vs. Private Ownership

In effect, the dual system of private and public ownership has been a historical attempt to apply to Canada the best of systems found in Great Britain and the United States. Whether this goal has been achieved is another matter. Nevertheless, the two sectors have provided Canadians with a balanced (some might say compromised) pattern of ownership where the sectors have competed with, as well as complemented, each other. When the physical presence of each sector in the country is examined, it is clear that the private sector is by far the largest of the two. Even a quick comparison of the figures in tables 7–1 and 7–2 offers

TABLE 7–3
Community Broadcasting

	AM Radio	FM Radio	TV	Totals
Remote communities and native broadcasting units	4	64	5	73
Communities other than those in remote areas	—	33	3	36
Student campus broadcasting units	11	24	—	35
TOTAL	15	121	8	144

Source: Compiled from data in CRTC, *Annual Report* 1989/1990 (Ottawa: Supply and Services, 1990), 82.

evidence of this. At the same time, one can really only speculate on the influence of this sector of the industry on political processes.

It is possible, however, to examine the public sector in terms of how its influence becomes manifest in the country. First, the Canadian Broadcasting Corporation (CBC) is in a favoured position in terms of disputes between the private and public sectors of the industry. The Broadcasting Act is very explicit in stating that the regulatory body is obliged to favour the public sector should such confrontations arise. Second, the national public system has been repeatedly recognized in studies of Canadian broadcasting as the so-called centrepiece of Canada's system in such areas as development of broadcasting standards and talent.[6] This recognition of the significant role that public broadcasting is to play has been evident from the 1920s to this day. Third, the CBC, its management, and its board of governors have been equally as influential, if not more so, than private broadcasters in fulfilling a consultative role for industry regulators. The sort of leadership that the public sector has demonstrated consistently with respect to talent development and the production of Canadian content has earned the CBC such importance in the consultative process. Fourth, the research and publishing the CBC has done about the direction of broadcasting at both the national and international levels have been significant and have had far-reaching effects.

For example, its early policies regarding matters of controversial broadcasting and fairness of expression, developed in the 1930s, have been adopted by regulators as standards appropriate for all broadcasters. As well, the UNESCO document published in 1980 (the MacBride Report), which has become recognized as the most comprehensive study ever made on international communication, was prepared by representatives from twelve of the hundred plus nations represented in UNESCO. One of these nations was Canada and Canada's representative was a staff member of the CBC, Betty Zimmermann. Fifth, the CBC maintains an extensive and sophisticated research and development centre in Montreal. Results from studies done at that centre have, on several occasions, influenced federal government initiatives, for example, offering technical and engineering aid for the development of communications in Third World nations. Sixth, the CBC has served as a pioneer in establishing television standards in parliamentary broadcasting, an area that has always been seen as politically delicate and having the potential for abuse. The parliamentary channel, now available to Canadians through cable distribution, attests to the success of the CBC in this area of broadcasting. Seventh, the CBC has served from 1945 to this day as the international broadcasting arm of the federal government, with its short-wave Radio Canada International Service.

A review of broadcasting legislation from 1932 (the date of Canada's first Broadcasting Act) to the present offers insight into how legislators have regarded the public and private sectors in terms of dominance. The 1932 act established a Canadian Radio Broadcasting Commission (CRBC), anticipating nationalization of the entire broadcasting industry, and indicated that the CRBC was empowered to lease or to buy any privately owned radio station. The 1936 act reiterated and strengthened this right. The 1958 act, which followed the introduction of television in 1952, did not contain the option to lease or purchase private stations, but it did empower the Board of Broadcast Governors to license privately owned broadcasting stations on the condition that these stations functioned as affiliates of the CBC—that is, privately owned stations were, in effect, being programmed in large part by the public sector. This affiliate status continues.

The effect of this public/private arrangement is that public and private sectors of the industry are similar in size. If the current twenty-nine CBC affiliate stations are regarded as extensions of the network, there would be a total of sixty originating TV stations with CBC programming and sixty privately owned originating stations. While the same situation does not hold true for radio, it is apparent that there is a strong programming presence on the part of the national TV service, which is at least equal to the private programming presence.

In sum, it is important to understand the dual ownership structure of the Canadian broadcasting system. In such an examination of Canadian media institutions, it quickly becomes apparent that the public sector, if less dominant than the private sector in terms of quantity of broadcasting units, capital investment, and sometimes popular programming, continues to function in a leadership role that has been its mandate from the earliest days of broadcasting.

Historical Overview

There are various approaches to the study of Canadian broadcasting, but it is perhaps most effective to examine its historical development as this has occurred through parliamentary legislation. Broadcasting has been regulated by five broadcasting acts, passed in 1932, 1936, 1958, 1967–68, and 1991. In each case, the enactment was preceded by some review of broadcasting (either through a commission or a committee), and in each case, these reviews altered the direction of the industry.

The 1929 Aird Royal Commission preceded and influenced the 1932 Broadcasting Act. The concerns expressed in the Aird Report continued to receive attention in subsequent reports and broadcasting acts: "At present the majority of programs heard are from sources outside of

Members of the Royal Commission on Broadcast-ing, c. 1928. Left to right: Charles Bowman, Sir John Aird (seated), Donald Manson (secretary), Dr. Augustin Frigon. (National Archives of Canada/PA 12227)

Canada. It has been emphasized to us that the continued reception of these has a tendency to mould the minds of the young people in the home to ideals and opinions that are not Canadian."[7]

The other tenet of Canadian broadcasting is outlined in the Aird Report as follows: "As a fundamental principle, we believe that any broadcasting organization must be operated on a basis of public service. The stations providing a service of this kind should be owned and operated by one national company."[8]

Regulations over the years have focussed on these two fundamental concerns of ownership and purpose of content, and the different approaches to them taken by legislators over time structure the discussion that follows.

The Canadian Radio Broadcasting Act, 1932

The 1932 act recommended the establishment of the Canadian Radio Broadcasting Commission (CRBC). This commission assumed some of the regulatory powers in the area of broadcasting held by the minister of marine and fisheries. While the commission was obliged to regulate and control Canadian broadcasting and to determine its overall shape and direction, the issuance of licences still remained the prerogative of the ministry, on the basis of the recommendation of the commission. Some of the additional powers of the CRBC are interesting to note. For example, in the thinking of the CRBC and the 1932 Parliament that legislated the act, the position of the private broadcaster was tenuous. The CRBC was empowered to make operating agreements as well as to take over all broadcasting in Canada (given the approval of Parliament).[9] Thus an ambiguous situation was established where the regulatory body over all broadcasting was also a national broadcasting service in its own right. This situation was to last for a quarter of a century.

What is absent from the act is a clear statement about the purposes of broadcasting, such as is found in subsequent legislation. However, the two statements cited from the Aird Report are appropriate substitutes for any other explicit statement of purpose.

The 1932 act, then, may be regarded as our first formal statement about where Canada was headed with respect to broadcasting, and the CRBC functioned primarily as an organization that began to establish standards of performance and to define the role that broadcasting was to play in Canadian society. In the interim, pressures in the country continued to be exerted, particularly by proponents of a public broadcasting system that would be fashioned in the mode of the BBC in the United Kingdom. Representatives of the Canadian Radio League expressed the concern that popular commercial broadcasting in the U.S. style was the dominant fare on the airwaves of the country. There was a need, the Radio League argued, to strengthen and establish for all time a national broadcasting system that would function as a public service. The essential arguments of the Radio League focussed on two main points: first, that private ownership of radio would result in a misplacement of its proper emphasis—the operation of businesses would overwhelm the fulfilment of a national purpose; second, a strong federal system of radio operation (supported by a well-developed network) could best oppose the numerous high-powered American stations broadcasting into Canada.[10]

Two prominent Canadians, Graham Spry and Alan Plaunt, were central to the establishment of the Canadian Radio League, which followed shortly after the publication of the Aird Report. Through the concentrated efforts of the membership of the League, which in 1932 represented a diverse number of Canadian organizations, the philosophy of public ownership of broadcasting was enunciated and defined.[11] With a membership of over one million, the League lobbied strongly and effectively for the establishment of the Canadian Broadcasting Corporation, a public corporation that would, it was anticipated, nationalize the entire radio industry so as to serve a national rather than a commercial purpose. As Spry argued, radio "is a majestic instrument of national unity and of national culture. Its potentialities are too great, its influence and significance are too vast to be left to the petty purpose of selling soap."[12]

The consequence of such public pressures, which included twenty-five Canadian newspapers supporting the Radio League, was further debate in Parliament. This in turn led to the establishment of a Special Committee on Broadcasting, which was created with a view to establishing a stronger public ownership presence in the industry. This committee, which was chaired by Raymond Morand, presented its report to Parliament in 1934.

Broadcasting Act, 1936

In the light of the intensity of pressures mounting for public broadcasting and the private sector's tendency to carry and emulate commercial programming of the U.S. industry, the Morand Committee reported to Parliament that it was imperative the public sector be strengthened in significant ways: the CBC was thus created by the act and had the dual responsibility of regulating the entire industry and developing and operating a strong national broadcasting network.

Prior to the passage of the new act, community and parliamentary debate had focussed on disappointments with the CRBC: while nationalization of the whole industry had been anticipated, the private sector had continued to grow. For example, it was indicated in Parliament that in 1932 there were sixty-nine private radio stations in the country, while by 1936 the number had increased to seventy-three.[13] The growth in numbers might not have been great, but, in light of contrary expectations, it fuelled greater demands for a dominant public sector.

The 1936 legislation was not much different from that of 1932—the Canadian Broadcasting Corporation, as a Crown corporation, replaced the CRBC in both its capacities as broadcaster and regulator of the industry. In terms of cabinet responsibility for broadcasting, the minister of transport replaced the minister of marine and fisheries, implying a more appropriate locus of supervision for the broadcasting industry.

Two particular changes in the 1932 act might be noted. First, the powers of the CBC became more explicit in that the CBC was mandated to control the "character" of any and all programs broadcast. Second, the corporation was obliged to review the activities of private stations each year before renewing their licences.[14]

The first annual report of the CBC (1938) highlights three particular matters. First, it was the intent of the CBC to improve relations between French-speaking and English-speaking Canadians. Consequently its development was to be planned around promoting cordial relations between "the two great mother races." Second, the corporation notes that it was keeping "careful watch" on the development of television so that in Canada the new medium "might be controlled in the public interest." Third, with respect to programs, the report indicates that a survey of Canada's radio programs had been done and that the object of the study had been to determine "the extent and character of Canadian resources." Perhaps for the first time in Canadian broadcasting, we find content policy the aim of which was to feature "characteristic Canadian material." In this self-imposed mandate, the CBC identified a problem that continues to exist: do Canadian-produced programs reveal Canadian character and consciousness?[15] Regulatory bodies continue to this day to confront the broadcasting industry with these production imperatives: there is an urgent need to repatriate Canadian audiences with domestic progamming. Equally important is the need to produce content that will reflect the Canadian character and consciousness.

In the years during which the CBC continued to regulate the industry (1936 to 1958), nationalization of all broadcasting did not occur as had been envisaged by at least some parliamentarians and by the Radio League and its large group of supporters. Rather, the corporation established the broadcasting system as a partnership arrangement between the private and public sectors, a partnership that had been started by the CRBC. What is evident is that nationalization might well have taken place if the CBC, or the CRBC before it, had been allocated sufficient sums of money. In 1935, a Member of Parliament noted, "I do not think the Radio Commission has made a great deal of headway in nationalizing radio broadcasting in Canada. . . . Undoubtedly the Commission has been handicapped by lack of funds."[16] Thus we have the pattern of development established in these early years that was clearly not industry-wide nationalization but rather a hybrid system of public/private stations that carried the national service.

The CBC, prior to the popularization of television in the country in 1952, operated three radio networks, and the structure of these networks offers insight into the nature of the public/private relationship: the Trans-Canada Network was made up of seven CBC-owned-and-operated stations and seventeen privately owned stations; the Dominion Network consisted of one CBC-owned and twenty-eight privately owned stations; and the French Network comprised three CBC-owned-and-operated stations and nine privately owned ones.[17] A similar

pattern continued when TV was first introduced: the CBC built its own stations in Canadian communities where capital funding permitted and then licensed private operators to build and operate stations when there was a shortage of public funds. Table 7–2 reveals, however, that while the public/private affiliation continues fairly consistently with respect to television, radio development is a different story. We see, for example, with respect to CBC-AM radio affiliation, there is a drop from ninety-four stations in 1977 to a current figure of fifteen. There is a corresponding increase in the number of independent radio stations along with a modest increase in the number of new CBC stations.

While the partnership between the two sectors continued, it was an occasionally rocky relationship. According to the Canadian Association of Broadcasters, the relationship was not really a case of equal partnership due to the fact that the CBC had a dual function as regulator and broadcaster. As the number of broadcasting units in Canada grew, particularly with the licensing of an increasing number of independent stations, the CAB pointed out that the corporation, in fact, competed with private broadcasters for audiences, frequencies, business, programs, and personnel.[18]

The pressures of the increasingly powerful CAB lobby continued, and references to the near conflict of interest situation of the CBC were points of discussion whenever broadcasters met. An analogy popular at the time was that the broadcasting situation was tantamount to one grocery chain dictating rules of operation for its competitor. The consequence at the parliamentary level was that a royal commission (the Fowler Commission) was created in 1955 to study the entire broadcasting situation, in particular the impact of television. The commission researched the industry intensively, giving special attention to the issues of Canadian content, Canadian talent, and threats to Canada's national identity inherent in foreign programming. The commission released its report in 1957, having arrived at several conclusions. Chief among these, it recommended that the CBC, after twenty-two years as a regulatory body, focus its resources on becoming a national public broadcasting entity and shed its regulatory responsibility. Further, in comparing the private and public sectors, it found that in 1956 the publicly owned CBC had spent $9.1 million in artists' fees, while the private sector only had a total talent expenditure of just over $2 million.[19] Moreover, the CBC expenditures had a greater impact as the corporation achieved Canadianization over a national system. Unlike the CBC, private broadcasters offered only the single program format for limited community audiences. The report concluded that "with some notable exceptions, the private stations have done little to encourage Canadian talent."[20]

Essentially, what the report underlined was that the private sector of broadcasting had succumbed to the pressures of the marketplace and the concomitant attractions of profitability by resorting to importing American radio and television programs. The cost of these programs was significantly less than would have been the cost of similar programming produced in Canadian studios. The details of the commission's research included a phrase that has figured in recent jargon concerning the responsibility of broadcasters to contribute to the imperative of national identity, that is, "the logic of the licence." In urging private broadcasters to share in an increased responsibility to Canadian society, the commission stated that "private stations should individually be required to justify the continued grant of a valuable public franchise by contributing to their societies in return."[21] The

Robert Fowler, 1906–80, March 1967
(D. Cameron/National Archives of Canada/
PA 129243)

principle of accountability thus became formalized in the commission's report.

Finally, the commission recommended the establishment of an independent regulatory body, not involved in broadcasting, to assume the regulatory responsibility that up to that time had been held by the CBC. The 1958 act, which resulted from the commission's report, named the Board of Broadcast Governors (BBG) to be that body.

Broadcasting Act, 1958

It is in the 1958 act that we find for the first time a statement of objectives for the broadcasting system. The basic regulatory responsibility would be to ensure the efficient operation of a national broadcasting system. This system would be expected to provide both varied and comprehensive broadcasting of a high standard that would be "basically Canadian in content and character."[22] At the same time, its regulations would apply to both the private and public sectors of broadcasting. As well, following the recommendations of the Fowler Commission, the act empowered the BBG to make regulations to promote and ensure "the greater use of Canadian talent by broadcasting stations."[23]

The new act further formalized the need for the regulatory body to hold public hearings when particular matters of interest to several parties were under discussion, for example, licensing issues. In effect, the principle of public access to the

hearing process became established under the act, and we are aware of the current extension of the principle, whereby citizens are invited to participate, in person or by written brief, in any matters arising from the way in which broadcasting stations conduct themselves.

The new act, too, permitted stations to apply for affiliation with a network other than the one operated by the CBC. (However, this had to be done following a required public hearing.) Implicit in this permission was the anticipated development of privately owned networks. What was also evident in this permission was a recognition of the Fowler Commission's intention that the mixed Canadian system of public and private ownership "is here to stay," and that private broadcasters should no longer fear "the bogey of nationalization that has filled them with suspicion and fear in the past."[24]

As one reads the proposals described above, it is possible to predict changes in direction for the Canadian broadcasting system. The act came into effect in September 1958, and the members of the new BBG were named shortly after that date. The newly appointed chair of the board, Dr. Andrew Stewart, wasted little time in taking several initiatives to translate the guidelines contained in the act into working principles for the industry. Within sixteen months of its establishment, the board announced a regulation that, more than any other, has reshaped the operational practices in the industry and offered a clear indication for its future. This regulation indicated that as of 1 July 1960, no less than 55 percent of the schedules of Canadian television stations or networks would be devoted to programs that "are basically Canadian in content and character."[25]

The board's new content regulation had been announced a full year earlier (28 July 1959) so as to permit public discussion of the matter. Broadcasters, particularly those from the private sector, reacted immediately, predicting that domestically produced programming would prove to be inferior in quality to imported materials. These broadcasters also claimed that costs to stations would be such as to drive them out of business at the same time as viewers would be driven to watch U.S. channels. Perhaps a more serious consequence, other Canadians asserted, would be the threat of the regulation to a normally developing national cultural identity. A culture could not be regulated into existence, the argument continued, and such regulation would result in a distinct threat to a natural cultural development.

Despite the complaints, the board continued to enforce the regulation and indicated that while a similar content quota for radio would not be introduced, it would monitor radio stations to ensure an increased commitment to Canadian content and to the use of Canadian talent.

As one reviews different parliamentary debates, annual reports, and documents relating to broadcasting in the 1960s, it becomes evident that the BBG and the CBC did not see eye to eye on several matters of importance. For example, early in the 1960s, second TV licences were issued by the BBG to private TV broadcasters, who in 1961 were permitted to form a second TV network: the Canadian Television Network (CTV). This initial private network was represented in eight of Canada's major cities and was clearly established as a second TV service that would compete with the CBC network.

Another of the difficulties in the often strained relationship between the BBG and the CBC was that the 1958 act continued to emphasize the distinct status of the CBC by specifying, obliquely, that both the CBC and the BBG reported to the same federal department—the minister of transport. Such a reporting responsibility weakened the stature of the BBG as the body supposedly responsible for regulating both sectors. Such a jurisdictional dispute, which found focus on several regulatory matters (including whether the CBC or the new CTV network had proprietary rights to televise the 1962 Grey Cup football game), made it apparent that legislation was needed to clarify the powers of a regulatory body that would in fact and in law be recognized as the authority by both private and public sectors. Thus, we find Parliament, in the spring of 1964, discussing the need for a new regulatory body and a new broadcasting act to define its powers.

Broadcasting Act, 1967–68

Although a royal commission was not struck in this instance, cabinet invited Robert M. Fowler, chair of the 1955 Royal Commission, to serve again, this time as chair of an advisory committee to review the complaints being heard in Parliament regarding the CBC, the BBG, and the general state of broadcasting.

In handing down its report in 1965, the Fowler Committee set the tone for the discussion with its often repeated introductory statement: "The only thing that really matters in broadcasting is program content; all the rest is housekeeping."[26] This particular statement not only indicated what was to follow in the report, but has offered a focus for action by regulatory bodies since that time.

The 1967–68 act, which resulted from the committee's report, spells out in detail what the purpose of content should be: all broadcasting undertakings should be regarded as a single system, which was to be "effectively owned or controlled by Canadians so as to safeguard, enrich and strengthen the cultural, political, social and economic fabric of Canada."[27] This particular statement must be emphasized because it identifies very clearly a link between Canadian ownership and an active role in promoting a distinct Canadian consciousness.

In the act, as well, we find a clear expression of the mandate of the CBC. First, to provide a balanced service of information, enlighten-ment, and entertainment for people of different ages, interests, and tastes. Second, to extend service to all Canadians (a subsequent regulation identified that areas for coverage should be those communities with at least five hundred residents). Third, CBC services should be extended to serve special needs of geographic regions in both English and French languages. Fourth, the CBC is "to contribute to the development of national unity and provide for a continuing expression of Canadian identity."[28] This latter specification concerning national unity has been problematic and it has been questioned since the time it was first offered to the CBC, whether in fact, broadcasting could accomplish what was essentially an awesome task. We find in the 1991 act recognition of this problem in that the mandate of promoting national unity for the CBC becomes modified.

The 1967–68 act further clarifies the relationship between the private and public sectors: it is the public sector that is to receive preferential treatment in the event of any conflict between the objectives of the CBC and the interests of private broadcasters. Thus, we can see a reassertion of the primacy of the public sector in Canadian broadcasting.

The act further makes it clear that the new regulatory body created therein, the Canadian Radio-Television Commission (CRTC), would be the "single independent public authority" over all broadcasting. In detailing the powers of the new detailing the powers of the new CRTC, the act entrusts to it three broad responsibilities: (1) to identify and issue (as well as to renew) different classes of broadcasting licences; (2) to regulate the entire broadcasting system; and (3) except in the case of a licence issued to the CBC, to revoke broadcasting licences. (In a case of a licence dispute involving the CBC, the CRTC was invited to make specific recommendations to cabinet.)

At the same time the act reinforces the principle of public access to hearings. Public hearings become mandatory with respect to issuing, revoking, or suspending licences, and the CRTC is given the latitude to hold hearings on amendments to licensing conditions or on public complaints, should it deem such hearings to be in the public interest.

Given such increased emphasis on responsibility of broadcasters and a specific mandate for the industry, the CRTC moved to strengthen the Canadianization of the industry. The Canadian content regulation for television was increased to 60 percent from the earlier BBG-directed 55 percent. The radio industry, as well, was issued a content quota, and radio stations were obliged to schedule a third of their music programming with Canadian content. The CRTC stipulated four conditions that would characterize Canadian content in music: (1) the music should be composed by a Canadian, (2) the lyrics should be written by a Canadian, (3) the music should be performed by Canadian artists, and (4)

the music should be performed or recorded in Canada. In fulfilling the requirement, broadcasters would have to observe any two of the conditions. The CRTC demonstrated a great deal of flexibility in quota enforcement, occasionally with good reason. For example, private broadcasters indicated that they were technically ill-equipped to produce quality recordings. In fact, it was found that with the exception of some U.S.-imported recording facilities (RCA in Montreal), there was little or nothing in the way of multitrack recording facilities in the country. Initially Canadian radio stations filled the airwaves with such well-known and successful artists as Gordon Lightfoot and Anne Murray, both of whom complained to the CRTC on the dangers of overexposure. A consequence of the content regulation was that Canadians understood that the CRTC was firm in its demands, and quickly began to invest in and construct quality technical recording facilities.

At the same time as television and radio quotas were modified and introduced by the CRTC, the commission, acting on an instruction by cabinet, specified that there would be a tightening of Canadian ownership and control of broadcasting: the 1967–68 act thus specified "effective ownership and control." The regulation stipulated that at least 80 percent of issued shares, to which at least 80 percent of voting rights were attached, must be owned by Canadian citizens.[29]

This regulation created considerable consternation in the Canadian broadcasting community, since it became apparent that there was, in fact, a great deal of non-Canadian ownership of Canadian broadcasting media. Nevertheless, the CRTC was resolute in enforcing the regulation and divestiture proceedings were started almost immediately. Over a period of five to six years, while many complications arose in the process, divestiture was completed so as to achieve the required 80/20 ratio. The process of changing ownership from foreign to Canadian hands often required substantial capital investments on the part of Canadians.[30] The consequence was that, in many parts of the country, owners whose media holdings were already of considerable scope and size increased their broadcasting holdings even more.

When the new act stipulated that all broadcasting undertakings would constitute a single system, operating under the same public service orientation as a mandate, it was unclear what the CRTC's role would be with respect to cable television. While the act implied that cable operations were as integral a part of the broadcasting system as radio and television, cable operations essentially involved distribution of content; conventional broadcasters were producers as well as distributers of content. Introducing an increased number of channels through cable distribution created two problems: the economic position of conventional broadcasters was threatened in that audiences for advertisers were splintered, and broadcasting signals were being distributed freely

in communities where these signals had not been licensed to operate. Thus, the previously mentioned logic of the licence principle was threatened in that the commercial bases of broadcasting stations were compromised, reducing the ability of stations to produce Canadian content. The CRTC, in attempting to resolve these problems, introduced several regulatory measures for CATV systems. Although such regulations began in 1970–71, the two problems we have just identified have never been satisfactorily resolved. It was possible to regulate conventional broadcasting by applying a direct quota system of a type that was simply not possible for CATV. What was developed by the CRTC was a system of "signal priorities" for cable.[31] This system of priorities indicated that particular community and national needs for information had to be fulfilled before distribution of non-Canadian signals would be permitted. While the system of priorities, or tiers, was thus instituted (and it continues to be modified), it is far from perfect with respect to the Canadian content demands implicit in the broadcasting act.

Although stations and the programs they offer can be regulated, audiences cannot be. As we saw in chapter 5, Canadians, when offered a choice, have almost always preferred foreign programming to domestically produced programming. While children and teens watched more foreign programming in 1989 than did adults, adults themselves were heavy consumers of non-Canadian programs: franco-phones spent two-thirds of their viewing time watching foreign content, and anglophones spent only one hour in twenty watching a Canadian show.[32]

It was not only cable television that created regulatory headaches for the CRTC. The 1960s and 1970s saw the birth and development of a variety of patterns of content distribution: satellites, the expansion of telegraph systems, and telephone lines as carriers of signals all demanded regulation.

The appropriate and conventional action to take was to consolidate various regulatory powers related to communications or telecommunications systems under the aegis of one body. That body was the CRTC, although under a slightly different name—Canadian Radio-Television and *Telecommunications* Commission. This restructured body was approved by Parliament in April 1975. While the commission now would be known in abbreviated form as CRTTC, government documents and other literature continue to use the earlier abbreviation, CRTC.[33]

Broadcasting Act, 1991

The 1991 act was long overdue, and there was no disagreement about this either on the part of the industry or politicians in Ottawa. The impact of technological developments had been so rapid, diverse, and revolutionary that this dynamism was not properly accommodated by the 1968 act. Broadcasting

has always been a changing rather than a stable industry, and measures attempted by regulatory bodies have often been outdated before they have come into effect.

The 1991 act, however, attempts to consolidate what has gone on before and to establish directions for the future. This is no easy task in the Canadian context at the best of times. How does one promote the development of a Canadian identity when only a relatively few of the increasing number of broadcasting signals available to Canadians are Canadian in origin? And, if overzealous protectionist barriers in the form of policies are enacted, might the consequence not be international retaliation in some other sphere of social or economic activity?

While the 1991 act was not preceded by a formal royal commission or committee inquiry, there was a document that might be termed a position paper that was issued by the Department of Communication in 1988. This document, *Canadian Voices: Canadian Choices*, begins with a statement that encompasses considerations related to nationhood: "Ultimately, a national, regional or ethnic culture is largely defined by shared experiences. Our culture is what we have in common."[34]

The new act, then, continues to express concern about Canada's national culture and its protection, but it strikes off in a new direction from its predecessors. The earlier acts focussed on growth and development of the broadcasting industry, on establishing appropriate relationships between private and public sectors, as well as on establishing quota systems for Canadian content and ownership principles and responsibilities. In contrast, the 1991 act is broader in scope and concerns itself as well with political and cultural sovereignty and how the cultural industries are expected to contribute to that sovereignty. The concern here extends beyond the broadcasting industry per se, and is reflected in the name of a parliamentary committee that earlier had its scope expanded to include the cultural industries—the Committee on Communication and Culture.

Canadian Voices: Canadian Choices touches on four main points. First, are concerns with respect to programming. On this question the position paper reflects the introductory statement of the earlier Fowler Committee about the centrality of program content, and this is the focus taken in the document. The purpose of programming is to provide quality choices to English-language and French-language audiences, without being concerned with mass audiences. Incentives for the production of Canadian content were to be developed. The CBC was to increase its content quota to 95 percent Canadian content in prime-time television. The second issue is fairness and access, whereby minorities' needs would be addressed. The multicultural nature of Canada and the special role of aboriginal people would be recognized in that access to the broadcasting system would be assured. The new Broadcast Act would "complement the *Charter of Rights and Freedoms* and its emphasis on the dignity and equality of all men and women."[35] The third element of the document focusses on communications technology and emphasizes that while regulatory jurisdiction will apply to hardware, the emphasis will be on the content that is produced by that hardware. Again, we find an echo of Fowler's statement regarding content and housekeeping. The fourth point discusses the operations and administration of the broadcasting system, and significant changes become apparent here. The document indicates that the new act would separate the offices of chair of the board of the CBC and that of president. Up to this point, the two functions were handled as one responsibility, creating, as critics indicated, a conflict of interest whereby the chair of the board would design policies for the corporation and that same person, wearing his or her second hat, would effect those policies as chief executive officer. Thus, we find, even before the new act was approved by Parliament, that the cabinet moved to appoint former broadcaster Patrick Watson as chairman of the CBC board under the new system and named Gerard Veilleux, a former senior civil servant, as president and chief executive officer.

The position paper contains a controversial recommendation. The document specifies that the CRTC would continue to be subject to policy direction from the cabinet, but the rationale creates concern: "To ensure that the overall policy development lies firmly in the hands of elected representatives, directly responsible to the people of Canada."[36] This could be construed as meaning that political concerns of the cabinet might threaten the independence of the CRTC, at least this was the position of CRTC chair André Bureau.[37] The two parliamentary committees that debated the act as it made its way through parliamentary procedures offered final unanimous approval once the threat of political interference was lessened with a change in wording.

The new act, reflecting the position paper discussed above, first makes no mistake regarding the responsibility of the CRTC to regulate both broadcasting and telecommunications industries. Clearing up earlier ambiguities in this regard, the act defines broadcasting as "any transmission of programs, whether or not encrypted, by radio waves or other means of telecommunications for reception by the public. . . . "[38]

But the pronounced and dominant changes in the new act are contained in an enlarged statement of "Broadcasting Policy for Canada," section 3 of the act. This policy statement is reproduced in the Appendix to this book along with a copy of the similar paragraph from the 1967–68 act because its understanding is basic to the role of the cultural industries as they are intended to serve a national purpose. A few highlights of this policy will be noted.

The demand that the Canadian broadcasting system should exist to safeguard and identify our culture was reiterated, as in the earlier act, but greater emphasis is placed on the development of programming that would reflect Canadian attitudes, opinions, ideas, values, and artistic creativity. What the act clearly recognizes with respect to Canadian content quotas is what broadcasters learned from the very day that such quotas were enacted: it was really not much of a challenge to produce a fixed amount of domestic content, but it *was* a challenge to produce content that Canadians would listen to or watch; not to mention the greatest production challenge of all, to develop content that contains values that are inherently Canadian. It has simply been easier, most producers of content found, to emulate production styles and value systems to which we have all become accustomed—those found in the U.S. entertainment industry. The policy statement emphasizes this particular problem.

A second matter in the policy statement that needs to be addressed is the mandate provided for the CBC. This mandate is more specific than that contained in the previous act, but students will note that a specific responsibility for helping to develop national unity has been changed, and now reads to "contribute to shared consciousness and identity."[39]

In the midst of debate on the new Broadcasting Act, the country found itself in another, more fundamental debate regarding the place of cultural industries in relation to the growing integration of the

North American economy. This was reflected in the Free Trade Agreement with the United States, which came into effect in 1989, and in the continuing discussions on free trade with Mexico.

The Free Trade Agreement, as well as the 1991 act, reaffirm in principle Canada's desire to continue to regulate cultural industries in order to protect its national identity. To what extent such protection will continue to be possible is problematic. There is no doubt that the U.S. will put increasing pressure on Canada to relax or abolish much, if not all, of its protective legislation. We can only speculate on how adamant Canada's stance will be in protecting its cultural industries. Given the history that we have recounted, it is unlikely that we will see a wholesale abandonment of the cultural industries to the international marketplace. The principles of cultural protection and the sensitivities regarding national identity are too deeply embedded in the Canadian psyche for a dramatic turnaround to occur at this point in our history. However, pressures to abandon protective measures will continue to be felt.

Budgets and Mandates: The CBC Dilemma

While some events in the 1930s—the birth of the Canadian Broadcasting Corporation, for example—caught the attention of the Canadian community regarding what should be the responsibilities of public (as opposed to private commercial) broadcasters, attempts by the federal government in the late 1980s to reduce the massive national deficit brought the issue back into focus. In the midst of budget cuts that affected everyone and every institution in Canada, the CBC, too, found itself faced with a need to reduce staff and programming and in the winter of 1984 eliminated some program plans and reduced its staff nationally by over 1000 persons.

Responding to such cuts, an ad hoc coalition of Canadians, which in rhetorical terms recall the Radio Broadcasting League of the 1930s, called on the federal government to re-establish a strong commitment to a Canadian public broadcasting system. Describing itself as the Friends of Public Broadcasting (later, Friends of Canadian Broadcasting), the coalition emphasized that only within the framework of a publicly owned system could the country's needs be properly served: "One of the few sustaining cultural links is the electronic bridge provided by the Canadian Broadcasting Corporation; without it we Canadians would have no cross-country sounding board, little opportunity to exchange facts, fantasies, opinions and trends—in other words, the shared values that create a distinctive society."[40] At the same time, the group cautioned the federal government to ensure that Canadian sovereignty over its cultural industries not be compromised in trade negotiations with the United States.

But it was a second budgetary cutback in December 1990 that

brought cries of anguish from the four corners of the country: a $108 million reduction in the budget for the year 1991 caused a further 1100 positions to be cut. The major net effect of the budget cuts was that three CBC-owned-and-operated stations were closed and eight others had their local community news and public affairs programming ended. Transmitters continued to function, telecasting nationally and regionally originating programs. The cities affected included Goose Bay, Corner Brook, Sydney, Matane, Rimouski, Sept-Isles, Toronto, Windsor, Saskatoon, and Calgary. The impact of these reductions, which were claimed to save $46 million, was that each province was to have one regional telecasting centre to provide news and public affairs programming for that province.

One community in particular—Windsor, Ontario—was left without any local programming, as there is no private TV operation in the city. The reaction of a community committee established to try to restore local television news services of any sort was that the CBC had reneged on its mandate and, in so doing, surrendered the southwest corner of Ontario to U.S. cultural forces. While it is true that people in Windsor continue to have access to local Canadian radio and newspapers, they have lost the ability to look to television for news of themselves.

Patrick Watson, chairman of the Board of Governors of the CBC, spoke to a Windsor-area Member of Parliament about the plight of the community. Although he was sympathetic, Watson indicated that he hoped that regional news broadcast from Toronto would be consolation for Windsorites.[41] What Watson was enunciating was a departure on the part of the corporation from its earlier mandate. A CBC spokesperson explained this change as follows: "We were a local service in television; we no longer are. In effect this is a change in our mandate. We had no choice."[42]

It was this change in mandate that caused community groups across the country to press the CRTC for a public hearing. The CRTC scheduled such a hearing in March 1991, at which the CBC presented its revised approach to community programming, which was summed up in the phrase "local reflection" by regional stations rather than by local stations.[43]

In the corporation's *Annual Report 1990–1991*, the president of the CBC explains a fundamental change in serving Canadians with programming:

> The new approach was to build on the complementary strengths of the French and English radio and television services. Radio would continue to be deeply rooted in the regions of Canada, and provide services at the local, regional, and national levels, but would withdraw from most international activities, except basic newsgathering. Television would complement radio by withdrawing from programming intended for purely local audiences, to concentrate on regional, national, and international programming.[44]

Telecommunications

The discussion so far has focussed on broadcasting and telecommunications as if the two entities were one and the same; and in some instances, given overlapping and converging technologies, they might indeed be regarded as one. The conventional view of broadcasting is that it uses over-the-air links between senders and receivers, while telecommunications has been viewed as using wired links between senders and receivers. However, such distinctions break down quickly when you consider that microwave operations, CATV operations, satellite transmissions, and telephone systems are content carriers for broadcasting systems. In light of this the difficulty of establishing a clear separation between broadcasting and telecommunications becomes evident. At this point, however, despite the technological convergences that are occurring between the two sectors, a brief overview of the telecommunications segment of the industry is in order.

There are four major sets of players in Canadian telecommunications activity.[45]

1. Telecom Canada is a consortium that comprises the following entities:
    (a) three provincially owned telephone systems (Alberta, Saskatchewan, and Manitoba),
    (b) six privately owned telephone systems, the largest of which is Bell Canada (Quebec and Ontario). The CRTC regu-lates only Bell telephones: the remaining systems fall under the jurisdictions of their respective provincial bodies.
    (c) Telesat Canada was established in 1969 and owns and operates Canada's domestic satellite communications systems. Telesat is jointly owned by the federal government and other Telecom Canada participants.

    Telesat Canada has been one of the world's pioneers in developing satellite carriers for domestic use. *Anik 1*, which was successfully launched in 1972, proved to be the world's first domestic satellite in geostationary orbit, that is, in fixed orbit with the rotation of the earth. The significance of Telesat Canada is linked to the overall national cultural environment: virtually all Canadians are linked as a national group with broadcasting, data, telegraph, and telephone signals.

2. Unitel (formerly CNCP Communications) was originally established in 1956 by two separate entities: Canadian National Telecommunications and Canada Pacific Telecommunications. In 1980 the two organizations, one public and the other private, formed a partnership, which, in effect, placed them into competition with Telecom Canada. In 1989 Rogers Communications bought out the CN portion of the partnership and in 1990 the company took on a new name, Unitel.

The services offered, both by Unitel and Telecom Canada, cover the broad range of voice transmissions, broadcasting signals, computer data applications, cellular telephone services, and variations of business teleconferencing. The two carrier organizations provide links from sea to sea in Canada and also interconnect to United States' carriers.

3. Teleglobe Canada was established in 1949 as the Canadian Overseas Telecommunications Corporation and adopted its current name in 1975. Teleglobe Canada is Canada's international carrier and connects Canadian and overseas networks. Teleglobe Canada also serves as Canada's representative on international bodies that operate sophisticated satellite and cable systems that interconnect the global community.

Originally established as a Crown corporation, Teleglobe Canada was privatized in 1987. The CRTC has jurisdiction over Teleglobe to the extent that user rates are fixed and modifications to rates require CRTC hearings.

4. CANCOM is a supplementary, privately owned satellite service and was licensed by the CRTC in 1981. CANCOM carries additional radio and television broadcasting programming to Canadians who live in remote areas of the country. It is a supplementary service in the sense that it is not regarded as a competitor to the more elaborate and extended services offered by Telesat Canada or Unitel.

The entry of American Telephone and Telegraph Company (AT&T) into the Canadian telecommunications industrial environment in the fall of 1990 introduced a new element of strong competition for the Canadian industry. AT&T, the world's largest telecommunications carrier corporation, had offered to join the Telecom consortium along with the other Canadian carrier companies. The offer was turned down due to the head-on competition that AT&T would provide to the domestic industry.[46]

New Canadian services (electronic mail and enhanced facsimile message capabilities) are part of an already existing global service that AT&T currently offers in the U.S., Britain, and Japan. As we discussed earlier with respect to the cultural industries, the free trade environment will be a decisive factor in determining how competitive the telecommunications industry will be in the future. As there is no clear cultural content to protect in this instance, open market tendencies favour "AT&T Canada Ltd."

Conclusion

The purpose of this discussion has been to show students that the history of broadcasting in Canada has been dominated and given direction by five major parliamentary pieces of legislation. To understand the character of the broadcasting/

telecommunications industries is to understand the importance, with respect to such significant questions as nationhood and sovereignty, that the highest political decision-making body in the land has given to these industries and their products.

Insofar as the telecommunications sector is concerned, Statistics Canada points out that Canada, on a per-capita basis, has the "most extensive telecommunications system in the world."[47] It should be pointed out as well that this is consistent with what Karl Deutsch and others have postulated regarding a society's prerequiste to nationhood: the society must be linked throughout every piece of its territory. Remember, however, that telecommunications systems are essentially carrier systems. In Canada the hardware is in place; whether the *content* carried by that hardware satisfies the needs of nationhood on the part of all Canadians is quite another matter.

Notes

1. See Frank W. Peers, *The Politics of Canadian Broadcasting: 1920–1951* (Toronto: University of Toronto Press, 1969), 4.
2. Canada, *Report of the Royal Commission on Radio Broadcasting 1929* (Ottawa: King's Printer, 1929).
3. Cited in Peers, *The Politics of Canadian Broadcasting*, 123.
4. Canada, House of Commons, *Debates*, 18 May 1932, 3035.
5. For insight into the early years of the CAB, see T. James Allard, *Straight Up: Private Broadcasting in Canada, 1918–1958* (Ottawa: Heritage House Publishers, 1979), 114–23.
6. *Report of the Task Force on Broadcasting Policy* (Ottawa: Supply and Services, 1986), 269.
7. *Report of the Royal Commission on Radio Broadcasting*, 6.
8. Ibid.
9. Canadian Radio Broadcasting Act, 1932, 4.
10. John Egli O'Brien, "A History of the Canadian Radio League, 1930–1936" (PhD. dissertation, University of Southern California, 1964), 105–14.
11. Ibid.
12. Graham Spry, "A Case for Nationalized Broadcasting," *Queen's Quarterly* 38 (Winter 1931): 169.
13. Canada, House of Commons, *Debates*, 15 June 1936, 3717–18.
14. Canada, Canadian Broadcasting Act, 1936, 22 (1) (c); 24 (1).
15. Canada, CBC, *Report of the Canadian Broadcasting Corporation for the Period November 2, 1936 to March 31, 1937* (Ottawa: J.O. Patenaude, 1938), 8–9.
16. Canada, House of Commons, *Debates*, 15 June 1935, 3717.
17. *Canada Year Book 1947* (Ottawa: King's Printer, 1947), 740.
18. Canadian Association of Broadcasters, *Supplement to Presentations to the Royal Commission on Broadcasting by the Canadian Association of Broadcasters, May 1956* (Ottawa, 1956), 3. For a detailed examination of the development of television in its formative years, see Paul Rutherford, *When Television Was Young: Primetime Canada, 1952–1967* (Toronto: University of Toronto Press, 1990).
19. Canada, *Royal Commission on Broadcasting 1957* (Ottawa: Queen's Printer, 1957), 64.
20. Ibid., 68–69.
21. Ibid., 13.
22. Canada, Broadcasting Act 1958, 10.

23. Ibid., 11 (1) (e).
24. *Royal Commission 1957*, 13.
25. Canada, Board of Broadcast Governors, *Board of Broadcast Governors' Announcement Regarding Radio (TV) Broadcasting Regulations, November 18, 1959* (Ottawa, 1959), 7.
26. Canada, *Report of the Committee on Broadcasting 1965* (Ottawa: Queen's Printer, 1965), 3.
27. Canada, Broadcasting Act 1967–68, 3(b).
28. Ibid., 3 (g) (iv).
29. Canada, *Order in Council PC 1969-2229, Direction to the Canadian Radio-Television Commission, 20 November 1969* (Ottawa: Queen's Printer, 1969), 4 (c).
30. Canada, CRTC, *Annual Report 1971–72* (Ottawa: Information Canada, 1972), 27.
31. Canada, Canadian Radio-Television Commission, *Canadian Broadcasting "A Single System": Policy Statement on Cable Television* (Ottawa, 1971), 14–19.
32. Jan Wong, "Nationalism Not the Key Issue for TV Fans, Survey Says," *Globe and Mail*, 26 March 1987, A8. Also see Canada, Statistics Canada, *Television Viewing: 1989 Culture Statistics* (Ottawa: Supply and Services, 1991), 8.
33. Canada, House of Commons, Bill C-5, 21 April 1975.
34. Canada, Department of Communication, *Canadian Voices: Canadian Choices A New Broadcasting Policy for Canada* (Ottawa: Supply and Services, 1988), 5.

35. Ibid., 9.
36. Ibid., 10.
37. Andre Bureau, "Opening Remarks before the House of Commons Legislative Committee on Bill C-136," (Ottawa: CRTC, 23 August 1988), 2–3.
38. Broadcasting Act 1991, 2 (1).
39. Ibid., 3 (l) (1) (vi).
40. Friends of Public Broadcasting, "An Open Letter to Prime Minister Brian Mulroney on Public Broadcasting" (advertisement), *Globe and Mail*, 14 December 1985, A15.
41. "Transcript Shows Watson Vague on CBET," *Windsor Star*, 13 December 1990, A1.
42. Christopher Harris, "TV's Mandate Abruptly Altered," *Globe and Mail*, 6 December 1990, A1.
43. "Broadcasting: Justifying the Cuts," *Maclean's*, 1 April 1991, 51.
44. Canadian Broadcasting Corporation, *Annual Report 1990–1991* (Ottawa, 1991), 5.
45. Details contained herein are, in large part, assembled from Statistics Canada, *Canada Year Books*. See specifically, *Canada Year Book 1985* (Ottawa: Supply and Services, 1985), 444; *Canada Year Book 1988* (Ottawa: Supply and Services, 1988), 14-2 to 14-3; *Canada Year Book 1990* (Ottawa: Supply and Services, 1989): 14-1 to 14-4.
46. Lawrence Surtees, "AT&T Brings Global Service to Canada," *Globe and Mail*, 11 September 1990, B6.
47. *Canada Year Book 1988* (Ottawa: Supply and Services, 1988), 14-2.

C H A P T E R   8

Canada's Film Industry

Introduction

The focus of this chapter is the film industry as it has developed in Canada, in large part guided by governmental involvement. The chapter does not attempt to discuss film as a mass medium as such, or its impact on society, as important as these considerations are. Such is the substance of several excellent books, one of which is written by two Canadians, Garth Jowett and James Linton. In their text, *Movies as Mass Communication*, they view movies "as a facet of mass culture and mass art"[1] and explore the relationship of the movies to their audiences. Our purpose here is to document, historically, the industry as it developed in Canada.

In comparison with many other nations, Canada has been slow to develop a film industry of its own. This should not be surprising since Canada is a neighbour to a society that has become the most prodigious producer of film and televi-sion entertainment in the world. Canadians have been predisposed to depend upon products from the United States in a variety of economic and social spheres, given the economic challenge of producing and distributing goods for a relatively small population. In the case of film, they depended almost totally upon Hollywood product in the earlier part of this century, and they came to accept U.S. films and Hollywood stars as if they were their own.

The rapid rise of the film industry in the United States occurred within the framework of international exchanges, as film artistry developed in several countries at the same time. We find exchanges of film and knowledge about film-making involving the United States, the United Kingdom, France, Italy, Germany, and Russia. Because of its dependence on the U.S. film industry, Canada benefitted from these exchanges, even though our contribution was nearly negligible.

Canadian Interest in Filmmaking

Since developments were occurring rapidly in the United States, it was inevitable that Canadian interest in filmmaking grew and that the importance of this new medium to nation building was not lost on Canadians. Commercial film production had an early beginning in Canada; as early as 1898 the Massey Harris Company engaged Thomas Edison to produce a brief promotional film about its farm implements.[2] Historians have also noted that federal government agencies began to produce films in order to promote trade and commerce. Some early Canadian "one-reelers" were played in the United Kingdom to encourage immigration to Canada.[3]

But it was during the First World War, in 1916, that the federal government took the initiative to develop what became known as the Exhibits and Publicity Bureau. This bureau was established by the Department of Trade and Commerce and it produced films to promote Canadian trade. C. Rodney James, whose study of the beginnings of the National Film Board (NFB) deals extensively with this early period in Canadian film history, notes that in 1921 the Exhibits and Publicity Bureau was renamed the Canadian Government Motion Picture Bureau.

This bureau functioned as a co-ordinator of government filmmaking until Parliament created the NFB in 1939.[4] Thus, by the time the NFB was established, a Canadian national film tradition had already been in the process of formation for nearly twenty-five years. In the main, the films produced were nontheatrical and included a wide range of educational, promotional, scenic, wildlife, and industrial themes. The films were distributed largely through schools, churches, and various community organizations in several nations. It was pointed out in discussions in the House of Commons that the scope of activities of the Motion Picture Bureau, in the period before the NFB was formed, included "6,000 copies of films in active circulation in about 30 countries with about 40,000,000 [persons] in audience per year."[5]

When the proposal was made in Parliament to establish the NFB, Parliamentarians asked why it was necessary to replace the successful Motion Picture Bureau with a new organization. The government's response was it was important that it expand this medium in a way "that other countries are adopting [it] for the promotion and spreading of intelligence, information and . . . entertainment for the working out of certain national interests . . . to sell the idea of a country in terms of national perspective, so as to build up an increased interest and favourable sentiment towards a nation and its people, at home and abroad."[6]

The National Film Board (NFB)

The National Film Board was created by an Act of Parliament on 2 May 1939. For a period of nearly two years, the NFB functioned in an advisory and supervisory capacity with respect to government films, while the basic tasks of production and distribution remained with the Motion Picture Bureau. The beginning of the Second World War in September 1939, and Canada's participation in it within days of the British declaration of war against Germany, emphasized for the government the need for a unified system of film production, distribution, and control. It was particularly important that Canada be able to document the contribution its armed forces were making to the war effort. Thus, in 1941, the NFB assumed the filmmaking responsibility previously assigned to the Bureau and began to produce documentaries and newsreels both overseas and on the home front. The two wartime series that caught the country's attention were *The World in Action* (1942–45) and *Canada Carries On* (1940–59). These were shown in theatres across the nation.

NFB Mandate

The 1939 act does not specify a mandate for the NFB. Rather, it is in the description of the duties of the commissioner (chief executive officer) of the NFB that the responsibilities of the Board are enumerated. The fundamental responsibility of the commissioner is to advise on the production and distribution of films "designed to help Canadians in all parts of Canada to understand the ways of living and the problems of Canadians in other parts."[7]

While other co-ordinating, advisory, and developmental responsibilities are mandated in the act for the commissioner, it is the statement quoted above that set the tone for the board's functioning from the very beginning, and it continues to be central to its functioning today. The statement, when examined closely, clearly designates a persuasive role for the NFB, and we find in these formative years of the NFB a second effort (the CBC had been created three years earlier) to harness media to the service of the country. While the popularity of the Hollywood product in Canada continued (joined by British films following the end of the war in 1945), the development of the documentary tradition by the NFB at this time is historically noteworthy.

Following the conclusion of World War II, it became clear that the purposes of the NFB could be enlarged, and in 1950 a new act for the Board was approved by Parliament. The new (and current) act provides explanations for responsibilities in greater detail than found in the 1939 act, and we find specific purposes of the Board enunciated. For example, the primary purpose of the Board is to initiate and promote development of films "in the national interest." This particular mandate enlarges the earlier statement "to help Canadians understand each other." The act goes on to specify that NFB films should not only interpret Canada for Canadians, but interpret Canada for other nations, thus further enlarging the role of the NFB. The act charges the NFB with the role of representing the government of Canada in international discussions concerning filmmaking. In addition, the NFB is charged with becoming involved in research concerning the developing technology of film production, and "to make available the results thereof to persons engaged in the production of films."[8] This responsibility to make research results available has had a significant impact on the Canadian filmmaking community because the NFB has interpreted it as a need to offer its assistance and training facilities to independent filmmakers across Canada.

The National Film Board received a strong measure of endorsement from the Royal Commission on National Development in the Arts, Letters and Sciences (the Massey Commission) in its report released in 1951. The terms of reference of this royal commission emphasized that it was "to give encouragement to institutions which express national feeling, promote common understanding and add variety and richness to Canadian life . . . [so as] to recommend the most effective conduct in the national interest. . . . "[9]

Accordingly, the commission noted the "unique" achievements of the NFB in its production and distribution of documentary materials and strongly recommended that funds be made available to expand its overall activities. At the same time, the commission recommended that the NFB be made responsible for maintaining a national film collection to serve as a historical record. Further, the commission endorsed the work initiated by the NFB with respect to the research and experimental work done in the area of informational instruction.[10] We find in the commission's supportive statements for the NFB, not only a large measure of praise, but also a delineation of where achievements might be strengthened. For example, in the production of film for instructional purposes, the NFB, since picking up on commission recommendations, has contributed significantly to changing the balance between foreign and domestic audiovisual materials used in our schools: the dominance of foreign (particularly U.S.) audiovisual instructional materials used in schools has been lessened considerably.

When the NFB celebrated its fiftieth anniversary in 1989, NFB chair Joan Pennefather commented in the Board's *Annual Report* on the success of the NFB as a national institution:

The praise accorded the NFB by the Canadian public and the filmmaking community stands out as a highlight of this special year and must rightfully go to the creators, directors, producers, technicians, distribution and support staff, and film librarians of the NFB. Their work has secured the lasting impact of the NFB on the daily lives of Canadians.[11]

NFB Productivity

There are likely to be few twentieth-century Canadians who have been untouched by the NFB in some aspect of their lives—whether at school, at work, or in social gatherings; and, there can be little question that the NFB has fulfilled its mandate enunciated in 1939 and enlarged in 1950. The high quality of its films is recognized throughout the world and its marketing/distribution efforts have left few nations unfamiliar with NFB products.

In its over half-century history, the NFB has produced 17 000 audio-visual documents (slides, filmstrips, stills), including more than 6500 original films,[12] in addition to wartime newsreels, vignettes, adaptations, revisions, and film clips.[13] Over this same period it has received more than 3000 international awards, including almost a hundred awards in its anniversary year alone. Among the broad array of awards are fifty-two Oscar nominations and eight Oscars from the Academy of Motion Picture Arts and Sciences. As well, the Board received a ninth, honourary Oscar in 1989 in recognition of its "artistic, creative and technological excellence" over the years of its existence.[14] In accepting the award, the Minister of Communications, Marcel Masse,

indicated that he was doing so "on behalf of the 26 million people of Canada to whom the Film Board belongs."[15]

In the post-World War II years the NFB grew rapidly under the direction of John Grierson. While his industry and inspiration fuelled the energies of NFB staffers, it is acknowledged that his most significant contribution was his creative management in assembling a team of dedicated filmmakers whose productivity began to put Canada on the world map. When television appeared on the scene in 1952, the Board began producing films and series for television audiences, in addition to its continuing distribution of films to schools, libraries, and the like. The 1954–55 *Annual Report* indicates that all twenty-five Canadian television stations in exis-

John Grierson, 1898–1972, c. 1940 (National Archives of Canada/PA 120568)

tence at the time had used NFB products, for a total of 2574 bookings—the previous year's bookings were 704. Distribution of films in other countries in the same year totalled 2482, of which 223 were for telecasts.[16] Audience growth continued in the 1960s and 1970s, and the 1973–74 *Annual Report* indicates a total world audience for NFB films at an estimated 794 million.[17]

Challenges Setting In

Despite the recognition that the Board was receiving at home and abroad, conditions for the functioning of the NFB had been in the process of change since the mid-1950s. For example, television systems and CATV systems, in both English and French languages, had developed rapidly. As well, independent, commercial filmmakers represented an important new component in the industry. Such independents developed largely through the creativity and initiatives of individual producers, given the active encouragement by both the BBG and the CRTC for broadcasters to open their schedules to accommodate audiovisual materials produced by individuals. Further, school boards, colleges, universities, as well as provincial bodies of education, were developing their own media centres and were becoming increasingly committed to the production of instructional materials. Finally, the establishment of federal and provincial funding agencies, which were aimed at fostering independent

film and video productions, were investing millions of dollars in such enterprises. All of these developments, within the space of about a dozen years in the 1960s and 1970s, brought changes in attitudes in Canada towards an area of activity that earlier had been almost the exclusive territory of the NFB. Moreover, many people who had gained world-class quality production skills as employees of the NFB were moving into private industries and bolstering the quality of the private film production industry.

Co-operation between the NFB and the private film sector has been, according to NFB *Annual Reports*, at a consistently high level: government departmental film requirements (the responsibility of the NFB) are often contracted out to independent filmmakers; the NFB has served from its inception as an unofficial film training school for filmmakers in the country; collaborative production efforts with independents, too, have been successful ventures; and a formally constituted program established in 1980 continues to provide direct assistance, when needed, to private film producers. In 1985–86, for example, the Program to Assist Filmmakers and Films in the Private Sector provided assistance to 159 projects that might otherwise not have been completed.[18]

Elements of doubt about the NFB's own status and direction, however, were apparent in the annual reports of NFB commissioners. Budgetary restraints, if not cutbacks, created low levels of morale in the Board:[19] as a consequence, creativity suffered, and as the 1970–71 *Annual Report* indicates, the Board's questions and doubts about itself abound: " . . . the Film Board, much admired the world over, too little known in Canada where it is supported and yet not unconditionally believed in, was beginning to ask itself a lot of questions. . . . What now the Film Board? What for, and why?"[20]

This attitude of questioning its own role in a changing Canadian media environment was continued at that same time as the NFB was launching highly successful new initiatives: the world-renowned animation Studio A; the *Challenge for Change/Société Nouvelle* series on social issues in 1967; the Environmental Studio to stimulate ecological awareness in 1974–75; and the internationally acclaimed Studio D, a program staffed by women that has focussed on women's issues since it was established in 1974. The latter program produced well over 100 films, winning three Oscars for the NFB.

It was in the rise of the private filmmaking sector that the NFB recognized its dilemma: first, the Canadian market for films is relatively small, and it is questionable how readily that market would be able to absorb the products of both the private and public sectors; second, both the NFB and a large proportion of the independent producers (commercial and noncommercial) receive funding from the same government sources, which were subjected to severe budgetary constraints.

The Task Force on Broadcasting Policy in its *Report* released in 1986 introduces its discussion of the NFB as follows:

> This venerable Canadian institution is at a precarious moment, its future highly uncertain. It is buffeted on all sides, its enemies clamorous, its defenders uncertain, its board and staff divided, its paymaster—the government of Canada—anxious for assorted reasons to reduce its budget. . . . Hardly anyone, friend or foe, is satisfied with the status quo. Many wonder whether the Board has not simply outlived its usefulness.[21]

There are ample reasons for such a pessimistic evaluation, for when one examines the recent context within which the NFB has been functioning, the question posed by the task force concerning whether the NFB has outlived its usefulness seems highly germane.

For example, as the task force points out, part of the problem experienced by the NFB relates to distribution of its product in the light of an increasingly competitive audiovisual production industry in Canada. For example there is no obligation on the part of Canadian television networks, or anyone else for that matter, to carry NFB material. Second, and related, the CBC insists that the controversial themes on which the NFB focusses are not suitable for broadcasting, where the requirement is to present equal treatment to points of view. As the

BOX 8-1

Neighbours

While several NFB filmmakers have gained worldwide reputations, none has made as forceful an impact on the film industry as has animator Norman McLaren. In his over forty-year association with the NFB, McLaren made sixty animated films and collected nearly 500 international awards, including the highly regarded Oscar in 1952 for his antiwar statement, *Neighbours*. The *Vancouver Sun* commented on the animation genre as follows: " . . . [since] the legendary Norman McLaren first put the place [the NFB] on the cinematic map with an Oscar-winning short called *Neighbours*, the NFB has been known as the place to make animated films that are more than just cartoons for kids."[a] McLaren's colleagues have, over the years, described him as the "Picasso of modern film" and critics have commented on his style in light of Hollywood's Walt Disney: " . . . in McLaren's work the cloying cuteness we associate with Walt Disney is undercut by a tougher, uncompromising outlook."[b] "Norman was lucky; he came along at the right time, when Disney had established our expectations for animated films. He [McLaren] turned everything upside down, broke all the rules"[c] in designing unique approaches to animation.

The deeply implanted animation tradition established by McLaren prompted the NFB to fund an Opportunities Program that gives young animators a chance to demonstrate their creative skills in the animation genre. More recently, the NFB named its main administration building in Montreal in honour of McLaren.

[a] "The NFB: Where Animated Films are More Than Cartoons For Kids," *Vancouver Sun*, 24 February 1988, B6.
[b] Martin Hunter, "Animated Magnetism," *Canadian Art* 4 (Winter 1987), 76.
[c] Michael Mills, cited in ibid., 77.

director on television news and current affairs for the CBC commented, "We'd love to run the high quality material produced by the Board. . . . But the coverage has to be balanced and fair. Their [NFB] films tend to be self-indulgent and they don't understand that as a broadcaster, we can't be."[22] Further, the CBC insists that the handling of controversial material is a news and public affairs responsibility, rather than that of general programming.

It is also possible to identify other reasons why the NFB is no longer as dominant as it once was. In its early years it developed a reputation for high levels of artistry and skill in filmmaking. But today, it no longer holds a monopoly on such skills, as there are others in the industry who possess the same skills. As well, the

Norman McLaren, 1915–87 (Richard Robitaille/Courtesy NFB)

broadcasters to schedule the products of these independent producers. Also, film–video distribution methods have altered significantly in the past two decades. There was a time when it was a novelty for a school, a church, or a social organization to schedule film showings. The rapid development of television and cable systems now provides viewers with many more channels of information than they can possibly watch. In effect, the novelty of NFB showings has worn off.

strategy of government funding bodies, along with that of the CRTC, has been to encourage a private film industry in the country. As the federal government has provided money for independent production, the CRTC seeks commitments from

Yet another factor that must be considered is that the NFB developed its reputation, in large part, by programming that challenged the status quo. The Board captured the attention of society by its handling of controversial matters. It is probable that the Board has antagonized

Still from Neighbours showing the two actors of the film. (Courtesy NFB)

political authority by insisting on exploring controversial issues. For example its statement that it has produced a series of films "that may well be unique in the history of government-assisted film-making, in that they openly and purposefully criticize the agencies that support them,"[23] while courageous, might also be seen as arrogant and politically naive. In this same vein, two decades later an NFB spokesman continued to stress that the Board "has a role to play, which is to take a point of view. If we give up that role we're no different from anyone else."[24] Point-of-view commentary suggests clearly that alternative points of view are being denied expression. It would follow that those whose points of view are not being represented are not likely to look at the National Film Board with very much favour when, for example, the budgetary axe is about to fall.

Documentary or Drama?

One final point needs to be made regarding the apparent fall from favour of the National Film Board. In 1982, the NFB produced a film on Canada's World War I air hero, Billy Bishop, entitled *The Kid Who Couldn't Miss.* It was not long after the film's showing that writer/producer Paul Cowan found himself and the NFB mired in controversy. His film was called "infamous," "libelous trash," "scandalous," "misleading," and a "spurious twisting of fact." Such reaction is found in parliamentary debates of the period. As

well, many petitions were presented to Parliament, criticizing the film and its producer, pointing out that there were "more than thirty-five factual and historical errors . . . in this so-called documentary."

At issue was the portrayal of several incidents in the life of Billy Bishop, but one of these stood out. Bishop had been awarded the Victoria Cross (the Empire's highest military honour) for a raid on a German aerodrome. The film depicts Bishop as having fabricated the raid and falsely taking credit for something that Cowan stresses did not occur. In the film itself, Cowan uses the dramatic device of a supposedly real interview with Bishop's aircraft mechanic. In this "docudramatic" interview, the mechanic suggests that the bullet holes in Bishop's biplane were made by Bishop himself.

The furore created by the film forced the minister of communications to request an internal review of the matter by the NFB. The result of the review was that the Film Board concluded that Cowan had been scrupulous in his research and the film was a fair presentation of the exploits of Billy Bishop. The decision was that the NFB "would not withdraw or revise the film."[25]

This, however, was not to be the final word. Giving in to petitions, letters, and pressures from a variety of sources in the country, the NFB agreed to what was labelled "an uneasy compromise," wherein it would make a second documentary on Billy Bishop. In reporting on the NFB decision, the Montreal *Gazette* stated that *The Kid Who Couldn't*

Miss did not accurately record history and played "fast and loose with chronology." The newspaper also indicated that Cowan had admitted that some details were inaccurate. But perhaps the most significant statement of all concerning this unhappy episode came from François Macerola, film commissioner of the NFB: "when you use a docudrama to say something that can't be proved in a documentary, I have problems with that."[26] While Macerola's leaving the NFB four months prior to the end of his contract might be attributed to dissatis-

faction on the part of NFB staffers with the decision to produce a second Billy Bishop film, the point is immaterial. What is material is that Macerola's statement regarding historical fact and docudrama focusses on a significant question: does artistic freedom of expression permit historical revisionism? The debate is far from over, but it should be pointed out that it is issues such as this that have come to bear on the NFB and its practices.

A report from a Senate Subcommittee on Veteran's Affairs, which reviewed the NFB production on

---

Billy Bishop–The Kid Who Couldn't Miss

"*The Kid Who Couldn't Miss* has been the subject of controversy since its release in 1982. It is the fascinating account of how a brash kid from Owen Sound, Ontario named William Avery

(Billy) Bishop became one of the leading fighter pilots of World War I. *This film is a docudrama and combines elements of both reality and fiction. It does not pretend to be a biography of Billy Bishop. Certain characters have been used to express certain doubts and reservations about Bishop's exploits. There is no evidence that these were shared by the actual characters.* At age 23, Bishop became a hero and Canada's most decorated military figure. Excerpts from John Gray's play *Billy Bishop Goes to War*, featuring Eric Peterson, provide a thread throughout the film."

Billy Bishop, c. 1917 (National Archives of Canada/PA 1654)

(Description from NFB promotional material. Courtesy NFB)

Billy Bishop, was tabled in the Senate in April 1986. The report, while not condoning the "debunking" of the heroism of Billy Bishop, recommended that a disclaimer be attached to the film, identifying it as a "docudrama," that combined reality and fiction. At the same time the report was emphatic in stating that no more action ought to be taken on the matter, regardless of how upset war veterans and their organizations might be. The final recommendation epitomizes the "libertarian tradition" discussed in chapter 2:

> Real formal censorship must not be attempted in the present case and in the present circumstances—it would violate a principle dear to the Canadian sense of freedom and democracy notwithstanding the risks entailed. . . . *The Kid Who Couldn't Miss* will be forgotten long, long before the memory of Billy Bishop starts to fade.[27]

The Future

What is in the future for the NFB remains to be seen. However, with respect to whether the NFB has fulfilled its mandate as envisioned by pioneers of the Board, two points are clear: first there is little doubt that the Board has fulfilled its mandate concerning John Grierson's interpretation of the Board's role "to explain the shape of events and to create loyalties in relation to the developing scene"[28] (that is, to portray and interpret Canada for Canadians); second, it might very well be the case that developing technolo-

gies, with their multidimensional production and distribution modes, have simply overwhelmed and overtaken the NFB as a production enterprise. Thus, it is not necessarily a case of having outlived its usefulness, but that the times have changed with respect to film production in Canada. There is an implicit irony when one examines the history of the NFB from 1939 to the present: it becomes apparent that the NFB has been one of the major sources of technology and human resources that have contributed to the development of the arts and sciences of film and video production in the country. Thus, in fulfilling its mandate, the Board might well have brought about the beginning of its changing role in Canadian society. However, it may be in the continuation of this resource and research strength that the future of the NFB might be realized. The *Report of the Federal Cultural Policy Review Committee 1982* (Applebaum-Hébert Committee) makes precisely that recommendation to the Department of Communications: that the mandate of the NFB be altered so as to permit the assignment of current NFB responsibilities to other federal agencies, and that the new NFB mandate assign the Board to become a centre with training activities that "extend and complement those of Canada's educational institutions" as the NFB becomes "transformed into a centre for advanced research and training in the art and science of film and video production."[29]

Nevertheless, a strong sense of faith in the NFB continues to be found within the Board itself. Colin Low, who joined the NFB in 1945, has been associated with many of the Board's successes over the years, and has developed a reputation as one of the Board's most proficient documentary producers. In commenting upon the future of the Board, Low indicates that he has seen "this place [NFB] on the edge of being destroyed several times. I say that the moment this place is destroyed, it is going to have to be reinvented or you can write off the country."[30] Indeed, such persuasion about the centrality of the role of the NFB in a national identity context cannot be ignored. However, it is not the destruction of the NFB that is anticipated or preferred; what does appear to be inevitable is a shift in direction for the Board and a modification of its earlier role as Canada's foremost and central film production facility. The multitude of mass media/telecommunications developments in Canada since the 1940s in themselves have functioned as agents of change for the NFB.

The Canadian Film Development Corporation (CFDC)

While we may believe that the NFB succeeded in its mandate to project a positive image of Canada to other Canadians and to other nations, a nagging question persists concerning the image of Canada presented by the Hollywood feature film industry. Pierre Berton comments on the possible impact of Hollywood with respect to the Canadian image:

... the only consistent impression of us that outsiders have received in this century has come from the motion pictures. Books, newspapers, magazines, radio and television have made scarcely any impact beyond our own borders. It is the movies that have projected our image to the world and also, to a considerable extent, to ourselves. And by "movies" I don't mean the earnest and often brilliant documentaries of the National Film Board. I mean the commercial pictures that Hollywood made [about Canada], scores of which are still being seen on smaller screens.[31]

The image of Canada at home and abroad, Berton contends, has been "blurred, distorted, and hidden ... under a celluloid mountain of misconceptions."[32] Berton indicates that insofar as he was able to determine, in the years 1907 to 1975 there were 507 movies produced in the United States in which the plots were set either entirely or mainly in Canada. These films would have seen distribution not only in North America, but overseas as well.[33]

While the NFB has been aware of the impact of the Hollywood movie, there has not been a great deal that it could do to lessen the distorted image that such movies have presented. The NFB has had some suc-

TABLE 8–1
Country of Origin of Films Newly Released in Canada 1966–83

Year	No. of Features Released	Canadian	U.S.	French	U.K.	Italy	Other
1966	637	11	228	157	62	108	71
		1.7%	35.7%	24.6%	9.7%	16.9%	11.1%
1969	669	10	235	34	165	98	109
		1.4%	37.8%	5.0%	24.6%	14.6%	16.2%
1972	719	35	294	134	71	116	69
		4.8%	40.8%	18.6%	9.8%	16.1%	9.5%
1976	690	40	380	109	43	32	86
		5.7%	55.0%	15.7%	6.2%	4.6%	12.4%
1979	662	24	330	134	11	28	135
		3.6%	50.0%	20.2%	1.6%	4.2%	20.4%
1983	474	69	256	88	12	27	22
		14.6%	54.0%	18.6%	2.5%	5.7%	4.6%

Source: Data assembled from *Canada Year Book*, vols. 1966–1983. Data beyond 1983 are not included because they are not comparable due to changes in Statistics Canada reporting.

cess in the field of feature film production, either with films that it made on its own or in co-operation with other Canadian partners. However, feature film production involves huge budgetary expenditures that are often associated with considerable capital risk. In addition there is the problem of a near monopolistic distribution system over which Canadians have little control. These difficulties have not been easy to surmount. The Board would have to use a substantial portion of its production budget to mount even one successful feature film on its own.

Canadians have produced some remarkably successful feature films for distribution in Canada, the U.S., and elsewhere. However, when considered in relation to the overall number of feature films being exhibited in Canadian movie houses, the number of these films is relatively small.

Data show a slight gain in Canadian participation in the film distribution industry from 1966, the year that Canadian Film Development Corporation (Telefilm) was proposed. However, when a calculation is made of newly released features (as shown in table 8–1) as well as previously released features (as in table 8–2), a somewhat different pattern of exhibition appears.

Canadian productions, in this more realistic enumeration of Canadian materials in movie theatres, show a considerable increase from the calculation based only on new releases. The data also indicate that exhibition of Canadian features in pay TV and cable TV is nearly a fifth, as in theatrical showings. However, in free TV schedules, that is, regular over-the-air television where most films are shown, exhibition of Canadian films is light when compared to that of U.S.-produced materials.

Part of the problem leading to such low levels of distribution has been the reluctance of movie houses to exhibit films dealing with themes unique to Canada. On the other hand, films produced in Canada that mirror Hollywood production styles and that have little or nothing to do with a Canadian consciousness have achieved (and continue to achieve) respectable measures of financial success in both Canadian and American movie houses.[34] In effect, such films might be considered as simple extensions of Hollywood, and their production in Canada may be explained by the need to locate a film somewhere. These films (for example, those in the horror mode) are quite unrelated to the attempt that Canada has made to take hold of media and cultural industries to help establish a national identity.

Students of Canada's film industry, while not pointedly commenting on Berton's complaint about the Americanization of Canada's national image, underline the essence of the problem in assessing Canada's policies concerning film production: "Canada is perhaps the only country in the advanced capitalist world that did not develop its film production capability. Until 1968 there was hardly any indige-

TABLE 8-2
Country of Origin of Previously Released Films and Videos

1987–88	Theatrical N=833	Pay/Cable N=904	Free TV N=5761
Canadian	168 (20.1%)	154 (17.0%)	293 (5.0%)
U.S.	303 (36.3%)	365 (40.3%)	4927 (85.5%)
France	123 (14.6%)	129 (14.2%)	138 (2.3%)
U.K.	21 (2.5%)	216 (23.8%)	261 (4.5%)
Other	218 (26.1%)	40 (4.4%)	142 (2.4%)

Source: Statistics Canada, "Film and Video in Canada, 1987–88" *Culture Statistics* (Ottawa 1990), 39.

nous [feature] film production in Canada."[35]

The U.S. film industry was of such magnitude and influence that an indigenous industry in Canada was thwarted, and in the sense that a cinema ought to reflect in some way the people viewing it, threats to Canadian identity have emerged as a consequence. At the same time, it becomes apparent that Canada had been missing out on a huge, multi-million dollar industry—an industry that could have employed several thousand members of Canada's creative community. It thus became evident that there was an urgent need for Canada to initiate a film production industry on a scale for which the NFB at the time was not equipped.

CFDC Mandate

In presenting the issue to Parliament in June 1966, Judy LaMarsh, the minister responsible for cultural development, emphasized the problem of the bankruptcy of Canada in such a critical area as feature film production. She indicated that the government was prepared to make a major effort and financial investment, in this instance by establishing a Crown corporation that would focus directly on the task of developing a feature film industry in the country. As she promised to do, the minister introduced a bill creating the Canadian Film Development Corporation (CFDC), which became law in September 1967. The act creating the CFDC specifies, without adornment, that the objective of the corporation is "to foster and promote the development of a feature film industry in Canada."[36]

To permit the new corporation to achieve its objectives, the act created a fund that would allow the CFDC to help film producers overcome the onerous problem of capital risk: for example, the act permitted the corporation to make investment loans and co-operative investments, as well as to give awards for accomplishments and grants to promising filmmakers. There were also provisions for professional advice and assistance for administrative and distributive functions of feature-film production. The initial "bank" was set up as a constant fund of $10 million, and this amount has grown over the years.

In the initial twelve months of its existence, the CFDC gave formal consideration to fifty-two requests for financial assistance. The following year offers an example of the quick successes achieved by the CFDC regarding its mandate. In the first two years, an amount of $4 mil-lion was invested with private film-makers and the result was forty-four feature films (either completed or in some stage of near completion). Of these forty-four films seventeen were in French and twenty-seven in English.[37]

Significantly, the CFDC recognized in its first *Annual Report* that many benefits were to be gained by Canadians coproducing films with partners in other countries. Several of these benefits are worthy of note: first, by putting together teams of creative persons from various nations, Canadians would obviously benefit by gaining expertise; second, coproduction automatically ensured that the resulting product would be distributed in Canada and at least one other nation, if not more; third, coproduction also permitted a larger film budget, avoiding the need to resort to low-budget production; fourth, big-budget films permitted entry into big league competition; finally, coproduction assured Canadian investors of the likelihood of increased financial return, as well as the safety of a shared risk. Within a few years, the CFDC had fostered co-production agreements with film producers in at least ten countries through avenues provided by the Department of External Affairs.

Over the years, the success rate, in terms of the number of features produced and in terms of CFDC investment has varied, as is evident in table 8–3. However, a domestic feature film industry has clearly gotten off the ground, and the vision

TABLE 8–3
The CFDC and the Growth of the Canadian Feature Film Industry

Year	Number of New Films in Production	Combined Total Film Budget	CFDC Contribution
1968, '69, '70	44	$12 million	$4 million
(3 years)	27 Eng/17 Fr		
1975–76	18	$6.2 million	$2.9 million
(1 year)	11 Eng/7 Fr		
1978–79	27	$50 million	$5.6 million
(1 year)	17 Eng/10 Fr		
1982–83	24	$28.3 million	$2.5 million
(1 year)	10 Eng/14 Fr		

Source: Compiled from data in *Annual Reports* of the Canadian Film Development Corporation.

of such an industry employing many artists in Canada is slowly being realized.

The Lack of a Filmmaking Tradition

Concurrent with this development has been a corresponding increase in the quality of films produced. However, the CFDC experienced growing pains in the early years of its existence. Although the philosophy of the corporation was praised by Canadians, some of the early productions that resulted from its "bankrolling" were not. The lack of a filmmaking tradition other than that associated with the NFB was very apparent. Writing in Canadian periodicals and newspapers, film critics indicated some of this early disapproval. For example, a *Maclean's* review of one of the early CFDC-supported productions, *Another Smith for Paradise*, comments that "it might well be the most painful Canadian movie ever made. . . . The film is meant to be an attack on big business, tax evasion, and God knows what else. It misses all of its targets."[38] An earlier *Maclean's* reviewer referred to another CFDC-sponsored film, *Flick*, as "the dumbest movie I've ever seen. . . . A grade-Z potboiler . . . which is with any luck going to disappear suddenly and beyond memory's recall, leaving the CFDC a $150,000 out of pocket." The title of the review captures the author's opinion: "You Helped Finance the Creation of a Big, Dumb Frankenstein."[39]

The CRTC consistently promoted Canadian products and encouraged broadcasters to schedule Canadian features as a part of their programming. In this early period, the then Chairman of the CRTC, Pierre Juneau, indicated in a public address in Victoria, B.C., that during the week of his visit the B.C.

capital *TV Guide* had listed eighty-three feature films on television. He noted that of those films not one was Canadian, leading him to comment: "Whether you consider it a favourable or an unfavourable situation, one thing is sure: no other country in the world is in a comparable situation. Not the United Kingdom, not France, not Japan, not the United States."[40]

Juneau's comments notwithstanding, where efforts were made to schedule Canadian feature films, broadcasters found that audiences reacted highly negatively to them, particularly to films characterized by the liberal use of nudity and profanity. In one instance, at least, the general manager of a Canadian cable system indicated that despite the willingness of his organization to promote the growth of Canada's new film industry, "the audience comments received . . . have led us to close off this outlet for Canadian production."[41] Despite the many disappointments of filmmakers, the CFDC, distributors, and Canadian audiences, it was clear that problems were just the earmarks of a new industry: better things lay down the road.

It is possible to look back and identify some outstanding breakthroughs achieved in this early period that signalled the establishment of a quality-based Canadian film production industry. For example, the purchase by Paramount Pictures in 1974 of the U.S. distribution rights to *The Apprenticeship of Duddy Kravitz* marked a clear turning point. The film, based on Cana-dian novelist Mordechai Richler's novel of the same name, received high praise from New York and Washington film critics, and was produced on a budget of $900 000 with CFDC support. While the budget for the film was substantial, it was not huge and offered evidence of the ability of the Canadian creative community to produce world-class entertainment.

More recently, a 1991 independent study confirmed that Telefilm-supported features were beginning to enjoy some notable theatrical successes, particularly in Canada's French-language market. Citing the report, the *Globe and Mail* indicated that twenty-six features produced for the French-language market over the four-year period 1986–90 gained a box office average of over half a million dollars. Two films in particular are cited in the report: *Jesus of Montreal* and *Cruising Bar*. These earned more than $3 million in their French-language versions.[42]

Noting the success of *Jesus of Montreal* in gaining a Hollywood Oscar nomination for Denys Arcand, the *Globe and Mail* commented in an editorial on the achievements of Arcand and other colleagues who have committed their creative energies to producing feature films in Canada:

> His is an original voice, as *Jesus of Montreal* reminded and his success has come from the willingness of people with money (including government agencies) to let that voice be heard. We write those sentences not only in praise of Mr. Arcand, but

in a general spirit of hope for the Canadian feature film industry. . . .[43]

The editorial goes on to point out a prominent characteristic of some current Canadian films, remarking that " . . . it seems Canada has witnessed a series of entertaining, often intellectually stimulating films recently, grounded firmly and unapologetically in Canadian settings."[44] Complaints in the recent past from regulators of Canada's broadcasting industry have been that films produced in Canada have been for the most part unapologetically grounded in U.S. settings.

Some earlier demands by filmmakers concerning distribution of their products should be noted. As we have seen, Canadian films were not at first enthusiastically greeted by cinema owners or by broadcast-

ers. Nevertheless, due to a prescribed Canadian content quota for TV stations and networks, television has served as an outlet for Canadian feature productions. Vocal demands for similar regulatory measures for cinemas were raised and film industry practitioners emphasized that "if Canadian films are to become a reality to the Canadian audiences, it is essential that they gain entry to the mainstream of commercial distribution. The only way to ensure that they do is to institute a content quota."[45]

Further demands were made by performers' associations and unions and these included proposals that imported films be regulated into making contributions in terms of a share of their gross earnings to fund production of Canadian films.[46] Negotiations concerning

---

BOX 8–3

Jesus of Montreal

Denys Arcand, director of *Jesus of Montreal*, has achieved success in Quebec cinema over the past twenty-five years. The highly acclaimed *Jesus of Montreal* is his sixth feature. His earlier film *The Decline of the American Empire* (1986) was also much praised internationally.[a]

In its 1989–90 *Annual Report*, Telefilm Canada indicates that in 1989 it sent 326 Canadian-produced films to 101 film festivals and events held all over the world. "The film *Jesus of Montreal* alone obtained ten international awards, including the Jury Prize at the 1989 Cannes International Film Festival. It also won 12 Genie awards in Toronto, was nominated for Best Foreign Language Film at the Oscars in Hollywood, and is highly successful at the Box Office."[b]

---

[a] Telefilm Canada, *Feature Film Catalogue*, 1989.
[b] Telefilm Canada, *Annual Report 1989–1990* (Montreal, 1990), 14.

Lothaire Bluteau as Jesus of Montreal. (Max Films)

audience support of the industry has not been easy to determine. Canadians, when polled, said they favoured a fixed quota system calling for the showing of eight weeks of Canadian films every two years. The breakdown of the response was 65 percent in favour, 17 percent opposed, and 18 percent undecided. In a follow-up question, Canadians were asked whether they would be interested in actually going to see a Canadian film: 37 percent they would, 47 percent said they would not.[48] The question of establishing a quota system for Canadian films is still being considered.

Telefilm and CBPDF

A significant development in the successful evolution of a Canadian entertainment feature film industry occurred in 1983. While the CFDC mandate in our view had been fulfilled, the need to build on CFDC successes was apparent in light of the continuing threat to Canada's cultural identity posed by foreign content. As a result the CFDC mandate was enlarged to include a broad range of film and video productions other than feature films. Specifically, the minister of communications indicated that there was a dearth of Canadian drama, children's programming, and variety programs showcasing Canadian talent in the schedules of Canada's TV stations. At the same time, there was no shortage of quiz shows, talk shows and the like to fill out Canadian content quotas. Thus, the Canadian Broadcast Program Devel-

both of these measures have continued from the 1970s and efforts have been made to introduce measures to ensure distribution of Canadian films co-operatively rather than through formal government regulation. Such measures have never been established and Canadian filmmakers are very much aware that competitiveness in the public market dictates the number of Canadian films shown.

An important further contribution to the development of the feature film industry was made when, in 1974, federal income tax regulations were amended to allow a capital cost allowance. This allowed investors to shelter part of their incomes by investing in the film industry. In a sense, the offering of this tax shelter represented a second level of support by taxpayers to the developing industry.[47]

While the industry developed rapidly due to the infusion of government funding, the extent of opment Fund (CBPDF) was established with an initial fund of $34 million. The fund was to be administered by the CFDC. In the following year, so as to accommodate the increased scope and variety of CFDC activities, the minister approved a change in name of the corporation to Telefilm Canada, the name under which it currently operates.[49]

In its 1989–90 *Annual Report*, Telefilm indicated that during that reporting year it had injected the largest sum ever into the Canadian film and television industries—a total of $166.5 million. That total represented parliamentary appropriations (about 90 percent), as well as reimbursements of advances made to film producers and revenues from productions (about 10 percent).[50] In the same report, Telefilm announced a new, detailed action plan, which defines its main goals for the near future:

- to help the film and television industry to define and reach its public through improved marketing, thus realizing greater impact and financial viability;
- to give priority to high-quality productions of original content that depict the diversity of Canadian cultural, intellectual, and creative life;
- to consolidate its partnership with the industry by supporting the development of strong and viable companies and by encouraging close collaboration between producers, distributors, and broadcasters.[51]

The *Annual Report* of Telefilm Canada for 1988–89 reflects the increased scope of the corporation. With increased budgets, Telefilm, in the reporting year, injected a total of $145.1 million into Canadian film, television, and video industries. In addition, the report indicates that in the following year, Telefilm would have at its disposal an additional $16.5 million for television production alone. In all, these expenditures represent a very significant leap from the original $10 million that had been identified as the CFDC "bank" when the corporation was first established. The executive director of Telefilm comments that "considering the belt-tightening implemented by the Canadian government, one must conclude that it has a great deal of confidence in the future of the industry."[52]

Conclusion

In Telefilm Canada's report to the 1986 Task Force on Broadcasting Policy a significant point is made concerning production financing and broadcaster participation. The point is related to a statement made by secretary of state Judy LaMarsh in earlier parliamentary debates on establishing the CFDC. That point was that the commercial film industry that was being developed must eventually prove itself commercially viable and that the products of the industry must eventually prove good enough to merit exhibition anywhere. The Telefilm report to the task force indicates that in Canada less than 10 percent of Canadian content in prime time for the five major networks (CBC, Radio-Canada, CTV, Global and Tele-Metropole) comes from independent Canadian producers, whereas in the U.S., in France, and with respect to Britain's Channel 4 network, up to 80 percent of such content comes from independent producers. The report concludes that the commitment of Canadian broadcasters in devoting less than 10 percent of their prime-time schedules to independently produced Canadian content is not enough to create the necessary economic conditions to guarantee the financial success anticipated by the independent film production industry in the country.[53] It becomes evident, then, that regulatory bodies for broadcasting have a greater role to play in the further successes of Telefilm.

Nevertheless, a commonly held view in Canada is that, given the massive degrees of competition in all facets of filmmaking and distribution, the original planners of CFDC/Telefilm have produced notable results—a firm and solid base for filmmaking in Canada has been established. At the same time, it's evident that some major problems still need to be overcome. A recent assessment of the successes of the Canadian film industry and Telefilm concurs. Stephen Godfrey's article "Telefilm: A Big Boon, a Bigger Bust," indicates that although Canadian feature films backed by Telefilm derive about 80 percent of their annual budgets from government

services, and despite government tax shelters for investors, Canadian features account for still only 3 percent of the screen market.[54]

The essential problem in this instance is that Canadians are not in control of the distribution modes for Canadian film. Canadian film producers find themselves in a situation where there is little competition, if any, in film exhibition and distribution in the North American market: such control continues to remain in the hands of the Motion Picture Export Association of America.[55]

While there have been pressures placed on the Department of Communications to institute quotas for Canadian movie houses, this has not yet taken place. Nor have attempts to negotiate entry of Canadian films into movie houses been successful. What has become abundantly clear is that Canadian films, if they are to become a significant part of movie theatres' schedules, will need to compete for audiences, openly and unabashedly, with U.S. films. This means, of course, that the Canadian industry, spearheaded by Telefilm as it has been in the past, will need to make stronger attempts to achieve more effective distribution than has been apparent to date.

In 1989–90 Telefilm injected $24.8 million into the distribution, marketing, and "versioning" (for example, dubbing dialogue in different languages) of feature films and TV programs, both in Canada and abroad. And for the second consecutive year, Telefilm has stepped up its marketing and distribution strategies on behalf of the films in which it has invested taxpayers' money. For the future Telefilm indicates that it will be more selective in its financing planning so as to "be able to give preference to the production and distribution companies with the best record. . . ." Thus, producers with established track records, companies where "previous productions have been good, well-managed and commercially profitable" are likely to be those singled out to advance the interests of the Canadian film industry.[56]

Associated with that approach, Telefilm has indicated that henceforth, it will want to see some return on its investment with filmmakers more rapidly than in the past. Whereas Telefilm has often been last on the list to recoup investments, and "in some cases had to wait seven years before seeing any money," the funding agency will now want to see some return on its money "within a year."[57]

What appears to be clear is that Telefilm Canada has evolved from its earlier strategy of trying to develop an industry from the ground, to a more professional stance of challenging the North American industry on its own terms with a clear view to ensuring the continuation of a firmly established, financially viable Canadian film industry.

Notes

1. Garth Jowett and James M. Linton, *Movies as Mass Communication*, 2nd ed. (Newbury Park, CA.: Sage Publications, 1989), 16.

2. C. Rodney James, *Film as a National Art: NFB of Canada and the Film Board Idea* (New York: Arno Press, 1977), 4.

3. Ibid.

4. Ibid., 29.

5. Canada, House of Commons, *Debates*, 13 March 1939, 1850.

6. Ibid., 1845.

7. Canada, National Film Act 1939 (Ottawa: King's Printer, 1939), 9(a).

8. Canada, National Film Act 1950 (Ottawa: King's Printer, 1950), 9(a), (b), (c).

9. Canada, *Report of the Royal Commission on National Development in the Arts, Letters and Sciences 1949-1951* (Ottawa: King's Printer, 1951), xvii.

10. Ibid., 308–12.

11. Canada, National Film Board, *Annual Report 1988-1989* (Montreal, 1989), 8.

12. Statistics Canada, *Canada Year Book 1990* (Ottawa: Supply and Services, 1990), 15–17

13. Bruce Blackadar, "The National Film Board At 50," *Toronto Star*, 29 April 1989, F1.

14. "Davis, Kline Win Oscars for Supporting Roles," *Gazette* (Montreal), 30 March 1989, E1.

15. Ibid.

16. Canada, National Film Board, *Annual Report 1954–1955* (Montreal, 1955), 7.

17. Canada, National Film Board, *Annual Report 1973–1974* (Montreal, 1974), 5.

18. Canada, National Film Board, *Annual Report 1985–1986* (Montreal, 1986), 4.

19. Canada, National Film Board, *Annual Report 1969–1970* (Montreal, 1970), 3.

20. Canada, National Film Board, *Annual Report 1970–1971* (Montreal, 1971), 5.

21. Canada, Department of Communications, *Report on the Task Force on*

Broadcasting Policy 1986 (Ottawa: Supply and Services, 1986), 345.

22. Lorena Bekar, "Strained Bedfellows," *Broadcaster* 47 (August 1988): 25.

23. Canada, National Film Board, *Annual Report 1969–1970*, 7.

24. Blackadar, "The National Film Board," F1.

25. Canada, House of Commons, *Debates*, 4 December 1984, 1244.

26. Mark Abley, "Why the NFB is Remaking Its Film of WWI Hero Billy Bishop," *Gazette* (Montreal), 20 March 1988, A1–A4. Similar concerns were raised in reviews of Oliver Stone's film *JFK.* See Lance Morrow, "When Artists Distort History," *Time* 138, 23 December 1991, 68.

27. Senator Jean Le Moyne, "The Case of 'The Kid Who Couldn't Miss'," *Canadian Parliamentary Review* 10 (Winter 1987–88): 5. Also see Canada, Senate, *Production and Distribution of the National Film Board Production "The Kid Who Couldn't Miss"* (Ottawa: Supply and Services, 1986).

28. Canada, National Film Board, *Annual Report 1977–1978* (Montreal, 1978), 5.

29. Canada, Department of Communications, *Report of the Federal Cultural Policy Review Committee 1982* (Ottawa: Supply and Services, 1982), 264.

30. "Colin Low Sees Future for the NFB and the Documentary," *Cinema Canada* 165 (July–August 1989): 34.

31. Pierre Berton, *Hollywood's Canada: The Americanization of Our National Image* (Toronto: McClelland and Stewart, 1975), 12.

32. Ibid.

33. Ibid., 16.

34. See Manjunath Pendakur, "Canadian Feature Films in the Chicago Theatrical Market, 1978-1981: Economic Relations and Some Public Policy Questions," in *Current Research in Film: Audiences, Economics, and Law*, ed. Bruce A. Austin, vol. 2 (Norwood, NJ: Ablex Publishing Co., 1986), 194–97.

35. Manjunath Pendakur, "Film Policies in Canada: In Whose Interest," *Media, Culture and Society* 3 (April 1981): 155.

36. Canada, Parliament, the Canadian Film Development Act, 10.1.

37. Canada, Canadian Film Development Corporation, *Annual Report 1970–1971* (Montreal, 1971), 4.

38. John Hofsess, "What Did Canadians Do To Deserve This?" *Maclean's*, August 1972, 68.

39. William Cameron, *Maclean's*, June 1970, 80.

40. Pierre Juneau, Address to the Chamber of Commerce, Victoria, B.C., March 1972.

41. "TV Station Bans Canadian Movies," *Toronto Star*, 30 June 1972, 33.

42. Christopher Harris, "Telefilm Study Confirms Market Differences," *Globe and Mail*, 26 July 1991, C8.

43. "Original Voices in Canadian Films," *Globe and Mail*, 29 March 1990, A6.

44. Ibid.

45. "Content Ruling Urged For Films," *Charlottetown Guardian*, 18 September 1972, 22.

46. Association of Canadian Television and Radio Artists (ACTRA), "Policy for the Seventies," (Toronto, 1973), 27.

47. *Report of the Federal Cultural Policy Review Committee*, 250.

48. Canada, Canadian Film Development Corporation, *Annual Report 1973–1974* (Montreal, 1974), 8.

49. See, Canadian Film Development Corporation, *Annual Report 1982–1983* (Montreal, 1984), 5;

also see, Canadian Film Development Corporation, *Annual Report 1983–1984*, 4.

50. Telefilm Canada, *Annual Report 1989–1990* (Montreal, 1990), 7.

51. Ibid.

52. Telefilm Canada, *Annual Report 1988–1989* (Montreal, 1989), 11.

53. Telefilm Canada, "Financing Canadian Television Production: A Paper Presented by Telefilm Canada to the Caplan-Sauvageau Task Force Committee" (December 1985), 26.

54. Stephen Godfrey, "Telefilm: A Big Boon, a Bigger Bust," *Globe and Mail*, 5 May 1990, C1.

55. Manjunath Pendakur, *Canadian Dreams and American Control: The Political Economy of the Canadian Film Industry* (Detroit: Wayne State University Press, 1990), 252–53.

56. Telefilm Canada, *Annual Report 1989–1990*, 14.

57. "$163 Million Invested in Movie Industry Telefilm Says," *Globe and Mail*, 30 August 1991, D6.

C H A P T E R 9

The Persuasion Industries

Introduction

In studies assessing the development of modern societies, a number of interrelated components have been identified: industrialization, urbanization, literacy, education, technological inventiveness as well as the effectiveness of institutions providing for our social and physical well-being, such as schools and hospitals. One component highly indicative of modernity tends to be either overlooked or underemphasized: the existence of highly sophisticated advertising and public relations industries. What we all recognize is that in modern societies we are all heavy consumers of goods and services. Furthermore, when we examine the persuasion industries—advertising and public relations—we find they are part and parcel of industrialization: the day that an individual produced two units of a product rather than the one that was needed was the day the persuasion industries were born.

Before we distinguish between advertising and public relations functions, it is necessary to point out one basic characteristic they share: the central concern of each industry is to link the interests of the "account" (the term refers to product/producer/seller, etc.) with the interests of the consumer.

Within this common framework, advertising agencies tend to be product/service oriented and focus on getting paid messages to the consumer, either in mass or segmented groups. Public relations firms, on the other hand, are producer/organization oriented and focus on achieving "positive press" (by means of press releases and/or press conferences) for the organizations they represent. Thus, their targets tend to be mass media organizations. While these are not hard and firm distinctions, they do tend to identify what is unique about each industry.

At the same time, it is important to understand that advertising/public relations industries do not function in society on their own. They are part of a broad socio-economic structure that begins with the purpose of producing a company's existence: to sell its product. Marketing textbook writers from the earliest days to the present refer to "the four P's"—Product, Price, Place, Promotion.[1]

(a) Product: a decision is made that a particular product or service is needed by some identifiable group in society.

(b) Price: the product, in order to produce profit for the manufacturer and to achieve acceptability with consumers, needs to be strategically priced.

(c) Place: a determination is made by the company as to where and in what manner the product is to become available.

(d) Promotion: broadly, promotion refers to activities that advise society about the product, perhaps its price and its place, and that enhance the transfer of the product/service to consumers.

There are four elements that may be part of the promotion process:

(i) merchandising: in-store aids to selling;

(ii) personal selling: usually direct contact by a company's representative to a would-be consumer;

(iii) public relations; and

(iv) advertising.

Thus, advertising and public relations can be seen to be essential parts of the entire marketing process.

Why Study Advertising and Public Relations?

In the first Canadian edition of their text, *Advertising*, Wright, Winter, Zeigler, and O'Dea begin their discussion by considering the reasons the industry is worthy of study. Such an examination is important here as well because it provides an opportunity for understanding the characteristics of the advertising/public relations industries.

First, the authors indicate that advertising is a "highly visible force" in society, one that affects us all on a daily basis. Second, advertising (and public relations) are influential in shaping popular standards. Third, as consumers who react to advertising messages, we should be aware of how the industry functions and how messages are designed. And fourth, advertising is having a recognizable impact on the international community.[2] Indeed, on this latter point the MacBride UNESCO Report of 1980 comments that:

> Advertising is seen by many as a threat to the cultural identity and self-realization of many developing countries; it brings to many people alien ethical values; it may deviate consumer demands in developing countries to areas which can inhibit development priorities; it affects and can often deform ways of life and life-styles.[3]

As one reads the UNESCO comment on the impact of advertising on the international community, it is possible to speculate on whether the citation also applies to the Canadian community in light of Canada's proximity to the United States.

The Impact of the Persuasion Industries on Society

There are many reasons in addition to those cited above why the advertising and public relations industries merit close examination. The persuasion industries not only shape popular standards, but they are also deliberately persuasive; they are value-laden message systems. As they provide us with information about products and services, they identify and justify from their own perspective both social aspirations and behavioural directions for us. And, because there is so little to counteract those massive information systems, we usually respond to messages directed at us. As well, the industries' volume of activity is huge and influential. While the dollar value of public relations activities is difficult to assess because the passing on of information to newspapers, for example, is not normally paid for, it is possible in the case of advertising to document the massive dollar expenditure involved. Table 9–1 indicates that in the 1980s, the industry in Canada more than doubled its gross revenues.

TABLE 9-1	
Gross Advertising Revenues	
Year	Revenues
1980	$ 4.01 billion
1982	4.93
1984	6.13
1986	7.24
1988	8.43
1990	10.86

Source: *A Report on Advertising Revenues in Canada* (Toronto: Maclean Hunter Research Bureau, 1987 and 1991).

The data cited in this table also point out that advertising is a growth industry. Further, this growth may be identified in three different ways: by dollar volume activity; by human activity (i.e., number of people employed in the industries); and the scope of industry activity in terms of involvement in all facets of a community's life. It should be noted, too, that the patterns of growth that we have discussed for Canada are also true in the United States, where over the same period gross advertising revenues increased from $66.6 billion to $118.8 billion. Per capita expenditure in Canada in 1978 stood at $127; a decade later, the figure had increased to $305.[4]

In Canada we accept that one of the bases of our pluralistic society is the persuasion process. During elections, for example, political parties and candidates compete to persuade us to support them. By studying advertising and public relations, we are in a position to gain a better understanding of the persuasion process, as citizens of any pluralistic society should.

Since the beginning of the 1980s, the federal government has become one of the largest advertising "accounts" in the country, as measured by dollar expenditure. In 1990, only the Thomson Group (The Bay, Zellers, Towers) and General Motors spent more on advertising than the federal government.[5] In 1990 its expenditure was measured at $67.3 million, not including money spent on political campaign advertising. It is important that as receivers of that huge volume of information from our federal government, we should understand the processes involved.

At the same time that the advertising/public relations industries present their messages, we are aware that their prime intent is to link consumers with products and services. Nevertheless, it is obvious that there have been some unintended consequences stemming from messages sent by the industries. For example, sex-role stereotyping and ethnic stereotyping, which provide the basis for some advertisements, have helped perpetuate sexist and racist attitudes. It is commendable that regulatory authorities have moved to enforce alteration of such messages, but we have to be constantly on the alert for such abuses in advertising.

Finally, in this brief examination of the characteristics of advertising and public relations, it is important to understand that with the exception of some public broadcasting activities (such as CBC Radio) and some few publications that exist as a result of government subsidy, mass media in Canada depend upon advertising for their existence. The relationship between mass media and advertising is one of complementarity, where each depends upon the other.

Factors Contributing to the Growth of Advertising

In an advertising course offered at the University of Windsor in 1989, students were asked to respond to a questionnaire. They agreed that advertising tended to distort the process of product selection (81 percent) and that advertising failed to present the true picture of the products advertised (88 percent). Nevertheless, 85 percent of these students indicated that they approved of advertising either "somewhat" or "a lot." While the figures cited here for university students are slightly higher than those recorded for other groups, there is consistency of response in whatever group in society is studied. Even if we concur that advertising tends to distort the information portrayed, we tend to approve of the existence of the industry. It is a curious paradox, but one that helps us appreciate why the persuasion industries today enjoy such large measure of success and continue to grow.

In their book, *Advertising: Its Role in Modern Marketing*, Dunn and Barban identify a set of social forces that contributed to the growth of advertising in the United States.[6] Reference to some of these points is appropriate here, since, as generalizations, they apply to the Canadian context as well.

First, twentieth-century technological developments have made possible more "units" of production. Since more product has had to be sold, more advertising has been needed. Rapid industrialization (measured in Gross National Product), has in fact been paralleled by a corresponding increase in advertising expenditures. The expansion of highway systems and the concomitant increase in automobile and truck use have created an effective means for manufacturing industries to distribute their products. This change has led to the construction of large, centralized production centres, which have added a measure of efficiency to productivity and distribution. More cars have also made it possible for more people to go shopping and in so doing to part with their money. As well, the rapid spread of consumer credit has been a key factor contributing to sales increases. We can speculate, then, that as the manufacturing sector (which now has accommodated robotics' assembly lines) continues to develop, the level of productivity will continue to increase, as will manufacturers' need for advertising. Thus, advertising growth is clearly linked with production capacity.[7]

The twentieth century has also seen the continuing evolution of a relatively prosperous middle class, with a corresponding growth in disposable income. It is, of course, this money available after basic necessities are looked after that is of particular interest to advertisers. It is sadly true that those who exist below or at the poverty level are becoming more numerous in North America. It is increasingly difficult for these people to live in a society that so heavily emphasizes the upscale lifestyle promoted by advertising. But most of the middle class, to whom advertising is generally aimed, have some disposable income.

Professional advertising organizations have been important as well in the growth of the persuasion industries. As Dunn and Barban point out, such organizations institutionalized and professionalized the industries. In Canada, organizations such as the Canadian Advertising Advisory Board, the Canadian Advertising Research Foundation, the Association of Canadian Advertisers, as well as several others associated with individual mass media, have all played a role in fixing a firm place in society for the persuasion industries. The prime concerns of such specialized associations are ethics and responsibility or product research.

In addition to the social forces identified by Dunn and Barban, it is important to consider the increases in levels of education in our society as these have affected advertising. Such increases have led very rapidly to two important considerations:

(a) the rise of consumer activism (which we shall discuss in the following chapter) and (b) the rise of criticism and informed commentary regarding advertising's place in society.

At the same time, the inclusion of advertising in curricula of business schools as well as in various disciplines in the humanities and the social sciences has increased our knowledge of the factors basic to successful advertising. Since the Second World War, the study of propaganda and communications theory, combined with the development of social science research methods, have contributed to advertisers' knowledge about consumers, thus providing a substantial stimulus to innovative retail methods and to the creative design of advertising messages.

Finally, changing work-force patterns have led to a growth in the numbers and kinds of retail shoppers. There are more men shopping today than ever before; as well,

the female teenager has become an important family shopper. The advertising industry has adapted accordingly to reach these markets.

Advertising's growth is evolutionary, in the same sense that society itself is dynamic and changing. Further, each social change—urbanization, for example—is likely to be reflected in an operational change within the advertising industry. While this discussion of the growth of advertising cannot be said to be complete, our purpose here has been to identify some of the dynamics of society as they are reflected in the advertising industry.

Definitions and Descriptions

Public Relations

Public relations (PR) as an industry, as indicated earlier, is a companion to advertising in that the end purpose is the same: to relate the inter-

TABLE 9-2
Advertising Revenues by Media

	$ Value (1990)		% Change from 1989
Daily Newspapers	2.30	Billion	+8.5
Catalogues and Direct Mail	2.23	Billion	+3.5
Television	1.45	Billion	+5.5
Directories	1.10	Billion	+12.1
Outdoor	764.00	Million	+6.4
Radio	751.00	Million	+4.7
Weekly Newspapers	690.00	Million	+5.2
General Magazines	252.00	Million	-0.8
Business/Farm Press	176.00	Million	-3.3

Source: *Advertising Revenues in Canada* (Toronto: Maclean Hunter Research Bureau, 1991).

ests of the client to the interests of consumers. It is in their operational methods that the two industries differ. The British Institute of Public Opinion indicates that PR is the "deliberate, planned, and sustained effort to establish and maintain mutual understanding between an organization and its publics."[8] This definition, while accurate, offers few specifics regarding the operations of public relations firms. A working definition has been adopted by the World Assembly of Public Relations practitioners, which offers an important description of PR behaviour as "the art and social science of analyzing trends, predicting their consequences, counselling organization leaders, and implementing planned programs of action which will serve both the organization's and the public's interest."[9] In looking at the public relations practitioner, we can summarize appropriate tasks in the following manner. The practitioner, as a counsellor to management in industry, clearly has a responsibility for being well informed about current events. Equally important, however, the practitioner must possess superior research skills, both quantitative (statistical) and qualitative (case study or history), in order to be able to extract information from the environment as needed. Further, the practitioner must possess sensitivity to public opinion and be able to translate society's opinions into sound advice to suit the purposes of a client. Finally, the practitioner must be able to project to society the goals and policies of the client organization. In carrying out these tasks (very often in the difficult circumstance of a public embarrassment for a firm), the PR practitioner must be able to rely on a sharply honed set of interpersonal and communication skills.

What is often overlooked by those who discuss public relations activities is that the practitioner always has two publics with which to contend. The first (and this is the area of activity often given inadequate attention) is the "internal public," that is, employees and associates of the organization. The tried-and-true maxim of public relations continues to be as important today as it has ever been: happy employees are well-informed employees. One of the sins of public relations practice is allowing employees to learn of events concerning that organization either from a neighbour or the news media. There is no difficulty in understanding how employees can quickly become disenchanted with their employers if the organization operates with an ineffective internal information system. Conversely, well-informed employees can be highly effective spokespersons for an organization's policies, its operational methods, and its products or services. The second public of import to the PR practitioner is the "mass" or "external public." In order to get across an effective message to this audience, the PR practitioner must be honest and candid. By and large, the modern-day public relations industry has learned this lesson. Less scrupulous public relations officers find to their sorrow that deviousness, subterfuge, or any warping of the truth are very likely to become quickly apparent. Because of the increased standard of education of the public, and because society is now supported in its quest for information by legal instruments—access-to-information acts, for example—the only route for public relations strategists in any organization should be the "high road" of truth.

Advertising

Advertising is a paid persuasive message about a product or service that is distributed on behalf of an account (a sponsor) conveyed in appropriately selected media, and aimed at a particular group of would-be consumers.

Advertising operates on two broad levels in Canada: "national" and "retail" accounts. A national account is distinguished from a retail account mainly by its mode and range of distribution. General Motors, for example, distributes its products nationally, and thus is a national account. Quality Cars Sales Ltd., however, which sells Chevrolets in a local community, is considered to be a retail or local account. Figure 9–1 illustrates the differences of each.

The parts of the advertising industry are apparent in the "information flow" of the national account. First, the sponsoring company is likely to have its own advertising department, with an advertising manager, and decisions regarding advertising needs are made at the company level on the basis of overall marketing strategies. When a specific advertising need is determined, a company will seek out the services of an advertising agency. Consultations between company officers and agency representatives will clarify communications needs (message design, audiences, the appropriate media to use, and timing). The agency is then likely to choose the appropriate media to carry the message with the assistance of media group representatives (those whose job it is to sell space and time for

FIGURE 9–1

National and Retail Advertising Accounts

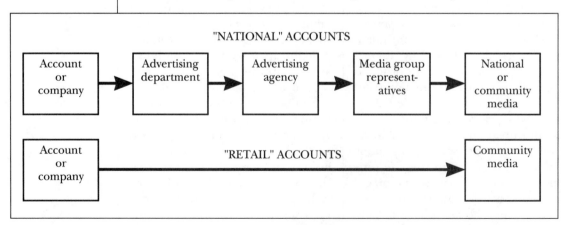

media organizations). Such organizations function in communities across the country. "Bookings" are made for time and for space in selected media, and advertising messages, which have been filtered through a comprehensive testing process, are then scheduled.

At the retail or local level, an account deals directly with representatives of community media. While the costs are not necessarily the same from community to community, or from medium to medium, the cost of placing an advertisement at the retail level is likely to be 15 to 25 percent less than would be the case for national accounts.

It is possible to identify national and retail account preferences for advertising media, with national accounts predominantly using television, and retail accounts preferring newspapers and radio.

Types of Advertising

There are four types of advertising, intended to reach certain audience/consumer groups:

- General consumer advertising: commercials and advertisements aimed at consumers wherever they might be.
- Trade advertising: overtures made by the account to retailers or wholesalers who would be distributors of the account's products or services.
- Industrial advertising: overtures made by product suppliers to

TABLE 9–3
Media Preferences of National and Retail Accounts

Type of Media	National Accounts	Retail Accounts
	(Media Expenditures)	
Radio	23.9%	76 %
Television	78.1	21.7
Daily Newspapers	21.5	78.4
Community Newspapers	6.6	93.3

Source: Compiled from data available in *Canadian Advertising Rates and Data* (April 1990).

manufacturers. For example, tire manufacturers make direct sales presentations to automobile plants, as do body-trim parts plants to automobile assembly plants.
- Professional advertising: messages that are aimed at certain professions, for example, doctors, dentists, architects, lawyers, and educators.

Our purpose in identifying these four kinds of advertising is to point out that not all advertising is placed in the mass media. It is evident from the above that often money is better spent in directing messages to specific audiences through non-mass media channels.

The decision of which medium or strategy to use in an advertising campaign is based on a rule of thumb referred to as "cost per thousand." It is applied at the start of an advertising campaign to identify the medium and strategy that will garner the largest audience for each dollar spent.

The following example demonstrates the cost-per-thousand formula (abbreviated as CPM):

Suppose that a thirty-second commercial in a Super Bowl network telecast would cost the advertiser $675 000. The anticipated audience for the event is 120 million. The calculation of CPM, then, involves dividing the cost of the commercial by the audience (in groups of 1000), resulting in a CPM of $5.60 (that is, 1000 people are reached for the cost of $5.60.)[10] The high cost of an advertisement that reaches such a large audience is clearly cost effective. If, for example, that same advertiser were to attempt to reach 1000 persons by mail, postage alone could amount to over $400.

A cautionary note needs to be introduced here: CPM, although extremely useful, is an estimate. In this particular example, a CPM of $5.60 would be achieved only for a product that each member of that huge audience would be likely to use—soap, soft drinks, and toothpaste, for instance. The reader should understand that the "true" CPM figure would be higher if the account's product were a bulldozer or a yacht. In these cases, a more direct and selective route from account to consumer would obviously have to be considered.

Concepts

A number of concepts from the public relations and advertising industries have found their way into common parlance. These are introduced here because they are necessary to understand contemporary public relations and advertising practices.

Targeted Audiences

The term *targeted* is used interchangeably with *segmented* and refers to the identification of a particular group of consumers within the broad society. The process of identification includes demographic study—age, education, and the like—as well as psychographic study—tastes, preferences, and lifestyles. However, to be of interest to an account, this identified group should possess at least the following features. First, the group must be accessible to the account's advertising message—that is, the group as a whole has to be available to be reached through some medium. Secondly, the group must also be sufficiently large to make it economically worthwhile for a firm to manufacture and distribute its product. Thirdly, individuals constituting the group must be able to benefit from the product or service purchased. If individuals are not able to use the product or service gainfully, then they have little or no continuing interest to the account. Finally, the target audience must be able to afford the product.[11]

The application of computer technology to research on target identification has achieved a particularly high level of sophistication and has caused a minor revolution in advertising agencies' methods. For example, copywriters, responsible for the essential message, have ready access to highly reliable information regarding which set of "appeals" is likely to work with which targeted groups for the benefit of the account.

Design and Preparation of Advertising Messages

There are three sites in the advertising industry where messages are designed and produced, and the purpose of this discussion is to provide a descriptive overview of this aspect of the industry.

First, advertising is produced "in house." The term means simply that retail stores or large accounts do their own advertising design and preparation. Typically, in large organizations, advertising departments are often as large as independent advertising agencies. An in-house department is normally supervised by an advertising manager, along with his or her creative and research directors. In effect, the in-house advertising department will perform all or most of the research tasks, create actual advertisements, and schedule its own advertisements in appropriate print and broadcast media. In large chain retail organizations, some centralized production processes take place, and advertising materials and plans are distributed to the company's branches across the country. Perhaps the most popular form of such centralized production is the multicoloured newspaper advertising insert. On occasion the in-house

department might need to engage a specialty service for art or photography of a unique kind.

As well, mass media are themselves producers of advertising messages. At the community level, a local broadcasting station or newspaper is likely to be well equipped to perform whatever services are required by a retail account. Such services could include audience research, readership studies, copywriting, production, layout, or whatever else might be required. Because retail accounts work very closely with local media, an important characteristic of such a relationship is the considerable flexibility in the production and scheduling of advertising messages.

The third site where messages are prepared is the advertising agency. These vary in size from what is known as "full-service" agencies (usually having international ties) to the single specialty houses, which provide unique services such as specialized research, artwork, or photography. Such specialty houses are known in the industry as "boutiques."

There are currently three trends affecting advertising agencies. First, there is a vast amount of merging and consolidation occurring among advertising agencies and boutiques. The second trend is towards internationalization. Of the larger agencies in Canada, there are few that do not have links with advertising firms in other countries. For example, McCann-Erickson, one of the largest agencies in the world, either owns outright or is in partnership with agencies in forty-nine countries.[12] A third trend is for advertising agencies to offer highly diversified services, in part because of mergers of specialty agencies. The consequence of these changes, overall, is that some agencies are becoming extremely large, to the detriment of the smaller independent sector.[13]

In summary, advertising agencies are experiencing dynamic activity and growth, and this growth is characterized by the volume of account billings, number of people employed, and by the scope of activities, both domestically and internationally. In an industry where accounts worth millions of dollars a year are often sought, the competitive stakes are high. Needless to say, it is not an industry where weak-hearted souls should enter.

Co-operative Advertising

There are two kinds of co-operative advertising: horizontal and vertical. In the first type, a group of similar accounts might bond together for a common purpose—to share the cost of expensive advertising, for example. A group is usually brought together by a common product or service that they have for sale, such as dairies sponsoring generic rather than brand-name commercials for milk. Vertical co-operative advertising is somewhat different: co-operation takes place between a parent company (a national account, perhaps) and a retail distributor of that company's product. The co-operative arrangement is likely to take one of three forms. First, a parent company will purchase a large newspaper advertisement, and the retail dealership will "tag" its name to that

TABLE 9-4
Canada's Top Advertising Agencies

Rank by revenue	Millions[a] 1990	Percentage of foreign ownership[b] (1989)
1. Cossette Communication Marketing	33 330	0
2. MacLaren: Lintas Inc.	32 341	100
3. Young & Rubicam	31 536	100
4. Baker Lovick Advertising	28 003	49
5. J. Walter Thomson Co.	24 620	100
6. Ogilvy & Mather (Canada) Ltd.	24 306	100
7. Grey Advertising Ltd.	22 497	100
8. FCB/Ronalds-Reynolds Ltd.	21 726	100
9. McCann-Ericson Advertising Ltd.	21 085	100
10. Saffer Advertising Ltd.	20 929	0

Source: [a] Heather D. Whyte, "Strength in Numbers," *Financial Post 500* 85 (Summer 1991), 164.
[b] Mark Evans, "Foreign Invasion," *Financial Post 500* 84 (Summer 1990), 191.

advertisement. Secondly, the parent company, often from its own in-house advertising department, will produce and distribute to its dealerships promotional advertising kits that contain written advertising copy, film/video prepared commercials for television, and prepared "mats" for newspaper advertising; because this package is professionally prepared, it involves a considerable cost saving to the retailer. Thirdly, the parent company and the retailer will share direct advertising costs in whatever proportion is agreed on.

Co-operative advertising is regulated under the Competition Act (earlier the Combines Investigation Act), administered by the federal department of Consumer and Corporate Affairs. Such regulation emphasizes that even though co-operative advertising is certainly permissible, the parent company may not offer some advantage to one retailer that is unavailable to another. Regulation paradoxically enforces the libertarian tradition of the open market, where the basis of behaviour is competition rather than favouritism. A more detailed examination of regulation in advertising follows in the next chapter.

Comparative Advertising

Comparative advertising is a popular format that has been in existence for decades, though it was in the 1970s and 1980s that the practice came into its own. Comparative advertising is simply the comparison of an account's product with that of a competitor, either identified as "Brand X" or directly, brand with brand.

Theoretically at least, comparative advertising is thought of as having a benefit for the consumer, in that (again hearkening back to the libertarian tradition) the "good" product ought to drive the "bad" one out of the market. Because, however, there are so many levels on which similar products compete (price, usefulness, reliability, and prestige, for example), it is questionable whether such an open marketplace phenomenon actually occurs.

Complaints by the industry itself about comparative advertising are numerous. Some critics claim that the strategy has the effect of degrading the credibility of the advertising industry itself. As well, raising matters of reliability and trustworthiness could make the entire industry suspect. Opponents of the strategy also say that direct and open comparison could cause some consumers to be confused about which product is intended to be the "superior" one. Finally, opponents indicate that comparative advertising has become in large part a defensive strategy, whereby producers of excellent products are forced into comparative advertising in self-defence.

Comparative advertising is rigidly controlled, as one might expect, especially for food or drug products. There is a large measure of industry self-regulatory activity as well, and the basic principles of such activities are the same in the

United States as they are in Canada. The American Association of Advertising Agencies in a recent policy statement indicated that when comparative advertising is used "truthfully and fairly," there is clear benefit for the consumer because less worthy products are identified. The directors of that association specify guidelines, and while all are important, two predominate: "the intent and connotation of the ad should be to inform and never to discredit or unfairly attack competitors, competing products or services" and "in all cases [the competitive product] test should be supportive of all claims made in the advertising that are based on the test."[14] In Canada, criteria for comparative advertising are similar and are contained in an Advertising Standards Council publication. These criteria stress that competitors must not be unfairly discredited or unjustly disparaged by the specific or overall impression created by the advertisement, and that advertisers must be prepared to provide support for whatever advertising claims are made.[15]

Despite the existence of such guidelines, lawsuits in the U.S. courts since 1988 have increased owing to increasingly more stringent legislation, and some substantial settlements have been awarded to accounts that have been attacked unfairly in comparative advertisements. A recent article reviewing the increased frequency of such suits described comparative advertising as having become "a hard-bitten, attention-grabbing way of saying we're better than the competition." The authors conclude that henceforth "every comparative advertiser should be ready to go to court."[16]

Research About Advertising

In an industry where millions of dollars are routinely at stake, the value of sound research is obvious. Research can be conducted at every level of the industry—by accounts, agencies, mass media, and professional research organizations. Six basic kinds of research are generally identified in textbooks on advertising, and most are in agreement that these are the major component parts of research in the industry. Within each type, several subcategories are possible; and there are likely to be as many variations of these, and of research strategies employed, as there are creative minds at work on them. Thus, the description here is a broad outline of the basic, researched information needs in the conduct of work in the advertising industry. (a) Market research is carried out in the community where products or services are to be available. The overall economic health of the community is vital. Factors such as family income, amount of disposable income, the local employment rate, and the general economic stability of the area are considered, as are social conditions, such as the crime rate. Even weather conditions are important to an account, since they might influence the acceptability of a product. (b) Research about the product itself is essential; for example, the product's usefulness to consumers is of vital importance. The manner in which it will be used and its durability must be determined. (c) The appropriateness of exposing a product in a particular medium is also important. For example, if a product's unique selling point is its application to a task, then clearly television provides an opportunity to demonstrate it in action. (d) Consumer research focusses on individuals and includes both demographic studies (physical characteristics) and psychographic studies (lifestyles) of the target group. (e) Message research is perhaps the most crucial and at the same time the most elusive: reliable research results are not easy to obtain. Normally, message research takes place at four different points during the message preparation/scheduling process. First, preliminary research is often conducted on message parts. For instance, persons to be used as models in commercials are tested to determine how they will be received. Linguistic and pictorial components are also tested before a completed commercial is produced. Finally, when the creative directors are sure that an audience will accept the parts of the commercial, the final message is assembled. Secondly, immediately prior to the scheduling of the advertising campaign, the completed commercial is tested. For example, the commerical's producers might prepare slightly different versions of the ad and test these before "jury panels" or "focus groups," collected groups

of potential consumers. Thirdly, concurrent testing refers to research about the campaign while it is in progress. Phone surveys might be used or retail outlets studied to determine product acceptability. Finally, postcampaign studies are routinely done. For instance, consumers might be tested for their recall of the advertising message, retail managers might be surveyed to gather data about sales successes they might have experienced with the product. Product sales are obviously a form of postcampaign measurement, though unreliable alone. There may be a time lapse between the ad campaign and consumer reaction. As well, factors such as sale price, companion shoppers, or availability of money are variables affecting measurement. (f) Specific research on audience and readership is perhaps the oldest research strategy in advertising because media managers need to know how many people are contained in a broadcast audience or constitute a newspaper's or magazine's readership.[17]

Among the major organizations that measure broadcast audiences in Canada are the Bureau of Broadcast Measurement (BBM) and A.C. Nielsen, a U.S.-based organization that services Canadian broadcasting as well. Generally three measurement strategies are employed: electronic surveillance devices, such as "audimeters" and "people-meters," which by agreement with the owners are placed in family TV sets to record viewing habits;[18] a written diary in which respondents record radio or television programs they've listened to or watched; and personal interviews, either by telephone or in person. Print circulation and readership are measured by a number of organizations. The best known and oldest is the Audit Bureau of Circulation (ABC), which focusses mainly on newspaper and magazine printing and distribution. The Starch readership technique interviews readers and concentrates on determining the parts of publications read and the intensity of that readership. Finally, there are various organizations that study long-range audience/readership trends. Elmo Roper Associates was a forerunner in such trend studies. It was among the first organizations to identify audience preferences for specific information and to ascertain which media people turned to for that information.

Advertising and the Corporation

Advertising, as a part of a corporation's marketing plan, normally has two purposes. The first is to support the product-manufacturing process and initiate the selling practice. The second is to support the corporation itself.

In chapter 4 we discussed the concept of persuasion and it is clear that a central key to success in advertising is not only the product's but also the producer's credibility. The term normally used to describe this activity is *institutional advertising*. A corporation may use advertising in a purely "halo-polishing" manner—

that is, to publicize its tradition, its health, its prosperity. Or a corporation may involve itself in what might be called good citizenship deeds. Oil companies, for example, often, as a natural extension of their refinery activities, become involved in chemical and medical research on behalf of society.[19]

Such image enhancement actually is important to a corporation's effective internal management, contributing to employees' sense of being part of a worthy corporation. The company's altruism, dependability, and trustworthiness may also be transmitted to consumers. As readers will appreciate, there are many ways for institutional advertising to fulfil these corporate objectives. Many corporations sponsor museums, works of art, cultural performances (the Stratford Shakespearean Festival is an excellent example), or sports teams. It is in this particular area that advertising closely resembles public relations.

Advocacy Advertising

A third corporate activity completes this discussion. Variously called issue advertising, "advertorials," opinion advertising, or most commonly advocacy advertising, the strategy has had an important impact on society over the past two decades. It clearly has an educational role, which corporations and other users have assigned to themselves.

Advocacy advertising, while not new, is normally thought of as having had a fresh beginning in the mid-1970s, when Mobil Oil was turned down by a U.S. network in a bid to place television commercials explaining Mobil's role in the 1973 oil crisis. In a 1982 program produced on advertising by TVOntario, the vice-president for public affairs of Mobil Oil discussed his reasons for employing advocacy advertising. He indicated that the company chose to buy advertising space on the back page of a newspaper because the story the company had to tell didn't appear on the front page. "Our views and facts weren't getting to the American public," he explained.[20]

Advocacy advertising can be defined as purchased advertising aimed at persuading society to a particular point of view and influencing policy reconsideration or change on behalf of the interest group conducting the campaign. In this sense, advocacy advertising may be seen as self-serving, but is also viewed by the advertisers as furthering important social causes.

Because advocacy advertising involves the purchase of space or time in the mass media, an important question is raised, particularly when governments are the clients: there is no opportunity for direct debate of a government's position in a television commercial or newspaper advertisement. Advocacy in the mass media is no debate at all: the party forming the government has access to taxpayers' dollars to finance its information campaign, while the opposition parties might have little other than campaign debts. The central question then becomes, does advocacy advertising

enhance freedom of expression (by permitting an interest group to state its position, as argued by the spokesperson for Mobil Oil), or is freedom of speech diminished or denied since alternative views are not presented in the ad?

No immediate answer is forthcoming; however, insight was provided by representatives of industry and the federal government at a 1982 Canadian conference on the subject.

The business community presented four arguments in favour of advocacy advertising. First, it is important, said supporters, to foster free enterprise and the value system underlying it. Second, an assumption is made on the basis of some public opinion polls that society generally does not hold the business community in high esteem. Supporters of business contend that low image can be counteracted by advertising campaigns. Third, the business sector finds problematic the dissemination of its point of view through mass media news organizations: its access to the public is only through purchase of time or space in the media. Finally, the perception exists in the business community that mass media organizations maintain a strong bias against them. This perception exists, regardless of how paradoxical it might appear, given that media are financially dependent on corporate advertising and are themselves high-profile business organizations. To underline this negative perception of business among the media, a conference participant related that in 1980 a nonprofit research group in the United States had conducted a study of fifty "top-rated" television programs and found that most businessmen were depicted "as crooks, moral wheeler-dealers, cheats, fools and clowns." The probusiness representative regarded advocacy advertising as the way to parry such broad media bias.[21]

Speaking on behalf of the federal government, and explaining the government's rationale for using advocacy advertising, was then minister of communications Gerald A. Regan. Four arguments were presented. First, citizens of Canada must have full, accurate, and timely information to enable them to take part in the democratic process. Second, emphasized the minister, Canadians have a right to access the government's record. Third, "the government has a duty to inform the public of its proposals before they have been decided by Parliament." Finally, the government has a responsibility "to learn of the concerns and views of Canadians . . . so as to inform itself in establishing priorities, in developing policies, and in implementing programs which serve the interests of Canada." The relationship between citizens and government with respect to the seeking of and providing of information should be co-operative.[22]

The minister argued accordingly that mass media advocacy advertising was mandatory. However, it is important that students be aware that to this end, the federal government budgeted and spent in excess of $67 million in 1990. Where can

groups opposing government positions raise equivalent amounts to present alternative points of view? It is clear that advocacy advertising has become embedded in Canada's political processes at both the provincial and federal levels. Moreover, it is carried out by governments regardless of which political party happens to be in power.

Direct Advertising

While direct advertising is not new, it is has experienced a revival and reshaping in the 1970s and 1980s. Grandparents and parents of readers, or perhaps readers themselves, will recall the regular distribution of product display catalogues, particularly in the rural areas of the country. Readers will also recall the development of book and record clubs on the continent, which are also in the catalogue tradition.

Recently with the application of computer technology, direct advertising has experienced phenomenal growth. Such growth might be attributed to several factors, but most important would be consumer mailing lists, which are constantly being updated on computers, credit card shopping, and the proliferation of toll-free 800 telephone numbers. These factors, which taken together allow the consumer to bypass retail store shopping, provide advertising accounts with an excellent cost-per-thousand delivery. There is always some waste circulation of the advertising messages, but the more effectively a company designs its principal tool, the consumer list, the more such waste is reduced.

The central tool of direct advertising is of course the effective consumer list. A retailer may develop over time a "house list"—the names and addresses of shoppers who patronize the store. At an opportune time, advertising pieces are mailed to these people rather than to the whole community. An organization may also order a list from companies that collect, categorize, and sell names to advertising accounts desiring a specialized list of potential consumers. Such businesses appear under "Mailing List" in the Yellow Pages of most telephone directories.

The development of direct advertising has been rapid. For example, percentage of share of all advertising revenues for catalogues and direct mail increased in 1987 from 19.2 percent to 23.4 percent. In that same year, daily newspapers dropped from their traditional first place in share of advertising revenues, from 28.6 percent to 23.3 percent.[23]

One final comment is in order. Direct mail, readers are well aware, is often described as "junk mail," and we all claim that such mail quickly finds its way to the garbage or recycling can. Nevertheless, while you and I may do that with *our* junk mail, the majority of Canadians do not. An A.C. Nielsen study in the late 1970s indicated that at least 75 percent of Canadians open and look at all direct mail; for fund-raising appeals, that percentage rose to 81 percent. Moreover, more than 75 percent reported using product samples received in the mail and more than 50 percent used coupons mailed to them.[24] In 1985, it was reported that over 80 percent of recipients in all age categories used the coupons they received.[25] It can be anticipated then, that with increasingly sophisticated methods of assembling mailing lists, resulting in more exact targeting of consumers, a high rate of positive response to junk mail will continue.

Ethics and Responsibility

There are a number of issues related to ethics and the responsibility of the industry in society. We do not intend to discuss all of these in full.[26] A few, however, are of particular importance.

An advertising message's potential to offend is one of the prime concerns in any examination of ethical issues and the industry. Even though advertisers would be the last people in the world who would want to offend any large groups of would-be purchasers of the product they represent, advertisers still appear to lack an understanding of the effects of stereotyping, or even worse, demonstrate a lack of concern. The professional advertiser is likely to argue that the target population for whom the product commercial is intended is not likely to be offended by stereotyped messages. However, the spouses, neighbours, or children of the target audience might be. And if stereotypes of race and gender especially are being perpetuated, the ad in fact perpetuates abuse.

Advertising and "Sexploitation"

Sexism in advertising continues apace in fact. It began and continues to be used as an attention-getting device and power symbol for male buyers. Its existence is clearly offensive to women, limiting their role in society. Approaches taken to deal with the problem differ. In Canada, the federal government responded in 1979 to pressure from women by raising the question of gender inequality in the media. The review began in the Department of Communications, quickly involved the CRTC, and a task force was established to examine the problem and report on it. The task force reported in 1982 *(Images of Women: Report of the Task Force on Sex-Role Stereotyping)*, and guidelines to eliminate stereotyping were quickly drawn up for broadcast programming as well as advertising and were put in place voluntarily by the industries. In 1986, the CRTC made adherence to these guidelines mandatory as a condition of licence for broadcasters.[27]

The guidelines specified:

Advertising, in keeping with the nature of the market and the product, should reflect the wide spectrum of Canadian life portraying men and women of various ages, backgrounds and appearances actively pursuing a wide range of interests, sports, hobbies and business, as well as home-centred activities.

and

Advertising should not exploit women or men purely for attention-getting purposes. Their presence should be relevant to the advertised product.[28]

To what extent sexism in advertising has been reduced is open to debate. Practitioners in the industry continue to maintain that sexual imagery associated with a product is effective in selling: "Use of sex as a metaphor for pleasure for a wide range of consumer products is something that we've known and will know as long as a market for those goods exist."[29] It was suggested by a reporter from *Marketing* that some advertisers do not take guidelines against sexist advertising very seriously and they continue to portray women as sex objects. The reporter describes a particular advertising campaign conducted in the fall of 1989. It featured a bathing-suit-clad young woman, and the movement of the camera over her body was described as blatant sexploitation.[30]

Advertising that overtly exploits women as sex objects is not limited to television commercials. In the fall of 1989 subway and bus shelters in Toronto featured advertising that was eventually removed, following complaints by women's groups. The reaction of the industry following the removal of the advertising was described in a newspaper account as follows: "Frustration—even anger—in the advertising industry is directed not only at the City of Toronto but at MediaWatch, a small feminist lobby group that was instrumental in getting two ads pulled."[31]

While the problem of sexploitation has been identified and some remedial action has taken place, it is evident that the advertising industry remains, at least to some degree, reactionary in continuing to perpetuate gender stereotypes.

After receiving a complaint from MediaWatch in July of 1990, the Toronto Transit Commission was quick to order that this ad be removed from subway cars for being sexually exploitive. (Courtesy Globe and Mail, Toronto)

Deception in Advertising

Whatever we might believe about advertising, it is not likely that an account would knowingly try to deceive purchasers of the product. The simple reason for this is that the account is more interested in long-range economic stability of a company or a brand, and overt deception might very well destroy that goal. Nevertheless, deception is occasionally found in the industry in the same way that we are likely to find fraudulent behaviour in any segment of society.

Interestingly, the laws that protect comsumers in Canada and in the United States are consistent in emphasizing that an advertisement may be found to be deceptive even if it contains only the possibility or capacity to be deceptive. Thus regulators stress that advertisements should not be ambiguous.

Children and Advertising

An important focus of research in the 1970s and 1980s has been the effects of advertising on children (i.e., ages two to twelve), and the results of this research are consistent in several respects. First, children do in fact find it difficult to distinguish between fiction and reality. Therefore, the Broadcast Code for Advertising to Children is emphatic in its statement that personalities, characters, and even puppets well known to children must not be used to endorse products.[32] As well, research points out that children readily accept the institution of advertising and they understand its inherent value systems. For example, response to advertising is very personal. Advertisements single out individuals and indicate to them how their lives, their power, or their status can be enhanced. It is well understood that material values, associated with personal property, are part of the value system of advertising. Such values are quickly learned by children.

Society has reacted to information of this kind, and overtures have been made to the advertising industry, to mass media, and to regulatory agencies in an attempt to curb advertising aimed at children. In most cases, these attempts have not been successful. For example, despite opposition by some parent groups, a sponsored newscast aimed at children in their classrooms was launched in the U.S. in 1989. The news program itself, it is argued, is a valuable instructional aid to teachers of social science studies. While that may be the case, some parent groups claim that the essential lesson children learn is that advertising is an integral part of all we do.[33]

On the other hand, some noted successes in reducing the influence of advertising on children have been made, and the Broadcast Code for Advertising to Children has been extremely stringent in setting guidelines in areas where abuses are most likely to take place. An outstanding success occurred in 1989, when the Supreme Court of Canada upheld legislation passed by the Quebec National Assembly prohibiting advertising to children under the age of thirteen.[34]

Advertising Influence on Media

It is evident that advertising has an effect on mass media, since the two industries are so heavily dependent on each other. But the central question focusses on the matter of undue or unfair influence that advertising might have; for example, influence on the news reporting behaviour of mass media. While in Canada's large markets, where advertisers might be lined up to buy time or space, such undue influence is not likely to be effective. On the other hand, in a smaller community, will a TV station or a newspaper report accurately on air pollution if the station's or newspaper's major advertiser is the chief polluter in the community? Cases of such influence have been both subtle and blatant. In a popular television police series a few years ago, police consistently and obviously drove one brand of vehicle, while the "bad guys" drove competing brands. Despite constant reminders of such ethical lapses, ethical behaviour is the norm in the media industries for no other reason than that those who function at the management level understand that over a long period of time ethical standards pay off. They are directly related to media credibility, and advertisers prefer to be associated with credible and creditable behaviour.

We are reminded in this instance of the apocryphal story concerning advertiser influence on a mass medium. A major newspaper advertiser whose son had been arrested and placed in jail visited the editor of the daily newspaper, suggesting that it would be appreciated if the editor would keep the name of the advertiser's son out of the newspaper. The editor listened patiently and then replied, "I'll make a deal with you. You keep your son out of jail and I'll keep his name out of the newspaper."

Subliminal Advertising

No discussion of ethics in advertising could be considered complete without some comment on subliminal advertising—a strategy that in every respect is considered to be unscrupulous and unethical. Subliminal advertising messages are those aimed at and perceived by us, but below the threshold of conscious perception, i.e., messages offered and absorbed without our awareness of having been "programmed."

It is strongly held that subliminal advertising is effective, and that, despite its illegality in Canada (by CRTC regulation), it is frequently used.[35] While the concept of subliminal advertising is not new, it was raised to new prominence in advertising in the early 1970s by Wilson Bryan Key. Key indicates that most "national advertising includes imbedding," which is the practice of hiding emotionally charged symbols (pictures and/or words) in advertisements. Moreover, the most popularly embedded word in the U.S. advertising industry is *sex*.[36] Presumably, when we are confronted with the hidden symbol, viewed beneath the threshold of perception, we experience sufficient pleasurable stimulus to move us to purchase the product.

Research dealing with subliminal advertising has consistently disclosed that subliminal devices, which would induce particular behaviour, have not been shown by evidence to have "the power ascribed to them by advocates of subliminal advertising."[37] At the same time, it is apparent that on occasion a message may be designed to contain a strong suggestion of a motivational image; this in turn may cause the viewer to fill in the pictures not explicitly present. But this phenomenon is well within the range of human perception. The strategy has been labelled "borderline simulation," and is a case apart from the use of hidden, subliminally perceived messages.[38]

Conclusion

The advertising and public relations industries are a massive force in our society and their activities affect every household on a daily basis. While adjustments of various kinds will continue to take place in the industries and in society, the pattern of growth and influence as discussed in this chapter is likely to continue.

Notes

1. See, for example, Keith A. Tuckwell, *Canadian Advertising in Action* (Scarborough: Prentice-Hall, 1988), 4.

2. John S. Wright, Willis L. Winter, Jr., Sherilyn K. Zeigler, P. Noel O'Dea, *Advertising, First Canadian Edition* (Toronto: McGraw-Hill Ryerson, 1984), 1–2.

3. UNESCO, *Many Voices, One World: Report by the International Commission for the Study of Communication Problems* (Paris, 1980), 111.

4. Canadian data from Maclean Hunter Research Bureau, *A Report on Advertising Revenues in Canada* (Toronto: Maclean Hunter Research Bureau, 1987), 11; U.S. data from McCann-Erickson, *Insider's Report* 17 (June 1988): 7.

5. Martin Mehr, "Thomson Overtakes Government As Top Advertiser," *Marketing* 96 (8 April 1991): 1.

6. S. Watson Dunn and Arnold M. Barban, *Advertising: Its Role in Modern Marketing*, 5th ed. (Toronto: The Dryden Press, 1982), 40–41.

7. Maclean Hunter Research Bureau, *A Report on Advertising Revenues in Canada*, 5.

8. As cited in Dennis L. Wilcox, Phillip Ault and Warren K. Agee, *Public Relations, Strategies and Tactics* (New York: Harper and Row, 1988), 5

9. W. Lawrence Nolte, *Fundamentals of Public Relations*, 2nd ed. (New York: Pergamon Press, 1979), 5.

10. William Lowther, "The Big Fourth Down: Football Is a Small Part of the Super Bowl," *Maclean's*, 23 January 1989, 19.

11. Dunn and Barban, *Advertising*, 241.

12. "Foreign Agencies by 1989 Gross Income," *Advertising Age* 61 (26 March 1990): S–25, S–44.

13. See "The Year in Review: Mosaic of Mergers and Account Shifts," *Marketing* 95 (1 January 1990): 1, 4.

14. Cited in J. Thomas Russell, Glenn Barrell, W. Ronald Lane, *Kleppner's Advertising Procedure*, 10th ed. (Englewood Cliffs, NJ: Prentice-Hall, 1988), 623.

15. See "Guidelines for the Use of Comparative Advertising in Food Commercials," cited in Tuckwell, *Canadian Advertising*, 577.

16. Bruce Buchanan and Doran Goldman, "Us vs. Them: The Minefield of Comparative Ads," *Harvard Business Review* (May–June 1989): 38.

17. For a more complete discussion of the role of research in advertising, see Don E. Schultz, Dennis Martin, William P. Brown, *Strategic Advertising Campaigns*, 2nd ed. (Chicago: Crain Books, 1984), 435–60.

18. Some very different figures regarding audiences have become apparent: "reported" audiences are lower than those recorded by earlier instruments of measurment, see Ann Borden, "Meter vs. Diary," *Marketing* 95 (26 March 1990): 14.

19. For a detailed discussion of such corporate activity, see Wright et al., *Advertising*, 18–19.

20. Interview with vice-president of Mobil Oil in a telecast produced by TVOntario, "Quarters: Advertising," 11 February 1982.

21. S. Prakash Sethi, "A Theoretical Framework for Business Advocacy Advertising," a report from a Conference Board of Canada–sponsored conference, *Advocacy Advertising: Propaganda or Democratic Right*, May 1982, 26–29.

22. Gerald A. Regan, "A Statement of the Federal Government's Position," in *Advocacy Advertising: Propaganda or Democratic Right*, 39–40.

23. Ken Riddell, "1987 A Record: Ad Revenues Top $7 Billion," *Marketing* 93 (8 February 1988): 1, 3.

24. Reported in Wright et al., *Advertising*, 306.

25. Nielsen Promotion Services, *Coupon Use by Grocery Shoppers* 4 (1986): 4.

26. Dunn and Barban, *Advertising*, chapter 5, 82–103.

27. For example, Canada, CRTC, "Renewal of Licence for Global Television Network: CRTC Decision 1986–1086" (Ottawa, 14 November 1986), 20.

28. As cited in George Speare and Kasia Seydegart, *The Portrayal of Sex-Roles in Canadian Television Advertising 1985* (Ottawa: Supply and Services, 1986), 69.

29. Reid Morris, "Treading the Fine Line between Risque and Responsible," *Marketing*, 94 (2 October 1989): C8–C9.

30. Jim McElgum, "Juicy Commercial is Example of Bad Taste," *Marketing*, 94 (30 October 1989): 8.

31. Marina Strauss, "Advertisers Have to Be Careful with Transit Shelter Messages," *Globe and Mail*, 23 November 1989, B5.

32. The Canadian Association of Broadcasters, *The Broadcast Code for Advertising to Children* (Ottawa, 1988), 2–5.

33. N.R. Kleinfield, reporting for the *New York Times*, "Quiet entrepreneur force behind high school's 'Channel One.'" *Detroit Free Press*, 2 April 1989, C1, C4.

34. Kirk Makin, "Supreme Court Backs Quebec Law Restricting Ads Aimed at Children," *Globe and Mail*, 28 April 1989, A1–A2. The court found in favour of the province and while expressing concerns regarding free speech concluded that freedom of speech ends where manipulative sales pitches reach the impressionable minds of children.

35. Benjamin D. Singer, *Advertising and Society* (Don Mills, ON: Addison-Wesley, 1986), 208.

36. Wilson Bryan Key, *Subliminal Seduction: Ad Media's Manipulation of a Not So Innocent America* (New York: New American Library, 1974), 108.

37. Timothy E. Moore, "Subliminal Advertising: What You See Is What You Get," *Journal of Marketing* 46 (Spring 1982): 45–46.

38. Singer, *Advertising and Society*, 212.

Regulation, Ownership, and Political Processes

C H A P T E R   1 0

Regulation and Social Control

Introduction

The beginning for a discussion of regulation in any society is its constitution, for a constitution, among other important functions, defines the relationship between individuals and groups and their government.

Canada's first constitution, the British North America Act, came into effect in 1867, following a process that began in Charlottetown, Prince Edward Island, in 1864. Subsequently, documents were added to the constitutional framework until 1982 when a new constitutional document, the Canada Act 1982, was approved by Parliament and became law. The Canada Act, then, represents a consolidation and synthesis of all that had gone on before; as well it strengthens individual rights and freedoms by entrenching these in the Charter of Rights and Freedoms.[1]

Students should especially note the following sections of the Constitution, since they reflect a strong commitment to individual rights with respect to fundamental freedoms.

Part I, Section 2
Fundamental Freedoms

2. Everyone has the following fundamental freedoms:

   (a) freedom of conscience and religion;

   (b) freedom of thought, belief, opinion and expression including freedom of the press and other media of communication;

   (c) freedom of peaceful assembly; and

   (d) freedom of association.[2]

These rights and freedoms are discussed in their legal contexts in part I, section 7 and section 15 (1) of the Canada Act.

These sections of the Constitution are relevant here since, in addition to detailing our individual rights, they provide the basis for the regulatory dilemma that exists with respect to government control of media institutions. On the surface, at least, there appears to be a conflict between the Constitution, which could be construed as libertarian (see chapter 2) in defining our individual freedoms, and legislation the government has passed regarding the conduct of mass media. This legislation states that Canada should exist as a society that is distinct from any other—socially, culturally, politically, and economically. And the government, as well as regulatory structures set up by government, affirm that mass media should support this aspiration for national distinctiveness. Thus, the concept of social responsibility collides with a narrow libertarian interpretation of the relationship between individuals and groups, on the one hand, and government on the other.

Some Canadians contend that regulation of media, both directly and indirectly, results in a restriction of "freedom of thought, belief, opinion and expression, including freedom of the press and other media of communication." The result, according to at least one critic is "prior restraint of the clearest kind."[3] At the same time, the Constitution makes it clear that whatever rights and freedoms might be guaranteed are not absolute, as they are subject to "such reasonable limits prescribed by law as can be demonstrably justified in a free and democratic society."[4]

It is consistent with the libertarian tradition that, in the case of a national crisis, priorities other than individual rights and freedoms

might prevail. In a sense, then, governments before and since the passage of the Canada Act 1982 have defended the need to regulate mass media, citing a higher priority. For example, in 1974, Pierre Juneau, then chairman of the CRTC, responded to complaints about Canadian content regulations as constituting censorship; he argued that due to Canadian broadcasters' decisions to schedule less expensive U.S.-produced television programs rather than producing their own using Canadian resources and talent, Canadians were denied access to, and expression through, their own mass media, which constituted a greater form of censorship in his view.[5]

The tension between individual freedoms, encompassing the libertarian tradition, and the need for control, embodied in the concept of social responsibility, is not unique to Canada. It is to be found in all democratic societies. John Merril describes that tension as it relates to freedom of the press:

So in spite of a few voices here and there trying to lure us back to the pristine libertarian days of Locke, Mill, and Jefferson, today there is a predisposition to redefine freedom of the press, to divorce it from independent determination by the media and infuse it with increased "guidance" of one type or another. . . . The attempt to make the press "responsible" or "accountable" is the synthesis of freedom and control, and the time for such a synthesis is at hand.[6]

In the case of Canada, however, we envision that the specific inclusion of the freedom of the press clause in the Constitution will result in a strengthening of the libertarian position. As Seymour Martin Lipset argues, the incorporation of a bill of rights in the Constitution, in fact, places "the power of the state under judicial restraint."[7] It would certainly not be surprising to see legal challenges to government restrictions on mass media over the next few years. Such challenges have recently occurred in the United States: in February 1989, a U.S. federal court upheld the action taken by the Federal Communications Commission, which had repealed the Fairness Doctrine.[8]

The Fairness Doctrine, which had been in existence since 1949, demanded that broadcasters devote time to the coverage of controversial social issues and that they present contrasting viewpoints. The Federal Communications Commission, in 1987, repealed the doctrine claiming that it inhibited rather than enhanced public access to diverse views since, to avoid public complaints, broadcasters tended to minimize airing controversial issues.

There are three forms of regulation: (1) governmental procedures and enactments of various sorts that are legally binding; (2) informal, nongovernmental actions taken by industry, which we call *self-regulation*; and (3) the expression of the will of the people, which we call *consumerism*. These three types of regulation, each of which we will discuss in turn, are obviously related, and

in the overall regulatory process there is a never-ending interaction between them.

For this discussion of regulation, two definitions are in order. The term *policy* is defined as a resolution that has a specific plan, selected from a set of options, so as to respond to a particular problem for the benefit of a designated social group. Thus, policy might be a resolution to produce more Canadian content for Canadian broadcasting in order to protect the national identity. *Regulations*, on the other hand, might be thought of as translating policy into practical terms and serve as operational guidelines in order to fulfil the designated policy. The Board of Broadcast Governors, for example, gave specific regulatory meaning to Canadian content policy. The Broadcasting Act specified that programming should be "Canadian in content and character." The BBG operationalized that *policy* by *regulating* that TV stations and networks would be required to schedule no less than 55 percent of their programming with content produced in Canada.

If they sense the government and public are concerned about a particular problem, media industries may well take the initiative to correct the problem in a defensive move designed to forestall government action. This self-regulation while lacking the force of law, cannot be dismissed. Not only are self-generated norms powerful in shaping behaviour, on occasion the government appears to prefer the informal channel and encourages self-regulatory measures through the power of persuasion.

Government Regulation

The Federal Department of Communications

The senior federal government department concerned with the operation of mass media and the cultural industries is Communications Canada. As the 1988–89 *Annual Report* proclaims in bold capital letters, the department's mission is "NATION BUILDING; helping Canadians share their ideas, information and dreams."[9] By any standard that is an exceedingly broad and all-encompassing mandate. The department's jurisdiction is remarkably wide and encompasses various broadcasting and filmmaking agencies as well as the national library, gallery, and archives. In addition it includes national museums and the agencies that fund all of these organizations.

Few aspects of the media industry and activities that comprise Canada's cultural environment are exempt from the minister's portfolio. Indeed, the oft-found references to the minister as Canada's "cultural Czar" are not out of order, since it is in the actions of this department that explications of Canada's aspirations concerning self-identity are to be found.

The Department of Communications was established as a separate entity in 1969 and has functioned since then in activating and developing a national communication system "that links Canadians from all regions through a variety of conventional and newer technologies. . . ."[10] The programs of arts and culture, earlier under the portfolio of the Secretary of State, were transferred to the Communications Department in 1980, thus extending its mandate over the broad range of social activities that are encompassed by the label, the media-cultural industries.

The department is highly influential in media–cultural activities and, on occasion, has been known to intervene in matters mandated to regulatory agencies under the department's jurisdiction. Several disputes over the role of the minister with respect to regulatory procedures of the CRTC demonstrate the department's influence and power. The twenty-four-hour news channel licence is a case in point. In the fall of 1988, the CRTC had awarded to the CBC, following an open competition with a private industry broadcaster, the right to build and operate a twenty-four-hour national television news service. At the request of private broadcasters, the minister, via cabinet, intervened and "set aside" the earlier CRTC decision, as the Broadcasting Act allowed, so as to permit a further review of the decision. When the CRTC reaffirmed its earlier decision, the communications minister intervened in the matter again, this time to outline conditions under which the licence would be operated by the CBC.[11] These conditions essentially created a compromise between the two sectors of the industry—public and private—and ensured that private industry participation in the TV news channel would be accommodated. As well, one of the conditions was that 70 percent of the news reporting would be from outside the Toronto region, thus ensuring broad regional participation. Clearly, the case indicated that the department is capable of overruling decisions made by appropriate regulatory bodies.

This type of forceful behaviour on the part of the department was envisioned years earlier in a document tabled in the House of Commons in March 1973 in the form of a policy Green Paper. Entitled *Proposals for a Communication Policy for Canada*, the paper set out the government's position and approach to the future regulation and development of communications in Canada. The then communications minister, Gerard Pelletier, indicated that it was important for the government, the communications industry, and the public to "mobilize Canadian creative, production and distribution resources" in order to protect Canadian cultural identity from "the massive generation of information and entertainment from across the border."[12]

To what extent that departmental "mobilization" of Canadian resources and creative capacities has

been successful is questionable at this time. In one instance, at least, the attempt to recruit resources in order to fulfil a national cultural purpose has been viewed as out of tune with the Canadian tradition of cultural freedom. When the Canadian Film Development Corporation was established in 1967, it diminished, in part, the mandate of the National Film Board. Three years later (a year after the establishment of the Department of Communications as a separate department), the NFB commissioner resigned, and in a press interview stated: "If our government decides to coordinate our whole cultural scene we are approaching the idea or possibility of state-voice culture. I'm not suggesting that M. Pelletier is trying to do this deliberately, but it is possible to move inadvertently into a situation where control is so concentrated that it becomes difficult to maintain cultural freedom."[13]

The purpose in bringing such comments to the attention of the reader is not to judge any of the department's actions related to the regulation of media industries. Indeed, government regulation, primarily through the instruments of the BBG and the CRTC, has fashioned a media industry of professional quality and of a scope needed by society, where one did not exist prior to the enactment of content quotas for broadcasting. However, when a governmental department describes communications infrastructure of the nation as "the very nervous system of the information society," and sees itself as the regulatory authority over that body, the danger of "state culture" should be apparent. These warnings may be underlined at a time when millions of Eastern Europeans are beginning to appreciate a pronounced relaxation of state intrusion in their everyday lives.

Advertising

The advertising industry provides an interesting focus of government regulation since advertising has such a pervasive influence in society. While advertising practices are normally thought of as being free-wheeling, creatively and competitively unrestricted, this is far from the truth. The element of competition is certainly a dominant characteristic of the industry, but the advertising market remains open and competitive largely *through* regulatory practices. Thus, we find that advertising, as a dynamic industry, is controlled by an equally dynamic regulatory system. Wright et al. identify eighteen federal statutes that regulate advertising,[14] and we find that at least a dozen federal departments and agencies are involved in enforcing these statutes. Of the latter, three predominate: the Department of National Health and Welfare, the Department of Consumer and Corporate Affairs, and the Canadian Radio-television Telecommunications Commission.

The concern of the Department of National Health and Welfare is to enforce the Food and Drugs Act legislation. Advertisements that discuss food and drug product claims must be cleared with and approved by that department. The term *claims* means that if any properties are attributed to food or drugs such advertisements require "copy" clearance. This is required for everything other than specifying the name of a product, where it might be purchased, and at what price. The department works very closely with the CRTC in enforcing this regulation.

The Department of Consumer and Corporate Affairs, through its Bureau of Competitive Policy and its Marketing Practices Branch, monitors advertising through the Competition Act (earlier the Combines Investigation Act). This act is unquestionably the most important single piece of legislation affecting advertising in Canada. It defines standards of conduct for the industry insofar as pricing practices and promotional allowances are concerned. It also treats offences under the rubric of misleading advertising. An example of how the marketplace is kept open and competitive is legislation relating to co-operative advertising (that is, advertising cost sharing between a product manufacturer and retail stores that sell the product), and investigations by Consumer and Corporate Affairs of co-operative advertising are commonplace. In effect, the legislation demands that the parent company that produces a product and shares advertising costs with retail distributors of the product must not favour one retailer over another.

At the same time, there is a large measure of regulation at the provincial level, and each province in Canada has its own set of requirements. In most cases, these regulations are similar from province to province, falling under the general term *consumer protection*. In some cases provincial regulations tend to be unique. An example of the latter would be Quebec's Charter of the French Language Act concerning linguistic labelling of products and packages.[15] In general, severe cases of violation of advertising ethics are considered to fall under the Criminal Code of Canada, and thus are within federal government jurisdiction. Table 10–1 lists the number of charges laid under the Competition Act for misleading and deceptive advertising practices. We note that, calculated as a percentage of legal actions initiated, conviction rates do not seem impressive; nor are the total fines levied, if divided by the number of convictions, of the magnitude likely to instill fear in those dealing with multimillion dollar accounts and willing to take risks.

The CRTC has a unique role to play in the control of advertising. First, it regulates the number of commercials permissible in a broadcast. Second, it regulates the type of product that can be advertised and charges broadcasters with responsibility for good taste in advertising. Third, the CRTC enforces copy clearance practices for particular advertisements, such as those dealing with food and drugs. As well, the CRTC has been forceful in its regulations concerning particular social problems and often holds open hearings to permit public dialogue concerning the social effects of advertising. This has been done in areas such as advocacy advertising, sex-role stereotyping, and advertising to children.

TABLE 10–1

Charges Laid Under the Competition Act for Misleading Advertising and Deceptive Marketing Practices

Fiscal Year	Cases Brought Before the Courts	Convictions %	$ Value of Fines
1979–80	244	41.8	378 380
1981–82	278	34.1	225 132
1983–84	332	41.8	1 654 640
1985–86	266	40.9	677 100
1987–88	245	34.2	661 500
1988–89	229	34.0	812 980
1989–90	195	25.1	907 850

Source: Data compiled from information in *Annual Reports* of the federal Department of Consumer and Corporate Affairs.

The Print Industry

In comparison with advertising and broadcasting, the print industries in Canada experience little in the way of formal government regulation. In chapter 6 we outlined attempts on the part of the government to regulate the print industry through the Davey Committee and the Kent Commission recommendations, but for a variety of reasons, the print industry is not subject to the same levels of control as the advertising and broadcasting industries. Nevertheless, it is clear that the government has used the instrument of the Income Tax Act both to protect the Canadian magazine industry in its pursuit of advertising revenue and to prevent non-Canadians from gaining ownership of newspapers and magazines. In the latter case, it is important to note that the mechanism of regulation is an indirect rather than a direct control of ownership. Given the provisions of the Income Tax Act, no foreigner would attempt to buy out a Canadian magazine or newspaper in the knowledge that Canadian accounts would not likely advertise in those publications and thus lose their tax advantage.

It is, however, the area of *concentration of ownership* in the print industry that has been a constant concern to government, and demands continually arise for formal investigations of this matter. One of the latest cases of increased concentration of ownership to attract political attention at the federal level involved Southam News's acquisition of 63 percent ownership of a British Columbia publishing company that owns twenty-four community newspapers and weekly specialty publications in the province. This is added to Southam's existing ownership of the *Sun* and the *Province*, both Vancouver newspapers. One opposition Member of Parliament in arguing that the House Committee on Communications and Culture should review the Southam purchase stated "there is no greater threat to a free press in Canada than the concentration of ownership in the hands of a few corporations."[16] The concentration of ownership keeps greater government involvement in the industry alive.

Broadcasting

Of all mass media, broadcasting is by far the most stringently regulated. Regulations have been in effect from the first day that a broadcasting signal was transmitted. Unlike print, the technology of broadcasting invites regulation. There needs to be a body or organization to allocate broadcasting frequencies, since some radio frequencies and television channels are more preferable than others. Left to their own devices, broadcasters would very quickly create technical chaos. But there are two further reasons why broadcasting has been subject to regulation. First, there has been an understanding that while publishers use their own presses to create their products, broadcasters utilize the public airwaves. The principle, then, has been established that the airwaves belong to the people, and that society "owns" broadcasting licences. Second, from the beginning days of broadcasting, it has been recognized that radio and television are instruments that affect audiences differently than does print. Although it may be a generalization, broadcasting continues to be regarded as a producer of signals that audiences respond to emotionally/sensually, rather than cognitively as is the case with print. With the recognition of broadcasting's power to persuade, Canadian governments felt obliged to regulate the industry and place broadcasting instruments into the service of society.

Regulatory bodies for Canadian broadcasting, as pointed out in chapter 7, have evolved over the past seventy-five years into the present CRTC. The commission represents a unique regulatory instrument, and an examination of its methods of regulation, along with some examples of how it conducts its business, are central to this discussion of government regulation.

The CRTC regulatory process begins with a philosophical rationale for its activities: "broadcasting is not an end itself. It is subject to higher and more general imperatives of national development and survival."[17] It is from such a philosophical touchstone that the Broadcasting Act outlines a mandate for the CRTC. In general, the commission will: regulate and establish rules of procedure for the industry; specify and issue licences to broadcasters, both public and private; renew, suspend, or revoke licences as needed; and hold public hearings to permit the Canadian community access to the regulatory process.

In terms of accountability the CRTC follows several reporting routes: It interacts with Parliament through the Standing Parliamentary Committee on Communication and Culture. It also reports to the federal Department of Communications (through the minister of that department); and finally the CRTC

BOX 10-2

Commitment of the CRTC

The commitment of the CRTC, the federal communications regulator, is to preserve and enhance communications systems in Canada in the interests of the Canadian public. In carrying out this commitment, the CRTC will foster an environment characterized by a wide diversity and availability of Canadian services and facilities offered by adequately resourced entities. Furthermore, in pursuit of the commitment, the CRTC will act in an efficient, proactive and adaptive manner supported by the fullest possible public participation.

Source: Canada, CRTC, *Annual Report 1987–1988* (Ottawa, 1988), 4.

often receives guidance and policy directions from cabinet.

The CRTC also has a commitment to the Canadian community and box 10–2 explains this commitment. To honour this commitment, the CRTC has used, and continues to use, various regulatory strategies. These are discussed below.

Station Logs

Each broadcasting station is required to report regularly on its activities through a station log. The log, which is simply a written document (now in computerized format), reports virtually every activity—down to the second—of each broadcast day. In Ottawa, the logs are studied with respect to program content and commercials. Obviously, the log is important in permitting the CRTC to regulate advertising and programming requirements. As well, the regular reporting of stations to the CRTC permits the commission to keep a finger on the pulse of the industry.

Monitoring Codes of Behaviour

The CRTC, in its interaction with consumers and the industry, is often in the position of co-operating with self-regulatory activities on the part of the industry. While the commission may agree to a self-regulatory process, it continues to monitor industry behaviour carefully. Should there be a need to harden the regulatory stance, the commission can make adherence to industry codes a condition of licence.

In the matter of sex-role stereotyping, the Canadian Association of

Broadcasters, in May 1988, volunteered to regulate its own activities through a national Canadian Broadcast Standards Council. In April 1990, the CAB announced the formation of five regional councils, which, in addition to discouraging sex-role stereotyping by its members, would handle public complaints about such stereotyping and administer any other self-regulatory codes.[18]

In its earlier agreement to the proposal, the commission endorsed the self-regulatory activity and indicated that it would closely monitor the behaviour of broadcasters to make sure they were adhering to their self-imposed code. If they stuck to it for a given period of time, the commission indicated that it would show its good faith in the self-regulation principle by allowing them to apply for a release from licensing requirements concerning sex-role stereotyping.[19]

Policy Guidelines

The CRTC regularly issues policy guidelines, which are usually based on information gathered at public hearings and from individuals and groups across the country. There are many of these guidelines and they tend to be addressed, as our earlier definition noted, to particular problems. Among others, a policy guideline was issued on the very contentious issue of "balanced programming." Section 3 (d) of the Broadcasting Act stipulates that broadcasters, in their programming, are expected to provide "reasonable, *balanced* opportunity for the expression of differing views on matters of public concern." The problem, at the operational level, is what is balance? Here the CRTC indicates that the requirement may be satisfied in the following way: "a variety of points of view will be made available . . . to a reasonably consistent viewer or listener over a reasonable period of time." In effect, broadcasters need not strike a "balance" in each and every single program; rather, offering varying points of view on contentious issues over a period of time would be seen as providing audiences with alternative perspectives.[20]

Canadian Talent

The CRTC has been committed to the policy of developing Canadian talent. Talent, in this case, includes all artistic, production, and administrative resources that have as their focus the production of worthwhile broadcast programming. It goes without saying that the regulatory bodies that preceded the CRTC, the Board of Broadcast Governors, and the CBC, were also dedicated to developing Canadian talent. In furthering its objectives, the CRTC has instituted four major strategies.

Content Quotas. A content quota has been in effect for television broadcasting since 1959/1960 and for radio broadcasting since 1970. In defining its concern about Canadian content, the CRTC has been careful to point out that it is unacceptable for Canadian content to be buried in "ghetto" periods. Rather, the objective of producing such

content is to "provide and exhibit in all broadcasting time periods, including the most popular viewing hours, a wide range of high-quality, Canadian-produced programs that a significant number of Canadians will choose to watch."[21]

The CRTC emphasized the importance of developing programs that will reflect the Canadian experience and compete for the attention of viewers domestically and internationally. The commission stressed that producing such programs is "no longer a matter of desirability but of necessity."[22] The quota system has been the commission's prime instrument in promoting Canadian talent.

While the amount of required Canadian content has varied over the years, the trend has always been to increase the quota requirements. The current requirement is that 30 percent of music played on AM and FM radio stations be Canadian. In calculating this quota, two of the following four conditions must be fulfilled: the music should be composed by a Canadian; the lyrics should be written by a Canadian; the performer(s) should be Canadian; and the performance should either take place or be recorded in Canada.

For television the current quota is 60 percent over an entire program schedule and 50 percent in prime time (6:00 p.m. to midnight) for private broadcasters, and 60 percent in prime time for the CBC. In this instance, it must be noted that the CBC has consistently programmed more than the required

BOX 10-3

What Is Canadian Content?

In some instances there appears to be a flaw in the four-point qualifying formula for Canadian music. In the fall of 1991, Canadian recording star Bryan Adams, who is a member of the Order of Canada, failed to meet Canadian content regulations for his new album *Waking Up the Neighbours*. The CRTC ruled that the album gained only one point on the four-point system. Adams gained one point for being Canadian. However, since he co-wrote the music and lyrics with British producer Robert Lange and the album was not recorded in Canada, he was not eligible to gain any additional points. As a result the album did not qualify as Canadian content.

Newspapers in Canada, not to mention Adams's fans, responded to the CRTC decision with varying degrees of disapproval, suggesting that it was time for the CRTC to review its Canadian content requirements.

The commission, in explaining its decision, conceded that "the system's not perfect. But it has worked pretty well for the past 20 years—and we have a pretty healthy music industry as a result."[a]

[a] Chris Dafoe, "Not Enough Can-Con, Adams Told," *Globe and Mail*, 13 September 1991, C1.

60 percent and, in co-operation with the CRTC, has set its sights on a 95 percent Canadian content quota.

The matter of defining what is "Canadian" for television has never been happily resolved for all parties concerned. Generally, whatever a Canadian station produces in its own studios is considered Canadian, but difficulties arise when an independent producer brings his or her program to a station or network to be telecast. In order for that program to qualify as Canadian, the following set of conditions apply. The producer must be Canadian. Thereafter six points must be earned. They are awarded as follows:

- two points each for a Canadian director and writer, either of whom must be part of the production team.
- one point each for a Canadian leading performer, second leading performer, head of art department, head of photography, music composer, and/or program editor.

As well at least 75 percent of the total salary paid must be to Canadians, and at least 75 percent of post-production costs (editing, dubbing, etc.) must be paid to Canadians. In addition to this detailed formula, the Task Force on Broadcasting Policy in 1986 offered the following more general view of what constitutes Canadian programming: "Canadian programs are those which are creatively controlled by Canadians and made primarily for Canadians."[23] While these regulations might appear to be a trivialization of a serious activity, when the formula is examined carefully, it becomes apparent how Canadian content regulations are aimed at the development of an industry as well as talent. It is clear that one cannot exist without the other.

In its desire to see more underrepresented content (particularly drama) in Canadian programming schedules, the CRTC has offered an unusual incentive to broadcasters. If a drama is produced and gains ten points using the above formula, and if that program is scheduled to commence between 7:00 and 10:00 p.m., the commission is prepared to calculate 150 percent Canadian content rather than 100 percent. This incentive, created by the CRTC in 1983, indicates an important change in calculating quota hours.[24] In effect, the commission is recognizing qualitative concerns, rather than only running times of programs.

Local Programming. The CRTC has always emphasized broadcasters' responsibilities to their communities and as applicants for new licences or renewed licences have appeared before the commission, their programming intentions have always been examined to see if they reflect a commitment to local community programming.

Generally, local programming has consisted of news, weather, sports, some publics affairs, talk shows and so on. With some notable exceptions, broadcasters have seldom produced programs that showcased community musical or dramatic talent. In March 1985, the CRTC announced a plan whereby greater flexibility would be introduced into producing content in such underrepresented categories as variety and drama. First, TV stations would be permitted to cooperate with other stations in their regions in production endeavours so long as each station spent no less money than it would have alone on such a production, and so long as the resulting co-operative program was relevant to the audiences of both regions. In such circumstances, each of the two stations would be entitled to claim that program as a local program.[25] Subsequently, the CRTC made co-operative productions more flexible by allowing independent producers who might have received funding from Telefilm Canada to join the production team.[26]

Canadian Content: Foreign Coproduction. Finally, with respect to defining Canadian content in a situation where a Canadian producer co-operates with a non-Canadian producer, the CRTC, while encouraging such coproduction efforts, nevertheless, set certain conditions for the resulting program to qualify as Canadian content. Among the most important are the following: the Canadian production company must be Canadian owned or controlled by Canadians; the budgets of the Canadian and foreign participants must be approximately equal; the Canadian partner must have equity interest and profit sharing in the production; and, most importantly, the production package programs are acceptable only in the under-represented content categories of drama, variety, documentary, and children's programming.[27]

Canadian Content: Enforced Budgeting. In the fall of 1988, the CRTC renewed the operating licences of seventy-five "originating" television stations in the country. The commission adopted an innovative regulatory approach with respect to Canadian content regulations by specifying that each privately owned station spend a fixed amount of money on Canadian production. The amount was determined by advertising revenues calculated over previous years. Examples of these stations' programming costs for the first year of the new licence period were: $17.4 million for CFCF-TV, Montreal; $17.3 million for CHAN-TV, Vancouver; and, $17.2 million for CFTO-TV, Toronto. Overall this regulatory approach was estimated to generate a minimum of $2 billion for the production of Canadian programs over a five-year period.[28]

CRTC Public Addresses: Friendly Persuasion

The annual meetings of the organizations that comprise the broadcasting industry usually feature keynote speakers who are invited to speak about the state of the industry. The chair of the CRTC is heavily in demand for these occasions. When the chair addresses the annual meeting of the CAB, for instance, speakers do not miss the opportunity either to identify some pressing problem facing the industry or to test the waters concerning some planned policy. It was in precisely this setting that the first public announcement of the proposal of the Board of Broadcast Governors to introduce a Canadian content quota for broadcasting was made. The identification of problem areas occurs within a particular business reality: members of the audience are very likely at some future date to be appearing before the keynote speaker to request a favourable response to some matter concerning a broadcast licence. Therefore it is simply sound business practice to pay close attention to these keynote addresses and to heed the implicit suggestions they contain.

In-House Research

In its Ottawa/Hull offices, the CRTC maintains its own research department and conducts its own day-to-day research activities in such areas as broadcast programming, audience studies, the financial status of broadcasting, and telecommunications companies, as well as other topics that are likely to yield hard numbers regarding the status of the industry. On occasion the commission engages independent researchers to undertake certain studies. For example, researchers have been hired to study sex-role stereotyping in broadcasting and broadcasting advertising. We mention this to emphasize that the CRTC, when it passes judgement on the behaviour of the industry, attempts to do so on the basis of sound knowledge.

The Private Sector: CRTC Concerns

In a variety of ways the CRTC pointedly offers guidance and direct assistance to the private broadcasting industry. This assistance often takes the form of regulatory protective measures. The commission has often accepted the brickbats thrown at it for what appears to be favouritism to the private sector. The commission's legitimate purpose in carrying out such regulatory protective measures is to permit private broadcasters to fulfil the objectives of the Broadcasting Act.

Broadcasting as an industry is profitable, and in some cases extremely so. But it is not in the ten major markets in the country in which the commission normally offers assistance. Some of the protective strategies are seen at public hearings; for example, when broadcasters appear for licence renewals, there are no competitors present for that particular broadcasting frequency or channel. When a broadcaster decides to sell his or her organization, while the CRTC does not "rubber stamp" the would-be buyer, neither does it invite new licence applicants. Such practices are often seen to be overly protec-

tive, but they are designed to ensure an orderly market.[29] One very important regulation protecting private broadcasters has been the requirement placed on cable companies for "simultaneous program substitution." This practice occurs when a cable company is running the same program as one shown on a local conventional channel. In such cases, the cable company is obliged to "dump" the distant (often non-Canadian) signal and in its place insert the local channel program, complete with commercials. This is done to protect the local Canadian station and its advertisers.

A variation of this regulation is seen in the protective device that has been in effect for the past twenty-five years requiring the deletion of commercials in programs that are received by cable companies over the air from U.S. sources. Cable operators who purchase such U.S. programs and then transmit them by cable into Canadian homes are required, on a random basis, to eliminate U.S. commercials accompanying these programs. The purpose of this practice has been to discourage Canadian advertisers from placing their commercials with American television stations near the Canadian border. Canadian advertisers were among the first to learn that in most cases, when given the choice, Canadians opt to view U.S. programs and channels rather than Canadian ones. The practice of eliminating U.S. commercials in cablecasts continues today. It might be noted that such protective strategies that affect U.S. broadcasters and programmers are currently being examined in the light of the U.S.–Canada Free Trade Agreement.

Public Comment

A very important part of the CRTC regulatory process is to respond to comments made by the public, either by letter, over the phone, or by personal representation. As the commission itself has noted, "the participation of the public is a central element of the Commission's decision-making process."[30] In 1988–89 the commission received nearly 6000 written complaints and inquiries. It encourages such feedback because it is regarded as a useful indicator of the level of public satisfaction.

When licensees are scheduled to appear before the commission on whatever issue, the CRTC tends to be helpful in permitting, and indeed inviting, public comment. It is not unusual, for example, for the commission to hold its public hearings in two dozen communities across the country in a single year. This practice brings the hearing process to the community level, often enabling personal intervention that might not be possible if hearings were only held in Ottawa, as they once were.

Interventions are also invited through public notice: not less than fifty days before the date of the public hearing, the commission publishes notices in *The Canada Gazette.* Announcements are also published in newspapers in areas that are affected by the commission's hearing agenda. In addition, broadcast licensees on the agenda of the commission at a particular hearing are obliged to broadcast announcements on at least four occasions within a ten-day period prior to the hearing.[31]

Such announcements also advise members of the public about where and how they may gain access to the licensee's written application for a new licence or a renewal, whichever the case may be. These written documents, which are also available for public reading at the hearing itself, are important, since prior to the hearing members of the public have an opportunity to familiarize themselves with a broadcaster's past performance or promises of performance. The latter furnishes the basis for the implicit contract broadcasters make with their communities.

The Hearing Process

In effect, the hearing process becomes an evaluative exercise regarding the fulfilment of promises of performance. These evaluations provide the basis of what several royal commissions and committees in the past have referred to as the "logic of the licence." Society makes known to the CRTC its expectations regarding national aspirations. The CRTC, in granting licences or renewals, expects broadcasters to fulfil these expectations. Thus, the logic of having a licensing process is to add emphasis to the role broadcasters are expected to play with respect to the demands of Broadcasting Act.

As readers are aware, the Broadcasting Act empowers the commission not only to issue licences but also to suspend or revoke them. A study of CRTC licensing decisions over the thirteen-year period 1968 to 1981 revealed that the commission denied twenty-eight licence renewals out of a total of several thousand applications. Of these twenty-eight denials, only three were related to inadequate programming standards. The remaining twenty-five nonrenewals were for various reasons unrelated to programming and generally involving business and finance. Thus, while the threat of nonrenewal is real, "it is clear that the CRTC uses its punitive power with considerable restraint and discretion," preferring instead strategies such as warnings, fines, and penalties, as well as short-term renewals as opposed to the conventional five- to seven-year licence period.[32]

Thus, the regulatory strategy of the CRTC, which finds its focus in the hearing itself, involves a continuous evaluation of a station's licence during the period from hearing to hearing. As a result when a broadcaster appears before the commission with a request for licence renewal, that broadcaster should not be surprised by the outcome of his or her application.

Overall, then, there are several aspects to CRTC regulatory activity. These include: a process of regular reporting on the part of the broadcaster; an opportunity for public participation with respect to formal interventions at hearings; indications of satisfactory broadcasting performance between hearings; as well as close monitoring activity on the part of the commission itself.

Self-regulation

Self-regulation processes in mass media industries occur at the local level, as mass media industries function in their own communities, and at the national level through national organizations that function as professional associations—for example, the Canadian Association of Broadcasters, the Canadian Daily Newspaper Publishers Association, and the Association of Canadian Advertisers.

In self-regulatory activities at the community media level, media managers are well aware of the need to behave in a responsible manner, for it is from their communities that many of their advertising accounts come. At the same time, media practitioners tend to practise standards of behaviour that are consistent with the expectations of their profession and the society at large.

Insofar as advertising is concerned, the regulatory authorities have made it clear that the station owner is responsible for the quality of the product that is broadcast. If a broadcaster is insensitive to accepted community standards, then complaint and intervention processes established for the purpose are likely to be used quickly to remedy the situation.

However, the principle of self-regulation has often come into question and for several reasons. First, there is no legal requirement for membership in professional organizations or for compliance with their codes of behaviour. Second, there are no apparent sanctions for noncompliance. The third vital consideration in self-regulation is the question of whether the process violates antitrust laws. In effect can an industry police itself?

Some examples of self-regulation show how the process operates. In 1963 the Canadian Advertising Foundation, based in Toronto and Montreal, established a Canadian Code of Advertising Standards. Regional councils were put in place to handle complaints and also became clearinghouses for inquiries, either from the public or from sectors of the industry themselves. Regional councils are located in Vancouver, Edmonton, Calgary, Regina, Winnipeg, and Halifax. The responsibilities of the councils go beyond handling complaints, in that they are constantly involved in liaising with government and public interest groups. Further, the councils develop, up-date, and publicize standards and codes and often initiate related research.

There are instances where advertisers fail to observe the codes of behaviour and fail to take corrective action. In such cases, the Advertising Standards Council is likely to use persuasive power to request compliance. Should such action also fail, the code offers the following scenario: " . . . the Council then notifies the media involved, or will sometimes ask that a bulletin be sent to all association members indicating that this message, in the Council's judgement, contravenes the Code. In effect, this means the media will not accept the message in its existing form."[33] It is understandable that to fall into disfavour with one's peers is not a position that anyone normally desires, either personally, or in a business context.

The Standards Code has received broad national acceptance and it tends to be highly regarded by organizations that participate in the affairs of the Canadian Advertising Foundation. Perhaps this is because the intention is "to make advertising more effective by continuing to raise the standard of advertising excellence and by ensuring integrity in advertising content."[34]

The extent and the breadth of self-regulation in the advertising industry is evidenced by the list of those organizations that endorse the code and function according to its standards. As is seen in box 10–3, those who endorse the Canadian Code of Advertising Standards include a number of mass media associations, such as the Canadian Daily Newspaper Association (CDNA) and the Canadian Community Newspapers Association. The Canadian Association of Broadcasters (CAB) represents the private sector owners and executive officers of

BOX 10–4

Organizations Participating in the Canadian Code of Advertising Standards

Advertising and Sales Executive Club of Montreal
Association of Canadian Advertisers
Association of Medical Advertising Agencies
Association of Quebec Advertising Agencies
Better Business Bureau of Canada
Brewers Association of Canada
Canadian Association of Broadcasters
Canadian Broadcasting Corporation
Canadian Business Press
Canadian Cable Television Association
Canadian Community Newspapers Association
Canadian Cosmetic, Toiletry and Fragrance Association
Canadian Daily Newspaper Association
Canadian Direct Marketing Association
Canadian Magazine Publishers Association
Canadian National Yellow Pages
Direct Sellers Association
Grocery Products Manufacturers of Canada
Institute of Canadian Advertising
Le Publicité Club de Montréal
Magazines Canada
Non-Prescription Drug Manufacturers of Canada
Ontario Funeral Service Association
Outdoor Advertising Association of Canada
Pharmaceutical Advertising Advisory Board
Retail Council of Canada
Society of Ontario Advertising Agencies
Telecaster Committee of Canada
Trans-Ad Limited
Trans-Canada Advertising Agency Network
Welcome Wagon Ltd.

Source: Canadian Advertising Foundation, *Canadian Code of Advertising Standards* (Toronto: Canadian Advertising Foundation, April 1991), 10.

broadcasting organizations. Whatever the medium, the respective association functions in a similar manner.

Associations

It is often a prime role for associations to perform a political lobbying activity. Lobbying in this case may be defined briefly as a liaison between mass media organizations and political structures in a society. The lobbyist has a central responsibility of explaining the interests of industry to government or, often, of government to industry. The form this explanation takes varies, but it certainly involves preparing and entering interventions in discussions and hearings of regulatory or political bodies. Second, the association normally provides a day-to-day information service to its members, to the public, and to government. This service operates in two modes: it feeds out information as would a public relations firm and it also responds to any requests for information. Thus, the publication of various informational materials is normally an important part of an association's activities. In a related way, because the association has a concern about distributing information, the association's officers have an influential role concerning the industry's technical, ethical, and content standards. Associations often schedule and promote meetings and seminars that serve as an educational resource for its members. These activities are normally associated with annual meetings of

the association, but may occur at other times as well. Finally, associations are likely to have their own publications, newsletters, bulletins, or magazines.

The CDNA, as a professional association, participates in all of the activities discussed above, and even a quick scanning of the content of any *CDNA Bulletin* reveals the educative role performed by the association. For example, one issue in February 1990 discusses legal cases dealing with the following themes: access to public records, disclosure of information; prior restraint (censorship), defamation, Charter of Rights, and copyright.[35] Other issues of the *Bulletin* usually contain information concerning new publishing technology, new photography methods, and uses of charts and graphs, so as to inform its membership about industrial and professional trends.

In broadcasting, the CAB performs the same functions of the associations outlined above and in addition has fostered the highly influential *Canadian Broadcaster*, a magazine that is sympathetic to the interests of the private sector, even though it is privately owned and published. The magazine is essential reading for anyone associated with or interested in the industry, as is *Broadcasting*, a magazine associated with the National Association of Broadcasters in the U.S.

Through such publications as the ones we have mentioned, both the CAB and the CDNA offer their members guidelines concerning appropriate behaviour. It is in this instructional role that associations and their members help to regulate themselves. It should be noted that association publications are not soley for the membership—they are available for all to see. As a consequence, they frequently elicit feedback from the public or from governmental bodies or agencies. This is one of the ways in which society, industry, and government interact in the process of regulation.

One final note concerning self-regulation should be added here, and that is the development of press councils in Canada, which has occurred since the publication of the Davey Committee *Report* in 1970. Press councils have been formed at the community and provincial levels as a result of initiatives taken by the industry at the suggestion of the Senate Committee.[36] While the history of press councils is a large subject in itself, at this point it is only necessary to indicate that this self-regulatory activity offers a direct route for the participation and protection of the public. Since many adjudications by press councils have favoured the complainants, such activity tends to define more clearly the boundaries of acceptable media behaviour.

Self-regulation: The Reporting of News

Self-regulation is firmly entrenched in Canada with respect to reporting of news—in both the print and broadcast media. In the case of broadcasting, government regula-

tory bodies have seldom entered the domain of journalists in any attempt to influence their behaviour. When they have done so, it has been to ensure that the news profession remains free from any restraints. An example will explain. In 1973, the Canadian Association of Broadcasters co-operated in an arrangement with the Canadian Association of Chiefs of Police that would, in effect, leave in the hands of police departments decisions concerning the release of crime information. The CRTC called a special meeting with representatives of the CAB to remind them of the very unwise arrangement they had agreed to with respect to journalistic responsibility. The arrangement was quickly dissolved by the CAB.[37]

There have been other instances when regulatory attempts to intervene in the journalistic process have been made. While the events surrounding Bill C-58 have been discussed in chapter 6, and while magazine nonadvertising content has been quantified as a result, newspapers have been relatively free of regulation. Enactments to regulate newspaper content have been short-lived or have failed to get off the ground. Three examples will explain.

In the Province of Alberta in 1937, the government of Premier Aberhart passed "An Act to Ensure the Publication of Accurate News and Information." The act, in effect, gave the government of the day the right to evaluate published news stories to see if they were truthful. The Canadian Supreme

Court disallowed the legislation. As a note of interest, the *Edmonton Journal*, in championing the cause of freedom of expression in this instance, was awarded a Pulitzer Prize for its exemplary behaviour.[38]

As discussed also in chapter 6, a central recommendation of the Royal Commission on Newspapers in 1981 was aimed at establishing a federal Canadian Newspaper Act. In the act, specifications were made that would have required the overseeing of the editorial behaviour of newspapers at the community level, and the reporting of this behaviour all the way to Parliament through the Ministry of Justice. As mentioned previously, the bill to legislate a Newspaper Act was introduced in Parliament, but no action was taken.[39]

Five years earlier, a Province of Ontario Royal Commission on Violence in the Communications Industry recommended that a national Freedom of Expression Act be written. Among other matters, the act would have focussed on censorship, libel, obscenity, breach of the official Secrets Act, and treason. As well, the recommendations proposed that the act would define the limits of free expression concerning "promulgating information that leads to incitement of violence or crime."[40] The report of that commission was not acted upon. With respect to messages that could lead to violence and crime, the recommendation was so broad in its scope that it could virtually eliminate the reporting of anything but "good" news. Thus far self-regulation,

largely through exhortations, by-laws, and professional codes, has had to suffice for the functioning of the print news industries.

The same may be said of broadcasting, and one notable example of self-regulation may be cited here. Since its inception in 1936, the Canadian Broadcasting Corporation has maintained a policy manual for its employees regarding the practice of journalism. The latest edition of the manual, entitled *Journalistic Policy*, identifies several areas of concern for broadcast journalists and programmers. Among other subjects discussed are: rights of the public; legal matters, such as the Canadian Charter, court reporting, copyright, official secrets; political reporting and so forth.

The CBC's journalistic policy is noteworthy since it sets out, without any ambiguity, both a philosophical and practical approach to journalistic behaviour. The manual outlines the following basic premises:[41]

(a) The air belongs to the people, who are entitled to hear the principal points of view on all questions of importance;

(b) The air must not fall under the control of individuals or groups influential because of their special position;

(c) The full interchange of opinion is one of the principal safeguards of free institutions;

(d) The Corporation maintains and exercises editorial authority, control, and responsibility for the contents of all programs broadcast on its facilities;

(e) The Corporation takes no editorial position in its programming.

With respect to the matter of "balance," the manual adds further that:

> programs dealing with an issue of substantial controversy on a one-time basis should give adequate recognition to the range of opinion on the subject. Fairness must be the guiding principle in presentation, so that the audience is enabled to make a judgment on the matter in question based on the facts.[42]

Thus far, in our recent history mass media have been largely free of formal governmental regulation with respect to news reporting. The development of instruments by the mass media themselves (codes, press councils, policies enacted by media associations) has served Canadian society reasonably well. Part and parcel of the self-regulatory process has been the capacity of media to take corrective actions when needed. While it is true that occasional lapses by the media in their reporting and analyzing the day's events have occurred, in most cases such lapses are not the fault of the systems of reporting. Rather, problems occur because news practitioners, like individuals working in other capacities, are mere mortals.

A climate in Canada has developed over the past twenty-five years wherein it has become apparent that the government is ready to entertain the notion of regulation with respect to the reporting of news. Self-regulatory measures currently in place, if consistenly adhered to, seem to offer a reasonable alternative to government regulation.

Consumerism

A third very influential regulatory activity is to be found in consumerism—a social process in which consumers join together to use group influence on governments and manufacturers. They do so in a manner that will result in protection for consumers as they interact in the marketplace with product manufacturers and sellers.

There are several reasons for the growth of consumerism in Canada and these do not differ markedly from those that prompted such growth in the United Kingdom and the United States. Post-Industrial Revolution Western society, in adopting mass production techniques, created surplus. In the midst of abundance, consumers often found that products were not always what advertisements claimed. Neither were the glowing pictures portrayed of society's industries by public relations practitioners always consistent with reality. While industrialists were creating a high standard of living, they were also polluting the land, water, and air, and doing little to aid the poor. Given the shocking evidence of the failure of capitalism during the Depression years, it was evident that all was not as healthy as we had been led to believe.

It is possible to describe a first phase of the development of consumerism beginning approximately in the 1920s. This phase was characterized by the growth of co-operative and labour union movements. Since individuals were at the mercy of the marketing process, it was found that groups employing defensive activities proved to be effective.

The Second World War marked a second phase of the development of consumerism in Canada; home-front mobilization of all social resources was instituted in effective support of Canada's war effort. While belt-tightening, rationing and organization of efforts were instituted, a paramount lesson learned was that governments under pressure are able to regulate fair trade practices. In addition to these insights, the Second World War also produced a group of highly experienced and self-sufficient women, who recognized their own effectiveness in protecting consumers in wartime. Two years following the end of the war, in 1947, the Canadian Association of Consumers, later changed to the Consumers Association of Canada (CAC), was established. CAC continued in peacetime what had been learned in wartime. Both at the federal and the provincial levels, CAC pressured governments to institute protective legislation concerning marketplace fraud, deception, price gouging, and imbalances in industrial competition. It should be noted that CAC was highly successful in its aggressive efforts and in 1963 began

to publish the magazines *Canadian Consumer* and *Le consommateur Canadien.* The magazines are owned and published by Canadian Consumer Inc., a subsidiary of CAC. The purpose of the publications is to keep members informed about CAC activity but, more importantly, they publish the results of the association's product-testing program. A recent issue of *Canadian Consumer* discusses the testing program: "Test reports are based on laboratory tests, controlled user tests, and/or experts' evaluations of the purchased sample."[43] The publication of product ratings are candid and highly regarded in the Canadian community and such ratings range from "very good" to "unacceptable" and products are scored (from best to worst).

In the same year that *Canadian Consumer* began, the federal government responded favourably to consumer activism in the country by establishing a Department of Consumer and Corporate Affairs. The *Globe and Mail* recently commented on the significance of this legislation:

When Parliament approved the establishment of the Department of Consumer and Corporate Affairs, Canada became the first nation in the world to respond to one of the significant social movements of the 1960s—consumerism—by providing a place at the Cabinet table where consumer interests could be represented along with those of agriculture, industry, and other producer groups.[44]

The establishment of the federal department might very well be regarded as the beginning of a third phase of consumerism in Canada, for we find its role somewhat altered after this point. The department moved quickly to introduce legislation ("twelve bills in three years"[45]) in response to consumer advocates' concerns related to matters of weights and measures, packaging and labelling, and hazardous products.

The federal minister at the time, Ron Basford, urged that an advisory consumer group to his department be created, and in particular pressed for a formal recognition of consumer rights in the manner that had been introduced in 1962 in the United States. In essence these were: the right of safety, the right to be informed, the right of choice, and the right to be heard.[46]

The minister's advisory group, which became known as the Canadian Consumer Council, responded by forwarding to the minister in 1972 a statement that enumerated consumer rights under a Canadian Charter. The document identified several consumer rights: the right to purchase, in terms of reasonable access; the right to information (the right to have accurate facts); the right to fair value; the right to choose freely; the right to safety; and the right to redress.[47]

It is possible to identify a fourth phase of consumerism in Canada, one that began in the early 1980s. The weekly *Financial Post* describes the current state of consumerism in Canada as "a mid-life crisis," and identifies such a crisis by a drop-off in membership of CAC, as well as a change in an earlier enthusiasm: "... the evangelical fire that once pervaded the North American consumer's movement is a fading ember today."[48]

The reasons for the apparent malaise of consumerism in Canada are not difficult to identify: earlier, there was much to do and there were many causes to address. When the corrective measures concerning basic consumer needs (for example, food prices, safety, fair trade practices) were achieved, consumerism moved on to attack a different set of social problems: pollution of the environment, broadcasting legislation, rights of women in the workplace, advertising to children, among others. Such issues, however, were no longer the exclusive territory of CAC. They were also taken up by various human rights groups. At the same time, it is evident that the federal and provincial governments have responded to consumers' demands and in this sense have taken some of the initiative away from consumer groups. Governments have seldom been known to shy away from exercises of authority, particularly if this is being done at the behest of the voting public. It might very well be that consumerism, on the large organized scale that has characterized CAC, has fulfilled a very useful purpose, and at this moment finds it difficult to formulate strategies clearly and with the zeal that was evident earlier. On the occasion of its fortieth anniversary in 1988, the *Globe and Mail* reported on CAC as follows: amid the celebrations, "the organization was insolvent, losing members and mismanaging its finances, which included almost a million dollars a year in government grants."[49] Ottawa responded to CAC's financial problems with an immediate $300 000 emergency bailout, as well as $1.7 million to discharge its debts.[50]

Consumerism, however, is not dead, even though it is not practised through CAC as it once was. There has been a shift from product monitoring to concerns of a broader nature that involve mass media behaviour. MediaWatch, for example, is a consumer group with a specific objective that is apparent in its name. It currently has found a high level of credibility with Ottawa regulators due to its sound research approaches to media behaviour. A similar form of consumerism is evident in the work of the Fraser Institute's National Media Archive. The archive puts out a research publication, *On Balance,* which contains analyses of media treatment of various public issues, such as free trade, the Meech Lake constitutional proposals and the Gulf War.

A special kind of consumer group has recently been formed in the U.S., an example of which is "Americans for Responsible Television." The full attention of this organization is aimed at gratuitous violence and exploitive sex, which appear in increasing amounts on U.S. television. In effect, the group concerns itself with what it terms "a violence epidemic" among juveniles. The strategies of such consumer groups are uncomplicated: they advise advertisers who sponsor television programs that depict gratuitous amounts of violence and sex that their products will be boycotted. In this sense, consumer power has again become mobilized against social problems. As a member of the American Family Association indicated, when pornography and violence are so abundant that they are considered to be dangerous to family values, consumers respond in a manner that "they [media] understand which is economic sanctions."[51] This strategy is endorsed by the popular columnist Ann Landers who notes, "The most effective blow is to the pocketbook."[52] The activities of these consumer groups and others like them have been described by the three major U.S. broadcasting networks as "attempts to manipulate our free society and democratic process."[53] It is certainly evident that consumer groups have moved into that arena.

The overall consumer movement represents a form of democratic activism that is mobilized when more formal regulatory interventions are absent. The inevitable consequence of consumerism is two-fold: either offenders correct their behaviour in order to alleviate consumer pressures, or governments will intervene through legislation or regulation. Again we note that the three participants in regulation (industry, government, and the public) are interactive and interdependent.

Notes

1. See Seymour Martin Lipset, *Continental Divide: The Values and Institutions of the United States and Canada* (New York: Routledge, Chapman and Hall, 1990), 225–27.

2. Parliament of Canada, Canada Act 1982, part I, section 2.

3. Lynda Ashley, "Future Freedoms: Festinger on the Charter, Broadcasting and the CRTC," *Broadcaster* 47 (August 1988): 17–18.

4. Canada Act 1982, part I, section 1.

5. See Canada, CRTC, "Radio Frequencies Are Public Property: Public Announcement and Decisions of the Commission on the Application for Renewal of the Canadian Broadcasting Corporation's Television and Radio Licences, 31 March 1974" (Ottawa, 1974), 28.

6. John C. Merrill, *The Dialectic in Journalism: Toward a Responsible Use of Press Freedom* (Baton Rouge: Louisiana State Press, 1989), 29.

7. Lipset, *Continental Divide*, 225.

8. The Fairness Doctrine was repealed in August 1987. See "Fairness Held Unfair," *Broadcasting* 113 (10 August 1987): 27–28, 62. Also see John H. Watkins, *The Mass Media and the Law* (Englewood Cliffs, NJ: Prentice-Hall, 1990), 413–26.

9. Communications Canada, *Annual Report 1989-1990* (Ottawa: Supply and Services, 1991), 4

10. Ibid., 3.

11. Hugh Winsor and John Partridge, "CBC's All-News Television Service Gets Cabinet Informal Go-Ahead," *Globe and Mail*, 18 October 1988, A1, A2. See also, Adam Mayers, "Outsiders To Have a Voice in TV News Channel," *Toronto Star*, 18 October 1988, B1.

12. Canada, Department of Communications, *Proposals for a Communication Policy for Canada* (Ottawa: Information Canada, 1973), 8.

13. "Towards an Official Culture," *Time* (Canadian edition), 3 August 1970, 7.

14. John S. Wright, Willis L. Winter, Jr., Sherilyn K. Zeigler, and P. Noel O'Dea, *Advertising, First Canadian Edition* (Toronto: McGraw-Hill Ryerson, 1984), 674.

15. Ibid., 703.

16. John Partridge, "Southam Stake in B.C. Chain Raises Concentration Issue," *Globe and Mail*, 11 May 1990, B5.

17. Canada, CRTC, *Annual Report 1970-1971* (Ottawa, 1971), 3.

18. Martin Mehr, "CRTC Computerizes: Broadcast Councils," *Marketing* 95 (16 April 1990): 14.

19. Canada, CRTC, *CRTC Public Notice, 1988-159* (22 September 1988).

20. Canada, CRTC, *CRTC Public Notice, 1988-161* (29 September 1988).

21. Canada, CRTC, *Policy Statement of Canadian Content in Television, Notice CRTC 83-18* (Ottawa, 1983), 3–7.

22. Ibid.

23. Communications Canada, *Report of the Task Force on Broadcasting Policy* (Ottawa: Supply and Services, 1986). The formulae for computing Canadian content are on p. 125 (for radio) and p. 113 (for television), while the quotation is found on p. 468.

24. Canada, CRTC, *Policy Statement on Canadian Content in Television, Notice CRTC 83-18* (Ottawa, 1983), 13.

25. Canada, CRTC, *CRTC Public Notice, 1985-58 (20 March 1985): Introducing Flexibility into the Concept of Local Television Programming* (Ottawa, 1985).

26. Canada, CRTC, *CRTC Public Notice, 1986-177 (23 July 1986): Local Television Programs* (Ottawa, 1986).

27. Canada, CRTC, *CRTC Public Notice, 1987-28 (30 June 1987): Recognition for Canadian Programs-Production Packages* (Ottawa, 1987).

28. See CRTC, *Annual Report, 1988–1989* (Ottawa, 1989), 24. Also see,

Jamie Portman, "'Spend or Close,' TV Stations Told," *Windsor Star*, 17 April 1989, A9.

29. Communications Canada, *Report of the Task Force on Broadcasting Policy* (Ottawa: Supply and Services, 1986), 459–60.

30. CRTC, *Annual Report, 1988–1989* (Ottawa, 1989), 18.

31. Ibid., 17.

32. Martin Romanow and Walter Romanow, "Broadcast Licence Non-Renewals: CRTC Practices," *Canadian Journal of Communication* 9 (December 1982): 71–72.

33. Canadian Advertising Foundation, Advertising Standards Council, *The Canadian Code of Advertising Standards* (Toronto, May 1986), 5.

34. Ibid., 6.

35. *CDNPA Bulletin* 18 (23 February 1990), 4. The name of the CDNA was recently changed from the Canadian Daily Newspaper Publishers Association.

36. Stanley B. Cunningham, "Press Councils in Canada" (paper presented at the Annual Meeting of the Canadian Communication Association, May 1987). In 1987, there were seven such bodies. In addition, a Canadian Conference of Press Councils has been formed at the national level.

37. Leonard R. Chandler "The Media and Law Enforcement: A Case Study Concerning an Agreement on the Public Release of Crime Information" (M.A. thesis, Department of Communication Studies, University of Windsor, 1979).

38. See G. Stuart Adam, "The Sovereignty of the Public System: The Case of the Alberta Press Act," in *Journalism Communication and the Law*, ed. G. Stuart Adam (Scarborough: Prentice-Hall, 1976), 154–71.

39. Canada, *Report of the Royal Commission on Newspapers* (Ottawa: Supply and Services, 1981), 245–52.

40. Ontario, *Report of the Royal Commission on Violence in the Communication Industry*, Volume 1, *Approaches, Conclusions and Recommendations* (Toronto: Queen's Printer for Ontario, 1976), 61.

41. Canada, CBC, *Journalistic Policy* (Ottawa, 1988), 5–6.

42. Ibid., 8.

43. See, "Consumers' Association of Canada: Our Recommendations," *Canadian Consumer* 20, 6 (1990): 49.

44. Tex Enemark, "Back to the Days of Buyer Beware," *Globe and Mail*, 22 January 1988, A7.

45. Ibid.

46. See Philip Kotler, *Principles of Marketing*, 2nd ed. (Englewood Cliffs, NJ: Prentice-Hall, 1983), 619.

47. Canadian Consumer Council, "The Canadian Charter of Consumer Rights," *Annual Report 1972* (Ottawa: Consumer and Corporate Affairs, 1972), 57.

48. David Hatter, "Consumerism's Midlife Crisis," *Financial Post*, 11–13 June 1988, A1.

49. Ellen Roseman, "40 Years Later, Consumerism Confronts a Quiet Crisis," *Globe and Mail*, 23 July 1988, D1.

50. Ibid.

51. Martin Mittelstaedt, "Consumer Activism Sweeping the U.S." *Globe and Mail*, 30 November 1989, B1.

52. Ann Landers, "Combat TV Violence by Using Economic Guns," *Edmonton Journal*, 15 July 1991, C2.

53. Jay Sharbutt, "Ignore Threats, TV Advertisers Told," *Globe and Mail*, 7 August 1991, C3.

C H A P T E R II

Access to
Information

Introduction

It was in the aftermath of the Second World War that positive steps were announced with respect to basic human rights as well as to rights of individuals as citizens. After a war that saw about 60 million lives lost (military and civilian) and suffering for countless others, it was no surprise that the Charter of the United Nations reflected such concerns.

> We the peoples of the United Nations determined to save succeeding generations from the scourge of war, which twice in our lifetime has brought untold sorrow to mankind, and to reaffirm faith in fundamental human rights, in the dignity and worth of the human person, in the equal rights of men and women and of nations large and small, and to establish conditions under which justice and respect for the obligations arising from treaties and other sources of international law can be maintained, and to promote social

progress and better standards of life in larger freedom . . . have resolved to combine our efforts to accomplish these aims.[1]

It is in this preamble that we find the basis for freedom of information concerns, which in 1948 later found expression in the Universal Declaration of Human Rights: "Everyone has the right to freedom of opinion and expression; this right includes freedom to hold opinions without interference and to seek, receive and impart information and ideas through any media and regardless of frontiers."[2]

It became evident that to implement such an international agreement, to which United Nations members including Canada were signatories, some guarantees were needed that Canadians themselves had access to information as citizens in their own country. In many societies this declaration did not assure citizens of rights of access to information or freedom of expression for that matter.

Access to Information Developments

The International Sphere

Insofar as access to information developments in the international community are concerned, two documents in particular are considered to have advanced the cause of freedom, and these, ultimately, are reflected in the 1948 Declaration of Human Rights, Article 19.[3]

The first, the Declaration of the Rights of Man and the Citizen (France, 1789) states: "The unrestrained communication of thoughts or opinions being one of the most precious rights of man, every citizen may speak, write and publish freely provided he be responsible for the abuse of this liberty, in cases determined by law." Second, the United States Bill of Rights (1791) states: "Congress shall make no law respecting an establishment of religion, or prohibiting the free exercise thereof; or abridging the freedom of speech, or of the press; or the right of the people to assemble and to petition for a redress of grievances."

Following the 1948 UN Declaration of Human Rights, a series of international meetings and conventions were held within the UN, and subsequently within UNESCO, over a period of thirty years. Agreements and resolutions of various sorts concerning freedom of expression, the role of the press, and access rights were drafted, each building on the conclusions of previous agreements and resolutions. The latest international declaration concerning freedom of information and rights of people and mass media is to be found in the 1980 report of a UNESCO Commission, entitled *Many Voices, One World*. Within this report one finds the basis for a continuing controversy regarding a need for a new world information and communication order. The controversy focusses essentially upon differing views of the role of media, journalism, and journalists held by proponents of the Western free press philosophy as opposed to those who defend the role of media as instruments of national development. (See chapter 2.)

As might be expected, freedom of information (FOI) legislation, whereby one has access to government documents and to one's own files held by governments, is more likely to be found in nations that support the Western philosophy rather than in nations with other political ideologies.

In one form or another, with varying degrees of individual access, and with differing criteria with respect to ensuring the necessary protection for governments, freedom of information legislation is to be found in the following countries: Australia, Austria, Canada, Denmark, Finland, France, the Netherlands, New Zealand, Papua New Guinea, Sweden, and the United States.[4] In some instances one finds the beginnings of legislation for access to government documents as early as 1776 (for example, in Sweden). However, it is predominantly in the post–World War II era that formal freedom of information legislation came into effect. In some Western societies, while formal legislation regarding access to information has not been introduced, a means of access for citizens has been provided by the appointment of ombudsmen and ombudswomen in lieu of legislation.

Noticeably absent from the list is Great Britain, where freedom of the press and freedom of expression hearken back to the seventeenth century. Although demands for access to information legislation are becoming increasingly frequent in the British Parliament, the philosophy and the strict provisions contained in the Official Secrets Act still prevail.

Finally, as collaborative structures in continental Europe become more formalized (for example, the Council of Europe, the European Community, and the European Parliament), there have been some urgings for legislation that would give people access to the documents of these new political bodies.[5]

While Canada's record with respect to freedom of expression and freedom of the press has generally been very positive, it was not until thirty-five years after the proclamation of the Universal Declaration of Human Rights that the Canadian government confirmed in legislation the particular right of access to information on the part of its citizens that is implicit in that declaration.

The United States Model

In describing the development of the U.S. Freedom of Information Act, a research librarian at the Library of Congress likens information to "the currency of democracy."[6] He emphasizes the central role of information in democratic communities by referring to the ideas of Founding Father and democratic theorist James Madison, who, in a letter in 1822, wrote: "A popular government without popular information or the means of acquiring it, is but a Prologue to a Farce or a Tragedy; or perhaps both. Knowledge will forever govern ignorance: And a people who mean to be their own governors, must arm themselves with the power which knowledge gives."[7] While Madison's prose may be somewhat archaic, his ideas are decidedly modern, and with a few alterations, students might well assume that his beliefs were expressed yesterday. It is due to such a tradition of thought concerning the value of information that the United States was among the first of modern democracies to champion the cause of freedom of information legislation for its citizens. In so doing, it established a model for others to follow.

Freedom of information legislation was introduced in Congress in 1964 and was signed into law on 4 July 1966. The FOI Act indicates that any person has a right to access to federal government agency records and that right is enforceable in the courts of the land. The act stipulates that agencies are required to publish information concerning where and how requests may be made, how application forms for information may be obtained, and any other information related to the public's access to government records. They must do this on a regular basis. Agencies are also required to advise an applicant within ten working days whether his or her application has been accepted. Should an application be denied, the agency must offer reasons for the denial and advise the applicant of routes of appeal.

There are exemptions concerning the compulsory disclosure of information by the federal government, and these relate to such matters as: national security; foreign relations interests; some federal government investigatory techniques; trade secrets; confidential information supplied to the government; information that would invade the personal privacy of citizens; law enforcement investigation records; and executive branch discussions that involve decision making, so as to preserve free and candid dialogue. (The Canadian equivalent to the last exemption would be cabinet secrecy.) Of course, all of these exemptions are open to different interpretations, depending on circumstances, and, on occasion, differences of interpretation of exemptions cause lengthy delays in responding to applications

for information: in some instances, such delays have been identified as "bureaucratic stonewalling."[8]

Users of the act are as follows: the business community is by far the greatest user, at 60 percent; the general public, 25 percent; finally, media and journalists account for about 8 percent of the requests.[9] Although most of the heavy usage by business is related to business conducted with the government, it also reflects an ongoing problem related to corporate secrecy. There is an attitude in the United States that stresses openness, and it is apparent that FOI legislation might contain a weakness, in that criminal elements have been known to use information gained through FOI legislation to circumvent police investigations. For example, information regarding ongoing criminal investigations has, on occasion, been revealed despite police efforts to suppress such information. It is no surprise, then, to read that amendments to the legislation are constantly under consideration.

Access to Information in Canada

Background

In his discussion of freedom of information developments in Canada, Arthur Siegel identifies what he calls "contradictory pressures for secrecy and openness in Canada."[10] The pressures for secrecy come from a long-established tradition. In the first place, this tradition carries over from the inherited British parliamentary system of government, with its Official Secrets Act. This act requires Cabinet members and some civil servants to take oaths of secrecy. Another element of secrecy derives from the relationship between the provinces and the federal government, where provinces, too, have constitutional powers. During negotiations between the two levels of government, as Siegel points out, there is on occasion "strategic withholding of information in the on-going federal-provincial bargaining."[11] A third factor contributing to secrecy is what is termed an "elite accommodation" style of politics, which has led to a dominance of bureaucracies over the individual, perpetuated by restricted access to information. The Canadian economic structure also encourages secrecy in that competition in business quite naturally gives rise to the withholding of information from competitors. And finally, the tradition of individual privacy is an important factor restricting open access to information about personal lives of citizens.

On the other hand, Siegel cites three factors that enhance openness. First, the nature of our society, wherein responsibility to the electorate is fundamental to the political process, demands openness if we are to make informed choices at the polls. Such openness includes, naturally, freedom of expression and freedom of the press. A second factor that provides pressure for openness, Siegel argues, is the bilingual and bicultural nature of Canadian society. The principle of national unity is served when linguistic and cultural groups are informed about each other and are able to converse with each other based on information they receive about each other. As well, our proximity to the U.S., where the principle of freedom of information flourishes, has had an influence on Canadians' desire for openness. Finally, trends towards openness, and the concomitant breakdown of government secrecy in other nations, have influenced our own society to move in the same direction.

The Access to Information Act

On 1 July 1983 two federal government acts took effect in Canada, the Access to Information Act and the Privacy Act. As in the neighbouring United States, the two acts are seen as complementary: while the government is prepared to make information available to the public, it also protects citizens from invasion of privacy.

The Access to Information Act specifies that its purpose is to extend the laws of Canada "to provide a right of access to information in records under control of a government institution in accordance with the principles that government information should be available to the public.... "[12] The act also specifies that there are necessary exemptions to the right of access to information and that reviews independent of government should be made concerning decisions regarding disclosure of information. In this sense, the Canadian act parallels the U.S. act.

Unlike the U.S. legislation, however, the right to request information under the act is limited to citizens and to declared permanent residents of Canada. The act provides that other persons may gain access to records, but approval would have to be given by the federal cabinet. If access is denied within a specified time limit, reasons for such denial must be offered. As in the case of the U.S. act, exemptions are cited and they are generally similar to those identified in the United States. Heads of government agencies either have the right to or are required to refuse applications for information in matters that relate to information provided to Canada in confidence by foreign states, provincial, regional, or municipal governments; information that could be injurious to the defence of Canada or to the suppression of subversive activities; intelligence gathered respecting foreign states; diplomatic correspondence with foreign states; information concerning crime investigations or investigations by the Canadian Security Intelligence Service; trade secrets or business information supplied in confidence to the government; and information that would compromise the privacy of individuals. Finally, information may be refused to applicants concerning "advice or recommendations developed by or for a government institution or a minister of the crown."[13] This ministerial exemption also extends to employees or staff members of a minister. The net effect of this exemption is that documents that are declared to be the property of any minister may be protected.

Table 11–1 shows the number of requests for information made under the act in each year since it has been in effect. The act also provides for complaints to be lodged when information is denied. Further, the act is explicit in indicating that a delay beyond the specified time limit without adequate expla-

TABLE 11–1
Requests for Access to Information, 1983–89

	1983/84*	1984/85	1985/86	1986/87	1987/88	1988/89
Requests received	1513	2229	3607	5450	7301	8853
Cost per request completed	$1984	$1705	$1182	$802	$679	$644
Fees collected per request completed	$11.85	$13.03	$11.25	$11.75	$10.81	$10.68

Source: Canada, Treasury Board Secretariat, *Access to Information Act/Privacy Act Second Consolidated Report by the President of the Treasury Board 1988–89* (Ottawa: Supply and Services, 1989), 8, 13.
*Data are from the *First Consolidated Annual Report 1987–88*.

nation constitutes a refusal on the part of a government agency to provide the requested information. Thus, within the act, a provision is made for an office of information commissioner, whose main role is to receive and investigate complaints from applicants who have either been refused access to a record or whose request has received an unreasonable delay, or who have been required to pay an unreasonable amount for their request. Currently the standard application fee of $5 provides for up to five free hours of search and preparation time, after which a charge of $10 per hour for research is applied.[14] The information commissioner is also empowered to investigate complaints "in respect of any other matter relating to or requesting or obtaining access to records" under the act.

Of the 3011 complaints that were processed from April 1989 to 31 March 1990 (see table 11–2), 69 percent dealt with delays (deemed to constitute refusal), 19 percent dealt with outright refusals, while 9 percent dealt with fee problems. Overall, 78 percent of complaints were found to have been justified, and 86 percent of these concerned the issue of undue delay. Of the 22 percent of complaints found not justified, the majority of these were in the categories of refusal (44 percent) and excessive fees (40 percent). These figures indicate that when the government has either not given access to information and provided reasons for such refusal or has given access to information and then charged the applicant fees that were perceived to be excessive, the commissioner sided with the government. However, in those instances where the government procrastinated in providing information to the extent that the delay was so long that it constituted refusal, the commissioner sided with the complainants. Indeed, in her final *Annual Report* commissioner Inger Hansen emphasized that "Delays to access remains one of the major problems under the

TABLE 11–2
Disposition of Complaints by the Information Commissioner

Reason for Complaint	Complaints deemed justified N=2340 78%	Complaints deemed not justified N=671 22%	Total N=3011
Refusal to disclose	12%	44%	N=569
Delay (deemed refusal)	86%	9%	N=2079
Excessive fees	.5%	40%	N=280
Other	1.5%	6%	N=83
	100%	100%	

Source: *Annual Report Information Officer 1989–90*

Act. . . . We believe access is useful and meaningful only if it provided in a timely fashion."[15]

Needs of Society for Access to Information

Access to information acts or freedom of information acts fulfil several important functions in democratic societies.

Society Participation

Modern Western societies are characterized by administrative complexity and by an increasing government involvement in our daily lives. This places a responsibility on individuals to be aware of such conditions and to understand the relationship that we all have with those who guide our lives at all levels of government. Increased standards of education in Western societies have enhanced our abilities to understand these day-to-day governing processes, but understanding itself may not be enough. We must have access to complete and accurate information base if we are going to use these democratic processes effectively. These principles entitle us to participate in our own open democratic processes, and in order to do so, we require assurance that the information we need is as complete as possible and that it is reliable. The acts work towards offering society these assurances. Thus, they serve a useful purpose.

The Nature of Bureaucracies

While acts respecting freedom of information are socially useful, they are so only when they function without undue restrictions. One of the concerns regarding freedom of information in a society is the manner in which bureaucracies function. Social science literature (particularly that of political science and public administration) contains many recent studies that indicate that government secrecy with respect to information tends to be inherent.

Studies frequently point out that bureaucracies have a strong tendency to function as *self systems*, that is, bureaucrats have a preference "for serving private ends over public ones."[16] The following impediments limit bureaucratic responsiveness to social interests: secretiveness, loyalty to agency (office) interests and procedures, a cultivation of private economic interests, and what is cited as a "passion for professional achievement without due respect to the public costs or broader social impacts."[17]

Freedom of information acts are tools to counteract this kind of secrecy and they also help to ensure the legitimacy of citizen participation in public policy processes. Indeed, such participatory practices have become mandatory in various public agencies such as the CRTC.[18] However, it is clear that in order for citizens to participate intelligently in any policy process, they need access to all the information that a policy manager needs to make a decision. "It is impossible for anyone—citizen, bureaucrat, or elected official—to make rational decisions without data and information pertinent to a particular program. . . . [The] material that is provided must therefore be complete [and must include] data that are comprehensible and organized, and materials that are timely and germane."[19]

Concerns about access to information, then, have a legitimate basis when one considers the processes of public management of our society and citizenship participation in those processes. Either as members of various types of public committees or boards or as commentators on public process, we are not likely to achieve any degree of effectiveness without the prerequisite information. In a sense, if we are invited to sit on public committees, or to comment at public meetings on our Constitution and are then denied the appropriate information we need in order to participate effectively, the government is being at best, deceitful, at worst, authoritarian.

At the conclusion of her seven-year term, information commissioner Inger Hansen summarized her convictions concerning secrecy in government in the following manner:

- The political will in support of freedom of information could be stronger.
- The bureaucratic resistance to freedom of information should be weaker.

- The tendency to withhold government information should give way to attitudes favouring its disclosure.[20]

Retention of Government Documents

In many municipalities in Canada, the decision to retain or destroy documents is largely based on the municipalities' capacity to store them. Under the Ontario Municipal Act, for example, municipalities are permitted to pass legislation indicating how their documents are to be retained. Time of retention may vary between two, three, or five years, and there are no firm provisions for microfilming. In many instances space becomes the dominant criterion affecting retention of records. We might well ask how our local historical heritage is being protected for future generations of scholars in this situation.

At the national level, Canada's latest Archival Act (1987), which replaced the 1912 act, increases the power of the Archivist of Canada with respect to decisions concerning the destruction or disposal of government records. In the discussions leading up to parliamentary debate and passage of the bill (Bill C-95—An Act Respecting the Archives of Canada), the Social Science Federation of Canada proposed that it should be mandatory that " . . . *all* records of the Government of Canada would require the Archivist's prior consent before their destruction, thus overriding the provision for non-release or mandatory destruction of certain classes of records contained in other legislation."[21]

This concern about extending the jurisdiction of the Archivist of Canada may be understood by an observation made in 1986 about the Public Archives of Canada by a study team report to the Task Force on Program Review. One volume of the task force report, *Culture and Communications*, points out that of all federal records, "an estimated 5 per cent are selected for preservation and transferred to Historical Archives; the remaining 95 per cent are destroyed either within a year of their creation or at the end of their active life cycle." The report adds that a retention rate of only 5 per cent "places Canada at the lower end of the spectrum among Western nations. At the other extreme, countries such as Luxembourg and Sweden preserve almost all government records." In a comment that underscores the severity of the problem of whether to retain or destroy government documents, the task force concluded "There does not exist a body of scientific knowledge or techniques, which could be used to determine the optimum rate of destruction."[22]

With the introduction of FOI legislation at the federal and provincial levels (and in the future at the municipal level), it is probable that the rate of retention of documents (and hence information) will be higher than in the past given the rapid development of computer technology. At the same time, access to information concerns, as they relate to the retention, storage, and access to historical documents require much thought and financial commitment on the part of governments. Thus in any discussion regarding society's needs in this area, we must understand that we are only making a beginning.

Some Continuing Concerns

In a sense, Canadians have done very well in gaining access to information generated and stored by federal and provincial governments. Since Member of Parliament Jed Baldwin first raised the matter in the House over thirty years ago, the federal government and six provinces have enacted access to information acts.

Many of the earlier apprehensions regarding how effectively the acts would work have been allayed by experience. For example, information and privacy commissioners (whose essential tasks are those of arbiters) are finding that their roles are becoming defined as they work with requests for information. As well, publicity regarding access rights of citizens has increased and Canadians are becoming more aware of what information is available and how to access it. The act provides for the release of descriptions of classes of records under the control of the government, and bulletins that update listings and provide other useful information to the public relating to the operations of the act are received at least twice a year by libraries. Applications for information can be made in person, by phone, or by writing to the appropriate government office. As well, a toll-free number is available for citizens to use.[23] Nor has misuse of the access laws materialized in Canada as it has in the United States, where most of the requests for information under the FOI Act are made by businesses seeking information about the secrets of their competitors.[24] At least this was the case in the initial years of the act.

Overall, then, the lot of the Canadian citizen who seeks information about himself or herself or about the operations of governments bodies has improved considerably over what it was even a brief decade ago, and we certainly look forward to continuing improvement.

Serious problems continue to exist, however. Two in particular may be identified: cabinet privilege and citizenship limitations.

Cabinet Privilege

The doctrine of cabinet privilege continues to be exercised by federal cabinet ministers. Section 69 of the Access to Information Act specifies that the act does not apply to confidences of the Queen's Privy Council of Canada (the cabinet), leaving the government with the final say concerning the release of documents. Then Communications Minister Francis Fox introduced the amendment to the act prior to its passage, which "excludes from public view all Cabinet documents and government documents that Cabinet Ministers say are part of the Cabinet record." In commenting on this amendment and the broad area of exemptions that might follow, parliamentarian Svend Robinson described it as "the Mack Truck clause of the bill."[25]

The information commissioner has indicated that her office does not have the authority to demand access to confidential cabinet documents, although on occasion further inquiries satisfied her that section 69 of the act had been used properly. "In other circumstances, [the Commissioner reported] a suspicion arose that, out of extreme caution, section 69 has been applied too broadly."[26]

T.M. Rankin has labelled the cabinet records clause "The Ultimate Exemption" and has interpreted the power of the courts with reference to cabinet documents in the following way: "[Under the Fox Amendment] courts will be allowed to inspect most sensitive national security information . . . [but] they will be unable, for any purpose whatsoever, to look at Cabinet documents."[27]

The celebrated case of the attempt of former auditor general Kenneth Dye to obtain documents of the Trudeau Liberal cabinet concerning the Petrofina purchase by PetroCanada illustrates the problem. While Dye's request for information was based on the auditor general's statutory and customary rights to have information, the essential challenge offered was on the basis of the concept of cabinet secrecy. In this instance, the Federal

Court of Canada confirmed the auditor general's right to see cabinet documents in the Petrofina matter, although specifying that this right was limited only to financial documents.[28]

In response to the Federal Court's decision, then Justice Minister John Crosbie indicated that it would be necessary to appeal the decision in order to support a fundamental principle, "Are there to be any Cabinet confidences at all? . . . We don't think that a Cabinet Government can function if this judgment stands as it is today."[29] In explaining his concerns further, Mr. Crosbie indicated: "We cannot give [Mr. Dye] any more access to matters in the past than we are already doing because Mr. Trudeau's administration does not wish us to. It doesn't matter to us. . . . But we have to observe the conventions of the Constitution, and the Trudeau Administration does not wish him to have access to Cabinet confidence about Petrocan."[30]

Cabinet documents, then, continue to be exempt from public scrutiny and the rights of courts in the matter appear to be limited. In essence, it seems that the auditor general is not going to be able to determine, on the basis of full access to both financial and political documents of cabinet, whether Canadians received adequate value for money spent in buying Petrofina.

Thus, Canadians will continue to be subjected to the perennial conflict with respect to release of information about what is "legitimate secrecy and what is stonewalling"[31]

(despite the existence of the Access to Information Act). Without changes to section 69, which excludes cabinet materials from public scrutiny, it is inevitable that Canadians will be left with the lingering feeling that a prominent weakness in the Access to Information Act remains.

Citizen Limitations

One further comment concerning the Access to Information Act must be made, and this is in reference to section 4, which specifies that only Canadian citizens or permanent residents are permitted access to records under control of the government.

Both the Canadian Bar Association and the Canadian Daily Newspaper Association (among other groups) argued unsuccessfully for elimination of this restriction before the Justice and Legal Affairs Committee of the House. The Newspaper Association made a particularly cogent argument: "If Canada opens its doors of information to include the public from other nations as well as our own, then our approach could have an impact on other nations also considering Freedom of Information legislation. This bill could help promote the free flow of information among nations, not Balkanize it."[32]

Had such advice been heeded by the government, the legislation would have been consistent with a major concern expressed earlier in the 1980 UNESCO MacBride Report—that freedom of information be considered a fundamental human right:

> All countries should take steps to assure admittance of foreign correspondents and facilitate their collection and transmission of news. . . . Free access to news sources by journalists is an indispensable requirement for accurate, faithful and balanced reporting. This necessarily involves access to unofficial, as well as official sources of information, that is, access to the entire spectrum of opinion within any country.[33]

That recommendation is a positive step toward fulfilling the intent of Article 19 of the UN Declaration of Human Rights, which, as we have seen, affirmed the freedom of individuals to seek, receive, and impart information and ideas through any media and *regardless of frontiers.*

By limiting access to government information to its own citizens under the Access to Information Act, Canada's behaviour is inconsistent with the intent of both the UN General Assembly Resolution and the recommendation of the MacBride Commission, bodies in which Canada has enjoyed active and forthright participation.

We are not suggesting that foreign journalists working in Canada lack access to information to the point where they have no materials on which to base stories. A study of foreign journalists working in Washington examines how they gain information from the host nation's media. As one journalist admitted: "I wrote quite a few articles on a lot of Supreme Court decisions by courtesy of *Washington Post* and *New York Times* legal reporters."[34]

But the matter takes on a more serious dimension, as the Canadian Bar Association points out, with respect to foreign scholars who want to conduct in-depth research on Canadian themes. In the case where they are denied ready access to prime-source materials, foreign scholars have no option but to use content prepared by their own nationals or by their own governments—that is, content prepared through foreign eyes rather than our own. Students may recall that several royal commissions and committees dealing with mass media (the Kent Commission and the Davey Committee, for example) have emphasized the need for Canadian media to have Canadian journalists reporting on international affairs rather than simply accepting reports from non-Canadian reporters. While this matter was discussed by the Parliamentary Committee on Justice and Legal Affairs before the Access to Information Bill was passed, the current version of section 4(1) of the act still has citizenship limitations. That particular section was also discussed in a 1987 response to a question raised on the matter by the Standing Committee on Justice and the solicitor general. The government response was that whereas the Standing Committee had recommended that access right be extended to any "natural or legal person regardless of where they are located in the world," and that while such a universal right of access might be a "desirable ideal, it is also important to recognize the very significant cost associated with such rights. . . ."[35] One can never ignore costs of government-provided services, but in the instance of extending the rights of access to the broader international community, costs would appear to be justifiable.

A recent amendment to section 4 of the Access to Information Act might alleviate the situation somewhat, although not entirely. The amendment, published in the *Canada Gazette* in 1989, indicates that the right to ask for information under the Access to Information Act would be extended to include "all individuals who are present in Canada but who are not Canadian citizens or permanent residents within the meaning of the Immigration Act and all corporations that are present in Canada."[36] In effect, one interpretation of the amendment is that non-Canadian corporations incorporated under the laws of Canada, and their non-Canadian employees who are resident in Canada, would be permitted to apply for federal government information under the Access Act. But, because access still does not pertain to *any persons* regardless of *where* they are "present," the Canadian government's hesitancy in the matter is still evident.

This hesitancy is difficult to understand given Canadian participation in the global community where Canadian representatives, along with other nations' representatives, have stressed that open, unrestricted access to information is a fundamental human right. It is also incomprehensible in light of the fact that the Canadian government has urged U.S. universities to establish Canadian studies programs. At present, due in no small measure to incentives provided by the Canadian government, approximately fifty universities and colleges in the U.S. have created such programs, and over five hundred offer courses dealing with Canada.[37] Having thus encouraged the study of Canada in the U.S., current access to information legislation discourages U.S. scholars from accessing prime-source materials.

To correct this situation and others like it that may arise, Canada's Access Act should be extended to any Canadian citizen or to a citizen of any other country with equal opportunity. Because sufficient exemptions prevail under the act to protect particular national interests, such an amendment would permit citizens of foreign countries to access prime-source documents as they conduct research studies about Canada. Primarily, however, such an amendment would bring Canadian behaviour in line with beliefs the country has expressed rhetorically concerning the value of freedom of information in a modern society.

Conclusion

In 1981, former prime minister Joe Clark, in parliamentary debate on the Access to Information Act, stated: "When the government operates in secrecy and refuses to let the public have certain documents, it creates an atmosphere of public mistrust. . . . It is a question of power and we all know that those who have information are those who wield real power."[38] In a foreword to a book published in Sweden related to access to government documents, Justice Michael Kirby of the Supreme Court of New South Wales in New Zealand echoed the Canadian prime minister's belief: "Political accountability with individual authority in an age of large public administration engined by the new technology is what FOI is all about. Ultimately, it is about the distribution of power in a modern state. Ultimately, it is a very modern issue of human rights, apt for our time."[39]

Our contention here has been that the importance of access to government-generated information cannot be overemphasized and that an open society is fundamental to human rights and to human dignity. However, we also recognize that such rights are accompanied by responsibility and that while basic rights are important, they are not absolute. There are some legitimate questions related to openness of government documents, the foremost of which—after "mechanical" hindrances to access have been removed, and after governments and their employees have facilitated openness—is: what is the point of balance between the right of the public to have information and the responsibility of the government to protect the welfare of the nation?

It is clear that more experience with the Access to Information and Privacy Acts is needed before this question can be satisfactorily answered.

Notes

1. See Ralph Townley, *The United Nations: A View from Within* (New York: Charles Scribner's Sons, 1968), Appendix I, 297–326.
2. Ibid. Appendix II, 327–31.
3. See Edward W. Ploman, *International Law Governing Communications and Information: A Collection of Basic Documents* (Westport, CT: Greenwood Press, 1982), 126–27. Further relevant articles of both documents are cited in this collection.
4. Tom Riley, "Acccessing Information: Recent International Developments," in *Access to Government Records: International Perspectives and Trends*, ed. Tom Riley (Lund, Sweden: Chartwell-Bratt, 1986), 85–103.
5. Ibid., 102.
6. Harold C. Relyea, "The Freedom of Information Act in America: A Profile," in *Access to Government Records*, ed. Riley, 17.
7. Quoted in Ibid.
8. Steve Weinberg, "Trashing the FOIA," in *Maincurrents in Mass Communications*, ed. Warren K. Agee, Phillip H. Ault, and Edwin Emery (New York: Harper & Row, 1986), 187. Also see Elaine English, "How To Use the FOIA," in *Maincurrents in Mass Communications*, 2nd ed., ed. Warren K. Agee, Phillip H. Ault, and Edwin Emery (New York: Harper & Row, 1989), 162–66.
9. Relyea, "The Freedom of Information Act," 24–25.
10. Arthur Siegel, *Politics and the Media in Canada* (Toronto: McGraw-Hill Ryerson, 1983), 37–55.
11. Ibid., 45.

12. Canada, Access to Information Act 2(1).

13. Ibid., 21(1)(a).

14. David Vienneau, "Changes to Information Access Law May Involve Much Higher User Fees," *Toronto Star*, 12 May 1990, C2. The concern in this article is that increased costs of access might in fact take away a fundamental democratic right from individuals.

15. Canada, *Annual Report Information Commissioner 1989–90* (Ottawa: Supply and Services), 9.

16. Walter A. Rosenbaum, "The Paradoxes of Public Participation," *Administration and Society* 8 (November 1976): 360.

17. Ibid. See also Rosenbaum's references to J.F. Coates, "Why Public Participation Is Essential in Technology Assessment," *Public Administration Review* 35 (January/February 1975): 67–69.

18. See Canada, Broadcasting Act 1967–68 (Ottawa: Supply and Services, 1968), section 19.

19. Elena C. Van Meter, "Third Party Perspectives: Citizen Participation in the Policy Management Process," *Public Administration Review* 35 (December 1975), 811.

20. Canada, *Annual Report of the Information Commissioner 1989–90* (Ottawa: Supply and Services, 1990), 2.

21. Social Science Federation of Canada, *A Brief on Bill C-95: An Act Respecting the Archives of Canada* (Ottawa: Social Science Federation of Canada, May 1986), 4–5.

22. Canada, Task Force on Program Review, *A Study Team Report to the Task Force on Program Review: Culture and Communications August 1985* (Ottawa: Supply and Services, 1986), 114–15.

23. The toll-free number for inquiries to the information commissioner regarding access to information is 1-800-267-0441.

24. "Corporate Freedom of Information Can Prove Costly," *Canadian Lawyer* 7 (May/June 1983): 23.

25. Jim Robb, "'Gutted' FOI Measure Heads to House," Ottawa *Citizen*, 9 June 1982, 1.

26. Canada, *Information Commissioner Annual Report 1984–85* (Ottawa: Supply and Services, 1985), 15.

27. T. Murray Rankin, "Information and Privacy Act: A Critical Annotation," *Ottawa Law Review* 15.1 (1983), 26.

28. "Blocking the Auditor," (editorial), *Globe and Mail*, 1 January 1986, A7.

29. Barbara Jaffe and Christopher Waddell, "Appeal Planning on Dye Ruling," *Globe and Mail*, 31 December 1985, 1–2.

30. Ibid.

31. "Blocking the Auditor," *Globe and Mail* (editorial).

32. Canada, House of Commons, *Minutes of Proceedings and Evidence of the Standing Committee on Justice and Legal Affairs Respecting Bill C-43, Wednesday 25 March 1981* (Ottawa: Supply and Services, 1981), Issue 22:27.

33. UNESCO, *Many Voices, One World: Towards a New More Just and Efficient Information Order* (Paris: UNESCO, 1980), 263.

34. Shailendre Ghorpade, "Sources and Access: How Foreign Correspondents Rate Washington D.C.," *Journal of Communication* 34 (Autumn 1984): 34.

35. Canada, Department of Justice, *Access and Privacy: The Steps Ahead* (Ottawa: Supply and Services, 1987), 33.

36. Canada, *Canada Gazette*, Part II, "Access to Information Act" 123, 9 (13 April 1989), 2287.

37. Association for Canadian Studies in the United States, *Annual Report 1989* (Washington, 1989), 2–3.

38. Joe Clark, 29 January 1981, on Second Reading of Bill C-43 (Access to

Information Act) cited in Canada, *Annual Report Information Commissioner 1988–89* (Ottawa: Supply and Services, 1989),1.

39. Justice Michael Kirby, "FOI and the Coming Counter-Reformation," in *Access to Government Records*, ed. Riley, 14.

C H A P T E R   12

Ownership

Introduction

If one were looking for words to describe the current state of the ownership of Canada's mass media, high on the list would be terms such as *buyout, takeover, amalgamation, acquisition,* and *monopoly.* The ownership trend identified by such words is not limited to Canada. Scholar and media critic Ben Bagdikian outlines parallel global trends in his provocatively titled article, "Lords of the Global Village."[1]

Chronicling the history of the press in Canada, Canadian historian Wilfred Kesterton describes the fourth press period (1900 to 1967) as one of consolidation and centralization of ownership.[2] Thus, the narrowing of the ownership base in Canada's mass media, which was brought to national attention by the Davey Committee *Report* in 1970, was in fact apparent in newspapers from the turn of the century, in radio from the 1920s and 1930s, and in television and cable systems from the 1950s.

Questions of who owns mass media and how widely distributed this ownership is are fundamental to any discussion of democratic theory as it applies to a society. While crucial and central, these questions are not easily dealt with, because the ownership profile of today may well differ from that of a month or two into the future. There are two reasons for this: first, acquisitions occur very rapidly and often are unannounced; second, when acquisitions take place, many of them are characterized by intercorporate stock trading. For example, company A will trade a parcel of its shares for an equivalent value of shares in one or two other companies. At the same time, companies B and C are doing the same thing. Because of the intertwined nature of media shareholding, it's often difficult to determine who actually controls the ownership of what company.[3]

As a consequence, in this chapter we are not going to attempt a precise inventory of who owns what mass media properties. Rather we will focus on the theoretical importance of ownership to the functioning of democracy, discuss ownership styles and trends as they have evolved and have been studied in Canada, review empirical research dealing with the effects of ownership on media behaviour, and, finally, discuss the question of social consequences of Canada's current ownership pattern.

Ownership and Democratic Theory

The fundamental social concern regarding concentration of mass media ownership has little to do with how many buildings, cameras, or presses individuals or companies own. Rather, the problem manifests itself in the products of media technology, that is, information in the broadest sense. Canadians are fortunate to live in a society where historically they have had freedom to select information that is consistent with their preferences and needs; in political terms we call this a pluralistic society. However, as James Winter has pointed out, extensive centralized corporate ownership threatens "our notions of [ourselves as] a pluralistic society. . . . There is now strong evidence to challenge the pluralistic view."[4]

The libertarian tradition we discussed earlier depends on the existence of multiple sources of competing information. Briefly, to review the argument, in a free marketplace of ideas, "good" (more popular) information will prevail over "bad" (less popular) information. Without painting a romantic picture of the past characterized by independent ownership as a golden age of information, it is clear that free market forces, whatever effect they have on information, also lead directly to consolidation and centralization of ownership. Leaving aside for the moment the question of the quality of information disseminated, as media systems develop and grow in number, the number of independently owned media outlets dwindles. Consequently, consolidating ownership reduces the number of independent, often divergent, views that are available to Canadians. In terms of democratic theory, we need to recognize the negative consequences inherent in a restricted ownership base.

Ownership Types and Trends

Types of Private Ownership

In the Canadian context a number of types of ownership exist in the private sphere and these will be discussed in turn.

Single Independent Ownership

Although less common today than previously, single independent ownership, where an individual or company owns one unit of mass media, does continue to exist. This form of ownership is typically found in community newspapers and smaller broadcasting organizations. Conditions tend to change, however; a medium might fail as a business, or a larger competitor might dominate a weaker one with respect to audience or circulation figures, or an owner might simply retire. The one-unit medium thus comes up for sale. It will be bought by whoever has the needed extra capital at hand—often the large media owner who may add the new acquisition to a chain of media outlets.

Broadcast or Newspaper Chains

Chain ownership occurs when one company owns a string of media outlets of the same kind, and this is known as *horizontal integration*. Chains develop very readily: a strong newspaper will either amalgamate with or buy out weaker competitors. As the buyout usually results in greater profits, these profits may in turn fuel similar media purchases in other communities, further enlarging the chain.

Cross-media Ownership

Cross-media ownership occurs when a company owns different types of mass media outlets. As profits accrue, a daily newspaper owner might buy a weekly newspaper or a radio or television station rather than another daily, diversifying his or her interests. Such cross-media ownership began to develop in the 1920s when radio appeared on the scene as a popular commercial medium to compete with print media.

Conglomerate Ownership

Conglomerate ownership involves an organization owning several, unrelated companies, which could include some mass media. As often happens, companies venture into various new areas. Diversifying holdings spreads the risk of one's investments. With respect to mass media, conglomerate ownership tends to present more potential problems than do other forms of ownership. Since making profits is the central and only *real* purpose of a conglomerate, printing and broadcasting philosophies and journalistic principles suffer. While such might be the case, generalizations do not apply to all conglomerate ownership: even as harsh a critic as the Davey Committee pointed out that "Some of Canada's best newspapers are owned by groups; some of the worst are owned by independents."[5]

Characteristic of conglomerate ownership, moreso than of the other types of private ownership, is the phenomenon of *vertical integration*. Although different, all four types of private ownership are subject to vertical integration. Simply put, vertical integration occurs when various component parts of an industry are owned by the same company. For example, a radio station may purchase or build a recording studio, and later acquire a retail outlet to sell these recordings. Indeed, early radio provided a classic case of vertical integration when companies such as RCA and Marconi established radio stations in order to sell radio receivers. A similar phenomenon is seen in the acquisition by Sony (an equipment-manufacturing corporation) of U.S. film and recording properties.

Types of Public Ownership

While all types of public ownership do not exist in Canada, it is important to review the kinds of extant ownership in the global community.

Totalitarian Ownership

In totalitarian societies, media are in fact a part of the governing apparatus and there is virtually no competition in these circumstances. For details regarding how the press behaves under totalitarian control, students can refer to the discussion in chapter 2.

Government Ownership in Non-totalitarian Societies

Examples of media systems owned and operated directly by government existed in various English-speaking Caribbean societies, such as Jamaica and Barbados in the 1960s and Belize in the 1980s.[6] In these circumstances, an agency of government ran broadcasting with broadcasters functioning as civil servants. While these governments ran media enterprises, at the same time they competed with privately owned and operated media outlets; hence, there was an element of competition in the system as a whole. Recent changes in the former Soviet Union associated with *Glasnost*, particularly in the post-1991 coup period, would seem to be moving that country in a similar direction.[7]

Crown Corporation/Public Monopoly

Prior to the introduction of commercial broadcasting in the United Kingdom in 1972, the British Broadcasting Corporation functioned as a public monopoly. However, it operated at arm's length from the government of the day, despite its Crown corporation status. Its objective was to perform a social, not a governmental role.

Crown Corporation/Non-monopoly

While originally constructed on the British model, i.e., as a Crown corporation functioning at arm's length from government, the Canadian Broadcasting Corporation has always operated in an environment of strong competition from privately owned stations. As we mentioned in chapter 2, the U.S. Public Broadcasting System (PBS) is less well funded than the CBC. Born and developed in a highly commercial environment, PBS is "publicly owned" in the sense that it operates on government subsidy but depends on public donations and subscriptions to stay on the air. The CBC, however, as a Crown corporation receives most of its funding from government (about 75 percent) while the remainder comes from advertising.

Community or Co-operative Ownership

Today CATV, more commonly known as cable TV, is largely privately owned. However, when it first began it involved community co-operation: individuals in a community purchased memberships in the co-operative and enjoyed the financial gains or suffered the losses. More popular than the co-operative has been the community broadcasting station, which again is owned and operated by a community, often in remote locations. Also, virtually all radio stations on college and university campuses in Canada are "owned" by their student bodies, in that broadcasting licences are held by student councils.

Trends Towards Concentration of Ownership

A variety of social, economic, and political forces have contributed to the concentration/consolidation trends reflected in ownership of Canadian mass media. It is important to understand that these forces operate on the sellers of media properties as well as on potential buyers.

Economic theory tells us that a transfer of ownership takes place when a particular property is worth more to the buyer than it is to the seller. For example, the buyer may be in a position to manage that property at considerably less cost than the current owner due to economies of scale.

There are other reasons why media owners buy more media property.[8] For example, a purpose may be for diversification. In addition, growth implies more borrowing power for yet further expansion. Because the situations of individual owners keep changing (their interests change, they retire, they die), media properties of such persons, or

companies controlled by such persons, often become attractive purchases for organizations that have already reached considerable size.

As well as financial considerations, the transfer of ownership could confer social status upon the buyer. Lord Thomson of Fleet, founder of the Thomson media empire, bought the *Times* of London because, as he told a group of students at Oxford University, he enjoyed being the owner of the greatest newspaper in the world, despite the fact that it was not profitable.

Media businesses generally have been founded and run by individuals or families. As long as members of these families possess the interest and the ability to maintain these businesses, this pattern of ownership can continue. However, at a particular point, considerations

Roy Thomson (Lord Thomson of Fleet) 1894–1976, c. 1960–64 (National Archives of Canada/ PA 052572)

about inheritance taxes enter the picture, and these may affect the decision to sell. Estate and capital gains taxes are indeed often so great that selling the business becomes a desirable option. If the business to be sold represents a substantial holding, only large companies will be able to afford it. The result is greater consolidation and concentration of ownership.[9]

From the buyer's perspective, the federal government, through the CRTC, has in fact encouraged large media owners to grow larger. First, in 1970, when the CRTC decreed that broadcasting systems would be "effectively" owned by Canadians, non-Canadian owners were obliged to sell. In some instances such holdings represented heavy financial investments, as was the case of Famous Players, a U.S. company that was forced to sell its properties. The only viable buyers for such properties were those with capital to buy and experience to operate them—namely, large Canadian media corporations. Second, when Canadian content regulations came into effect, first for television and subsequently for radio, broadcasters and other content producers felt pressure to develop Canadian content of a high quality. To do this, several companies argued that they required a strong and broad financial base: they needed to expand their financial bases to be able to fulfil the requirements of the content regulations. And, because the argument was realistic, regulatory bodies acceded to several such requests for growth, in part if not in

whole, for the sake of developing quality Canadian content.

The transfer of shares of AM, FM, and TV stations in Sherbrooke, Quebec, in 1966 to Power Corporation was one case in point. In granting approval, the BBG indicated that Power Corporation had expressed its concerns about the need to develop talent and to upgrade the quality of broadcasting programs.[10]

Three years later, Pierre Juneau, chair of the newly created CRTC, reiterated earlier sentiments: "We need some groups in Canada that will be large enough to be able to compete in the entertainment, the cultural, the informational and the educational fields with the enormous entities that are being created in other parts of the world and particularly by our neighbour [the United States]."[11]

Bushnell Communications Limited was also granted permission to expand. The Bushnell company, in 1970, applied for approval to acquire ownership and/or control of seventeen cable television systems, four television stations, seven AM radio stations, four FM stations, and one shortwave station. While not all of these proposed acquisitions were approved by the CRTC, and some that were approved were not realized, the rationale behind approving some of Bushnell's requests was that the company had pressed the matter of "improving and increasing [Canadian] program production."[12]

New technologies also promote the growth of mass media empires: satellite distribution systems and research into high definition television, for example, have attracted the interest and financial resources of global "big money" players. In a sense, to enter the game is a big money gamble, but the payoff, if there is one, can be enormous.

Finally, economies of scale encourage the large to become larger. Such economies can be achieved by horizontal chains, by mixed media owners, and certainly by conglomerates. For example, buying raw materials in bulk for a dozen newspapers rather than making twelve individual purchases allows the buyer to negotiate a more favourable price. Other more subtle factors come into play. Reporting the news tends to be expensive, and chains and networks are able to distribute the cost of one sought-after journalist over a number of media outlets. Also, this sought-after journalist might have been attracted by the opportunity for greater national exposure, financial rewards, and career advancement available in large organizations. Obviously, hiring talented people results in a better quality product and, in this sense, the argument presented to the CRTC to permit expansion in order to develop better quality content can be justified.

Theoretically, at least, a strong economic base can also sustain experimentation. For example, Roy Megarry, publisher of the *Globe and Mail*, proposed to develop the *Globe* as Canada's "national newspaper" through satellite printing. As well, he proposed to the newspaper's previous owners the extension of for-

eign bureaus. The proposals were turned down on financial grounds. At a later date—after the paper was purchased by Thomson, a considerably larger organization—the same proposals were accepted.[13]

Considerations Regarding Large Owners

Clearly there are advantages to media consumers that derive from large media ownership. Large organizations, for instance, can readily evade the sometimes pernicious influences of advertisers; small organizations often cannot. In some circumstances large organizations can afford to press for access to particular information that is useful for society to have. They also possess the necessary legal resources to challenge political authority on behalf of society. Those who challenged President Nixon at the time of the Watergate scandal were not local community radio stations or small-town newspapers. Despite threats, challenges to the president and his administration came from the *Washington Post* and the CBS network, media organizations of considerable size and scope.

While there are some positive aspects to large media organizations, it is necessary to look at the other side of the coin. While economies of scale are possible for large ownership, the question really must be asked, who benefits from these economies? There is evidence that in some situations where takeovers have occurred, prices and costs for customers have, in fact, gone up. This was the case with business advertising rates that, when increased following a takeover, were passed on to consumers.[14]

Large, strong corporate ownership of a conglomerate nature often has the result of discouraging, or even preventing, new initiatives or new entrants into the field. This is particularly true when strong vertical integration characterizes the conglomerate. In Canada, the federal government (through Telefilm and the CRTC, for example) has introduced incentives for networks and large broadcasting organizations to use the products of small, independent producers. Under unregulated economies of scale, large companies would be unlikely to use such independently produced content. Finally, large ownership tends to be concerned with profit margins, often critical in large operations where operating costs are great. The tendency, then, is to pay greater attention to effective business management than to the quality of product. This emphasis can result in content with a broadly based appeal that ignores cultural considerations.[15]

Investigations into the Ownership Question

Three landmark studies stand out in the history of investigations into the question of the ownership of Canada's mass media. The Davey Committee (1970) examined ownership in all forms of mass media, the Kent Commission (1981) was concerned exclusively with ownership of newspapers, while the Task Force on Broadcasting Policy (1986) reported, among other matters, on the question of ownership in broadcasting media, as well as examining the phenomenon of cross-media ownership. While all of these studies have been referred to previously, at this point we want simply to review the context in which they took place, summarize their major findings, and evaluate their impact on trends in media ownership.

The Davey Committee

The trend towards concentration of ownership of Canada's mass media began in the early decades of this century. However, it was really only after the introduction of television in the early 1950s and the recognition of its political influence in the 1960s that concern focussed on this question. Senator Keith Davey mobilized this concern in the form of a Special Senate Committee to study mass media in 1968. The committee's *Report* (released in three volumes in 1970)[16] set the tone for the subsequent debate on media ownership in Canada.

The context for the Davey Committee Report was provided by a post-World War II society upon which television had made a massive impact in a short period of time, by major studies in the U.S. and the U.K. that focussed on mass media responsibility, and by the continuing trend towards concentration of ownership that had been going on uninterruptedly since the turn of the century. As the introductory volume of the *Report* indicates, such a trend raises several vital questions. How is it possible to reconcile the trend towards monopoly ownership of media with a pluralistic society's need for diversity? How can we ensure "diverse and antagonistic sources" of information, which are central to the process of free and open debate, when the ownership base of media is narrowing rapidly? Given the implicit concerns regarding growing media conglomerates, where "bottom-line" concerns tend to dominate, how can society be assured about the "quality and relevancy of the product" produced by mass media?

The committee convincingly documented the extent of chain ownership of Canada's mass media. It also revealed the number of newspapers held by chains and the percentage of circulation they controlled in a series of tables that have since formed the basis of countless student essays. As well, the committee's research revealed that in 1958 the three largest chains (Southam, Thomson, and FP Publications) controlled 25 percent of total Canadian circulation; twelve years later, in 1970, they controlled 45 percent. And of Canada's daily newspapers, 66 percent were owned or controlled by chains; in terms of circulation the figure was 77 percent.[17] Thomson, at the time, owned thirty

daily and fifteen weekly papers in Canada; Southam owned eleven daily newspapers and had minority interest in three other dailies, in addition to owning 50 percent of Pacific Press, which published the *Vancouver Sun* and the *Vancouver Province*; while FP Publications owned or controlled eight dailies, including the prestigious *Globe and Mail*, and was the largest newspaper chain in the country due to a slightly higher margin of circulation than the others.

In contrast to newspaper groups, ownership of broadcast media, the committee reported, was more widely distributed, as just under half of radio and TV outlets were controlled by groups.[18] In some instances, group ownership had extended to all three media types, raising the spectre of cross-media ownership.

The Davey Committee made a number of recommendations, some of which were eventually reflected in legislation—Bill C-58 referred to in chapter 6, for example. However, the crucial recommendation for the creation of a press ownership review board, which would have controlled the growth of newspaper chains, was never acted upon. Twenty years after the publication of his Senate Committee's *Report*, Senator Davey, in addressing an annual meeting of the Canadian Advertising Foundation, noted that the trend towards concentration of ownership had continued unabated and that the situation had gone from "bad to worse." He indicated that it was not too late to rectify the situation and suggested that it "may be in the public interest to have some form of unbundling," that is, to begin a process of breaking up the large chains.[19]

The Kent Commission

A decade later, with the establishment of the Royal Commission on Newspapers (the Kent Commission), earlier concerns about the concentration of ownership were emphatically raised again. As mentioned in chapter 6, the commission had been created in a climate of deep concern. It was established within a week of the simultaneous closing of the *Winnipeg Tribune* and the *Ottawa Journal* in August 1980, as a result of an arrangement between the Thomson and Southam groups. The closing of the papers left each company in a monopoly situation. In addition to numerous other newspaper ownership changes over the preceding decade, Thomson had just acquired the eight daily newspapers of FP Publications, which included the *Globe and Mail* and the *Winnipeg Free Press*, two of Canada's premier newspapers. Thus, Ben Bagdikian's prediction that as the consolidation of ownership progressed, chains would begin devouring chains had come true.[20] Such changes left Thomson with forty of Canada's 117 daily newspapers. Southam owned fourteen, although Southam emerged as the largest newspaper group in Canada in terms of daily circulation.[21]

The Kent Commission, in its main report issued in 1981, points out that chains then owned 75 percent of Canada's newspapers.[22] Meanwhile, in the same decade, circulation of English-language dailies controlled by chains had increased from 60 percent in 1970 to 75 percent in 1980, and circulation of the chain-owned French-language dailies jumped from 50 percent in 1970 to an extraordinary 90 percent in 1980. These figures meant that chains controlled 77 percent of national daily circulation.[23]

More recently, in 1987, McPhail and McPhail reported that the chain-controlled circulation stood at 79 percent.[24] Three years later, Kesterton and Bird calculated the figure to be 82.8 percent.[25] The latest calculation, made by the authors in August 1991, indicated that chain-controlled circulation had risen to 85.6 percent. As well, of the 109 daily newspapers publishing in Canada in August 1991, chains owned 97 papers (89 percent), while independents owned but 12 papers (11 percent).

There is a reality here that deserves our attention: in 1970, the Davey Committee made several recommendations, some of which have had a lasting impact on media ownership, especially non-Canadian ownership of Canada's print media. In comparison, the recommendations of the Kent Commission, had they been acted upon, would have had an even more profound effect than those of the Davey Committee. For example, had the Canadian Newspaper Act become law, the effect would have been dramatic. Changes would have taken place in ownership and, without a doubt, concentration of ownership would have been stemmed, if not reversed.

In discussing concentration of newspaper ownership as a problem, Ross Eaman identifies four possible approaches that Canada can take in dealing with it. First is the laissez-faire approach, i.e., leave things as they are. The second approach involves "limited controls." In this approach, Eaman suggests that the effective use of press councils, for example, could eliminate some of what he terms, the "worst effects of concentrated newspaper ownership." A third position identified by Eaman is that the whole matter of concentration of ownership should be brought to a halt through the establishment of a monitoring group (not unlike the Davey Committee's Press Ownership Review Board) that would have the authority to approve or disapprove any buyout or merger. Finally, Eaman's fourth position, which he labels the "counter-measures" approach, is aimed at reversing large group ownership and control of circulation. This could take place in the manner suggested by the Kent Commission, whereby the proposed Newspaper Act would require that the Thomson organization either sell the *Globe and Mail* or the remainder of its newspaper holdings in Canada.[26]

In spite of a high level of awareness and concern about the problem of the concentration of newspaper ownership in Canada, very little has been done to alter the situation. Indeed, concentration has proceeded to such an extent that Eaman's proposed monitoring group would now have little left to monitor, as the bulk of consolidation has already taken place. In terms of rectifying the situation, in our view, little else is left but Eaman's fourth position, and here we are reminded of the fate of the Kent Commission's recommendations, which achieved little except to raise the ire of virtually every newspaper executive in the country. With the exception of the creation of some voluntary press councils, laissez-faire seems to have won the day by default.

The Task Force on Broadcasting Policy

As the Davey Committee pointed out, the extent of group ownership in broadcasting media is not as high as that found in publishing. In part, at least, we believe this is due to the existence of legislation (the Broadcasting Act), which, since the very beginning, made a government agency responsible for the matter of ownership. Thus, the broadcaster was never considered to "own" a licence; rather the licence was granted on the condition of "promise of performance" on the part of the licensee. At the same time, there has always been a concern in broadcasting about the local community in which a station was located. As a result, even today, broadcasting groups tend to function on a regional, rather than a national level.

In its 1978 study of corporate concentration in Canada, the Bryce Commission recommended that the CRTC should be permitted, whenever appropriate, "not only to constrain print media from controlling broadcast and electronic media . . . but also to prevent broadcast media from acquiring or controlling major print media." Through its regulatory practices, the CRTC has been seeing that these situations do not arise.[27]

There are a few examples of cross-media ownership: the Irving family holdings in the Maritimes (broadcasting and print); the Blackburn family holdings in the London, Ontario area (broadcasting and print). Both families have held these properties since the earliest days of television and radio. More recently, Southam, through its minority ownerhip of Selkirk Broadcasting, has been publishing newspapers in five cities where Selkirk has stations.[28]

To some extent, the problems of cross-media ownership exist because we have no firm regulatory measures that limit this kind of ownership. In the U.S., for example, newspaper owners are prohibited from holding broadcasting licences in the same communities where they publish papers. As well, the Federal Communications Commission (FCC) limits the number of broadcasting stations an individual or company can own. Since 1984 the limit has been twelve AM, twelve FM, and twelve TV stations (up

from an earlier seven/seven/seven limit).[29] In contrast, in Canada, with a population one-tenth that of the U.S., CHUM, based in Toronto, alone owns twenty-four radio stations and six television stations.[30] In the U.S., in addition to the twelve-station ownership limit, the FCC has imposed three other restrictions to prevent concentration of ownership: "the duopoly rule" prevents an individual or company from owning two commercial stations that have overlapping signals; the "one-to-a-market rule" forbids an individual or company from owning both a radio and a TV station that serve the same area; individuals or companies cannot own a broadcasting station and a daily newspaper in the same community.[31] These kinds of detailed regulations do not exist in Canada.

The regulatory approach taken in Canada, as the task force on Broadcasting Policy points out, has been a case-by-case approach, often lacking consistency.[32] But the Canadian approach towards concentration of ownership is not as casual as it might appear to be. First, the CBC is a strong national broadcasting entity with well-designed regional broadcasting structures. Thus, unless something drastic were to occur, such as the privatization of the CBC (which was debated and passed at the 1991 Progressive Conservative policy convention), the element of competition offered by publicly owned media outlets is guaranteed and is likely to continue. Second, the financial base of Canadian producers has to be as sound as possible. It has been apparent for a number of years, particularly since 1960 when the Canadian content quota for television was first introduced, that Canadian producers would be facing increasingly strong competition from the U.S. and the global community. In most cases, such competition was the product of large and financially secure production organizations. Thus, the BBG and the CRTC have been acutely aware of the danger of weakening the operative financial base of Canadian broadcasters. Nevertheless, the Task Force on Broadcasting Policy strongly underlines the need for a comprehensive policy with respect to broadcasting ownership in Canada, despite the clear recognition of the financial resources needed to compete in the context of worldwide growing concentration of ownership.[33]

In 1985, the calculation of concentration in broadcasting ownership differed according to the basis of measurement. For example, of 446 radio stations (AM and FM), 133 were owned by radio groups, roughly 30 percent. However, in this instance, a radio group was defined by the task force as a group owning seven or more stations. Clearly, if the same criteria used for television groups (two or more stations) were applied to radio, this percentage would increase dramatically. For television, sixty-four of Canada's eighty-one TV-program-originating stations (79 percent) were group owned.[34] Trends since 1985 indicate further consolidation of broadcasting ownership.

Research on the Effects of Concentrated Ownership

A crucial question with respect to concentration of ownership (which virtually every investigator recognizes as being too high) is the relationship between ownership and media behaviour as reflected both in business practice and content. Research has been done in this area in the United States and in Canada, and a discussion of some of these studies follows.

Ownership and Advertising Rates

While not a subject that has prompted a great deal of research, studies done in the U.S. and in Canada conclude that when a monopoly either exists or occurs through the buyout of a competitor, advertising rates tend to increase. On the basis of empirical studies done in the U.S., Picard arrives at three conclusions: (1) chain-owned newspapers, Joint Operation Agreement (JOA) newspapers, and newspaper monopolies tend to charge higher prices for advertising than do papers that publish in a competitive environment; (2) in those instances where economies of scale are realized, the financial benefits tend not to be passed on either to newspaper consumers or advertising accounts; (3)

cross-ownership of media properties does not apparently affect pricing behaviour as it relates to unit costs or advertising costs to consumers.[35]

In a comprehensive study of the effects of ownership on advertising rates in Canada, based on nine cases of chain-acquisition and three cases of newspaper terminations occurring over the years 1966 to 1980, Charrette et al. found no consistent pattern. In cases where a monopoly was created by the termination of a competing newspaper, the surviving newspaper charged higher advertising rates. Acquisition of a paper by a chain did not result in a change in advertising rates.[36] A termination of a competing newspaper in Winnipeg in 1980 confirmed the study cited above, in that the surviving newspaper increased its advertising revenue by 5 percent, despite a decrease of 27 percent in the overall amount of advertising.[37]

Content

In a study of the impact of Southam News's acquisition of the previously independently owned *Windsor Star*, content changes were examined in a number of areas, such as the front page, editorials, features, sources of content, areas of interest, and political partisanship. The study, employing a before-and-after design, revealed that changes in the *Windsor Star* had indeed coincided with the ownership change, but that whether one viewed these changes as positive or negative was largely a matter of one's own preference. With respect to particular areas of interest, there

was a drop-off in front page stories, editorials, and features dealing with the United States and an increase in local, provincial, and national Canadian material, but not in all categories of content. Predictably, the use of Southam News Wire Service increased dramatically (an example of economies of scale). It must also be pointed out that while the corporation benefitted from these economies of scale, so, too, did newspaper readers who now had access to Canadian national and foreign correspondents in a manner and frequency that they had not had before. With respect to political partisanship, it was found that under independent ownership the *Windsor Star* tended to balance its favourable and unfavourable comments on all political parties, with a slight tendency to favour the party in power, at both the federal and provincial levels. Under Southam, the newspaper assumed the traditional "critical" role of the press; that is, it opposed the party in power (the PCs at the provincial level and the Liberals at the federal level).[38]

The 1980 acquisition of the *Globe and Mail* by Thomson Newspapers was not a case of a chain taking over an independent newspaper. However, in that it involved the country's premier newspaper being taken over by a chain that had a questionable reputation (according to both the Davey Committee[39] and the Kent Commission)[40] with respect to its commitment to journalistic quality, it was a contentious acquisition. A thorough empirical examination of the effects of the "Thomsonization" of the *Globe* was warranted. The final four years of *Globe* content prior to the ownership change and the first four years following it were examined. Again, as with the *Windsor Star*, changes were evident, and again, it is difficult to judge whether these changes are positive or negative. In summary, what happened to the *Globe* under Thomson is that it became "Canada's National Newspaper" not only in name but also in terms of its content. Dramatic decreases in local, Toronto-based material were evident, as well as concomitant increases in both national and international material. Sources of material used by the paper did not change. Nor did patterns of political partisanship. The *Globe* under FP ownership had an anti-Liberal persuasion at the federal level and an anti-Conservative persuasion at the provincial level. These persuasions, consistent with the adversarial role of the press, continued under Thomson ownership.[41]

Candussi and Winter's examination of the *Winnipeg Free Press* differs from both of the previously noted studies since it looks at the content of a newspaper under the same ownership in two periods of time: a pre-monopoly situation and a post-monopoly situation. They found that following the closing of the rival *Winnipeg Tribune*, the *Free Press* experienced a 7 percent decrease in the amount of space devoted to news. However, when the authors controlled for actual space, it was found that the newshole had increased by 5 percent (i.e., the total newspaper got smaller, and news made up a greater percentage of that smaller newspaper). The percentage of local material actually increased slightly (contrary to the hypothesized trend), while both national and international coverage declined. The authors point out that these changes in area of interest may be related to factors other than the change in monopoly situation.[42] For example, the salience of particular news events might well have affected such changes.

An American study that examined editorial pages of twenty-eight daily newspapers before and after the papers were purchased by chains in 1985 (a total of fifty-six daily newspapers in the U.S. were acquired by chains in that year alone) arrived at definitive conclusions.

> The primary purpose of the study was to search for evidence of diminished commitment to the editorial page by chains that are characterized as greedy and profit-minded. It was anticipated that chains would devote fewer pages to editorials and commentary, would publish fewer local and regional editorials and letters, and would publish more advertisements and canned editorials. But this did not happen. With one minor exception, there simply were no statistically significant differences for the 16 variables that measured the quality of editorial pages.[43]

The author concludes that it appears as if "both [chain and independent newspapers] are equally committed to an editorial page."

Another line of inquiry related to the effects of chain-ownership on media content is found in the behaviour of mass media in times of election. Presumably, if the owner's influence were to be evident, it would more than likely be in times of heightened political activity such as elections. Studies that go back to the 1972 Canadian election indicate that it is difficult to document an owner's influence on papers within a chain through studies of content. In the 1972 election, Wagenberg and Soderlund compared election editorials in four FP Publications newspapers and three control newspapers. No evidence was found to indicate similarities in editorial judgement on the part of the editors of the FP papers.[44]

For the 1974 election, the same authors conducted a more detailed study, this time examining the editorial behaviour of three chains: FP, Southam, and Thomson. Conclusions were similar. "While there [were] some indications that chain ownership would foster within a chain a community of attitudes on social values and political philosophy, this [did] not take the form of central direction of editorial policies. . . ."[45]

The 1979 and 1980 campaigns presented the opportunity to study, on a more comprehensive basis, election coverage in both electronic and print media. Thus Soderlund et al. were able to comment on effects of private vs. public ownership in electronic media and chain ownership (in both French and English) for print media. Following the election of a PC minority government in 1979, the government's failure to win a vote of confidence necessitated an election in the following year. Thus we have two elections, held in consecutive years, with different political parties in power and in opposition in each election. The dominant conclusion emerging from the study is that the nation's media presented a highly homogeneous account of the election campaigns concerning parties, party leaders, and issues. In a re-analysis of those data for the Royal Commission on Newspapers, designed to highlight the effects of chain ownership, similar conclusions were apparent: there was no direct link to be found between chain owners and identifiable patterns of election coverage on the part of their papers.[46]

Ownership Intrusion

Before he ceased publication of the *Toronto Telegram* in 1971, owner and publisher John Bassett publicly commented on a criticism made of his habit of writing occasional editorials and articles for that newspaper; his comment was to the effect that there was nothing wrong with him doing that—after all, it was his newspaper. More recently, Conrad Black, who owns newspapers globally, on occasion writes columns for his publications. It has also been noted that Rupert Murdoch openly supported Ronald Reagan and Margaret Thatcher through his media properties in the U.S. and the U.K.[47]

Further, let it not be forgotten as we examine ownership influence on media content that, in the case of most weekly newspapers in the country, the roles of owner, publisher, editor, and even reporter are often played by the same person. As well, when we examine the history of newspapers in particular, it quickly becomes apparent that "taking sides" was a historical tradition that is still to be found today, albeit, rarely or in a less obvious manner. Nevertheless, the *Toronto Star*, Canada's largest circulation daily, has openly and clearly supported the Liberal Party (with the exception of one federal election) since the earliest days of the newspaper.

With respect to broadcasting, the question of ownership influence on content is less contentious a matter than is the case with newspapers, given the obligation of stations to offer fair treatment to divergent views on matters of public interest. While occasional lapses might occur, the norm is that broadcasters do observe that obligation.

Nevertheless, it is important to look at how ownership intrusion is likely to occur. Seldom, research has pointed out, do corporate owners in Canada enter their newsrooms and tell editors and reporters how they should "play" a particular issue. And, owners who have appeared before special committees, royal commissions and the like, have consistently indicated that they are not concerned with the political direction of their publications. Rather, they are satisfied if their newspapers operate effectively in their communities, and, of course, in a profitable manner. Crude and arbitrary intrusions on the part of media owners are rare indeed.

However, ownership interference in the newsroom may occur in less overt ways. Two case studies in particular are worthy of note in exploring these more subtle means of exercising influence.

Power Corporation and La Presse

In 1972, in Quebec, Power Corporation acquired the influential daily *La Presse* of Montreal. This acquisition created considerable adverse commentary concerning the anticipated increase in that corporation's influence over public opinion in the province. Five years later, when a federal royal commission was established to study corporate concentration (the Bryce Commission), the Power Corporation/*La Presse* relationship came under close scrutiny.

The study looked at the different types of power and control between the corporate owners and the newspaper. The researchers identified three ways in which Power Corporation management could intervene so as to affect news content: first, they could intervene through selective hiring and training, which could be aimed at creating "a profile of journalistic resources"; second, they could selectively allocate human and financial resources to the newspaper's coverage of areas and events; and third, they could control psychological and financial rewards. These three types of intervention could result in a media organization that is highly compliant with the values of its owner.[48]

The researchers concluded that the management at *La Presse* had been "circumspect" in the use of ownership controls, and when there had been direct intervention, it tended to be with respect to industrial relations rather than content.[49]

Beland H. Honderich and the Toronto Star

A study of the *Toronto Star* newsroom in 1988 produced some interesting results concerning ownership intervention. The case is especially significant as the *Star* has a history of vigorous ownership involvement in the running of the paper going back to its founder, Joseph S. Atkinson. As well, the *Star* has been openly committed to a philosophy of "liberalism and Canadian nationalism."

Three broad findings are relevant: first, many journalists on the paper had never met the publisher, and the publisher rarely issued statements concerning the direction news should take; second, newcomers to the newsroom tended to learn appropriate behaviour through daily practices rather than through a handbook on policy (even though such a publication does exist at the *Star*); and third, a budding journalist with the *Star*, and certainly those long in the employ of the paper, would be quite familiar with the "liberal" tradition of the newspaper, and in this sense that tradition would influence their work.[50]

Conclusion

Where does this overview of problems associated with ownership of Canadian media bring us? We began the chapter with a discussion of the role of mass media in the context of democratic theory and practice, highlighting the assumption that democracy depends on multiple, independent, and diverse voices. This assumption of course reflects pure libertarian thinking. While the contemporary reality of mass media ownership has departed in significant ways from this libertarian ideal, has Canadian democracy diminished in its vitality? We need to be very careful not to jump to conclusions in attempting to answer this question.

In truth, the effects of concentrated media ownership on democratic governance are unclear. No one would properly argue that the levels of concentration currently in existence in Canada represent a "healthy" situation. As the Kent Commission pointed out, there is simply too much power over public opinion held in too few hands for anyone to be comfortable. This is our instinctive reaction to bigness.

On the other hand, Canadian mass media are businesses and moreover are businesses that have to compete on a global scale. Worldwide trends towards concentration of ownership in industry, in general, and in the mass media industries, in particular are unmistakably clear, as we shall see in the following chapter. Whatever the precise reasons, ownership units are increasing in size and in diversity of activities. The large conglomerate is a reality, and this is most likely so because this form of ownership is most competitive economically.

Second, the actual track record of concentrated ownership of Canada's mass media does not point to a situation where owners of mass media empires have harnessed their clear potential to shape public opinion. Research in the United States as well has shown that there is little difference in the news and editorial content between competing papers in a community and a monopoly newspaper. These studies go back to the 1950s.[51] Current research continues to support them. Most remarkably perhaps, "the presence or absence of daily newspaper competition does not seem to make much difference" to the readership.[52]

Tomorrow is another day, however, and past practice may prove to be an imperfect indicator of future behaviour. For the moment at least, we can take consolation from the fact that insofar as "diverse voices" are concerned, if anything, there are increasingly *more* voices, given the multiplication of domestic and global broadcasting sources—cable systems, satellites, and the increased ease in receiving short-wave news broadcasts.

To what extent such multiplication of sources of programming results in "diverse" voices being heard by audiences is largely a matter of opinion: detailed content and audience studies would be required to ascertain the amount of diversity and its impact. While this is true for today's media, there is no assurance that diversity has ever existed in Canadian media, beyond that period in the mid- to late 1800s and extending into the early 1900s, when newspapers were explicitly Grit or Tory in their views.

As well, judgements as to whether diversity exists depend to a certain extent on one's expectations. If one expects the media to express opposing views, one can certainly find instances of this. For example, the *Globe and Mail* and the *Toronto Star* took opposite positions on the issue of free trade in the 1988 election. Network news on Canadian TV has been shown to differ in measurable ways from that on the American networks and coverage of Canadian issues by Canada's two major English-language TV networks—CBC and CTV—has, on occasion, reflected broadly disparate views.[53] On the other hand, studies have also shown media treatments of events to be highly homogeneous.[54] But, if one expects that people in society should be able to express their views through media, certainly a great deal of that exists: a myriad of talk shows on both radio and television accommodate countless opposing and controversial points of view; op-ed page features in most Canadian newspapers express a fairly wide spectrum of political interests; letters to the editors of newspapers are usually supportive of or openly confrontational to any and all current issues.

We foresee a continuing increase, across a broad spectrum of media, of flows of information into Canada from non-Canadian sources. While this increased flow of foreign information strongly challenges the intent of Canadian content regulations—to protect the national identity—it also presages an increase in the multiplicity and diversity of ideas and opinions current in our society. In our view, this content from other societies presents a formidable threat to the maintenance of any cultural distinctiveness they might prefer for their own society. Moreover, this threat is likely to be much more profound than has been or will be the impact of the narrowing ownership base of Canadian media on "diverse" ideas and opinions: indeed, in comparison, the ownership factor will be slight.

Notes

1. Ben Bagdikian, "Lords of the Global Village: Cornering Hearts and Minds," *The Nation* 248 (12 June 1989), 805–20.
2. Wilfred Kesterton, *A History of Journalism in Canada* (Ottawa: Carleton University Press, 1984), 64–83.
3. The stock trading between Southam News and Torstar (the company controlling the *Toronto Star* serves as an example. See Edward Greenspon, "Southam's Tenets Cited in Defense of Swap," *Globe and Mail*, 2 April 1986, B4; and Ian Austen, "Torstar's Pact with Southam Ends," *Toronto Star*, 30 June 1990, C3.
4. James P. Winter, "Interlocking Directorships and Economic Power," *Press Concentration and Monopoly: New Perspectives on Newspaper Ownership and Operation*, ed. Robert G. Picard, James P. Winter, Maxwell E. McCombs and Stephen Lacy (Norwood, NJ: Ablex Publishing, 1989), 115.
5. Canada, Senate, *The Uncertain Mirror: Report of the Special Senate Committee on Mass Media*, vol. 1 (Ottawa: Information Canada, 1970), 15.
6. See, for example, descriptions in *Mass Media and the Caribbean*, ed. Stuart H. Surlin and Walter C. Soderlund (New York: Gordon and Breach, 1990), 13–20; 56–64; 105–13.
7. "Glasnost Extended to Radio, TV," *Windsor Star*, 16 July 1990, A10.
8. For a detailed discussion of this topic, see Rowland Lorimer and Jean McNulty, *Mass Communication in Canada*, 2nd ed. (Toronto: McClelland and Stewart, 1991), 183–217.
9. See discussion in Michael Charette, C.L. Brown-John, W.I. Romanow and W.C. Soderlund, "Acquisition et fermeture de journeaux par des chaînes de journeaux: effets sur les tarifs de publicité," *Communication Information* 6, 1 (1984): 50–54.
10. Canada, Board of Broadcast Governors, *Announcement of 24 November, 1966* (Ottawa, 1966).
11. Pierre Juneau, "Address to the Canadian Television Association," 14 May 1969.
12. Canada, Canadian Radio-Television Commission, *Public Announcement: Decision CRTC 70-156, 6 July 1970* (Ottawa, 1970).
13. Author Interview with A. Roy Megarry, publisher, *Globe and Mail*, 7 November 1986.
14. Charette et al., "Acquisition et fermeture," 58.
15. See, for example, David Waterman, "The Failure of Cultural Programming on Cable TV: An Economic

Interpretation," *Journal of Communication* 36 (Summer 1986): 92–107; and Joseph Turow, "Corporate Planning and Media Culture," in *Communication Yearbook 7*, ed. Robert Bostrom and Bruce H. Westley (Beverly Hills: Sage Publications, 1983): 432–42.

16. In addition to the already cited *The Uncertain Mirror*, vol. 1, see *Words, Music and Dollars: A Study of the Economics of Publishing and Broadcasting in Canada*, vol. 2 (Ottawa: Information Canada, 1970); and *Good, Bad or Simply Inevitable: Selected Research Studies*, vol. 3 (Ottawa: Information Canada, 1970).

17. *The Uncertain Mirror*, 20–21. In 1991, two chains, Southam and Thomson, controlled 49 percent of daily newspaper circulation. (See chapter 6.)

18. Ibid., 5.

19. Randy Scotland, "Media Concentration Increasing," *Marketing* 95 (May 1990): 9.

20. Ben Bagdikian, "Newspaper Mergers: The Final Phase," *Columbia Journalism Review* 15 (March–April 1977): 17.

21. Andrew M. Osler, "From Vincent Massey to Thomas Kent: The Evolution of a National Press Policy in Canada," in *Communications in Canadian Society*, ed. Benjamin Singer (Don Mills: Addison-Wesley, 1983), 103.

22. Canada, *Royal Commission on Newspapers* (Ottawa: Supply and Services, 1981). Students should be aware that eight separate research publications of the commission accompanied the main report and are generally available in university and community libraries.

23. Ibid., 1–14.

24. Thomas L. McPhail and Brenda M. McPhail, *Communication: The Canadian Experience* (Toronto: Copp Clark Pitman, 1990), 95.

25. See Wilfred Kesterton and Roger Bird, "The Press in Canada," in *Communications in Canadian Society*, ed. Benjamin Singer (Scarborough: Nelson Canada, 1991), 46. The authors' calculation was based on August 1991 circulation figures available in *Canadian Advertising Rates and Data*. In this calculation the *Toronto Star* was counted as an independent paper. Figures used are the Monday–Saturday average daily circulation.

26. Ross A. Eaman, *The Media Society: Basic Issues and Controversies* (Toronto: Butterworth, 1987), 91–110.

27. Canada, *Report of the Royal Commission on Corporate Concentration* (Ottawa: Supply and Services, 1978), 353.

28. Canada, *Report of the Task Force on Broadcasting Policy* (Ottawa: Supply and Services, 1986), 644.

29. Jeremy Tunstall, *Communication Deregulation: The Unleashing of America's Communications Industry* (New York: Basil Blackwell, 1986), 151.

30. *Task Force on Broadcasting Policy*, 620–26.

31. Jack W. Whitley and Gregg P. Skall, *The Broadcaster's Survival Guide: A Handbook of FCC Rules and Regulations for Radio and TV Stations* (New York: Scripps Howard Books, 1988), 63–64.

32. *Task Force on Broadcasting Policy*, 644.

33. Ibid., 645

34. Ibid. Data are compiled from tables found on pp. 620 and 626.

35. Robert G. Picard, "Pricing Behaviour of Newspapers," in *Press Concentration and Monopoly*, ed. Picard et al., 68.

36. Charette et al., "Acquisition et fermeture," 59.

37. Dores A. Candussi and James A. Winter, "Monopoly and Content in Winnipeg," in *Press Concentration*

and Monopoly, ed. Picard et al., 144–45.

38. W.I. Romanow and W.C. Soderlund, "The Southam Press Acquisition of *The Windsor Star*: A Canadian Case Study of Change," *Gazette* 22, 4 (1978): 26–37.

39. "The dailies published in Canada by the Thomson chain are uniformly disappointing." See *The Uncertain Mirror*, 85.

40. The Royal Commission on Newspapers cited a former Thomson editorial employee who charged the company with "'indifference' to the need for editorial quality throughout its operations." See *Report of the Royal Commission on Newspapers*, 131.

41. W.I. Romanow and W.C. Soderlund, "Thomson Newspapers' Acquisition of *The Globe and Mail*: A Case Study of Content Change," *Gazette* 41, 1 (1988): 5–17.

42. Candussi and Winter, "Monopoly and Content," 139–45.

43. F. Dennis Hale, "Editorial Diversity and Concentration," in *Press Concentration and Monopoly*, ed. Picard et al., 174.

44. R.H. Wagenberg and W.C. Soderlund, "The Influence of Chain-Ownership on Editorial Comment in Canada," *Journalism Quarterly* 52 (Spring 1975): 93–98.

45. R.H. Wagenberg and W.C. Soderlund, "The Effects of Chain Ownership on Editorial Coverage: The Case of the 1974 Canadian Federal Election," *Canadian Journal of Political Science* 9 (December 1976): 689.

46. W.C. Soderlund, W.I. Romanow, R.H. Wagenberg, E.D. Briggs, *Media and Elections in Canada* (Toronto: Holt, Rinehart and Winston, 1984), 69, 90. See also by the same authors, "Correlates of Newspaper Coverage of the 1979 Canadian Election: Chain-ownership, Competitiveness of Market and Circulation," study prepared for the Royal Commission on Newspapers, 1980.

47. Thomas Kiernan, *Citizen Murdoch* (New York: Dodd Mead & Co., 1986), 261.

48. Yvan Allaire, Roger-Emile Miller and Paul Dell'Aniello, *Royal Commission on Corporate Concentration, Study No. 23, The Newspaper Firm and Freedom on Information: A Technical Study* (Ottawa: Supply and Services, 1977), 63–65.

49. Ibid., 83–87.

50. Joe Fox, "Social Influences on Decision-Making in *The Toronto Star* Newsroom" (M.A. thesis, University of Windsor), 1988.

51. Raymond B. Nixon and Robert L. Jones, "The Content of Non-Competitive vs. Competitive Newspapers," *Journalism Quarterly* 33 (Summer 1956): 299–314. Also see, Maxwell McCombs, "Concentration, Monopoly, and Content," in *Press Concentration and Monopoly*, ed. Picard et al., 129–37.

52. John C. Schweitzer and Elaine Goldman, "Does Newspaper Competition Make a Difference to Readers?" *Journalism Quarterly* 52 (Winter 1975): 710.

53. Stuart H. Surlin, W.I. Romanow, W.C. Soderlund, "TV Network News: A Canadian-American Comparison," *The American Review of Canadian Studies* 17 (Winter 1988): 465–75; see also "Persian Gulf Crisis: Part I," *On Balance* 4 (April 1991).

54. Soderlund et al., *Media and Elections*, 49–95.

Media Ownership Profiles

Introduction

In order to understand further the ownership of Canadian mass media, in this chapter we will present profiles of major corporate media owners, international and domestic.[1] Our purpose in identifying particular individuals and companies is to offer students insights into the kinds of media ownership that are currently operative, to identify strategies for growth and expansion employed by media owners, and to shed some light on ownership trends in Canada.

What quickly becomes apparent from even a brief study of ownership is that the ownership strands of one company become entangled with those of a second company, or a third, often to the point where it becomes difficult to sort out what is whose and in what amounts. Further complicating this situation is that the penchant for growth (profits are seldom pocketed by owners or shareholders), which is a dominant characteristic of the media business community, is occasionally characterized by venturesome investments—for such is the attraction of new and developing technologies. In such instances, venturesome investments occasionally result in an overextension of ownership obligations. And, in economic recessionary periods, creditors seldom hesitate to ask for loan repayments. Thus, selling strategies, in order to pay off loans, become as important as growth strategies. The ownership profiles that we discuss in this chapter, then, tend to be snapshots of the moment rather than lasting descriptions of particular companies.

Major International Owners

Time Warner Incorporated

The merger of Warner Communications and Time Inc. in January 1990 resulted in the formation of "the world's biggest entertainment corporation," with an annual cash flow of $2.3 billion.[2]

In addition to their normal distribution of products into Canada from the U.S., both companies, prior to their merger, owned Canadian publishing interests: Warner Publisher's Services (Canada) Inc. and Time's Little, Brown and Company (Canada) Ltd. Globally Time Warner is active in areas such as book and magazine publishing, record, film, and TV program production, cable TV (owning 19 percent of CNN), studio production facilities, and entertainment content distribution facilities. The economies of scale realized through vertical integration by the merger of these two content production and distribution giants are readily apparent.[3]

In the global business environment, described as "deal or be dealt," Time Warner in May 1991 was "engaged in nearly two dozen discussions in Europe and Asia that could link most of the world's entertainment and media companies in a complex web of relationships."[4]

In the fall of 1991, Time Warner announced that it had concluded an arrangement whereby Toshiba Corporation and C. Itoh (consumer electronics and broadcasting distribution hardware), both of Japan, would join with Time Warner Entertainment. The majority share and operating and creative control of the new film, cable, and cable programming company would be held by Time Warner.[5]

Sony Corporation

In the fall of 1989, the Sony Corporation of Japan announced its acquisition, for $3.4 billion, of Columbia Pictures Entertainment, Inc.[6] The purchase by Sony was considered to be part of an elaborate strategy on the part of the firm to become Japan's first truly global company, with a vertical integration scheme encompassing programming and electronic equipment production—that is, ownership of both "software" and "hardware" components of the entertainment industry.

A year earlier, Sony flagged its intention to move more vigorously in acquiring North American entertainment industry assets when it purchased, for $2 billion, CBS Records, the world's largest recording company.[7]

These acquisitions by Sony, one of the world's largest and most successful electronic equipment (radio, television, VCR) firms, added emphasis to the seriousness of the "globalization game" currently underway: huge corporate structures are in the process of merging with, or purchasing outright, other huge corporate structures, irrespective of national boundaries or distances. The Sony acquisitions also raise the particular problem that accompanies intercultural/international mergers: one may ask whether "the trend presents an opportunity for foreign companies to exert influence on American public opinion and politics."[8]

News Corporation Ltd./ Rupert Murdoch

Rupert "Digger" Murdoch, originally an Australian press baron, now American (in order to be able to purchase U.S. broadcasting interests—the Fox Network and Metromedia television stations), moves his money and influence wherever attractive media properties and opportunities become available. In 1969 he moved to Britain (where he owns about 34 percent of total newspaper circulation) and purchased the *News of the World*, with its six million readers whose interests focus on the "never-failing English formula of sex, sin, and soccer."[9] He quickly added the *London Sun*, and raised its daily circulation from a faltering 800 000 to four million,[10] using the same formula. As the former editor of the *Times* of London (now also a Murdoch property) was moved to comment, "He's [Murdoch] not in newspapers to make the world a better place."[11]

Currently, his holdings include newspapers, film, and TV production facilities (20th Century Fox Film Corporation); TV satellite distribution facilities (Sky Television Channel), which distribute programs to the U.K. with planned expansion into continental Europe; book publishing (Harper Collins); and sundry other properties, for example, *TV Guide* and *Soap Opera Digest*. During the 1980s Murdoch established a holding company (News Corporation Ltd.) that has rapidly become a global giant. In the spring of 1990, he announced that he would hold back on further acquisitions so as to permit him to focus on his current holdings "for the next two or three years."[12]

Maxwell Corporation/ Mirror Group Newspapers/ Robert Maxwell

Up to the time of his unexpected death in the fall of 1991, Robert Maxwell might well have typified the global media tycoon of the latter part of the twentieth century. Described as "bombastic and mercurial" and as "the Citizen Kane of his time,"[13] Maxwell's empire extended to four continents and no media ownership opportunity related to new technologies appeared to be beyond his interest and grasp.

While a recent plan to publish an English-language daily newspaper from Japan (with distribution via satellite in the U.K., U.S., as well as Tokyo) has been delayed, Maxwell unabashedly proclaimed in 1988 that it was his intention to turn U.K.-based Maxwell Communications into a global information empire.[14]

With his broadcasting and cable TV, printing and publishing interests through much of Western Europe (in addition to the U.K. where in London his *Daily Mirror* boasts a daily circulation of three million), Maxwell recently extended his financial investments into Canada. While limited in the amount of newspaper ownership available to him (under the federal Income Tax Act), he joined forces with Quebec publisher Pierre Péladeau (Quebecor) to extend his Canadian interests to pulp and paper (Domtar), book publishing (formerly Collier Macmillan, now Maxwell Macmillan), and newspaper investments. As Maxwell indicated, he had an interest in every area of Canada's communication business, "from the timber to the postal stamp."[15] He commented further that he saw his new investment firm of Maxwell Communications of Canada making substantial investments "over the next 10 years in selected industries."[16]

One of his last ventures, the *European*, a pan-European English-language weekend newspaper, is published in London, Paris, and Hanover, and he envisioned future publishing sites in the U.S. In terms of distribution of the paper (with sections on general news, business, culture, sports), Maxwell looked at the possibility of a single market in the twelve-nation European community as well as further distribution into Eastern European nations where communism is no longer the dominant political force.[17]

With respect to his intent to extend his interests into the North American market (the New York *Daily News* has been a Maxwell Group-owned newspaper), Maxwell indicated his awareness of the non-Canadian ownership restrictions currently in force regarding broadcasting and publishing. However, in an open press conference in early 1989, he also stated that he had met with federal government representatives, who would re-examine such ownership limits so as to permit him to invest more heavily in Canadian media.[18]

Such may have been Maxwell's plans at that time. However, his death by drowning (presumed accidental) while vacationing on his yacht in the Canary Islands in November 1991 halted these plans and created a considerable stir in United Kingdom banking circles and wherever Maxwell's interests extended. To what extent media properties will continue to be in the hands of the Maxwell family is questionable. A month after his death, the family's shares in Maxwell Communications Corporation and Mirror Group Newspapers were declared for sale.[19]

Turner Broadcasting Systems, Inc./Ted Turner

In the summer of 1990, a total of over 2500 athletes from more than fifty countries participated in Ted Turner's second version of his global "Goodwill Games," which were established by Turner and his CNN empire to promote world friendship rather than competition that characterizes the Olympics. None of the participants come from *foreign* countries it was noted, as the word *foreign* has been barred from use on Turner's network.[20] As the Goodwill Games executive producer explained, "we will not use the word 'foreign.' There are just friends waiting to be made."

Ted Turner (© 1990, Turner Broadcasting System Inc. All rights reserved.)

In assembling his empire, consisting of broadcasting (CNN), film, and broadcasting production companies (MGM and United Artists), Turner has parlayed the assets of one property to beget others. The influential *Economist* has explained that in pursuing new purchases, Turner has had more gall than cash. When he put together a financial offer to buy the U.S. CBS network, it consisted of $5.4 billion in "junk bonds" plus a smattering of shares in Turner Broadcasting. As well, the arrangement included some future plans to sell off some CBS holdings, such as record publishing, radio and TV stations. Had the deal gone through, Turner would have achieved ownership of

CBS without putting up "one red cent of cash."[21]

Nonetheless, despite the failure of that purchase, Turner has accumulated properties to the point where his programming has been extended to all of North America and Western Europe, with plans for Eastern Europe. Eventually, Turner wishes to extend his "goodwill" influences globally. His programming causes are important to him, as he points with particular pride to "Voices of the Planet," an environmental TV series. "You'll have to admit that we do have a theme at Turner Broadcasting, that we do stand for something a little bit better."[22] Turner's CNN gained worldwide attention and recognition for its in-depth, extensive, live coverage of the US–UN war against the Iraqi invasion and occupation of Kuwait in early 1991. Broadcasters around the globe carried CNN coverage of that military conflict, and most broadcasters and critics conceded that CNN established new standards of live, remote coverage of spectacular international events.

For its coverage of the Gulf War, and for CNN's coverage of the rapidly changing momentous events in Eastern Europe in 1991, *Time* magazine editors were moved to comment, "The very definition of news was re-written [by CNN]— from something that *has happened* to something that *is happening* at the very moment you are hearing it." Therefore, *Time* editors indicated, "For influencing the dynamic of events and turning viewers in 150 countries into instant witnesses of history, Robert Edward Turner III is *Time*'s Man of the Year for 1991."[23]

In an earlier interview with *New Republic* magazine, Turner explains that his purpose is to "become a large mass media owner. . . . I'm a great and patriotic American. . . . But, I am also, first and foremost, a citizen of this planet. The national interest today is subservient to the international interest."[24] Further, in a cover story profile in *Fortune*, Turner extends the rationale behind his drive to become a global public servant: "I'm not concerned with myself. I'm trying to get bigger so I'll have more influence. It's almost like a religious fervor."[25]

Bertelsmann/ Reinhard Mohn

Reinhard Mohn of West Germany, who, through his European and recently acquired U.S. properties, is described as one who "dwarfs" such a media giant as Rupert Murdoch, or "any other U.S. conglomerate." With annual expected sales exceeding $7 billion, Mohn's company, Bertelsmann, is the second largest media company in the world behind Time Warner. Properties of the Mohn family operation include vast European publishing and broadcasting interests, as well as U.S. holdings, including Doubleday publishing, *Parents Magazine*, RCA Records, and Bantam Books.[26]

The company was founded by the Mohn family in 1835 to print

hymn and prayer books, and the family still retains nearly 90 percent of the company stock.[27] The company acted quickly on media opportunities in 1989 and 1990, after the Berlin Wall came down, buying a major daily newspaper in Berlin, establishing three other dailies in the former East Germany, and founding a book club that within three years boasted 400 000 members.[28] Citing increasing internationalization as its aim, Bertelsmann is exploring opportunities in East Asia; however, the company continues to indicate interest in strengthening its presence in the United States, in the magazine industry in particular.[29]

Some Others

The media moguls who function in the global community are not limited to those cited above: there are other ambitious and active individuals and corporations competing in the international communications sweepstakes. Two others are worthy of note.

ALCATEL N.V.

A recent merger of a U.S. private and a French government corporation (ITT in the U.S. and French state-owned General Electric) has created what has been described as the second largest signals carrier system in the world, second only to AT&T. The new jointly owned company, registered in the Netherlands, is called ALCATEL N.V., and is now in a position to compete for growth with any other company in the global community.[30]

Silvio Berlusconi

Silvio Berlusconi of Italy, in the fall of 1989, joined with a West German company and with U.S. Capital Cities/ABC Video Enterprises to share in the operation of Tele 5, a satellite-delivered cable and television service that reaches 8 million homes with off-air programming and an additional four million homes with cable distributed programming. Such a two-continent, three-nation co-operative arrangement is a harbinger of the future with the coming of a unified European market.[31] Berlusconi's holding company (FININVEST), includes TV networks, film and TV production, a daily newspaper, several periodicals (including Italy's version of *TV Guide*), and a record company. His businesses are scattered through several Western and Eastern European countries. Berlusconi is credited with having established Europe's commercial TV market.[32]

Major Canadian Owners

The identification of prominent Canadians and their media companies could have resulted in a lengthy list, for there are many of them. Moreover, their impact on the development of media in a country as large as Canada has been

made in various pronounced ways since first newspapers, then broadcasting and films, have developed in Canada. But, in keeping with our persuasion that Canadian readers and audiences are becoming more and more exposed to media content that is the product of ownership that extends beyond the boundaries of a single nation, our selection reflects that ownership dynamic. Thus, the Canadian companies that are described here are those that function in an international context rather than in simply a Canadian one.

Hollinger Incorporated/ Conrad Black

Hollinger Incorporated is the media holding company of the Conrad Black family. In the winter of 1989, a *Globe and Mail* story offered indications about the growth strategy employed by Black in amassing his media empire. The story indicated that Hollinger had acquired "16 more U.S. newspapers."[33] This purchase brought into the company's fold six more daily papers and ten more weekly papers. The total numbers of daily newspapers thus was increased to seventy—fifty-five in the U.S., thirteen in Canada, one in the Cayman Islands, and one in the U.K. (the flagship *Daily Telegraph* in London is the largest circulation broadsheet newspaper in the U.K.). Of an additional 122 free distribution and weekly papers owned by Black, ninety-eight are in the U.S., twenty-three are in

Canada, and one in England. In an earlier purchase of U.S. papers, Black indicated that his concern is to buy vulnerable print media and convert them into healthy, competitive media properties. He added, "The only changes will be growth changes."[34]

As with the London-based *Daily Telegraph*, Black's approach has been to install new presses and state-of-the-art computer typesetting technology, thereby raising productivity while reducing labour costs. Overall, Black's ownership of the *Telegraph* has caused a "most spectacular turnaround"—circulation is up to 1.2 million, and in July 1989 it was reported that the paper had become a profitable enterprise for the first time since the Black takeover in 1985.[35]

Conrad Black (Canapress Photo Service)

Hollinger has investments in additional newspapers (*Daily Express* in London, England, *Le Soleil* in Quebec City, *Le Droit* in Ottawa/Hull, and *Le Quotidien* in Chicoutimi).[36] The latter three are owned by Hollinger Subsidiary UniMédia Inc. Hollinger also owns Sterling Newspapers Ltd., which publishes nine daily newspapers as well as an assortment of weekly and community newspapers mainly in western Canada. Perhaps one of Black's more high visibility takeovers occurred in the spring of 1989, when he acquired control of the *Jerusalem Post*, described by Hollinger executives as "the voice of Israel." While offering assurances that editorial freedom for the *Post* would continue, Hollinger executives also indicated that the *Post* was expected to become a profitable newspaper. At the same time, they conceded that "the *Post* is one of the great titles in the world, and we enjoy owning great newspapers."[37]

That same rationale was reportedly Black's motivation for purchasing the money-losing Canadian magazine *Saturday Night*, established in 1887 and as such Canada's oldest magazine. In the 1987 newspaper story that reported the magazine's sale, it was claimed that "Black is now the instant proprietor of an institution." And, the editor-in-chief of the *Globe and Mail* was reported as saying, "Clearly Hollinger isn't making the investment because it's a great money-making vehicle."[38]

In the fall of 1991, a new form of distribution for *Saturday Night* was started. In addition to subscription sales, the magazine was distributed in Southam-owned daily newspapers in Vancouver, Edmonton, Calgary, Ottawa, and Montreal. As well, it was included in home subscriber copies of the *Globe and Mail*. Overall, the plan increased circulation of the magazine from 127 000 to 400 000.[39]

What appears evident from Hollinger's approach to publishing is that, in addition to buying publications that have difficulty turning a profit, a particular strategy is employed. As Black describes it, "we do have an identifiable strategy that has served us well to date. We will not move from our long-standing practices of not overpaying for assets, and of neither strangling our franchises for short-term return nor tolerating under-performance."[40] Presumably, the strategy will continue to work well for Hollinger as the corporation continues to scan the globe for media properties to purchase. In September 1991 it was reported that Hollinger was part of a consortium bidding for control of the Australian newspaper chain John Fairfax Group Pty. Ltd. Figures cited for the purchase ranged from $975 million to $1.15 billion (Canadian). The deal ran into opposition from the Australian government, which expressed concern with Hollinger's reported 30 percent equity. In order to satisfy the Australian government, it was reported that Hollinger was willing to drop its equity share to 20 percent, the maximum permissible

degree of foreign investment in Australia. When that change was made and the deal was "sweetened" by Hollinger, the seven-month battle for control of the Fairfax group ended with another victory for Black's consortium.[41]

The Thomson Corporation (Canada)/Kenneth Thomson

"I can't imagine any publishing company anywhere in the world that would be beyond our ability to acquire," stated Kenneth Thomson, chairman of the newly named The Thomson Corporation.[42] This new corporation resulted from a merger of Thomson Newspapers and International Thomson, two earlier separate holding companies of the Thomson family. The merger was announced in March 1989 and resulted in a new entity with assets "bigger than the empires of global media magnates Rupert Murdoch and Robert Maxwell, making Thomson the fourth largest media empire in the world."[43] Less than two months later, the company announced the acquisition of about forty medical and health magazines from a Toronto publishing house for $8.5 million,[44] and a legal publishing firm in the U.S. for an estimated $810 million. With respect to the purchase of the U.S. property, the Thomson company announced that "legal publishing, professional publishing, is high on our list of priorities."[45]

BOX 13-1

The Thomson Family of Companies*

HUDSON'S BAY COMPANY

- The Bay (89 stores)
- Zellers (274 stores)
- Fields (124 stores)

MARKBOROUGH PROPERTIES INC.

- real estate development in Canada, U.S., and U.K.

THE THOMSON CORPORATION

- Thomson Newspapers
  164 dailies, 70 weeklies in North America

- UK Travel
  – Britannia Airways
  – Thomson Tour Operations
  – Lunn Poly Travel Shops

- Information and Publishing Group
  – UK Regional Newspapers
    13 dailies, 4 Sunday papers, 15 magazines, 134 weeklies
  – Thomson Professional Publishing
  – Thomson Business Information
  – Thomson Book/Reference Group
  – Thomson Financial Services
  – Thomson Informational Services

  Almost 40 000 individual products including magazines, newspapers, books, and directories (over 32 000 on-line microfilm and software packages, newsletters, and assorted controlled circulation papers and magazines) and UK newspapers.

Sources: *Financial Post Information Services: Thomson Corporation,* July 1991.
Thomson Corporation Annual Report, 1989.
Who Owns Whom 1991 (in North America).
Jamie Hubbard, "Merger at Thomson Creates Media Giant," *Financial Post,* 16 March 1989, 1.

* Holdings in: Australia, Belgium, Bermuda, Canada, Denmark, England, Finland, Greece, Hong Kong, Ireland, Kenya, Liechtenstein, Malta, Norway, Netherlands Antilles, New Zealand, Scotland, Spain, Sweden, Switzerland, Tunisia, U.S.A., Wales.

The Thomson family holdings, both before and after the merger, have been vast. Selling off its North Sea oil business two weeks before the merger may have been a signal that the large Thomson multi-industry conglomerate was planning to consolidate its holdings (which also include the huge Bay and Zellers department store chains). While such appears to be the case, as the emphasis on printing and publishing consolidation has been apparent, the consequent strategy for acquiring further properties, at least those in the U.S., will be to go after groups of newspapers rather than seeking out individual ones.[46] And, following the merger, there has been no shortage of funding to pursue such purchases. The merger created a holding company with a stock market capitalization of more than $7 billion (U.S.), shareholders' equity of over $2 billion, assets of about $5.3 billion, and annual revenues approaching $5 billion.[47]

At the time of the merger, Thomson's properties included 156 daily newspapers in Canada and the United States (including the *Globe and Mail*) and 36 weeklies in the two countries. In addition, the corporation owned vast magazine and newspaper holdings in the U.K. One of the purposes of the merger, explained Kenneth Thomson, was to give the companies "the financial clout to go after media targets that are growing even larger as the industry consolidates around the world."[48] At the same time, it was clear that the domestic scene was not being overlooked. In the fall of 1989, the company announced the purchase of eight community newspapers, one in Ontario and seven in British Columbia. The publisher of five of these papers commented on the ownership transfer: "in our long-range plans for the company we recognize that to progress, grow and keep on the leading edge of technological advances into 1990s and beyond would require the involvement of a large company such as Thomson Newspapers." [49] The Thomson acquisitions strategy, then, is not unlike that of Conrad Black—to buy newspapers that are failing, or that lack the resources to up-grade their technology, and with an infusion of capital, corporate management, and economies of scale, convert them into profitable publishing organizations. Indeed, Thomson Newspapers publishes more daily newspapers than any other group either in Canada or in the United States.

Reported in September 1991 was the Thomson Corporation's deal to purchase a portion of the publishing assets of Maxwell Macmillan Inc. (U.S.), a property held by Maxwell Communications Corp., which is headquartered in Great Britain. While an executive with Thomson remarked that the purchase "is not earth-shattering," it still could "add up to several tens of millions of dollars." The *Globe and Mail* story concluded with a May 1991 quote from a Thomson top executive "that the company has the financial resources to make any acquisitions that come up that we regard as compelling."[50]

Maclean Hunter Incorporated

Long regarded as one of Canada's largest media conglomerates, Maclean Hunter's properties in 1970 were described in the Davey Committee's *Report* as including about one hundred trade, consumer, and business periodicals. These were located in Canada, the U.S., the U.K., Western Europe—in English and French languages. In addition, in Canada, Maclean Hunter owned two TV stations and five radio stations and controlling interest in CATV systems in seventeen Ontario communities. Twenty years later, the holdings of Maclean Hunter were described as comprising about 200 consumer and trade magazines in Canada, the U.S., Britain, and Europe: it also controlled or owned twenty-three radio and two TV stations in Canada, CATV holdings in Ontario, and 62 percent of Toronto Sun Publishing Corporation (publisher of the *Sun* newspapers in Toronto, Ottawa, Calgary, and Edmonton).[51]

Perhaps more than any other media holding company, Maclean Hunter can be cited for instances of cross-media ownership within the same communities. The corporation owns multiple forms of mass media in three Canadian communities—Calgary, Edmonton, and Toronto—a situation that would not have been permitted if U.S. regulations concerning cross-media ownership were in effect in Canada. Nevertheless, such multiple media ownership in a single community has existed before in Canada, although not in same degree and not in three different communities, as is the case with Maclean Hunter.

It was in the fall of 1989 that Maclean Hunter persuaded the CRTC to grant permission for the corporation to purchase Selkirk Communications Limited and its holdings of sixteen radio stations, four TV stations, and two CATV systems. The purchase price was pegged at $606 million and constituted at the time the largest single ownership transaction in Canadian broadcasting history.[52] The purchase, in itself, was a contentious matter with respect to the prospect of the increased concentration of media ownership in particular communities, and the loss of a competitive broadcasting voice in several Alberta and British Columbia communities. However, what made the CRTC approval of the purchase highly unusual was the proposal that Maclean Hunter presented to the commission to sell off some of Selkirk properties to third parties—a process labelled as "licence trafficking"—at a profit. The full request of Maclean Hunter was not granted by the CRTC, but, nevertheless, the whole arrangement was a profitable one for the corporation, in that it gained ownership of an FM station in Toronto and two cable systems in Ottawa.[53] While not requiring CRTC approval, Maclean Hunter also acquired a Selkirk-owned cable system in Fort Lauderdale, Florida.

The "licence trafficking" complaints made to the CRTC by members of the public raise an important consideration with respect to licensing strategies followed by regulatory bodies. To buy and resell station properties might be one thing: but in this instance, Maclean Hunter bought and then resold permission to broadcast as well. As a consequence, the extent to which the "logic-of-the-licence" strategy is still operative in Canada is open to question. That particular strategy assumes that licences are issued and renewed to broadcasters so long as they demonstrate their preparedness to fulfill the obligations of the Broadcasting Act. In the past, evaluation regarding fulfilment of such responsibilities has been assigned to the CRTC, and certainly not to fellow broadcasters. Maclean Hunter was required to "plow back" the $21.1 million profit it made on the trafficking ploy involved in the purchase of Selkirk Broadcasting into a fund that would be used to "strengthen and improve Canadian broadcasting."[54] Nevertheless, Maclean Hunter has been a clear winner in this instance and has likely established a precedent in licence trafficking. This is so since the future concerning ownership will be more and more characterized by corporations merging with or buying out each other.

In the interim, Maclean Hunter growth continues unabated, adding further trade publications to its fold,[55] and with plans to form a "mini-network" of one of its TV sta-tions in Ontario with two others of a second company, so as to pool their resources and programming.[56] Such plans have not materialized.

Rogers Communications Incorporated/Ted Rogers

The 1968 Broadcasting Act introduced a new requirement into the Canadian scene when it stipulated, for the first time, that broadcasting outlets in the country were to be "effectively" owned by Canadians. The transfer of properties from non-Canadian owners to Canadians was begun. Ted Rogers, principal shareholder in the company that bears his name, began as an FM broadcaster in 1960, and took off from there. In 1979, he acquired the properties of Canadian Cablesystems, which had previously bought cable holdings from U.S. Famous Players when that company had been forced to sell under the new Canadian ownership stipulation.[57] Further acquisitions, as a consequence of the new ownership regulations, placed Rogers, by 1980, in first place in terms of size of all cable companies in the country.

More recently, Rogers formed a consortium (CANTEL), a cellular phone service company. He owns 25 percent of YTV (a youth cable programming service) and a majority ownership in Canadian Home Shopping Network Limited. His cable systems, in addition to serving well over a million subscribers with programming, provide high-speed cable links for business. Buying into the coast-to-coast resources of CNCP Telecommunications (renamed UNITEL), Rogers has challenged Bell Canada's long-distance telephone monopoly.[58] Currently as chairman of CANTEL, Rogers plans to be at the forefront, in terms of ownership, of fiber optics and cellular technological developments in the future.

In preparing for that future, and to raise the money necessary to buy the 40 percent share of CNCP (at an estimated cost of between $250 and $275 million), Rogers sold his cable holdings in the U.S. to a Texas company for $1.63 billion (U.S.).[59] His intent with respect to future U.S. investments, however, was clear: "we have no intention of not being diversified geographically."[60]

In a manner that has been described as a "feeding frenzy," Rogers has made good on his word to invest more money in Canadian communication industries. As well as buying up market shares in his own holdings, he has invested in various corporations across Canada, including Montreal-based Astral Bellevue Pathé Incorporated, which has interests in pay-TV, film distribution, video wholesaling, and photo finishing. As part of the Maclean Hunter–Selkirk blockbuster deal, Rogers participated in the Selkirk buyout by purchasing twelve of the Selkirk radio stations after they were sold to Maclean Hunter.[61]

In all, Rogers has been active in extending his holdings in the media–telecommunications industry and, apparently, has built market confidence in his companies. Overall, the three-year period from 1987 through 1989 has been described as a "free-wheeling shopping spree" with a "dizzying" number of transactions. Rogers Communications Incorporated grew by a staggering 319 percent between 1987 and 1989.[62] With that kind of market confidence, it is not likely that Rogers' acquisitions are complete. While some of his working colleagues describe Rogers as "a visionary," he speaks of himself as follows: "I tend to go from one project to another quickly . . . and I get enthusiastic. I do the best I can and I spend long hours at it."[63]

Southam Newspapers

With its ownership of only seventeen daily newspapers in 1991, the Southam Newspaper Group claimed a 28.1 percent share of Canadian daily newspaper circulation. Thomson, with forty papers, had 21.1 percent of daily circulation while Torstar and Quebecor had 9.8 percent and 8.9 percent respectively.[64] The two dominant publishers, then, claimed nearly 50 percent of daily newspaper circulation in the country.

Historically, Southam has been one of the largest and most diversified media-holding groups in Canada: the company's diversification strategy, however, has been limited to what former Southam president Gordon Fisher described as "the communication–information industry,"[65] rather than to the broad industrialization that characterizes the holdings of giants such as Thomson and K.C. Irving. Southam investments have included daily and community newspapers, printing establishments, the giant Coles Book Store chain, and, for a number of years, a large (although minority) share in Selkirk Broadcasting, which in 1989 was acquired by Maclean Hunter. With respect to its printing arm, Southam announced in the fall of 1991 that it was shutting down one of its printing firms, Norgraphics, Inc., a seventy-seven-year-old company with a hundred employees. A Southam representative indicated that the firm lacked state-of-the-art equipment and that there was an "overcapacity" of printing firms in the industry at this time. The printing firm had been purchased two years earlier and had been losing money.[66]

Southam was the subject of an inquiry (along with Thomson Newspapers) under the Combines Investigation Act when, in 1980, both organizations agreed to close down competing newspapers in Winnipeg and Ottawa, claiming that competition for advertising was so severe that such a move was necessary. The argument of the newspapers was sustained.

In 1986, Southam agreed to a share exchange with the publisher of the *Toronto Star*, Torstar Corporation. Southam acquired a 30 percent interest in Torstar and in exchange Torstar took a 23 percent interest in Southam. Several questions were raised concerning the

exchange, and shareholders in Southam claimed that the value of their stock had been diminished. In defending their action before a hearing of the Ontario Securities Commission,[67] Southam claimed that the trade was a defensive measure aimed at preventing any hostile takeover. At the same time, Southam defended their action by inviting Tom Kent, chairman of the 1980 Royal Commission on Newspapers, to comment on Southam's publishing policies. Kent defended Southam's record by indicating to the Securities Commission that the company's concern was to protect its strong publishing position—that the trade with Torstar was not profit motivated. Kent commented that Southam has "always had a policy of sacrificing profit performance in order to publish higher quality newspapers."[68] The exchange of stock has not squelched rumours of a takeover of Southam by other organizations. Torstar itself, Conrad Black, Power Corporation of Montreal, and the Molson Companies have been mentioned as prospective buyers.[69]

In the meantime, Southam owners have not been idle. In the fall of 1989, the company acquired the properties of the holding company of the daily *Kitchener-Waterloo Record*;[70] earlier that year, Southam had bought a controlling 60 percent share in the Angus Reid Group, a public opinion polling company with properties in Canada and with expansion plans for the U.S.;[71] in the spring of 1990,

Southam completed an arrangement to buy a 63 percent share of a new company owning twenty-four community newspapers and fourteen weekly specialty publications, all in British Columbia;[72] and early in 1991 Southam acquired the assets of the Kingston *Whig-Standard.* At the same time, a 1989 report revealed that Southam has plans that go considerably beyond its current status as a leading Canadian newspaper publisher. Along with its Torstar partner, Southam claimed that "we're a pretty big player. . . . Our oyster is the world."[73] The Southam spokesperson added that there was potential in the Southam/Torstar partnership to become another group on the order of Thomson, Maxwell, or Murdoch. While the Southam/Torstar stock trade was originally a defensive market move to prevent a takeover, it now appears that such thinking has shifted to offensive strategies and has extended beyond Canada to the global arena.

A further strengthening of ties between the two organizations was reached in December 1991 with an agreement that permitted the exchange, without cost, of "major domestic and international stories" prepared by reporters of both organizations. The stories would be exchanged through Southam News's satellite service and would be available to Southam newspapers as well as to the *Toronto Star.* The agreement was seen as a cost-effective plan to enrich the quality of newspapers of the two organizations.[74]

Torstar Corporation

The Torstar Cororation, with headquarters in Toronto, consists of three main operational entities. First, the organization publishes the *Toronto Star*, Canada's largest daily circulation newspaper. As well, the newspaper publishing arm of Torstar publishes, through its Metroland Publishing Subsidiary, twenty-four community newspapers. The weekly papers are published in the urban centres that surround Toronto.[75] Second, Torstar owns Harlequin Enterprises, the world's largest publisher of romance fiction. Harlequin romances are distributed in more than one hundred countries in nineteen languages.[76] Third, Torstar, through its ownership of the Miles Kimball Company in Wisconsin, has become one of the largest direct mail catalogue marketers in the United States, distributing about thirty-nine million gift catalogues.[77]

Finally, as explained above, Torstar, through a share-trading agreement in 1986, currently has a 23 percent interest in Southam Newspapers. In sum, Torstar ranks next to those Canadian corporations that are currently bidding for recognition in the global publishing community.

Télémédia (Québec) Limitée/Philippe de Gaspé Beaubien

Media concentration has been a continuing concern of Canadians and, from time to time, commissions and/or committees have made recommendations that seem to have little effect on either halting or reversing the trend. In one instance, however, in response to public concern and the establishment of a Special Committee on Freedom of the Press in the late 1960s by the Quebec government,[78] Power Corporation of Canada Limited sold most of its media holdings (eighteen newspapers and ten broadcasting stations). Télémédia, now the second largest radio station owner in Canada, with 20 wholly owned stations in Quebec and Ontario, originally was the radio station arm of Power Corporation. In 1970, the broadcasting properties were purchased from Power Corporation, and the former subsidiary continues with its original name of Télémédia, although now under the ownership of Philippe de Gaspé Beaubien.[79] Power Corporation continues with its major enterprises, retaining only a handful of media holdings through a subsidiary, Gesca Limitée.

Télémédia operates a French-language radio network in Quebec that supplies news, sports, and entertainment content to thirty-seven AM radio stations in Quebec and New Brunswick (five of its own and thirty-two owned by other organizations). As well, Télémédia was one of the founding shareholders in Canadian Satellite Communications Incorporated. In terms of publishing, Télémédia prints the two leading English- and French-language TV-listing magazines in Canada— *TV Guide* and *TV Hebdo*.[80] Télémé-

dia also owns Camden House, an Ontario-based publisher of *Harrowsmith* and *Equinox* magazines. In the midst of an apparent drop-off in advertising revenues in the late 1980s and early 1990s, Télémédia publications have reportedly done well, with *TV Hebdo*, for example, posting a 35 percent increase in advertising pages in 1990.[81]

In January 1989, Télémédia's majority shareholder Beaubien entered the Ontario radio market and also acquired two western Canadian city lifestyles magazines. On the international scene he has agreed to an arrangement with Hachette-Filipacchi Publishers of France to publish a Quebec edition of *Paris Match* magazine *(Québec Match)* and has added a 75 percent stake in Camden House Publishing in Vermont, which produces the U.S. edition of *Harrowsmith* magazine.[82] Further, Beaubien indicated that he saw his new publishing base in Vancouver as an entry point into the U.S. West Coast media market. Perhaps more importantly, Beaubien was reported as saying that his company had its sights on the huge Pacific Rim market as well.[83]

The Irving Group/ K.C. Irving Family

With an industrial empire valued at $10 billion, K.C. Irving of Saint John, New Brunswick, has been described by *Forbes*, the U.S. business magazine, as the world's third-richest nonmonarch.[84] With an acquisition strategy based on the principle of vertical integration ("K.C. Irving did it earlier—and better—than anyone else"),[85] Irving amassed a huge empire. This empire includes, among other diversified holdings, shipping, ship building, oil refining, gasoline stations, pulp and paper, and, while not dominant financial properties in the totality of his holdings, broadcasting and publishing. Included in the Irving media holdings in New Brunswick are the morning and evening dailies in St. John, two dailies in Moncton, one in Fredericton, a radio station in St. John, and a television station in St. John with seven TV rebroadcasting stations.[86]

Often pointed to as an example of excessive concentration and of oppressive cross-media ownership in a single community, Irving has managed to hold at bay those who would intervene in his media holdings in New Brunswick. While a federal government directive to the CRTC in 1982 was aimed at preventing a renewal of broadcasting licences to daily newspaper owners in the same community, the directive, which would have applied to the Irving situation in St. John, was eventually overturned.[87]

In a precedent-setting court case that took five years to resolve, Irving was found guilty in 1974, by the New Brunswick Supreme Court, of operating a monopoly with his ownership of all English-language daily newspapers in the province. The case was precedent setting in that this was the first newspaper monopoly trial held under the federal Combines Investigation Act. The Irving Companies were fined a sum of \$150 000, but the judge agreed to delay his decision for dissolution of the monopoly on which the conviction was based, pending appeal of the matter.[88]

Irving's appeal was successful and was eventually upheld in the Supreme Court of Canada. The outcome of the case was evidence, according to *Maclean's* magazine, of the "impotence of the Combines Act."[89] In part, that might have been the case. However, as the Supreme Court Justice who handed down the final ruling stipulated, there was a question of whether anticombines legislation applied to the content of newspapers, as distinct from physical objects of a company, such as a publishing plant.[90] He left this matter open, and adjudicated the appeal on evidence that it was clear that editorial control of the five Irving papers was in the hands of their editors and publishers, rather than in the hands of the owner. Thus, it was not proven that public detriment had resulted from Irving's ownership of the papers. At the same time, however, in commenting on the importance of newspapers in a democratic society, the Supreme Court Justice added that newspapers "are so different from other commercial ventures as to require the courts to view any alleged merger or monopoly in the newspaper field with greater concern for maintenance of freedom in the communication or dissemination of news and ideas."[91]

Quebecor/Pierre Péladeau

When he appeared before the Royal Commission on Newspapers in 1980, Pierre Péladeau, the principal shareholder of Quebecor, a steadily growing media holding company (owner of the tabloids *Le Journal de Montréal* and *Le Journal de Québec*—with an aggregate weekly circulation of 2.7 million), confirmed that his plans were for expansion whenever opportunities for profit became apparent. Such plans, he added, could include other newspapers in Quebec and in the U.S., where, in 1988, Quebecor established the Philadelphia *Journal*, and in radio and television.[92]

While broadcasting properties have not yet materialized in Quebecor's expansion plans, printing, publishing, and publication distribution certainly have. In February of 1989, through a merger of Quebecor with some of the late Robert Maxwell's North American holdings, Quebecor changed from a "modest publisher of Quebec tabloids and magazines into North America's second biggest commercial printer."[93] Further, a merger with the newspaper and magazine distribution operations of Benjamin News Incorporated of Montreal in 1989 resulted in a new company of which Quebecor now owns 62.5 percent and which has yielded about $200 million annually in newsstand sales.[94]

It is the merger, however, with Maxwell's printing subsidiaries in the U.S.—valued at about $500 million—that has put Quebecor on the ownership map. The Quebecor-Maxwell Graphics merger will have annual sales of $1.5 billion and assets of $1.1 billion. As described by the *Globe and Mail*, Maxwell Graphics, with its extensive network of printing plants in the U.S., has long-term contracts to print the magazines *Sports Illustrated* and *Time*, newspapers the *Boston Globe* and the New York *Daily News*, weekend newspaper magazines *USA Weekend* and *Parade*, and catalogues for retailers Sears and Roebuck and J.C. Penney.[95] In the wake of the Canada–U.S. Free Trade Agreement, Quebecor has targeted the United States and Mexico for expansion. The report on the Quebecor–Maxwell merger indicates that Quebecor, now with five daily and fifty-three weekly newspapers, is in a position to launch more U.S. newspapers in the future.[96] And, in the fall of 1991, a representative of Quebecor Printing, Inc., indicated that an agreement had already been reached to purchase a Mexican printing company that has annual sales of about $10 million.[97]

On the home front, however, Quebecor was forced to close its newly launched tabloid English-language daily, the *Montreal Daily News*, after only twenty-one months. Originally seen as a competitor to Southam's Montreal *Gazette*, the *Daily News* did not reach its intended circulation figures. The launching of the paper was considered poorly timed since newspapers and magazines in North America are seen to be suffering a decline in advertising revenues.[98] Neverthe-

302 PART THREE ✳ Regulation, Ownership, and Political Processes

less, the general manager of Quebecor's magazine division was optimistic about the future as he reported that "we'll grow either through acquisition or development, and it could come faster than we think."[99]

Conclusion

What becomes evident from even a brief overview of mass media ownership such as this is that the idyllic view of media ownership, linking one owner with one medium, is a thing of the past. In earlier times, the mass media owner was seen to be in touch with a community's needs, rubbing elbows with fellow citizens, often a benevolent pillar of the community: that picture is not today's reality. While there may still be found such a warm neighbourly relationship between media owners and their immediate communities in the instance of some daily and weekly newspapers, more typically, the owner is likely to be a distant corporate board chairperson, accepting reports from directors about financial operating effectiveness of diverse media groups spread out around the world. But even in the case of the weekly newspaper, which has economic and editorial strength because of the intimacy of its relationship with its community, local ownership is less evident. These newspapers have grouped together in order to achieve economies of scale and to remain profitable; as a consequence they have become ready targets for acquisition by large chains or conglomerates.

In our research on the ownership of Canadian mass media, we were particularly struck by the fixation on growth that was revealed in the comments of owners and corporate spokespersons. Five factors seem to characterize the current environment. (1) There is a desire to grow, with success measured by corporate size. Quality of product tends to be popularly associated with sophisticated corporate structures. (2) As in the case of Ted Turner and others, owners are on occasion "mission oriented." Even if many are not driven to this extent, it is still a dimension to be considered in assessing corporate growth. (3) Mergers, which are means of growth, are also a defence against hostile takeovers. This occurs when two companies that consider themselves potential targets link their assets to achieve a size that would discourage the normal patterns of takeover. (4) Mass media are businesses. Businesses make profits, which are usually invested in other businesses. When opportunities present themselves, in the manner that Conrad Black, Kenneth Thomson, and others have demonstrated, money and managerial skills can be injected into underfinanced media properties, which in a few years can become profitable. (5) Growth has proven to be most effective when it has followed a pattern of vertical integration; that is, where the producer of a product and the buyer of the product are part of the same corporate structure.

A final comment is in order. Most nations have some sort of protection against buyout of their industries by foreign investors. In such instances, this type of buyout, which is symptomatic of global industrial behaviour, is thwarted by the installation of quota systems or the establishment of national review agencies. Canadian mass media are good examples of quota system protection: broadcasting ownership is directly controlled by regulation (a 20 percent limit for non-Canadians), and publishing is controlled indirectly through a provision of the Income Tax Act (a 25 percent limit for non-Canadian ownership).

The current global economic environment offers great challenges to the strategy of protectionism. Western societies are going through a period of deregulation and expanding free trade. While protectionist policies have been enacted by the federal government, Canadian industrialists do not always co-operate with the spirit of such policies. Further the availability of Canadian stocks on foreign exchanges invites foreign participation in the economy. Two trends are unmistakable: (1) increased growth of media organizations in terms of both size and diversity; (2) interconnection of various kinds in ownership and programming. Thus, Canadian media are caught up in global patterns, and it is uncertain whether their ownership base will continue to be secure. Pressure continues to be placed on Canada to ease such protective strategies as have been in place for its media–cultural indus-

tries. Given the penhant for free trading and economic integration in Western societies, it is clear that such pressures will increase in strength and scope.

Notes

1. Corporate ownership, given the high level of buyouts, mergers, and creation of subsidiaries, etc., is not an easy topic to research. As well, today's research can literally become tomorrow's history. If students wish to follow the Canadian media ownership scene, in addition to specific footnotes in the chapter that indicate the sources from which we derived pertinent data, they are directed to company annual reports (usually sent on request), the directory *Who Owns Whom,* and *The Financial Post Publications* series on corporate structure.

2. Bruce Nussbaum, "The Worldwide Web Steve Ross is Weaving," *Business Week* (13 May 1991): 82–84.

3. Michael Connor, "Time May Sell Assets to Finance Warner Deal," *Globe and Mail,* 20 July 1989, B9; John Partridge, "Time/Warner Deal May Need Government's Blessing," *Globe and Mail,* 7 March 1989, B2; and Samuel Perry, "Time, Warner Merging to Create Media Giant," *Globe and Mail,* 6 March 1989, B1–2.

4. Nussbaum, "Worldwide Web."

5. "Time Warner Links Up With Toshiba, C. Itoh," *Globe and Mail,* 30 October 1991, B18.

6. Bill Carter, "The Networks Find One Opportunity in Sony Deal," *New York Times,* 2 October 1989, D10.

7. Stefan Wagstyl and James Buchanan, "Sony Out to Peddle Dreams with 'Daring' Columbia

Buy," *Financial Post*, 2 October 1989, 11.

8. Paul Farhi and Stuart Auerbach, "Hollywood Buyout Stirs Cultural Protectionism in U.S.," *Toronto Star*, 1 October 1989, F1–4.

9. Allan Fotheringham, "Birds of a Feather: Press Barons Prove Knowledge is Power—and Also Profit," *Financial Post*, 16 October 1989, 13, 20.

10. Ibid.

11. Ibid.

12. See Laura Landro and Dennis Kneale, "Murdoch Curbs Buying Habits at News Corp.," *Globe and Mail*, 14 April 1990, B5. Also see Marc Gunther, "Time Inc. Takeover Fight Will Affect All Audiences," *Detroit Free Press*, 15 June 1989, 6D.

13. Paul Koring, "Media Giant Maxwell Dies in Yacht Mishap," *Globe and Mail*, 6 November 1991, A1, A2.

14. "Maxwell's Japanese Venture in Doubt," *International Press Institute Report* 37 (January 1988): 14–15.

15. Kevin Dougherty, "Peladeau–Maxwell Match Unites Two Unpredictables," *Financial Post*, 13 February 1989, 27–29.

16. "Quebec Language Stand Backed by U.K. Tycoon," *Globe and Mail*, 7 February 1989, A4.

17. Steven Prokesh, "Maxwell Prepares for Introduction of European Paper," *Globe and Mail*, 10 May 1990, B2.

18. Dougherty, "Peladeau–Maxwell Match." Also see Mary McIver and Philip Winslow, "Publishing: Money and Happiness," *Maclean's*, 21 March 1988, 58–59.

19. Madeline Droham, "Maxwell Empire Crushed By Debts," *Globe and Mail*, 6 December 1991, B1, B2.

20. Marc Gunther, "Turner's Programming Centers on His Causes," *Detroit Free Press*, 13 July 1990, 8F.

21. "When Junketing Has Got To Stop," *The Economist*, 27 April 1985, 91–92.

22. Gunther, "Turner's Programming."

23. "*Time* Man of the Year: Prince of the Global Village," *Time* 139 (6 January 1992), 15.

24. Adam Paul Weisman, "As Ted Turns: Odyssey of the Cable Mogul," *New Republic*, 29 December 1986, 16–18.

25. Stratford P. Sherman, "Ted Turner: Back from the Brink," *Fortune* (July 1986): 24–31.

26. Edward Greenspon, "Communications Giant Inspired by His Time as POW," *Globe and Mail*, 2 November 1987, C1.

27. "The Media Company That Makes Murdoch's Empire Look Small," *The Economist*, 9 April 1988, 63–64.

28. "Bertelsmann: When Being a Giant Isn't Enough," *Business Week*, 12 November 1990, 72–75.

29. *The Economist*, 64.

30. Paul Lewis, "French–ITT Venture Predicts Profit of $260 Million for the Year," *New York Times*, 8 January 1987, D5.

31. Elizabeth Guider, "Cap Cities/ABC Buys into Europe, Invests in Munich's Tele 5," *Variety* (22–28 February 1989): 407.

32. Anna Carugati, "Italian Broadcasters Fight TV Bill" and "Italian Broadcast Bill Targets Berlusconi," *Broadcasting Abroad* 2 (May 1990): 6, 8.

33. "Hollinger Acquires 16 More U.S. Newspapers," *Globe and Mail*, 10 January 1989, B11.

34. "Conrad Black Purchased 4 Small U.S. Publications," *Globe and Mail*, 12 November 1987, B6.

35. Mathew Horsman, "Battling Press Barons Locked in Market War," *Financial Post*, 25 July 1989, 13.

36. "Quebec Language Stand Backed by U.K. Tycoon," *Globe and Mail*, 7 February 1989, A4.

37. Patrick Martin, "Black Takes Over the 'Voice of Israel,'" *Globe and Mail*, 6 May 1989, D3.

38. Ian Pearson, "Black Buys Saturday Night," *Globe and Mail*, 19 June 1987, A19.

39. This change was reported earlier. See, "Saturday Night Extends Distribution," *McCann Media News*, 16 July 1991, 1.

40. Christopher Donville, "Hollinger Wants 'Benign' Role at United Not Control, Black Tells Annual Meeting," *Globe and Mail*, 15 June 1989, B15.

41. Tom Burton, "New Media Laws May Stall Black's Australian Foray," *Globe and Mail*, 5 September 1991, B19. Also see "Black's Tourang Group Wins Control of Fairfax" *Globe and Mail*, 16 December 1991, B1, B2.

42. John Partridge and Dan Westell, "Thomson Merger to Create Vast Acquisition Opportunities," *Globe and Mail*, 16 March 1989, B1, B4, also see Jamie Hubbard, "Merger at Thomson Creates Media Giant," *Financial Post*, 16 March 1989, 1.

43. Partridge and Westell, "Thomson Merger," B1, B4.

44. "Trimel to Sell 40 Magazines to Thomson," *Globe and Mail*, 4 April 1989, B5.

45. Dan Westel, "Thomson Buys Legal Publisher for $810 Million," *Globe and Mail*, 3 May 1989, B1, B4.

46. Partridge and Westell, "Thomson Merger," B1.

47. John Partridge, "Market Gives Approval to Thomson Merger," *Globe and Mail*, 17 March 1989, B1, B3.

48. Ibid.

49. "Thomson Makes Major Newspaper Purchases," *Canadian Community Newspaper Association Publisher*, August/September 1989, 14.

50. John Partridge, "Thomson To Buy Maxwell Unit," *Globe and Mail*, 13 September 1991, B7

51. John Partridge, "Maclean Hunter Takes Advantage of Lower U.S. Rates to Cut Debt," *Globe and Mail*, 24 April 1990, B10.

52. "Issues and Events: Deal of Century," *Broadcaster* 49 (January 1990): 12.

53. "Mega Media Marriage Approved: Maclean Hunter Acquired Selkirk," *Windsor Star*, 29 September 1989, D7.

54. Ibid.

55. Jamie Hubbard, "Maclean Hunter Gains Control of CB Magazines," *Financial Post*, 16 July 1990, 3.

56. John Partridge, "New Television Ballgame Possible," *Globe and Mail*, 10 July 1990, B1.

57. Canada, *Report of the Task Force on Broadcasting Policy* (Ottawa: Supply and Services, 1986), 629.

58. See Daniel Stoffman, "Great Connections," *Report on Business Magazine* 6 (September 1989): 37–44.

59. Jamie Hubbard, "Tough, Brilliant Rogers Quests for Birthright," *Financial Post*, 24 April 1989, 4.

60. John Partridge, "Rogers Sad To Leave the U.S. But Promises To Return," *Globe and Mail*, 11 August 1989, 86.

61. John Partridge, "Rogers Buys More Stock in Two Communications Companies," *Globe and Mail*, 22 March 1989, B16. Also see, "Deals to End a Decade," *Broadcaster* 49 (January 1990): 18.

62. Ted Davis, "Business Takes a Breather: Broadcast Sector Growth Relaxes its Breakneck Pace," *Broadcaster* 49 (January 1990): 14.

63. Hubbard, "Tough, Brilliant Rogers."

64. Data cited are computed from *Canadian Advertising Rates and Data* (August 1991).

65. Cited in Canada, *The Royal Commission on Newspapers* (Ottawa: Supply and Services, 1981), 92.

66. "Southam to Close Norgraphics," *Globe and Mail*, 11 September 1991, B8.

67. Edward Greenspon, "Southam's Tenets Cited in Defense of Swap," *Globe and Mail*, 2 April 1986, B4.

68. Ibid.

69. Ian Austen, "Torstar's Pact with Southam Ends," *Toronto Star*, 30 June 1990, C3.

70. "Southam Buys K-W Record," *Financial Post*, 27 November 1989, 5.

71. "Southam Buys 60 Percent Stake in Pollster in Move Geared to U.S. Expansion," *Globe and Mail*, 22 March 1989, B14.

72. John Partridge, "Southam Buys Giant Stake in B.C.'s Regional Publishing Industry," *Globe and Mail*, 9 May 1990, B13.

73. Dan Westell, "Big League Role Hinted for Southam, Torstar," *Globe and Mail*, 7 April 1989, B8.

74. John Partridge, "Southam, Torstar Ink Deal To Exchange Editorial Copy," *Globe and Mail*, 5 December 1991, B9.

75. Torstar, *Annual Report 1989* (Toronto: Torstar Corporation, 1989), 11.

76. Financial Post, "Torstar Corporation" (Toronto: Financial Post Publications, 1991), 11.

77. Ibid.

78. *The Uncertain Mirror*, 28.

79. *Report of the Task Force on Broadcasting*, 638.

80. Ibid.

81. Patricia Chisholm et al., "Losses For Words: Newspapers and Magazines Are Suffering from a Decline in Advertising Revenues," *Maclean's*, 14 May 1990, 43.

82. Bertrand Marotte, "Telemedia Hopes to Buy 2 Money-Losing Stations from London Broadcaster," *Globe and Mail*, 11 January 1990, B3.

83. Ibid.

84. John Dumont, "The Tough Tycoons: A New Brunswick Family Pushes to Expand One of the World's Richest Empires," *Maclean's*, 6 February 1989, 32.

85. Ibid., 36.

86. *Report of the Task Force on Broadcasting*, 634.

87. Ibid.

88. "Irving Newspapers Fined $150,000 On Combines Counts," *Globe and Mail*, 3 April 1974, 31.

89. Dumont, "The Tough Tycoons," 36.

90. Mary Trueman, "Irving Ruling Sidesteps Effect of Editorial Content," *Globe and Mail*, 17 November 1976, B2.

91. Ibid.

92. *Royal Commission on Newspapers*, 97–98.

93. Dougherty, "Peladeau–Maxwell Match," 27, 29.

94. Harry Enchin, "Quebecor and Benjamin Merging Distribution Units," *Globe and Mail*, 14 July 1989, B14.

95. Barrie McKenna, "Quebecor Acquires Maxwell Subsidiary," *Globe and Mail*, 31 October 1989, B1.

96. Ibid., B7.

97. Alan Freeman, "Quebecor Printing Spins Web to Mexico," *Globe and Mail*, 30 November 1991, B1.

98. Chisholm et al., "Losses for Words," 43.

99. Gail Chaisson, "Quebecor: A Rags to Riches Story of a Publishing House," *Marketing* 95 (9 April 1990): 39.

C H A P T E R   14

Mass Media and Politics

Introduction

In any examination of the relationship between mass media and politics it is important to point out that this interaction occurs at two distinct levels: at a basic level, providing the attitudinal components necessary for the formation and preservation of a "political community," and at the day-to-day practical level, serving as a link between citizens and government in the process of democratic governance. These two roles are shown in box 14-1. In that mass media are central to the activities of a people coming together in common causes and values, as well as in their continuing ability to solve their national problems democratically within a shared system of values, the role played by mass media at each of these levels needs to be fully understood.

BOX 14–1

Political Roles of Mass Media

Role 1: media providing attitudinal supports for the concept of a "national political community"

Activities: helping to create and reinforce a distinct political culture through political socialization

Role 2: media serving as a conduit in the interaction between government and citizenry

Activities: providing information, analysis, agenda setting, and image building

Media's Role in the Formation and Continuation of a Political Community

There are several theorists who have made significant contributions to the subject of community formation, but it was Karl Deutsch who linked the concept of nationality specifically to social communication. Deutsch argued that a national community could be identified by communication patterns—that is, people who formed a national community interacted more frequently and on more issues than they did with those outside the community.[1] It is in this sense that early proponents of a national broadcasting system for Canada correctly argued that modern communications systems should provide the sea-to-sea link that railroads did in the pre-electronic age.

In his adaptation of systems theory to politics, David Easton speaks of the concept of *political community*.[2] This means that, in order to co-operate sufficiently to make democracy workable, a people must share basic values and beliefs, specifically the belief that the problems that beset the political community should be solved through the mechanism of legitimate debate and negotiation, rather than through the application of force.

Communications, and mass media in particular, are important in the establishment and preservation of a sense of political community. Two concepts are important in understanding this role: *political culture* and *political socialization*. *Political culture* refers to the values, beliefs, and norms shared by a people with respect to their political governance: what is important, what is appropriate, and what is proscribed. It is necessary to remind students that values tend to be defined differently in different cultures, and behaviour that is considered normal and appropriate in Canada may be out of place when practised in a different cultural setting.

Assuming that Canada does have a unique political culture, the attributes of that culture have to be disseminated and learned by new generations of Canadians in order for that culture to survive. This is the process of *political socialization,* and herein lies the importance of mass communication: in addition to the family, schools, and churches, mass communication, particularly television, is a powerful agent of socialization. Symbols, values, beliefs that are uniquely Canadian have to appear in mass communication products in sufficient volume and in positive contexts in order for the underlying culture to be perpetuated. Thus we see the rationale for the "defensive posture" that we have argued is evident in Canadian mass media policy. If mass media fail to transmit a unique Canadian culture, the vitality of that culture will be diminished.

Several differences between Canadian and American cultures are examined in detail by Seymour Martin Lipset,[3] but there is one cultural difference between the two societies that we will use to demonstrate the role of mass media at this basic social level. We believe that Canadian political culture has been more accepting of ethnic and linguistic diversity than has been American culture. This difference is sometimes illustrated by the American concept of the "melting pot" as opposed to the Canadian concept of the "mosaic."[4]

In the debate surrounding the attempted ratification of the Meech Lake Accord in the spring of 1990, there were a number of instances where media behaviour could be seen as undermining the values of tolerance in Canadian culture. Two examples stand out. One is the high level of media attention given to communities formally declaring themselves to be unilingual Anglophone. The other, and especially important because of the visual symbolism involved, was the despoiling of the Quebec flag, the *fleur-de-lis*, in an eastern Ontario community. While that incident can be interpreted in the context of news, in the sense of indicating dissatisfaction on the part of a small group of Anglo-Canadians with the proposed constitutional changes, of far more significance was its symbolic importance to the continuation of the Canadian community. In that the incident was replayed time and again on Quebec television, the message that was transmitted to

Quebeckers (nationalist and federalist alike) was one of profound disrespect for a cultural symbol held in high regard by the French-speaking community.[5] It seemed that Anglophone Canada cared little whether Quebec separated. Thus the incident had the potential to fracture the national political community. In a similar fashion, over the summer of 1991 media coverage of the Great Whale hydro-electric project took on a significance beyond that of informational reporting on environmental concerns. According to Lucien Bouchard, leader of the sovereignist Bloc Québécois, "James Bay has become a symbol of an intolerant Quebec that oppresses the native minority," and Bouchard accused the federal government of not defending Quebec against this "malicious propaganda."[6]

Anti-French protestors in Brockville, Ontario, take turns stomping on the Quebec provincial flag, the fleur-de-lis. 7 September 1989. (The Brockville Recorder and Times)

Media's Role in the Politics of Democratic Governance

Without entering into a philosophical discussion of democratic theory, it is our view that democracy entails the notion that society has a basic responsibility (usually carried out through elections) to select its leaders and thereby, indirectly at least, to influence fundamental policy directions.[7] And, as Carl J. Friedrich maintained, "freedom of the press is a cornerstone of constitutional democracy."[8] Further, our preference in Canada is that political choices are typically made in an open forum, where the electorate is provided ample opportunity to select among parties that vie for our attention and our votes.

Media may be visualized as a set of conduits that link the governed with those who govern. Historically, information tended to flow in greater volume from those who govern to the governed, rather than the other way around. More recently, however, media function as conduits for information flow in both directions. And, if we consider the often high volume of media reporting on public opinion polling, on occasion the information flow from the citizenry to government becomes voluminous. This dual role of mass media is depicted in figure 14-1.

In general, scholars have pointed to the increased importance of mass media in the democratic process. John Meisel, in particular, has advanced the argument that as political parties have declined in importance as a link between individuals and their government, mass media have correspondingly increased in importance.[9] Indeed, one would be hard pressed to find any contemporary political commentator who would argue that mass media are not central institutions of democratic government. As well, there appears to be a consensus that among competing types of mass media, television has emerged as dominant. There are a number of factors contributing to television's preeminence: 98 percent of Canadian homes have at least one TV;

FIGURE 14–1

Media as a Conduit Between Citizens and Government

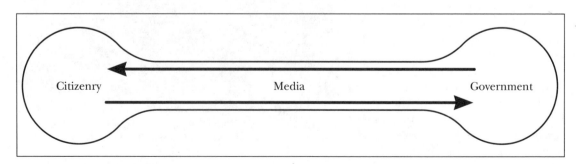

Citizenry — Media — Government

viewer attention to television increases each year; and in at least one study it is clearly the medium with the greatest "credibility," judged by Canadians to be most "fair and objective" (TV—42 percent, newspapers—18 percent, radio—15 percent, magazines—10 percent, don't know—15 percent).[10] These considerations offer insight into what today has become the essence of the political process, the emphasis on sensory (emotional) rather than cognitive processes.

While television has gained preeminence in terms of attention paid to it by audiences, there is an interactive relationship between broadcasting and newspapers that continues to be played out. In the 1920s and 1930s, radio stations often made a practice of reading newspaper stories over the air. Such is no longer the case. However, in a study done for the Royal Commission on Newspapers in 1980, Frederick Fletcher reports that 91 percent of media executives interviewed reported that they read the *Globe and Mail* regularly. According to Fletcher, "it seems reasonable to conclude, therefore, that the *Globe*'s major news stories, features and even editorials can serve to set the agenda not only for policy makers but also for other media as well."[11]

The roles that mass media play in democratic societies need to be examined in two broad situations: the period of time between elections, when a particular party and leader in fact govern; and the relatively brief but extremely important period of election campaigns, when the government is in the process of being selected.

The Role of Mass Media During Periods of Governing

During nonelection periods, domestic politics as news has to compete with a variety of other types of news such as international incidents, domestic tragedies, as well as entertainment and sporting events; in short, a whole range of social, economic, cultural, and human interest issues. While domestic politics tends to be considered important, there is no guarantee, as is the case during elections, that an issue deemed to be important by the government will attract substantial journalistic attention. Thus it is necessary to examine the relationship between politicians and journalists in the process of deciding what is news.[12]

This relationship has been described as a symbiotic one, in that each party needs the other in order to thrive. Politicians need exposure in the media to promote continued name recognition as well as to call attention to their positions on various issues. Journalists, on the other hand, require access to information regarding what is going on; hence they must cultivate news makers at every level. There is an obvious tension in this relationship, as politicians attempt to "use" journalists to project a desired image, and journalists in turn "pump" politicians for revealing pieces of information that may put them on the trail of a significant story. This relationship can lead to excesses on the part of both politicians and journalists. The former "leak" stories to the press, they "plant" stories with journalists, and in some instances covertly attempt to use media in a carefully planned manner. Journalists are also not without fault. Motivated by the lure of career rewards, they will often focus in an exploitative manner on items of scandal and personal misadventure involving politically prominent persons. As mass media have risen in importance as a political force, so too have the stakes in controlling what will be covered and what elements in a story will receive emphasis. While this symbiotic relationship can be abused by either of the participants, thoroughly professional politicians and thoroughly professional journalists are aware that the accepted standard of behaviour for each is the moral high road.

In nonelection periods there exist no special regulations or expectations for mass media other than the basic principles of balance and fair play, particularly on the reporting of controversial matters. The research literature on media coverage of public policy issues outside of election campaigns is not large. However, beginning in 1988, we have seen an important media development in the form of the National Media Archives publication *On Balance*. This publication, using carefully designed research methods, has reported on media

coverage of a number of public policy issues. The February 1989 issue, for example, examines coverage of health care by the CBC and the *Globe and Mail* from December 1987 to November 1988. Among significant findings were that, in spite of widespread public concern as indicated in public opinion polls, "this issue comprised only 1 percent of CBC television's agenda." Within this health-care coverage, strikes were the focus of major attention by both CBC (45.8 percent) and the *Globe and Mail* (43.5 percent). Questions regarding quality of care occupied 24.9 percent of *Globe* coverage as opposed to 18.9 percent of CBC coverage, while costs were discussed in 23.1 percent of *Globe* coverage and only 9.5 percent of CBC coverage. In terms of "news makers" (i.e., those who were interviewed for material), doctors and government spokespersons predominated, with doctors being especially sought out by CBC, and government officials given preference in the *Globe*. In terms of specific illnesses, in spite of the fact that heart disease and cancer are by far the largest killers of Canadians, AIDS garnered the lion's share (61.3 percent) of CBC's attention.[13]

These findings are not unexpected in light of what we know about criteria for selecting news. Strikes, as conflict situations, are naturally attractive to the media. Elite spokespersons (doctors and government officials) who stand out because of professional or social position, are most likely to be approached for their views on a particular topic. The extraordinary attention given to AIDS is also characteristic of media reporting, which thrives on shock and drama. In essence, the reporting function is characterized by a search for information that is important to the reader, listener, or viewer but that, at the same time, is characterized by its unique nature. Thus "news" must stand out in the informational environment.

Media's Role During Elections

Elections are crucial times for democratic societies on a number of levels. Jon Pammett argues that elections provide the political system with the means whereby rulers are selected, they provide political parties opportunities for organization building, and they serve as an avenue for the exercise of political power for individuals.[14] In discussing mass media in times of elections, a number of issues must be considered. These are identified below.

The Canada Elections Act

For most competitive events there exists a set of rules. In the case of elections, these are found in the Canada Elections Act. It is a lengthy piece of legislation (280 pages) and deals with everything pertaining to the "franchise of electors and the election of members to the House of Commons."[15] Readers will understand that a document with such a mandate is both extensive

and detailed. For example, the act, among other items, defines the period of an election campaign, the rules for the registration of political parties, the identification of eligible voters, the definition of electoral boundaries, the periods in a campaign within which parties and candidates may advertise, the calculation of limits on and the reporting of election expenses, the allocation of "free time" to political parties, as well as limits to contributions that may be made to political parties. In addition to the Canada Elections Act itself, the CRTC, on the occasion of a provincial or federal election, issues to all broadcasters details regarding expected behaviour in the campaign. It is our intent here to highlight important features of the act and CRTC guidelines as these affect media behaviour.

Spending and Advertising Limits

The Elections Act and the CRTC regulate campaign spending and advertising. The regulations are rigid and the penalties for violation are specified. Two principles underlie controls on spending and advertising. The first is to establish a limit on permissible campaign spending by candidates and parties so as to preclude the "buying" of an electoral victory. This amount is calculated for all parties according to a fixed formula that has as its basic component the numbers of voters in an electoral riding. The spending split between "national" and "local" campaigns is determined by each party. The second principle is related to equitable treatment to all parties and candidates: all contenders must be offered an equal opportunity to purchase programming and advertising time. In the 1988 election, this amounted to an aggregate of six and a half hours of prime broadcasting time, and it was the responsibility of each station to program such a schedule (see table 14–1) either alone as a station or through network affiliation. It should be noted that this particular regulation with respect to advertising is directed at broadcasters rather than at newspapers. However, no advertising, in broadcasting or print, is permitted in advance of the twenty-ninth day before polling day, on polling day itself, or one day immediately preceding polling day. Thus, in a normal eight-week federal campaign, roughly half is free of political advertising. The Elections Act is also specific regarding the requirement for candidates to report their election expenses through formally identified auditors within four months of election day. It is also illegal to use foreign broadcast facilities for Canadian election purposes.

In addition to paid program and commercial advertising time, networks are also obliged under the Canada Elections Act to provide "free time" to political parties for campaign purposes. In calculating party expenses, the commercial value of any free broadcast time is not taken into consideration.

The complexity involved in allocating time to political parties cannot be underestimated. The

complaint has often been raised that because time allocations are related to parliamentary representation, which is based on past performance, the system is disadvantageous to new and competing points of view. In the 1988 election, twelve political parties were recognized under the act. In addition to the three major parties (the Progressive Conservatives, the Liberals, and the New Democrats), also given official status in the election were the Libertarian Party of Canada, which ran 88 candidates; the Rhinoceros Party, which ran 72 candidates; the Reform Party, which also ran 72; the Green Party (68); the Christian Heritage Party (63); the Party for the Commonwealth of Canada (60); the Communist Party of Canada (52); the Confederation of Regions Western Party (52); and the Social Credit Party (9).[16]

Unhappy with its treatment by major TV networks with respect to time allocations, the Green Party brought charges against the networks under the Broadcasting Act, arguing that the party's national leader was not included in the telecast leaders' debates. In addition, the charge claimed that the networks had not provided adequate news coverage of the party. Two years later, the complaint was quashed by the Ontario provincial court, citing the argument that "the right to speak does not carry the right to have someone listen."[17]

Third Party Advertising
The 1988 federal election introduced into the Canadian electoral process on a major scale the phe-

nomenon of so-called *third party advertising*—that is, advertising sponsored by anyone other than registered political parties and their representatives. Such practices had been outlawed by the Canada Elections Act but were successfully challenged in 1984 as a violation of the Charter of Rights' guarantee of free speech. Thus, in the 1988 election, groups other than registered political parties advertised throughout the entire election period, including the periods where registered parties were prohibited from advertising. As well, there were no controls on the amount of money spent by such groups. The net effect of unrestricted third party advertising was to undermine the rationale for the strict budgeting and reporting demands placed on political parties. In fact, third party advertising in the 1988 election turned campaign spending regulations into a mockery, in that it was widely perceived that such advertising favoured one party over the others.

In the 1988 campaign the bulk of third party advertising focussed on the issue of the Free Trade Agreement between Canada and the United States. On the one side, opposing the agreement, was an alliance of trade unions, churches, and cultural and women's groups. In support of free trade, and by far the biggest third party spenders in the campaign, was the national lobby that represented the business community.[18]

In light of third party advertising, which appeared to violate the fundamental principle of equality, as well

TABLE 14-1	
Allocation of Broadcasting Time in the 1988 Election	
Party	**Minutes**
Progressive Conservative Party	195
Liberal Party	89
New Democratic Party	67
Rhinoceros Party	7
Libertarian Party	5
Green Party	4
Confederation of the Regions Western Party	4
Party for the Commonwealth of Canada	4
Social Credit Party	3
Communist Party	3
Christian Heritage Party	3
Reform Party	3

Source: CRTC Circular No. 352, *Allocation of Federal Election Broadcast Time* (Ottawa: CRTC, 4 October 1988).

as the existence of other shortcomings in the Canada Elections Act, the federal government, in the fall of 1989, created a Royal Commission on Electoral Reform and Party Financing. As expected, hearings before that royal commission have focussed heavily on resolving the dilemma between the right to free speech, on the one hand, and the desirability of maintaining a "level playing field" for electoral contests, on the other. As of this writing, the final report of the royal commission has not been released, but significant changes regarding third party advertising are anticipated.

Negative Advertising

Negative advertising consists of featuring an opposing party or candidate in a bad light. In a book dealing with media and elections in

Canada, published in 1984, we wrote as follows with respect to campaign negativism:

> In a democratic society a healthy skepticism about power and those who wield it is a useful tool for maintaining a responsive government. However, when those who occupy decision-making positions are constantly portrayed as lacking both morality and intelligence, the legitimacy of the decisions taken by the government may soon be called into question and the stability of the political system itself may be jeopardized.[19]

We based these observations on poll data that showed confidence levels in government ranging from 42 to 57 percent and confidence in the press at 44 percent. A Gallup Poll released in June 1990 indicates that, while confidence in newspapers remained constant at 45 percent, only 27 percent indicated confidence in the House of Commons, while a mere 14 percent had confidence in political parties.[20] It is data such as these that appear to confirm our worst fears. While we do not suggest a direct cause-and-effect relationship between negative advertising and such frighteningly low levels of confidence in our political institutions, it is a relationship that clearly bears looking into. Negative advertising, while not necessarily predominant in the 1988 Canadian campaign, did according to one study, form a significant part of each major party's ad campaign.[21]

Negative advertising arises out of campaign strategies that focus on image making and image destruction. Given the extraordinary brevity of television commercials—twenty, thirty, and sixty seconds in length—there is no real opportunity to elaborate on issues. Also, given television's superior ability to project the human dimension, it is not surprising to see the focus on party leaders. What is unique about negative advertising, however, is that parties spend large amounts of their precious advertising dollars linking the faces and names of opposition candidates to some negative attribute. This gives rise to concern.

While negative advertising has not been studied extensively in Canada, a number of U.S. studies have investigated the phenomenon. Conclusions, although tentative, appear to be the following:

- an attack by a candidate is likely to elicit some unfavourable backlash on the attacker;[22]
- on occasion, enhancement of the candidate under attack might occur;[23]
- it is safer and more effective to attack a candidate's capability (for example, management skill) rather than a candidate's character;[24]
- to avoid backlash, it might be preferable to use third parties as attackers;[25]
- in general, the electorate tends not to approve of attack campaigns.

The last conclusion suggests the need to "determine the social costs of such advertising, particularly potential costs in terms of increased cynicism toward the political process and decreased political participation."[26]

These conclusions notwithstanding, as with advertising in general, money is spent on what works, and it is clear that in electoral campaigns negative advertising tends to work despite the backlash noted above. Negative information appears to be far more powerful than positive information in crystalizing decisions for the electorate. This is significant in light of the obvious conflict between the short-term goals of electoral victory and long-term needs for a political system to enjoy reasonable levels of public support. Another dimension of the problem is that, every two years, Canadians participate as observers of elections (congressional and presidential) in the United States. Many Canadians will recall the 1988 American presidential campaign in which Republican advertisements associated the images of pollution in Boston Harbor and the face of a convicted killer (released and turned rapist) with Democratic candidate Michael Dukakis. The frequency with which these two commercials were scheduled suggests that Republican campaign strategists perceived them as highly effective in damaging the credibility of Governor Dukakis. Because Canadians continue to be heavy viewers of American television, even in the event that our own campaigns might become less characterized by negative advertising, it is entirely possible that Canadians would experience some spillover in terms of mistrust of politicians.

Leader Debates

In a post-1988-election poll, when invited to rate various factors in terms of their importance in influencing voting decisions, a national sample of 1000 Canadians ranked TV debates second only to general media coverage. This is really not surprising, although the relative ranking of debates as opposed to such seemingly prominent factors as advertising and polls is worthy of note (see table 14–2).

Research on Canadian voting behaviour has shown that party identification historically has been weaker in Canada than in the United States and Great Britain. Also, as the influence of political parties has declined over the years, short-term factors associated with a particular campaign have gained influence. Thus, highly publicized and confrontational debates between the major leaders have emerged as a significant determinant of electoral choice.

TABLE 14–2
Importance of Factors in Deciding How to Vote

	Helpful (%)	Unhelpful (%)	No Difference (%)
Media Coverage	51	12	37
TV Debates	45	6	49
Local Meetings	31	7	61
TV Commercials	26	15	58
Leader Tours	24	7	69
Published Polls	23	12	65

Source: "The Voters Reflect," *Maclean's*, 5 December 1988, 19.

Research on the effects of leader debates in the 1988 election points to differences in importance of the debates on the outcome. According to the team that conducted the 1988 national election study, leader debates were clearly an important factor:

> On the eve of the debates an impartial observer . . . would have concluded that a Conservative victory was overwhelmingly probable. The Debates changed more than parties' standings. They also ushered in uncertainty about what the frontrunners' (now numbering two) relative standing was. Clearly the Conservatives had dropped and the Liberals had surged.[27]

Lawrence LeDuc and Richard Price are more restrained in their assessment of the impact of the 1988 debates. They argue that

> [while] debates are important events in campaigns . . . they do not really act to change the perceptions of leaders that individuals hold in any fundamental way, and in some instances may merely serve to reinforce these. Where the public perceptions of debate performance are sharply out of line with established images or expectations, debates can produce measurable effects on public opinion. But these tend to be short-lived, and generally cannot be sustained through an entire campaign.[28]

Evidence supporting the conclusion offered by LeDuc and Price is to be found in the debate between John Turner and Brian Mulroney in the 1988 campaign. It was perceived that Turner was clearly the winner, as he successfully attacked the prime minister for "selling out" Canada on the free trade issue. Polls reflected an upsurge in Liberal fortunes, but the Progressive Conservatives were able to regroup, refocus their campaign strategy, and emerge as the clear winners.[29] Despite a significant body of research over the years, the jury is still out regarding the one-on-one relationship between TV debates and election outcomes.

An important aspect of leader debates is that they offer the opportunity for influential journalists to give an interpretational "spin" to the contest. Pointed journalistic evaluations have to be considered as a part of the debate context, colouring in not so subtle ways what viewers themselves initially thought of the candidates' performances.

Canada's first televised debate occurred during the 1968 election between Pierre Trudeau, Robert

Prime Minister Brian Mulroney and Liberal leader John Turner go head-to-head during the French-language debate as NDP leader Ed Broadbent looks on. (24 October 1988) (Canapress Photo Service/Fred Chartrand)

Stanfield, Tommy Douglas, and Réal Caouette. As described by highly regarded national columnist Peter Newman, it was "anti-climactic and depressing to watch this miraculous medium brought to an unimaginable level of dreariness as our politicians rehashed old statistics and went at each other with about as much wit, grace and style, as a group of awkward contestants on a quiz show."[30]

Writing in *Time* on the 1988 debate between George Bush and Michael Dukakis, Walter Shapiro indicates that the debate "may have been lost by Dukakis in the opening two minutes," in that Dukakis failed to respond adequately to an emotionally charged question that Shapiro describes as "being in ghoulish taste": Dukakis was asked to reconcile his stand opposing capital punishment in light of a hypothetical situation in which his wife had been raped and murdered. According to Shapiro, "even as his political dreams hung in the balance, Dukakis mustered all the emotion of a time-and-temperature recording."[31]

Research on debates reinforces our earlier emphasis on images being crucial to the electoral process. Debates focus on personalities, style, and appearance, as well as on dramatic slips of the tongue, basic factual errors, and peculiar patterns of speech or demeanour. All of these are dramatically emphasized by the television camera. If these factors are perceived as positive or negative by audiences (not to mention the "spin" factor), they can

Governor Michael Dukakis (right) gestures as he speaks during the presidential debate. Vice President George Bush listens at left. (AP/Wide World Photos)

make or break a campaign. All of this is supported by the truism agreed upon by candidates, party strategists, and pundits, that if you are ahead in the polls during a campaign, avoid TV debates as strenuously as possible; if you are behind in the polls, insist just as strenuously that a debate is a must. If, as the frontrunner, you are forced into a debate, be sure to schedule it early in the campaign so as to allow plenty of time for damage control.[32]

Polls

In our study of mass media coverage of the 1984 Canadian election campaign we speculated that, in spite of a research literature that suggested a "no effects" or "minimal effects" impact of polls on voting, the particular circumstances of that campaign—one party clearly in the lead over many weeks, combined with an extraordinary amount of media coverage devoted to the results of polls—led to a situation where polls would indeed have an impact.[33]

While it would be premature to conclude that such a position has carried the day in the controversy regarding effects of polls, a paper based on the 1988 Canadian national election study appears to have made a convincing case for just such a conclusion. Data confirm "that expectations are affected by polls, but the exact effect varies across parties. Conservative and Liberal expectations both responded to the most recent poll. For each party a unit gain in poll share percentage point produced an immediate expectational gain of just over one-quarter of a point."[34] Thus, in spite of research reported on the 1984 election,[35] and the June 1990 Gallup study that indicated that 82 percent of Canadians *do not* believe polls influence electoral choice,[36] the question of the impact of polls seems to be alive and well.

There are a number of dimensions to the issue of polls. First is the matter of their frequency. In the 1980 election, there were four published polls; in 1984 there were twelve; in 1988, twenty-four polls were published.[37] Clearly the sheer number of polls commissioned and published is a factor that bears consideration. It is debatable whether four polls reported over an eight-week campaign would have a significant impact on voters. Twenty-four polls reported over the same period, however, result in a blitz that voters cannot ignore. And,

given that mass media often sponsor polls (CBC, CTV, CFTO, Southam Newspapers, the *Toronto Star*, the *Globe and Mail*, and *La Presse*, for example),[38] it is extremely likely that poll results will be given prominent media attention. There are two primary attractions involved in media organizations' sponsorship of polls. First, the release of a poll is a highly exciting "news" event, and second, poll data offer reporters evidence on which they are able to base analyses.[39] Critics of poll publication have argued that mass media are in effect creating news stories and then reporting on their own creations. Regardless of how one feels about the morality of the issue, because polls are expensive and are often sponsored by media organizations, it is highly likely that media will continue to give them prominence in order to derive full value from their investment.

Another concern regarding polls deals with their accuracy. A common format for reporting polls includes a caveat to the effect that "This poll is accurate within plus or minus three percentage points, 19 times out of 20." Over the past decade, journalists (both broadcast and print) appear to alert their audiences to this basic question of accuracy. Despite occasional references to the "twentieth poll" (the so-called rogue poll in the 1988 election, which showed the Liberals ahead), polling is becoming more accurate. However, there are, as identified by Alan Frizzell, a number of problems with polling that deserve attention. Among the most significant are the adequacy of sample size, especially when regional analyses are attempted, effects of question wording and placement of questions in the questionnaire on responses, and the manner in which "undecided" voters are dealt with in statistical manipulation (for example, are they included and, if so, how are they reported).[40] Concerns regarding the effects of polls on voting choice have been raised by parliamentarians, who have called for either elimination or regulation of polls during elections. Frizzell suggests self-regulation on the part of the polling industry.

The question of the need and desirability for formal government regulation of polls during election campaigns is raised not so much by technical problems with polling as by the effect of polls. Member of Parliament Patrick Boyer identifies four negative effects: (1) they tend to trivialize campaigns by emphasizing their "horse race" features; (2) their broadcasting and publication use up valuable news space and air time better devoted to substantive issues; (3) if a candidate is behind in the polls, workers are likely to become discouraged; and (4) polling contributes to campaign negativism, in that those who find themselves behind in the polls succumb to the temptation to attack opposing candidates.[41]

While these effects might be true, polls also have advantages from the perspective of the electorate. Polls are becoming an increasingly reliable source of information concerning evaluation of events, issues, and parties. How can one argue that a society should be denied these data and thus be forced to make decisions on demonstrably worse information? Also, those who advocate the banning or regulation of polls tend to view them as an activity carried out solely by professionals working at the national level. However, what of controls on more informal "polls" conducted at the local level, using either methods similar to those used at the national level or what might be labeled "casual" polling— on-the-street interviews, radio call-in programs, or even studio audience discussions? These are also forms of canvassing public opinion and are used with regularity by newspapers and broadcasting stations. In any regulation of polls, what will happen to this kind of activity?

More fundamental than these technical problems, however, is that any suppression of poll information by the government, for example in the Canada Elections Act, not only would likely be challenged as violation of constitutional guarantees of both freedom of speech and freedom of the press, but would constitute an example of censorship by most definitions of the term.

Campaign Styles: U.S. and Canadian

There is no clear consensus as to how great an influence American campaigns have had on their Canadian counterparts. It is evident that there are characteristics that are unique to the Canadian electoral processes: most notably, Canada has a parliamentary system of government wherein the prime minister is not elected directly by the people (except in a particular riding), but rather holds the position by gaining the leadership of the party that either achieves or constructs a majority in parliament. The American president, although elected by an electoral college, actually runs as a candidate nation-wide.

The length of time of the electoral campaign also differs, and this affects the behaviour of politicians, parties, and the media. Constitutionally, Canadian elections must be called at least once every five years, but the timing of any one election is influenced by many factors. Hence, the exact date of an election cannot be predicted with certainty. The time period of the actual campaign is normally about eight weeks. American presidential elections are fixed every four years and, with the extensive system of primaries, some presidential campaigns go on for two years or more.

The two political systems vary in a number of other ways. In the U.S. there are fifty states and one commonwealth spread over a smaller geographical area than Canada. This implies greater political power exercised by only ten provinces and two territories in a huge geographic area.

But when we come to the election process itself, particularly in the area of style, we find a growing number of similarities, especially in those aspects of the campaign that involve mass media. Whether these trends are due to "Americanization" or simply "mediaization" (i.e., a similar shaping of elections worldwide by television) is impossible to determine. Nevertheless, there are several similarities between contemporary Canadian and American political campaigns that appear attributable to one or the other of these phenomena.

Perhaps the most obvious similarity is seen in the journalistic focus on party leaders. "Nowhere is the change in style of Canadian campaigning more apparent than in the concentration on leadership. . . . Modern electoral contests, abetted by television especially, have concentrated attention on . . . the party leaders, almost as if they were elected directly like the US president."[42]

Televised press conferences and addresses have been characteristic of U.S. presidential style since the late 1950s and early 1960s. Canadian Prime Minister Trudeau used this strategy effectively in the 1970s and early 1980s. Canadian political scientists claimed that the use of regional television networks by provincial premiers imitated American politics. "It has presidential connotations. It's not in our tradition to do it."[43]

Broadcast debates in the two countries are highly similar in style, in that both centre on major party leaders and candidates. Typically, these leaders are forced into confrontation with each other. This serves to magnify the role of leader, which in a presidential system is probably appropriate, but distorts the role of a prime minister in a cabinet/parliamentary system.

Further, when we look at the style of advertising in campaigns in the two countries, there is little to differentiate one from the other. Canadian parties have their versions of attack campaigns, as do parties in the United States. This is partly because advertising is North American; most agencies in Canada are either wholly or partially owned and controlled by U.S. agencies. Further, Canadians have tended to borrow freely from American sources. The NDP, for example, in the 1988 federal campaign hired the U.S. polling organization Fingerhut/ Madison Opinion Research to do its private polling.

The "follow-the-leader" behaviour of U.S. and Canadian media further contributes to the perceived importance of leadership. There are two apparent results that flow from this syndrome. First, the movements and statements of the party leaders, as they travel from province to province, in essence become the campaign. John Crosbie, a Conservative cabinet minister, complained that in the 1980 campaign, on a day when he had given a major address on economic matters in Toronto, TV news of the day featured Prime Minister Joe Clark getting his hair cut in Vancouver, where he was resting for the day.[44] The organization of press personnel and the logistics involved in following the leaders across the country, not only make the leaders the focus of coverage, but also contribute to "pack journalism" as reporters interact with each other in relatively cramped and tense circumstances for weeks at a time. A type of "group think" sets in as a consequence.[45]

The follow-the-leader campaign and consequent style of journalism have led to a similar problem within the journalistic community in the two nations. In the midst of an atmosphere of cameras, lights, microphones, and cables strung on the floor, print journalists have complained that the television camera has come to dominate over the note pad.

A case in point was seen during the week in June 1990 when the prime minister and the provincial premiers were involved in tense discussions in a race with a deadline to secure an agreement on the Meech Lake Accord. A Southam News reporter describes the scene as the premiers emerged from the meetings to be surrounded by media reporters with their note pads, microphones, cameras, and lights:

Day after day, print journalists were leaving the conference centre fuming over the way in which the electronic media—especially the CBC— controlled the proceedings.

Television equipment created a major physical barrier to making contact with the key political players when they came out to face reporters. When reporters tried to fight their way to the front of the crowd, they were frequently shoved back by officious government and TV types.

The majority of journalists had no opportunity to ask questions. They were forced by default to rely on the exchanges enacted before the cameras, exchanges primarily initiated by the CBC.[46]

Veteran U.S. political and media analyst Jeff Greenfield, commenting on political campaigning and the media, confirms that print media have been late in realizing that campaigns today are conducted largely through television. Stemming from that realization, Greenfield contends that the print press has two choices: to figure out something else to do in covering elections that television cannot do or to play second fiddle.[47]

Canadians participate vicariously in American politics through mass media. It is not surprising, therefore, to see Canadians making comparisons between the election of a president and the selection of a prime minister. When such comparisons are made, as they have been for several decades, Canadians tend to point to what they perceive as inadequacies in the Canadian system—that only a small group of Canadians, apart from those who live in the party leader's riding, participate in the prime ministerial selection process. Thus, as a Canadian political scientist has pointed out, the majority of Canadians are passive spectators. One solution that has been offered to this inadequate representation is for Canada

to adopt the practice of holding prime ministerial primary elections similar to the U.S. system.[48] Of course not all commentators on the American system of presidential primaries are impressed either with the process or its results.

Premature Release of Voting Results

The Canada Elections Act and the CRTC both prohibit the release of election results nationally until voting is concluded in British Columbia, which is in the Pacific time zone. The purpose of this prohibition is obvious: to prevent "bandwagon" voting in western parts of the country based on results from Atlantic Canada, Quebec, and Ontario. Indeed, in many federal elections, given the heavy proportion of seats in Quebec and Ontario, there might be little point in westerners casting their ballots.

The legislation, while attempting to protect a principle, is often violated, given today's capacity for the rapid movement of information. As polls close from region to region the temptation to advise Western Canadians about results obtained in Eastern Canada is difficult to suppress. Such information has been routinely distributed by telephone. At the same time, because broadcasting signals observe technical power considerations rather than electoral boundaries, "fringe" listeners and viewers unavoidably gain awareness about election results in constituencies east of them. As well, news reports about Canadian elections have been broadcast by U.S.

stations and networks, and Canadians continue to listen to and view American stations. In sum, while the prohibition regarding the release of voting results is still in force, violations of the legislation are inevitable.

The current situation does not appear to be satisfactory, in that the principle of a "free" vote is violated. There are two options for resolving the situation. The first is to remove all barriers to the release of election results, as is the case in the U.S., and to live with the consequences. It is clear that the main impact of such a move would be that Western Canadian votes would be cast with the knowledge of which party would likely be able to form the government. The second option would be to adopt a suggestion that has been made several times in the past: to readjust poll opening and closing hours from province to province so that the entire country would be voting during the same "real time" hours on election day. The latest suggestion in this regard has come from Canada's chief electoral officer and was reported in January 1989.[49] The newspaper story, while offering a suggestion about how "real time" hours could be scheduled, also indicated that in the 1988 federal election, Canadian TV networks projected election results and announced a PC majority government two hours and twenty minutes before the polls closed in British Columbia. It is not difficult to imagine that a significant proportion of British Columbians were aware of this result and that this knowledge affected their voting behaviour.

Role of the CRTC: Broadcasting and Elections

In addition to the Canada Elections Act, wherein details are specified concerning the conduct of media, political parties, and candidates, CRTC policies also play an important role in guiding the behaviour of broadcasting during times of elections, whether these be municipal, provincial, or federal. Typically, when elections are announced, the CRTC issues to broadcasting stations in areas concerned, sets of guidelines that outline all expectations regarding the conduct of radio and television stations. A case in point is *A Policy with Respect to Election Campaign Broadcasting*,[50] which was issued when the 1988 federal election was called. A brief review of that policy is appropriate in this discussion, since it will offer students insights into philosophical as well as practical contexts within which broadcasting media function during election periods.

The CRTC points out that its policy encompasses four categories of broadcasting content: paid time (program and advertising content on behalf of parties, candidates, and any advocacy groups); free time (time allocated to the parties and candidates on the basis of a Canada Elections Act formula into which are factored party seats held, percentage of the popular vote received, and the number of candidates nominated by each party during the previous election); news (programs that emanate from a station's news department); and public affairs programming (which normally provides analysis of news items, candidates, parties, and issues).

In each instance, the CRTC underlines that the general governing principle for the behaviour of stations is to be found in subsection 3 (iv) of the Broadcasting Act, which emphasizes that stations are obliged to "provide reasonable, balanced opportunity for the expression of differing views on matters of public concern." Out of that principle flow several particular responsibilities for broadcasters to observe: they have a responsibility "to become involved in controversial issues of public concern"; they should ensure opportunities for presentation of different points of view related to controversial issues; and by equitable, fair and, objective presentations, the public should be "placed in a position to make its own informed judgment on controversial issues."[51]

More specifically, however, and applying the general principle from the Broadcasting Act to election programming, the CRTC explicates a particular rationale for its policy:

> The purpose of these requirements [fair, just, and equitable treatment of parties, candidates, and the discussion of issues] is to ensure the public's right to be informed of the issues involved so that it has sufficient knowledge to make an informed choice from among the

various parties and candidates. This right is a quintessential one for the effective functioning of a democracy, particularly at election time. The broadcaster's obligation as a trustee of the public airwaves is seldom greater than it is in respect of this exercise of the most fundamental democratic freedom.[52]

Thus the broadcasters are reminded that they are not "owners" rather they are entrusted with an interim licence that obliges them to perform for the benefit of the community rather than out of any self-serving interest. They are placed directly at the centre of the political process that characterizes the pluralistic nature of Canadian society. The responsibility that broadcasters bear is onerous:

> It is the broadcaster's duty to ensure that the public has adequate knowledge of the issues surrounding an election and the position of parties and candidates. The broadcaster does not enjoy the position of a benevolent censor who is able to give the public only what it "should" know. Nor is it the broadcaster's role to decide in advance which candidates are "worthy" of broadcast time.[53]

In its design of current policy, the CRTC had sought public comment on election campaign broadcasting. A matter that had been raised in public dialogue was that of news programming and the obligation of broadcast journalists to conform to specific, almost formulaic, guidelines.

The commission explained its policy position. First, it agrees that news coverage during elections should "generally be left to the editorial judgment of the broadcast licensee." Nevertheless, even in their news coverage, broadcasters are again reminded that the demands of the Broadcasting Act prevail; that is, that broadcasters are expected to provide "reasonable, balanced opportunity for the expression of differing views on matters of public concern." Second, the commission indicated that it had approached the federal government with a request for an amendment to the section of the Broadcasting Act that had prohibited airing news and public affairs programming during periods when election programming and campaigning are prohibited (on election day itself and on the day preceding the election). The 1991 act reflects this amendment. The commission's rationale in this instance, with respect to journalistic behaviour, is that while equitable treatment of all is required, and while the public has a right to be informed on matters of public concern, there is also a need not to restrict broadcasters' and candidates' freedom of expression.

The commission's policy in matters of election broadcasting content is explicit and rigid, and, in conjunction with the Canada Elections Act, it is particularly demanding of broadcasters. At the same time, the policy is based on fundamental democratic principles that, of necessity, permit latitude on the part of broadcasters, so long as their performance is consistent with the democratic requirements of justice and fairness.

Conclusion

We live in an age when mass media play an increasing, some say central, role in the way in which we understand social and political reality. In this chapter we have discussed the ways in which mass media affect political life, pointing out that these effects are many and occur at different levels. Given the centrality of the notion of political community to contemporary Canadian politics, it is important for students to appreciate the impact of mass media at this fundamental level. With respect to day-to-day media coverage of political events, we have emphasized the roles that mass media play at times of heightened political activity—that is, times of elections. But it should be understood that, given the increased awareness by parties and their representatives regarding the power of mass media, political campaigning really never ends. It is also abundantly clear that, of all media, television has gained the central position in terms of attention by the public and by politicians alike.

The responsibility that is placed on broadcasters in their day-to-day political behaviour cannot be underestimated. While the Canada Elections Act and CRTC policies regarding the expected behaviour of broadcasters at election time are explicit, there is no reason to assume that broadcasters should behave any differently in periods between elections. Students should be aware that not all that happens becomes "news," and that what does become news influences the way in which we see and evaluate events and leaders. In chapter 4 we discussed the concepts of gatekeeping and agenda setting. When one considers the importance of selecting particular items from the information environment, and thus advising people what to think about, one becomes increasingly aware of the importance of institutions such as MediaWatch and the National Media Archive, which systematically monitor our mass media. If there are systematic biases in nonelection media coverage (and there have been some), these are discoverable by means of research and society as well as the mass medium concerned are made aware that someone is paying attention to what is happening.

Our views of the world, nation, province, and municipality are increasingly dependent on the mass media. Given this dependence it is little wonder that broadcast licensees in particular are closely monitored through their logs by government agencies literally every day of the year. While not a particular problem in Canada, where we live within broad parameters of political freedom, this is not always the case throughout the rest of the world. In the vast majority of cases where repression of the press occurs, it is the government that is the violator. Even with the recent relaxation of political restrictions in Eastern Europe and the former Soviet Union, Canada, its citizens, and its mass media function with an enviable level of freedom that the majority of the world's population still does not enjoy.

Notes

1. Karl W. Deutsch, *Nationalism and Social Communication: An Inquiry into the Foundations of Nationality* (Cambridge: MIT Press, 1966).
2. David Easton, "An Approach to the Analysis of Political Systems," *World Politics* 9 (April 1957): 383–400.
3. Seymour Martin Lipset, *Continental Divide: The Values and Institutions of the United States and Canada* (New York: Routledge, Chapman and Hall, 1990), 42–56.
4. Ibid., 172–92.
5. Peter Desbarats, "Television and Surveys are Playing a New Part in Politics," *Globe and Mail*, 8 June 1990, A7. See also Michael S. Serrill, "Getting their Pact Together," *Time*, 18 June 1990, 20.
6. Estanislas Oziewicz, "Bouchard Criticizes Canadian Diplomats," *Globe and Mail*, 13 September 1991, A5.
7. For an enlightened discussion of democracy see, Robert A. Dahl, *Preface to Democratic Theory* (Chicago: University of Chicago Press, 1956).
8. Carl J. Friedrich, *Constitutional Government and Democracy: Theory and Practice in Europe and America*, 4th ed. (Waltham, MA: Blaisdell Publishing, 1968), 502.
9. John Meisel, "The Decline of Party in Canada" in *Party Politics in Canada*, 5th ed., ed. Hugh G. Thorburn (Scarborough: Prentice-Hall, 1985), 98–114.

10. Michael Adams and Jordan Leviten, "Media Bias as Viewed by the Canadian Public" in *Canadian Legislators 1987–1988*, ed. Robert J. Fleming (Ottawa: Ampersand Communications Services, 1988), 10.

11. Frederick J. Fletcher, *The Newspaper and Public Affairs*, Vol. 7, *Research Publications of the Royal Commission on Newspapers* (Ottawa: Supply and Services, 1981), 20.

12. This relationship is examined in depth in David Taras, *The Newsmakers: The Media's Influence on Politics* (Toronto: Nelson Canada, 1990).

13. "Health Care," *On Balance: Media Treatment of Public Policy Issues* 2 (February 1989), 1, 3–6.

14. Jon H. Pammett, "Elections" in *Canadian Politics in the 1990s*, 3rd ed., ed. Michael S. Whittington and Glen Williams (Toronto: Nelson, 1990), 268–69.

15. Canada, House of Commons, Canada Elections Act, Revised Statutes of Canada, 1985.

16. Stephen Brunt, "12 Political Parties Granted Official Standing," *Globe and Mail*, 26 October 1988, A12.

17. Donn Downey, "Green Party Advisor Lays Criminal Charges Against TV Networks," *Globe and Mail*, 19 May 1989, A3. See also Gary Loewen, "Green Party Loses TV Debate Bid," *Globe and Mail*, 28 March 1991, A8.

18. Charlotte Gray, "Politics: Purchasing Power," *Saturday Night* 104 (March 1989): 15–18.

19. Walter C. Soderlund, Walter I. Romanow, E. Donald Briggs, Ronald H. Wagenberg, *Media and Elections in Canada* (Toronto: Holt, Rinehart and Winston, 1984), 132.

20. "Surveys Impotent, Poll on Polls Shows," *Windsor Star*, 5 June 1990, A2.

21. Arlene Shwetz, "A Discussion of Leadership Portrayal Within Political Advertising: A Case Study of Party Produced Televison Ads from the 1988 Canadian General Election" (paper presented at the Annual Meeting of the Canadian Political Science Association, University of Victoria, May 1990), 19–25.

22. G.M. Garramone, "Voter Responses to Negative Political Ads," *Journalism Quarterly* 61 (Summer 1984): 251.

23. G.M. Garramone, "Effects of Negative Political Advertising: The Roles of Sponsor and Rebuttal," *Journal of Broadcasting & Electronic Media* 29 (Spring 1985): 148.

24. Brian L. Roddy and Gina M. Garramone, "Appeals and Strategies of Negative Political Advertising," *Journal of Broadcasting & Electronic Media* 32 (Fall 1988): 417.

25. Lynda Lee Kaid and John Boydston, "An Experimental Study of the Effectiveness of Negative Political Advertisements," *Communications Quarterly* 35 (Spring 1987): 193–94

26. Roddy and Garramone, "Appeals and Strategies," 426.

27. André Blais, Richard Johnston, Henry E. Brady, Jean Crête, "The Dynamics of Horse Race Expectations in the 1988 Canadian Election" (paper presented at the Annual Meeting of the Canadian Political Science Association, University of Victoria, May 1990).

28. Lawrence LeDuc and Richard Price, "Campaign Debates and Party Leader Images: the 'Encounter '88' Case" (paper presented at the Annual Meeting of the Canadian Political Science Association, University of Victoria, May 1990).

29. Robert Krause, "The Progressive Conservative Campaign Mission Accomplished" in *The Canadian General Election 1988*, ed. Alan

Frizzell, Jon H. Pammett, Anthony Westell (Ottawa: Carleton University Press, 1989), 20–24.

30. Cited in Lynda Hurst, "TV Debates Changed Politics Forever," *Gazette* (Montreal), 22 October 1988, A1.

31. Walter Shapiro, "Bush Scores a Warm Win," *Time*, 24 October 1988, 16.

32. Seth Feldman, "So Near But Yet So Close: American Television Politics in the Canadian Election," *Canadian Forum* 69 (April 1989): 1–12.

33. R. H. Wagenberg, W.C. Soderlund, W.I. Romanow, E.D. Briggs, "Campaigns, Images and Polls: Mass Media Coverage of the 1984 Canadian Election," *Canadian Journal of Political Science* 20 (March 1988): 126–29.

34. Blais et al., "The Dynamics of Horse Race Expectations," 7.

35. Alan Frizzell and Anthony Westell, *The Canadian General Election of 1984: Politicians, Parties, Press and Polls* (Ottawa: Carleton University Press, 1984), 85.

36. "Surveys Impotent, Poll on Polls Shows," *Windsor Star*, 5 June 1990, A2.

37. Frizzell et al., *The Canadian General Election of 1988*, 95.

38. Gregory Wirick, "Sounding and Shaping Opinion: The Impact of Polling," *Parliamentary Government* 8 (Spring 1989): 5.

39. Ibid.

40. Frizzell et al., *The Canadian General Election of 1988*, 98–102.

41. Patrick Boyer, "The Case for Election Law Reform," *Parliamentary Government* 8 (Summer 1989): 14.

42. Soderlund et al., *Media and Elections*, 128.

43. Cited by Geoffrey York, "U.S. Influence Seen as Devine Turns to TV, Bypasses Legislature," *Globe and Mail*, 7 March 1990, A8.

44. John Crosbie, "Politics and the Media: Is the Public Well Served?" in *Politics and the Media* (Toronto: Erindale College, University of Toronto, and Reader's Digest Foundation of Canada, 1981), 10.

45. For the classic portrayal of the pack journalism phenomenon as it developed in a presidential campaign, see Timothy Crouse, *The Boys on the Bus* (New York: Ballentine Books, 1973); and for a comparable Canadian treatment, Clive Cocking, *Following the Leaders: A Media Watcher's Diary of Campaign '79* (Toronto: Doubleday, 1980).

46. Jamie Portman, "Meech Lake and the Role of the Media: Print Journalists Fumed," *Windsor Star*, 15 June 1990, A7.

47. Jeff Greenfield, "The Impact of Television Coverage on the Print Press," in *Covering the Candidates: Role and Responsibilities of the Press* (Reston, VA: American Press Institute, 1987), 86.

48. William Christian, "Time for a Change in Choosing the PM," *Globe and Mail*, 14 August 1989, A7.

49. Robert Matas and Susan Delacourt, "Election Officer Urges Same Voting Hours Across Canada," *Globe and Mail*, 10 January 1989, A1, A4.

50. CRTC, *A Policy With Respect to Election Campaign Broadcasting: Public Notice CRTC 1988-142* (Ottawa, 1988).

51. Ibid., 6.

52. Ibid., 8.

53. Ibid.

A P P E N D I X *

In chapter 7, "Broadcasting," we discuss the evolution of the five broadcasting acts that have been in effect in Canada since the first act was introduced in 1932. The subsequent acts (1936, 1957, 1967–68, 1991) are discussed in broad outline in the chapter, and significant changes, from act to act, are noted. But by far the most extensive of these acts is the 1991 act: it is considerably longer and more detailed than any of the previous acts, and it identifies with greater specificity the responsibilities of the industry with respect to its purposeful functioning in Canada. Of particular interest to readers here would be section 3 in each of the 1967–68 and 1991 acts, in each case entitled "Broadcasting Policy for Canada." This paragraph, more than any other, focusses on the role that broadcasters and their programs are expected to play so as to "safeguard, enrich and strengthen the cultural, political, social and economic fabric of Canada." A careful comparative study of section 3 of the 1967–68 and 1991 acts, reproduced below, will offer readers insight into the current status of the broadcasting system concerning the system's contribution to "nation building," as that concept has been identified by the federal minister of communications.

CHAPTER B-11

An Act to implement a broadcasting policy for Canada

SHORT TITLE

1. This Act may be cited as the *Broadcasting Act.* 1967–68, c. 25, s. 1.

PART I
GENERAL

. . .

Broadcasting Policy for Canada

3. It is hereby declared that
(a) broadcasting undertakings in Canada make use of radio frequen-

38–39 ELIZABETH II
CHAPTER 11

An Act respecting broadcasting and to amend certain Acts in relation thereto and in relation to radio-communication

[Assented to 1st February, 1991]

Her Majesty, by and with the advice and consent of the Senate and House of Commons of Canada, enacts as follows:

SHORT TITLE

1. This Act may be cited as the

---

* Department of Justice Canada, Broadcasting Act 1967–68 and 1991. Reproduced with the permission of the Queen's Printer for Canada, 1991.

cies that are public property and such undertakings constitute a single system, herein referred to as the Canadian broadcasting system, comprising public and private elements;

(b) the Canadian broadcasting system should be effectively owned and controlled by Canadians so as to safeguard, enrich and strengthen the cultural, political, social and economic fabric of Canada;

(c) all persons licensed to carry on broadcasting undertakings have a responsibility for programs they broadcast but the right to freedom of expression and the right of persons to receive programs, subject only to generally applicable statutes and regulations, is unquestioned;

(d) the programming provided by the Canadian broadcasting system should be varied and comprehensive and should provide reasonable, balanced opportunity for the expression of differing views on matters of public concern, and the programming provided by each broadcaster should be of high standard, using predominantly Canadian creative and other resources;

(e) all Canadians are entitled to broadcasting service in English and French as public funds become available;

(f) there should be provided, through a corporation established by Parliament for the purpose, a national broadcasting service that is predominantly Canadian in content and character;

(g) the national broadcasting service should

Broadcasting Act.

PART I
GENERAL

. . .

Broadcasting Policy for Canada

3. (1) It is hereby declared as the broadcasting policy for Canada that

(a) the Canadian broadcasting system shall be effectively owned and controlled by Canadians;

(b) the Canadian broadcasting system, operating primarily in the English and French languages and comprising public, private and community elements, makes use of radio frequencies that are public property and provides, through its programming, a public service essential to the maintenance and enhancement of national identify and cultural sovereignty;

(c) English and French language broadcasting, while sharing common aspects, operate under different conditions and may have different requirements;

(d) the Canadian broadcasting system should

(i) serve to safeguard, enrich and strengthen the cultural, political, social and economic fabric of Canada,

(ii) encourage the development of Canadian expression by providing a wide range of programming that reflects Canadian attitudes, opinions, ideas, values and artistic creativity, by displaying Canadian talent in entertainment programming and by

(i) be a balanced service of information, enlightenment and entertainment for people of different ages, interests and tastes covering the whole range of programming in fair proportion,

(ii) be extended to all parts of Canada, as public funds become available,

(iii) be in English and French, serving the special needs of geographic regions, and actively contributing to the flow and exchange of cultural and regional information and entertainment, and

(iv) contribute to the development of national unity and provide for a continuing expression of Canadian identity;

(h) where any conflict arises between the objectives of the national broadcasting service and the interests of the private element of the Canadian broadcasting system, it shall be resolved in the public interest but paramount consideration shall be given to the objectives of the national broadcasting service;

(i) facilities should be provided within the Canadian broadcasting system for educational broadcasting; and

(j) the regulation and supervision of the Canadian broadcasting system should be flexible and readily adaptable to scientific and technical advances;

and that the objectives of the broadcasting policy for Canada enunciated in this section can best be achieved by providing for the

offering information and analysis concerning Canada and other countries from a Canadian point of view,

(iii) through its programming and the employment opportunities arising out of its operations, serve the needs and interests, and reflect the circumstances and aspirations, of Canadian men, women and children, including equal rights, the linguistic duality and multicultural and multiracial nature of Canadian society and the special place of aboriginal peoples within that society, and

(iv) be readily adaptable to scientific and technological change;

(e) each element of the Canadian broadcasting system shall contribute in an appropriate manner to the creation and presentation of Canadian programming;

(f) each broadcasting undertaking shall make maximum use, and in no case less than predominant use, of Canadian creative and other resources in the creation and presentation of programming, unless the nature of the service provided by the undertaking, such as specialized content or format or the use of languages other than French and English, renders that use impracticable, in which case the undertaking shall make the greatest practicable use of those resources;

(g) the programming originated by broadcasting undertakings should be of high standard;

(h) all persons who are licensed to carry on broadcasting undertakings

regulation and supervision of the Canadian broadcasting system by a single independent public authority. 1967–68, c. 25, s. 2.

have a responsibility for the programs they broadcast;

(i) the programming provided by the Canadian broadcasting system should

(i) be varied and comprehensive, providing a balance of information, enlightenment and entertainment for men, women and children of all ages, interests and tastes,

(ii) be drawn from local, regional, national and international sources,

(iii) include educational and community programs,

(iv) provide a reasonable opportunity for the public to be exposed to the expression of differing views on matters of public concern, and

(v) include a significant contribution from the Canadian independent production sector;

(j) educational programming, particularly where provided through the facilities of an independent educational authority, is an integral part of the Canadian broadcasting system;

(k) a range of broadcasting services in English and in French shall be extended to all Canadians as resources become available;

(l) the Canadian Broadcasting Corporation, as the national public broadcaster, should provide radio and television services incorporating a wide range of programming that informs, enlightens and entertains;

(m) the programming provided by the Corporation should

(i) be predominantly and distinctively Canadian,

(ii) reflect Canada and its regions to national and regional audiences, while serving the special needs of those regions,

(iii) actively contribute to the flow and exchange of cultural expression,

(iv) be in English and in French, reflecting the different needs and circumstances of each official language community, including the particular needs and circumstances of English and French linguistic minorities,

(v) strive to be of equivalent quality in English and in French,

(vi) contribute to shared national consciousness and identity,

(vii) be made available throughout Canada by the most appropriate and efficient means and as resources become available for the purpose, and

(viii) reflect the multicultural and multiracial nature of Canada;

(n) where any conflict arises between the objectives of the Corporation set out in paragraphs (l) and (m) and the interests of any other broadcasting undertaking of the Canadian broadcasting system, it shall be resolved in the public interest, and where the public interest would be equally served by resolving the conflict in favour of either, it shall be resolved in favour of the objectives set out in paragraphs (l) and (m);

(o) programming that reflects the aboriginal cultures of Canada should be provided within the Canadian broadcasting system as resources become available for the purpose;

(p) programming accessible by disabled persons should be provided within the Canadian broadcasting system as resources become available for the purpose;

(q) without limiting any obligation of a broadcasting undertaking to provide the programming contemplated by paragraph (i), alternative television programming services in English and in French should be provided where necessary to ensure that the full range of programming contemplated by that paragraph is made available through the Canadian broadcasting system;

(r) the programming provided by alternative television programming services should

(i) be innovative and be complementary to the programming provided for mass audiences,

(ii) cater to tastes and interests not adequately provided for by the programming provided for mass audiences, and include programming devoted to culture and the arts,

(iii) reflect Canada's regions and multicultural nature,

(iv) as far as possible, be acquired rather than produced by those services, and

(v) be made available throughout Canada by the most cost-efficient means;

(s) private networks and programming undertakings should, to an extent consistent with the financial and other resources available to them,

(i) contribute significantly to the creation and presentation of Canadian programming, and

(ii) be responsive to the evolving demands of the public; and

(t) distribution undertakings

(i) should give priority to the carriage of Canadian programming services and, in particular, to the carriage of local Canadian stations,

(ii) should provide efficient delivery of programming at affordable rates, using the most effective technologies available at reasonable cost,

(iii) should, where programming services are supplied to them by broadcasting undertakings pursuant to contractual arrangements, provide reasonable terms for the carriage, packaging and retailing of those programming services, and

(iv) may, where the Commission considers it appropriate, originate programming, including local programming, on such terms as are conducive to the achievement of the objectives of the broadcasting policy set out in this subsection, and in particular provide access for underserved linguistic and cultural minority communities.

(2) It is further declared that the Canadian broadcasting system constitutes a single system and that the objectives of the broadcasting policy set out in subsection (1) can

best be achieved by providing for the regulation and supervision of the Canadian broadcasting system by a single independent public authority.

Name Index

Subject Index